Kafka
Judaism, Politics, and Literature

KAFKA,

Judaism, Politics, and Literature

RITCHIE ROBERTSON

WITHDRAWN

CLARENDON PRESS · OXFORD
1985

Oxford University Press, Walton Street, Oxford OX2 6DP

Oxford New York Toronto
Delhi Bombay Calcutta Madras Karachi
Kuala Lumpar Singapore Hong Kong Tokyo
Nairobi Dar es Salaam Cape Town
Melbourne Auckland

and associated companies in
Beirut Berlin Ibadan Mexico City Nicosia

Oxford is a trade mark of Oxford University Press

Published in the United States
by Oxford University Press, New York

British Library Cataloguing in Publication Data
Robertson, Ritchie
Kafka: Judaism, politics and literature
1. Kafka, Franz—Criticism and interpretation
I. Title
833'.912   PT2621.A26Z/
ISBN 0–19–815830–0

Library of Congress Cataloging in Publication Data
Robertson, Ritchie
Kafka: Judaism, politics and literature.
Bibliography: p.
Includes index
1. Kafka, Franz, 1883–1924—Criticism and interpretation
I. Title
PT2621.A26Z857 1985   833'.912   85–4120
ISBN 0–19–815830–0

Set by DMB Typesetting, Oxford
Printed in Great Britain
at the University Press, Oxford
by David Stanford
Printer to the University

To my mother
and the memory
of my father

Preface

THE subtitle of this book gives at best a rough idea of its scope.
'Judaism', which normally denotes the Judaic religion, is here being
used in a wider sense, close to that of the German *Judentum*, which
connotes both Jewish culture and the sense of Jewish identity. These
were what mattered to Kafka. His interest in Jewish culture was
aroused by the Yiddish actors who performed in Prague in the winter
of 1911–12, and extended to Jewish history and literature and eventually to the Hasidic traditions which still survived among the Jews of
Eastern Europe. During the same period, his identity as a Jew became
increasingly important to him. The awakening of his interest in
Jewish culture and in his own Jewish identity was closely connected,
as I try to show in Ch. 1, to the sudden breakthrough which enabled
him to write *Das Urteil*, his first major work of literature, in a single
night in the autumn of 1912. In order to demonstrate this connection,
I have discussed in some detail the principal documents of Kafka's
exploration of Judaism, which have largely been ignored by previous
Kafka scholarship. These are his notes on Pinès' *Histoire de la littérature judéo-allemande*, his public talk on the Yiddish language, and,
above all, the essay on minor literatures which he wrote in his diary in
December 1911 and which expressed his views about the desirable
relation between the writer and society. The chapter ends with an
interpretation of *Das Urteil* as the product of Kafka's divided allegiance
to German and Jewish culture.

During the following years Jewish images and allusions appear occasionally in Kafka's works, but they do not become prominent until
the beginning of 1917, in *Ein Landarzt, Schakale und Araber*, and subsequent works. From then on Kafka draws heavily on Jewish traditions, especially in *Das Schloß*, while his last story, *Josefine, die Sängerin
oder das Volk der Mäuse*, written a few weeks before his death in 1924,
returns to the theme of the 1911 diary entries by examining the relationship between artist and public within a specifically Jewish context.
In order to shed new light on these works, I have tried to show how
much they incorporate of Jewish history and tradition. I have given
particular attention to Kafka's interest in the Hasidic movement,

which he knew about through his reading and through his friendship with the Hasid, poet, and cabbalistic scholar Jiří Langer.

Politics, in the form of the Zionist movement, represented one obvious way in which a sense of Jewish identity could find expression. At first Kafka held himself aloof from Zionism, and he never took much interest in the day-to-day business of politics, 'the flat ephemeral pamphlet and the boring meeting', even though he did sometimes read political pamphlets and attend political meetings. Nevertheless, he thought deeply about the state of modern society. He was dubious about its secular and humanitarian ideals, and deplored the break-up of older communities through commercialism and the subordination of human beings to technology. In its place he wanted to see a genuine community established on a religious basis. From about 1916 on he sympathized strongly with Zionism, because he thought it could help to bring such a community into being. In Ch. 2 I have discussed *Der Verschollene* and *Die Verwandlung* as deliberate critiques of modern society, while in Ch. 4 I have tried to reconstruct the political assumptions held by the Zionists, especially Martin Buber, with whom Kafka came in contact.

Literature, the third member of my triad, refers to Kafka's reading as well as his writing. His extensive reading supplied him with many different types of source-material. In discussing Kafka's sources, both those that are already familiar and those that I have myself noticed, I have tried always to bear in mind Leszek Kolakowski's maxim that, in cases of influence, the active partner is not the one who exerts the influence, but the one on whom the influence is exerted. Accordingly, my concern has been to show how material from Kafka's reading was absorbed by his imagination and assimilated to his own central themes. I have also borne in mind that Kafka's writings are first and foremost literature. The diverse materials assembled in this book are all intended, therefore, to serve the elucidation and appreciation of Kafka's literary works, and I have tried, without going over too much familiar ground, to give due attention to his language, to irony and word-play, to the texture of his fictional worlds, to narrative method, and, surprisingly perhaps, to characterization. In particular I have emphasized an aspect of Kafka's works that has hitherto been largely neglected, namely their generic relationships. Now that explicit genre-systems have for the most part broken down, genres have become implicit and subliminal, permitting the illusion of direct access to literature. Yet, since one cannot approach a work of literature without a set of expectations about the kind to which it belongs, genre-concepts remain indispensable to mediate between the work and the world, and it is as important as ever to ensure that one's generic expectations correspond to the author's intentions. I have accordingly tried to reconstruct the genres of Kafka's three novels, and of some of the shorter works, in the belief that some at least of the bewilderment caused by Kafka's fiction results from the inappropriate assumptions about its genres made by his readers.

Under these three headings—Judaism, politics, and literature—I have tried to present a coherent account of Kafka's literary career. In doing so I have been concerned to oppose certain widespread notions about how to interpret his works. One is the view that Kafka's writings form a code which could easily be cracked if only the right key could be found. Fortunately, such approaches are now pretty well discredited, and new efforts at code-breaking are likely to meet with the same response as new attempts to 'solve' the 'mystery' of Shakespeare's sonnets. They have been displaced, however, by the equally depressing belief that Kafka's writings are insoluble riddles about which nothing can be known and therefore anything can be said. In a more sophisticated and austere form, this view is currently popular among academic interpreters of Kafka, who contend that his writings have nothing substantive to say, however indirectly, about the world, but are designed to frustrate the reader's desire for meaning and force him to reflect on the unreliability of his own mental operations. Neither of these views seems compatible with admiration for Kafka as a great writer. Still, both respond to genuine difficulties in interpreting Kafka, and it will be as well to consider briefly what the main difficulties are.

Kafka's writing is subtle, multi-layered, and allusive. His allusions, however, are not coded messages, but more like a delicate web which surrounds the central images of his stories, extending and controlling their implications. They ensure that, to borrow a metaphor from Conrad's *Heart of Darkness*, 'the meaning of an episode was not inside like a kernel but outside, enveloping the tale which brought it out only as a glow brings out a haze'. Subtlety is not vagueness, however, and interpretation of Kafka need not be hazy; but the interpreter does have to treat Kafka's allusions with due caution, to distinguish between a pointed reference and a glancing hint, and to avoid tearing the delicate web by heavy-handed over-interpretation.

As for Kafka's novels, much of the bewilderment among their readers results from failure to understand their narrative method.

I have tried, especially in Ch. 3, to oppose the widely held view that the novels are told from the standpoint of the hero, leaving the reader no option but to share the hero's perplexity. Rather, Kafka's novels are exercises in sustained irony, designed to induce a fine balance in the reader between emotional participation and the poise of superior knowledge. *Der Prozeß*, in particular, is a masterpiece of artful and ironic construction, and once the secret of its construction has been understood, many details which baffle Josef K. fall into place for the reader.

The most basic, irremovable difficulty in Kafka's work, however, is that he writes about matters which are intrinsically difficult. Not only is he a subtle and profound thinker, but he makes it his business to think through some of the most intractable problems of religion. His thinking finds expression in aphorisms, not in sustained philosophical argument, and I have tried to do justice to this neglected part of his work by devoting Ch. 5 to a detailed analysis of the large body of aphorisms he composed during the winter of 1917–18. Kafka's thinking is dualist. He assumes that there is an irreconcilable antithesis between two aspects of reality, which, throughout this study, I have labelled 'being' and 'consciousness'. Being can never become one with consciousness. The reconciliation of the two is indeed conceivable, but 'leider nur im Gleichnis': it cannot be brought about in reality, so that the gap between being and consciousness must remain unbridgeable. This may sound abstruse, but it is not, and for two reasons. First, Kafka has a gift for translating his thought into imagery and narrative. Second, he is concerned with the implications of his thought for ordinary human life. I have tried in Chs. 3 and 6 to show how his thought provides the intellectual underpinning for *Der Prozeß* and *Das Schloß*, in which he treats the problems of knowledge (especially self-knowledge) and of conduct that occur in everyday experience. The settings of Kafka's fiction may be grotesque, but its themes, if rightly understood, are of the kind to which every bosom returns an echo.

Kafka is often thought of as an exceptionally isolated figure. He certainly stylized himself in this way, as in the letter to Felice Bauer in which he unfolds a fantasy of living and writing in a vast cellar, where his only exercise would consist in walking to the door to pick up a tray of food that someone had left outside for him. Such self-stylizations have been accepted at face value by many critics, including Marthe Robert, whose recent book *Seul, comme Franz Kafka* takes its title from

a probably apocryphal remark ascribed to Kafka by the less than
trustworthy Gustav Janouch. It has too seldom been pointed out that
Kafka's actual life was less isolated than the lives of most writers.
Although he was a close friend of Max Brod and Franz Werfel, he did
not spend much of his time among writers, and was not a professional
literary man: he had to earn his living as a civil servant specializing in
accident insurance, which forced the social effects of technology and
industrialization upon his attention. He was keenly interested in the
world around him, especially in new technical developments such as
the cinema and the aeroplane. The First World War, the growth of
anti-Semitism, and the Zionist movement all impinged on his life.
One of my chief aims has been to show how these social and political
realities affected his writing. In doing so, I have drawn amply and
gratefully on the biographical and historical research done by Klaus
Wagenbach, Hartmut Binder, Christoph Stölzl, A. D. Northey, and
Gary B. Cohen. Much of the information they have uncovered has
already been presented to the English-speaking world in two recent
and readable biographies: Ronald Hayman's *K.: A Biography of Kafka*
(London, 1981), and Ernst Pawel's *The Nightmare of Reason: A Life of
Franz Kafka* (London, 1984). Both Hayman and Pawel are, however,
very timid about applying this information to elucidate Kafka's works.
This is what I have tried to do.

My debts to previous interpreters of Kafka are also great. The
references, though extensive, mention only a small proportion of the
material I have looked at and a far smaller proportion of the secondary
literature in existence. They are intended to document my indebtedness and to draw the reader's attention to the work on Kafka that
I have myself found most valuable. I should perhaps explain my attitude to two biographical sources, the work of Max Brod and Gustav
Janouch. In using Brod's copious and important writings on Kafka,
my rule of thumb has been to consider him more trustworthy as a biographer than as an interpreter, and to consider his earlier biographical
writings more trustworthy than his later ones. In the latter, especially
his own autobiography *Streitbares Leben* (Munich, 1960), he is sometimes led astray by a desire to exaggerate his own importance, as when
he claims to have launched Werfel's literary career. In all his writings
on Kafka he is concerned to stylize Kafka into a saintly figure and to
simplify Kafka's relationship to the Zionist movement and to modern
Judaic thought. In interpreting Kafka's works he is too much inclined
to ride his own hobby-horses, as in his notorious Kierkegaardian

interpretation of the Amalia episode of *Das Schloß*. Some of his remarks, however, are valuable as revealing the assumptions common to Kafka and Kafka's first readers, which now have to be reconstructed: an example is his description of *Ein Bericht für eine Akademie* as a satire on Jewish assimilation. If used with caution, Brod's writings are of great value. The same cannot be said for Janouch's *Gespräche mit Kafka*, first published in 1951 and reissued in an enlarged edition in 1968, since their unreliability has been demonstrated by Eduard Gold-stücker. Janouch certainly knew Kafka, and some of the remarks he records are no doubt authentic, but even in the first edition the bulk of the conversations, especially the solemn banalities that Janouch's Kafka so often utters, is unquestionably fictitious, while the new material in the revised edition, the provenance of which has never been clarified, need not be taken seriously. Accordingly I have avoided using Janouch as a biographical source.

In writing this book I have incurred many personal obligations. Most of the work was done during my tenure of the Montgomery Fellowship in German at Lincoln College, Oxford, and I wish to thank the Rector and Fellows for granting me two terms of sabbatical leave. I am grateful to the editors of *Oxford German Studies* for permission to use material that first appeared in vols. 14 (1983) and 16 (1985), and to the Institute of Germanic Studies, London, for permission to use material from J. P. Stern and J. J. White (eds.), *Paths and Labyrinths: Nine Papers from a Kafka Symposium* (London, 1985). I also wish to thank the staff of the Taylorian Library at Oxford and the Deutsches Lite-raturarchiv at Marbach, as well as Professor Jürgen Born and his col-leagues at the Kafka-Forschungsstelle at the University of Wuppertal, for their kindness and helpfulness. I am grateful also to Sir Malcolm Pasley, for help, encouragement, and advice at every stage of this project; to Dr Dovid Katz, for teaching me the rudiments of Yiddish; to Leofranc Holford-Strevens of the Oxford University Press, for his learned and meticulous copy-editing; to T. J. Reed, Professor J. B. Segal, Dr Naomi Segal, and Dr Jonathan Webber, for reading and commenting on parts of the manuscript; and to the Oxford under-graduates who for five years compelled me to think hard and long about Kafka.

RITCHIE ROBERTSON

Contents

1

Kafka's Exploration of Judaism
The Context of *Das Urteil* (1912)

KAFKA'S upbringing as a German-speaking Jew in predominantly Czech-speaking Prague has been described in two different, and indeed mutually incompatible ways. Even the recollections of people who were at school with Kafka contradict one another. His close friend Felix Weltsch, who was in the class below his at the Altstädter Gymnasium, asserts that their generation participated in a 'Jewish–German symbiosis': that is, they identified themselves naïvely and unthinkingly with the German minority in Prague, until, as Weltsch puts it, 'the repressed streams of the ethnic and religious factors forced their way through to the surface of active consciousness from the deepest sources of the soul', making them rediscover their Jewish identity and join the Zionist movement.[1] A different account, however, is given by Kafka's class-mate Emil Utitz. In his recollection, the Prague Jews lived in 'inselhafte Abgeschlossenheit': with no contact with the Germans, and scarcely any with the Czechs, they formed a kind of voluntary ghetto.[2] The latter view has been made into one of the commonplaces of Kafka studies by another emigrant from Prague, Heinz Politzer, who maintains in his widely read and influential *Franz Kafka: Parable and Paradox* that the Prague Jews were not allowed to mix with the Germans and were hated by the Czechs:

As a German Jew in Czech Prague, Kafka lived in a triple ghetto: the Jewish community was encircled by hostile Slavs, who in turn were hemmed in and held down by the Austrian bureaucracy that ruled the city in the name of the Habsburg empire until the revolution of 1918.[3]

Although both these descriptions of Kafka's Prague come from people who were born and bred there, it is impossible that both can be true. Weltsch's 'Jewish–German symbiosis' is incompatible with Utitz's 'voluntary ghetto'. The contradiction needs to be resolved, however, if we are to understand how Kafka's fiction is related to his social circumstances and, in particular, to his gradual exploration of the implications of being a Jew. The recollections of memoirists must therefore be supplemented and, where necessary, corrected by the extensive research into Kafka's social environment which has been done in the past twenty-five years by both literary scholars and professional historians. With this aid, I intend now to sketch a picture of what being a Jew in Kafka's Prague was actually like; to disclose some of the complicated ways in which three cultures—German, Czech, and Jewish—interpenetrated in Kafka's upbringing; and, finally, to suggest how his exploration of Jewish culture was related to his breakthrough into major literary achievement with *Das Urteil*, the story he wrote at a single sitting on the night of 22–3 September 1912.[4]

The Jews of Prague were a small group: in 1900 they numbered 26,342. Though some had Czech as their native language, the majority spoke German and probably formed between a third and a half of the city's German-speaking community. Offical statistics indicate that the number of German speakers dwindled from 38,591 in 1880 to 32,332 in 1910, so that they represented an ever-decreasing fraction of the city's total population, which swelled during the same period from 255,928 to 442,017. This population increase kept pace with the expansion of industry in Bohemia, a process in which neither the Jews nor the Germans played much part, since they belonged mostly to the middle or upper-middle classes and worked in commerce, finance or the professions. Unlike Berlin, Vienna, and Budapest, Prague had virtually no Jewish proletariat, and, until the First World War, very few immigrants from Galicia or other regions with large Jewish populations. Towards the upper end of their social range, the Prague Jews seem to have mixed freely in public life with the Prague Germans: the records of social clubs and similar voluntary organizations show a number of Jews among the members that corresponds roughly to their proportion of the German-speaking population. But if something of a symbiosis did exist in the public sphere, in private life things were different. Jews tended to have Jewish neighbours: the tenants in a single block of flats would be predominantly Jewish or predominantly German. Yet, since no complaints of discrimination are recorded, the Prague Jews seem not to have minded their separate identity and to have experienced no tension between their being Jewish and their belonging to the German-speaking community.

Jews at the lower end of the social range, like Kafka's father, had a more difficult time. Hermann Kafka[5] had come to Prague in 1881 from the village of Wossek (now Osek) in southern Bohemia, where

he had begun his career as a pedlar and undergone great hardships—
which later he never tired of describing to his children—before
acquiring enough capital to open a fancy-goods shop in the centre of
Prague. He and his wife Julie, who was also from the country, seem
to have betrayed their origins by using a number of Yiddish expressions in both speech and writing. Hermann Kafka once described
Max Brod as a 'meschuggenen Ritoch' (T 132), a phrase which Brod
himself translates as 'verrückter Brausekopf' (T 700), and a surviving
letter from Julie Kafka uses the Yiddish word 'Mischpoche' ('family',
F 614). This form of German had been extinct in Prague since about
1860 and was known by the pejorative term *Mauscheldeutsch*.[6] Their
retention of it would have helped to make the elder Kafkas socially
unacceptable to many Germans and to some Jews. They were, admittedly, anxious to enhance their social status by taking summer holidays
in resorts, outside Prague, rather than with relatives, engaging a French
governess for their son, and giving their children a German education
to increase their chances of social mobility. Nevertheless, it was difficult for Jews to scale the heights of Prague society. One of the main
characters in Brod's novel *Jüdinnen* (1911), an upper-middle-class
Prague Jewess named Irene Popper, talks about the complicated
gradations of Prague society and decides that even the richest Jews
are only on the level of the Gentile professional class.[7]

Not only social ascent but even acceptance on their own social level
was difficult for the Kafkas. The employees in Hermann Kafka's
shop, like many of his customers, were Czech, and anti-Semitic feeling was widespread among them. Recalling how his father referred to
the employees as 'bezahlte Feinde' (H 186), Kafka was later to blame
him for antagonizing them by his outbursts of rage. But it is probable
that many of them resented working for a Jew whose preferred
language was German, and that Hermann Kafka's incessant rows
with his staff—once he summarily dismissed them all, and Kafka
junior had to visit them one by one and persuade them to return—
may have resulted as much from their nationalistic ill-feeling as from
his irascibility.

In order to conciliate both Czechs and Germans, Hermann Kafka
had to perform a difficult balancing act which is conveniently symbolized by his own name. His Christian name is aggressively German,
since 'Hermann' is the customary German equivalent for Arminius,
the name of the Germanic leader who defeated the Romans in AD 9
and had been a potent nationalist image since the late eighteenth

century. 'Kafka', by contrast, is Jewish in origin, derived from
'Yakov' ('Jacob'), with a suffix that could be either German or Czech.
By a fortunate coincidence *kavka* is the Czech word for a jackdaw, and
a not uncommon Czech surname. The emblem of Hermann Kafka's
shop alluded to the Czech meaning of his name by depicting a jackdaw, but for the benefit of his German customers the jackdaw was
perching on the branch of an oak-tree. This policy of camouflage paid
off during the anti-German and anti-Semitic riots of December 1897,
in which many Jewish families, including that of Max Brod, had their
homes attacked or at the very least their windows broken, for it was
most probably on this occasion that passers-by restrained rioters from
plundering the Kafka shop by saying: 'Leave Kafka alone, he's a
Czech.'[8]

In the long term, however, the position of the Prague Jews was
untenable. Their loyalty to German culture was first and foremost a
loyalty to liberalism, to which they owed their civil rights and their
chances of social mobility. Yet by 1883, the year of Kafka's birth,
Austrian liberalism was already a lost cause. The last liberal cabinet
had fallen in 1879 and had been replaced by the Catholic, conservative, pro-Slav government of Count Taaffe. The Enlightenment
ideals of humanism and tolerance were in retreat, while nationalism,
anti-Semitism, and revolutionary socialism were on the advance.
Though not many Jews realized it, the society to which they wished to
assimilate was already crumbling. It took the exceptional figure of
Theodor Herzl to conclude, in the 1890s, that Jewish assimilation was
ultimately impracticable and that the Jews could only combat nationalism by adopting some of its principles and setting up a Jewish
national state.[9] But, although *Der Judenstaat* was published in 1896,
when Kafka was thirteen, it would be some twenty years before he
accepted the Zionist case.

Even in the 1890s, some unease among the Prague Jews can be inferred from the census-returns which Gary B. Cohen has recently
analysed. In 1900, when Kafka was in his last year at the Altstädter
Gymnasium, he was among the 90 per cent of Jewish students who
were receiving their education in German. Since 1880 the decennial
census had included a question about the language habitually used
outside the home (*Umgangssprache*), to which, in 1890, 74 per cent of
the Prague Jews had answered 'German'; yet in 1900 only 45 per
cent gave this answer, while the rest replied 'Czech'. So great a change
within ten years cannot be explained simply by the increasing pres-

ence of Czechs in business and professional life. These replies more probably represent a tactical attempt to conciliate the Czechs by demonstrating the Jews' willingness to mix with them on their terms, which casts grave doubt on Weltsch's notion of a Jewish–German symbiosis. Hermann Kafka did in fact speak Czech better than German. Kafka himself was fluent in Czech and read it with ease. He first learnt the language from his nurse, Marie Werner, a Jewess, who despite her name could speak only Czech. During his first two years at secondary school he attended lessons in Czech. He had to speak it to the employees and customers in his father's shop, and during his affair with his Czech translator Milena Jesenská she wrote to him in Czech, at his own request (M 9). 'Deutsch ist meine Muttersprache und deshalb mir natürlich,' he told her, 'aber das tschechische ist mir viel herzlicher' (M 17).

At school and university Kafka had almost no contact with Czechs and comparatively little with Germans.[10] Most Czechs attended schools in which Czech was the language of instruction. At the German-speaking Altstädter Gymnasium, only two of the twenty-four pupils in Kafka's final year were native speakers of Czech, and seventeen out of the twenty-four were Jews. Even stricter segregation existed at the Charles University, which in 1882 had been divided into two entirely separate institutions, one for Czechs and the other for speakers of German. In the latter, where a quarter of the students were Jews, there were two main student associations, the German-nationalist *Germania*, which did not admit Jews, and the liberal *Lese- und Redehalle*, where Jews were in the majority, and where Kafka and Brod, who had attended different schools, first got to know each other. It is not surprising, therefore, that all Kafka's close friends were Jews; Milena Jesenská was the only Gentile with whom he ever had a close and lasting relationship.

Kafka and those of his contemporaries who learnt Czech did so mainly because they had to. Their native language was German, and, though their social contact with Germans might be limited, they had no doubt of their allegiance to German culture. Jewish culture and tradition held no interest for them. Their parents had retained only a residual attachment to Jewish religious practices. The recollections of Hans Kohn, one of Kafka's contemporaries, are typical: 'My father went to the synagogue only on the high holidays, my mother almost never. None of the ceremonial laws were observed in our home. Yiddish [. . .] was not spoken in Prague [. . .]; the Eastern

European Jews were regarded more as aliens than as "brothers".[11] *Seder*, the first night of Passover, was celebrated in the Kafka household, but as the children grew older the occasion ceased to be taken at all seriously and degenerated into a 'Komödie mit Lachkrämpfen' (H 199). Kafka's father took him to the synagogue on the high holidays, but made no secret of his own indifference, and Kafka recalled later that he had never been so bored except in dancing-classes (H 198). The religious education he received at school appears to have been so incompetent as to stifle any interest in Judaism that he might have developed; indeed, it seems to have made an atheist of him, for he and his friend Hugo Bergmann used to have arguments in which Kafka attacked Bergmann's religious beliefs.[12] Earlier, at the age of thirteen, Kafka had his bar mitzvah, though on the invitation cards that his parents sent out it was called *Confirmation* in order to play down its Jewish character,[13] and Kafka himself regarded it merely as an exercise in rote-learning. On 24 December 1911 Kafka's nephew was circumcised; Kafka in his diary gives a detailed description of the operation performed by the *mohel*, or circumciser, and notes that none of his family, except for his father, showed any understanding of the prayers offered up by the *mohel*'s assistant. Since these ceremonies were already regarded as a mere antiquated survival, Kafka reflects ironically that it will not be long before their complete disappearance lends them a nostalgic interest for the very people who now watch them with indifference (T 205).

As a result of these experiences, Kafka came to feel that his parents' residual Judaism had been drained of its religious content and was merely part of the complex of Jewish middle-class values to which they adhered unquestioningly. One of the charges he levels in his *Brief an den Vater* runs: 'Im Grund bestand der Dein Leben führende Glaube darin, daß Du an die unbedingte Richtigkeit der Meinungen einer bestimmten jüdischen Gesellschaftsklasse glaubtest und eigentlich also, da diese Meinungen zu Deinem Wesen gehörten, Dir selbst glaubtest' (H 199–200).[14] The lower-middle-class status of Kafka's parents was perhaps the basic reason for the estrangement between them and their son. By acquiring a university education and adopting a profession, Kafka had distanced himself from them socially and had little in common with them. His father's difficult personality exacerbated this breakdown of communication, but did not cause it. One does not need to be Jewish or German to recognize this problem and sympathize with both parties. In many ways Kafka's situation typifies the marginal position of the intellectual in modern Western society; and, as the following chapters will argue, Kafka not only recognized his marginality, the 'Grenzland zwischen Einsamkeit und Gemeinschaft' (T 548) that he inhabited, but sought to overcome it through his writing.

The first means of escape from his parents' milieu that presented itself to Kafka was German culture, above all literature. At the Altstädter Gymnasium he received a grounding in German literature from the *Hildebrandslied* down to Grillparzer and Lenau. At university he read law, a subject traditionally chosen by Jews in search of a secure professional career, but in his first semester (winter 1901–2) he also attended the lectures on Grillparzer given by the distinguished scholar August Sauer, and in his second he attended several seminars on *Germanistik* given by Sauer and others. In his spare time Kafka kept up with contemporary literature mainly by reading the *Neue Rundschau*, to which he later subscribed. His literary tastes were conservative.[15] He disliked the 'decadent' posturing of such writers as Meyrink and Heinrich Mann, and later he objected to the shrillness of the Expressionists. Among his contemporaries he particularly admired Hofmannsthal, Robert Walser, and Thomas Mann. *Tonio Kröger* was among his favourite works, and one wonders how far Mann's presentation of Tonio as loving the healthy, blonde, blue-eyed types just because he is cut off from them, contributed to Kafka's understanding of himself as a necessarily isolated artist, drawn to the practical Felice Bauer because she was his antithesis, yet unable to marry her without sacrificing his vocation. Further back, Kafka was very fond of nineteenth-century *Novellen*, especially those of Kleist, Grillparzer, and Stifter, the tales of Johann Peter Hebel, and lyric poetry of a quietly reflective kind. His favourite poem appears to have been Justinus Kerner's 'Der Wanderer in der Sägemühle', closely followed by Eichendorff's 'O Täler weit, o Höhen' (M 305). But the foremost German writer in his eyes was of course Goethe.

Kafka's love of Goethe goes back to his schooldays. In his last year at school, when each member of the class had to prepare a talk on some literary topic and deliver it during one of the German lessons, Kafka was the only one to speak on Goethe, the title of his talk being 'Wie haben wir den Schluß von Goethes *Tasso* aufzunehmen?' In August 1902, at the end of his first year at university, he wrote to his friend Oskar Pollak reproaching the latter for describing a visit to

Weimar in insufficiently reverential terms:

Denn was Du vom Arbeitszimmer, Deinem Allerheiligsten, schreibst, ist wieder nichts anderes als eine Einbildung und ein Schulgedanke und ein klein wenig Germanistik, in der Hölle soll sie braten.[. . .] Weißt Du aber [Kafka continues in the precious style characteristic of his early letters to Pollak], was das Allerheiligste ist, das wir überhaupt von Goethe haben können, als Andenken . . . die Fußspuren seiner einsamen Gänge durch das Land . . . die wären es. (Br 12.)

Since Goethe's footprints were irrecoverable, Kafka turned to the next best thing, his works, diaries, and recorded conversations, and read and reread them avidly. He probably knew Goethe's personal writings quite as thoroughly as his literary works, but of the latter he seems to have had a particular affection for *Hermann und Dorothea*, and an admiration—not unmixed with criticism—for the stylistic purity of *Iphigenie auf Tauris*, on which he comments in 1910: 'Darin ist wirklich, von einzelnen offen fehlerhaften Stellen abgesehen, die ausgetrocknete deutsche Sprache im Munde eines reinen Knaben förmlich anzustaunen' (T 26). The cool, qualified tone of this judgement shows, as does the letter to Pollak, that Kafka wanted his admiration for Goethe not to be infected by the stereotyped adulation conventionally paid to Goethe by professors of German. He and Brod visited Weimar in the summer of 1912, but the detailed notes with which Kafka recorded the visit in his travel diary are free from conventional sentiments and show, instead, considerable interest in the attractive daughter of the custodian of the Goethehaus. Of the study and bedroom in the house, Kafka remarks concisely: 'Trauriger, an tote Großväter erinnernder Anblick' (T 654); and his tendency to regard Goethe as an ancestral figure is also mentioned by Max Brod in describing Kafka's reverence for Goethe:

Kafka mit Andacht über Goethe sprechen zu hören,—das war etwas ganz Besonderes; es war, als spreche ein Kind von seinem Ahnherrn, der in glücklicheren, reineren Zeiten und in unmittelbarer Berührung mit dem Göttlichen gelebt habe. Und um nun gleich wieder die kleine Bosheit zu Wort kommen zu lassen: Kafka betonte gelegentlich, er sei sehr erstaunt, daß mancher Schriftsteller so unvorsichtig sei, Goethe zu zitieren,—ein Satz von Goethe leuchte doch unfehlbar aus dem sonstigen Text jedes Autors allzu blendend hervor.[16]

Here Brod confirms that Kafka's admiration for Goethe was not professorial but professional. Rather than paying conventional homage to Goethe as a literary idol, Kafka regarded him as a supreme expo-nent of the art of writing which he himself practised. Membership of the same craft therefore entitled Kafka to criticize the 'offen fehlerhaften Stellen' in *Iphigenie* and to feel the intimacy implied by the image of Goethe as an ancestor.

As far as education and culture went, Kafka was fully assimilated to his German environment. But, as Cohen has usefully pointed out, acculturation need not be accompanied by social acceptance.[17] Even if he led as much as possible of his mental life in the world of German literature, Kafka's physical life was largely confined to Jewish Prague, and did not allow him to forget that he was likewise a Jew. Not that he himself was ever the victim of anti-Semitic prejudice. The only occasion in his life when he encountered such feelings directed against him personally—and then only in a comparatively mild form —was in April 1920, when he was staying in a hotel in Merano. His fellow diners, all old ladies and retired military officers of the purest 'deutsch-christlich' extraction (Br 270), caused him exquisite embar-rassment by trying to place his accent, and then reacted frostily on learning that he was a Jew. In November of the same year Kafka wit-nessed anti-Semitic riots in Prague. They lasted for three days, during which a mob stormed the Jüdisches Rathaus and Hebrew parchments were burnt in the street outside the Altneu synagogue. 'Ist es nicht das Selbstverständliche, daß man von dort weggeht, wo man so gehaßt wird (Zionismus oder Volksgefühl ist dafür gar nicht nötig)?', he wrote to Milena, watching from his window mounted police and gendarmes with fixed bayonets dispersing a screaming crowd (M 288).

For the most part, however, Kafka's day-to-day life was not seriously affected by his being a Jew.[18] He became one of the very few Jews employed in the public service when he left a private insurance com-pany, the Assicurazioni Generali, to join the state-run Arbeiter-Unfall-Versicherungs-Anstalt. What made his move possible was the coincidence that the manager of the Anstalt, a Czech-speaking Jew named Příbram who had officially severed his connections with the Jewish community, was the father of one of Kafka's school-friends, and agreed to use his influence to secure the post for Kafka. Some years later Kafka informed Brod that there was not the remotest chance of any more Jews being taken on: 'Die Anstalt ist für Juden unzugänglich' (Br 194).

By being so unusual, Kafka's good fortune could only help to remind him of the disadvantages of being a Jew. His early travel diaries show how self-conscious he was about this, for they include several descriptions of Jews encountered *en route*. In January 1911, for example, Kafka shared a railway compartment with a Jew from a Bohemian country town who showed himself to be under-assimilated by his exclamations about the price of the ticket and the slowness of the train; Kafka, defensively and a little uneasily, joined with another passenger in quietly laughing at him (T 589). When passing through Switzerland in August 1911, Kafka and Brod were struck by the prosperity of the country and the absence of Jews, and Brod remarked: 'Die Juden haben sich dieses große Geschäft entgehen lassen' (T 602). The same motive lies behind this remark as behind Kafka's mockery of his fellow passenger, namely the desire to dissociate oneself from the kind of Jew who embarrasses one by what are felt to be characteristically Jewish shortcomings like bad manners or commercial greed. Early in 1914 Kafka read the lively memoirs of Countess Thürheim; one of his diary entries on it, 'Juden' (T 358), refers to a passage in which she describes the embarrassment caused her by some Galician Jews. When travelling through Galicia with its Governor, Count Goëss, who was her brother-in-law, the Countess and her companion went ahead of the rest of the party in order to avoid the local officials who kept turning out to welcome the Governor:

Vor Rzeszow fuhren Nany und ich dem Wagen der Goëß vor, doch o Schrecken, bei dem Orte standen zwei Reihen von Juden, die uns wie Besessene mit Vivatrufen und Schwenken ihrer Fahnen empfingen und uns zum Schlusse ihre Thora zum Kusse reichten. In meiner Bescheidenheit wußte ich nicht, wohin mich verkriechen, doch Nany beantwortete diese Ehrenbezeigungen mit lautem Gelächter. Da wir uns mit den Juden nicht verständigen konnten, mußten wir notgedrungen auf den nachfolgenden Wagen warten. Als dieser endlich erschien, wandte sich ihm die Aufmerksamkeit der Israeliten sofort zu; sie ließen uns mitten auf der Straße im Stiche und eilten mit ihren Fahnen und Tafeln des Moses davon, um ihren Irrtum wieder gutzumachen.[19]

Kafka would have appreciated this incident from both points of view. As a Westernized Jew he could sympathize with the Countess's embarrassed incomprehension of the Jews' behaviour, and her annoyance at their apparent rudeness. In 1916 he was to describe the antics of the followers of the Belzer Rabbi in a similar tone. But, having met and made friends with several Galician Jews, he had acquired some insight into their world and could understand the motives behind the ludicrously inappropriate display of homage described here.

Kafka knew, of course, that some Jews were suffering worse things than social embarrassment or job discrimination. During his lifetime there were many revivals of the blood-libel, the charge that Jews murdered Gentiles in order to use their blood for ritual purposes, especially for the preparation of unleavened bread for Passover. This medieval superstition is most familiar to English readers from the story of St Hugh of Lincoln, which Chaucer retold in the *Prioress's Tale*. Heine describes it in his fragmentary novel *Der Rabbi von Bacherach*, which he began in 1824 and published in 1840 in response to the Damascus blood-libel. An elderly Capuchin monk in Damascus had disappeared, and rumours arose that the local Jews had murdered him for ritual purposes. Many Jews were hideously tortured to extort confessions of complicity. The charge was supported by the French consul in Damascus and even by Adolphe Thiers, then President of the Council of Ministers, who was anxious to conciliate clerical opinion in France. The affair ended in October 1840 when Syria was returned to Turkey and the Sultan issued an edict exculpating the Jews. Heine, who denounced the anti-Semites in a series of letters written for the *Augsburger Allgemeine Zeitung*, was horrified by the recrudescence of medieval superstition and by the readiness of many Westerners to believe in such charges.[20]

Kafka's contemporaries were no less credulous. In 1883 the Jews of Tiszaeszlár, a small town in Hungary, were accused of murdering a Gentile child, and the Professor of Semitic Languages at Prague University, August Rohling, was on hand to claim that such practices were enjoined by the Talmud.[21] Another such case occurred in Bohemia itself in 1899. A nineteen-year-old girl was found murdered in the village of Polna, and a local shoemaker's assistant, Leopold Hilsner, was charged with committing the murder for ritual purposes. The prosecuting counsel, Dr Karel Baxa, a nationalist politician who later became Mayor of Prague, succeeded in obtaining a conviction. Hilsner was sentenced to death, but a public campaign led by Thomas G. Masaryk obtained a retrial; Hilsner was again sentenced to death, but had his sentence commuted to life imprisonment in 1901 and was finally pardoned in 1916. The Hilsner case was described at the time as 'the Austrian Dreyfus affair'.[22] We can form some faint idea of the emotions whipped up by such cases if we recall the Moors murders or the affair of the 'Yorkshire Ripper'. In 1914 Arnold Zweig made the Tiszaeszlár affair the subject of his play *Ritualmord in Ungarn*; Kafka read it in 1916 and was moved to tears (F 735–6).

In 1911–13 Kafka was following the Beilis affair in the newspapers.[23] A Russian Jew, Mendel Beilis, was accused of murdering a Gentile child in Kiev, and kept in prison for two years before his acquittal. The trial provoked many anti-Semitic riots in Russia. The harrowing story of Beilis has now been told in Bernard Malamud's novel *The Fixer*; but Kafka, towards the end of his life, also wrote a story about the Beilis affair. It was among the manuscripts that Dora Dymant reported having burnt on his instructions.[24] The affair seems also to have left its mark on *Das Urteil*, where Kiev, the scene of Beilis' alleged crime, is mentioned as the place where Georg's friend witnessed a revolutionary demonstration addressed by a priest (E 62); and later Georg imagines his friend standing 'an der Türe des leeren, ausgeraubten Geschäftes' (E 64), as though the shop had been plundered in an anti-Semitic riot. A deleted sentence from the manuscript, 'Trampelndes Volksgetümmel zog reihenweise vorbei',[25] helps to suggest that Kafka had in mind reports of Russian pogroms.

Kafka, then, could not and did not forget that he was himself a Jew. Several distinctively Jewish forms of social involvement were available to him, including the Zionist movement. The degree of his interest in Zionism has been much debated: Brod and Weltsch maintain that he was whole-heartedly committed to it, and the same case has recently been argued by Klara Carmely.[26] Kafka does not help the biographer with the curious diary entry for 23 January 1922, in which he lists the many undertakings begun and then dropped in the course of his life: amid this oddly assorted catalogue, which starts with piano lessons and ends with his abortive plans to get married and set up a home of his own, we find the pair 'Antizionismus, Zionismus' (T 560). Till his late twenties, however, Kafka seems to have regarded Zionism neither with sympathy nor hostility, but with almost total indifference. Little reliance can be placed on the testimony of a fellow pupil, Zdenko Vaněk, who claimed in 1965 that while still at school Kafka had become an ardent Zionist. Bergmann, a much closer school-friend, at first confirmed this report but later undermined its value by stating that while he himself became a Zionist, the young Kafka adopted Socialism.[27] This entitles us only to conclude that at school Kafka took part in discussions about Zionism, Socialism, and kindred topics; and it would have been surprising if he had not.

In 1899 Jewish students at Prague University founded a Zionist society, named the Bar Kochba after the Jewish leader of the second century AD, which was to become the most important Zionist organization in Central Europe. Since Bergmann was one of its most active members, Kafka must have been dimly aware of its existence, but both he and Brod ignored it until 1909, when a writer in its journal, *Selbstwehr*, attacked the omission of Zionism from Brod's treatment of nationality problems in one of his innumerable novels, *Ein tschechisches Dienstmädchen*.[28] The resulting dispute taught Brod the principles of Zionism, and despite his initial reserve he had been won over to unconditional support of the movement by 1913 at the latest. His efforts to proselytize Kafka, however, were worse than ineffectual, for they led to a temporary estrangement between the two. In a conversation in August 1913 Kafka professed to be entirely without a sense of community,[29] and in his diary four months later he writes (perhaps in response to further attempts at persuasion): 'Was habe ich mit Juden gemeinsam? Ich habe kaum etwas mit mir gemeinsam' (T 350). Even in 1916, when his interest in Zionism had undoubtedly developed and he was urging Felice to help in a Zionist-run home for refugee children, he told her that if put to the test he might well prove not to be a true Zionist (F 698), and in 1918, in a passage from his notebooks not cited by Klara Carmely, he mentions that, unlike the Zionists, he had no contact with Jewish religious practice: '[ich] habe nicht den letzten Zipfel des davonfliegenden jüdischen Gebetmantels noch gefangen wie die Zionisten' (H 121). As Helen Milfull has noted, Kafka never mentions the Balfour Declaration, which to any Zionist would have been an epoch-making event.[30] However, in a letter of 13 February 1917 to Martin Buber, Brod speaks of 'mein Freund Franz Kafka (mit dem ich nicht diskutiere und auf den zu meiner Freude das Judentum langsam, unvermerkt übergeht)',[31] and in that year we find Kafka contemplating emigration to Palestine, where he would work as a book-binder (Br 277). As will be shown in later chapters, his broad sympathy with Zionism during the last seven or eight years of his life cannot be doubted, but his attitude to the movement was much more complex, qualified, and individual than the one ascribed to him by Brod and Weltsch.

    The period from about 1909 to 1915, when Kafka was fighting a rearguard action against Brod's efforts to enlist him in the Zionist ranks, may be that of what he later called 'Antizionismus'. Yet his professions of indifference did not prevent Kafka from attending at least ten lectures and recitals organized by the Bar Kochba between 1910 and 1914; and in a draft review of Brod's *Jüdinnen*, dating from March 1911, he implied that Zionism was at least a possible solution to the Jewish question (T 52–4). But the form of sociability offered by the Bar Kochba was uncongenial to Kafka, who was not a clubbable man and felt ill at ease at Zionist or other gatherings. 'Ich wie aus Holz, ein in die Mitte des Saales geschobener Kleiderhalter' (T 466) is how he describes his demeanour on one such occasion, and when he took advantage of a visit to Vienna in 1913, where he had to attend an international conference on industrial safety and hygiene, to look in on the Eleventh World Zionist Congress, he felt uncomfortable, 'wie bei einer gänzlich fremden Veranstaltung' (Br 120).[32]

There was, however, another form of social contact with Jews that did appeal to Kafka very strongly, and it was provided by the Yiddish theatre. In May 1910 he went to see a troupe of Yiddish actors from Lemberg, the capital of Galicia (the most north-easterly province of the Austrian Empire, bordering on Russia, with a large Jewish population), who were performing in Prague. Nothing more is known about this troupe, which Kafka and Brod refer to only fleetingly in their diaries,[33] but we know a great deal about another troupe of Yiddish actors from Lemberg who visited Prague in the winter of 1911–12, for Kafka went to about twenty of their performances, describes the plays at great length in his diary, and became a close friend of one of the actors, a Polish Jew named Jizchok Löwy. Kafka's interest in these actors proves his independence of mind, for it was shared by none of the Prague Zionists except Brod. Only one member of the Bar Kochba, Bergmann, had ever visited the Jewish communities of Eastern Europe. The Prague Zionists were dedicated to learning Hebrew, and regarded Yiddish as a shameful relic of Jewish subjection. At this stage, too, they were more devoted to consciousness-raising among themselves than to any practical involvement with the Jewish people. The Jews in Prague were scarcely aware that to the east, in a vast area stretching from the Baltic to the Black Sea, there were communities of Yiddish-speaking Jews comprising some five million people.[34] They had been settled there since the late Middle Ages, when persecution and commercial rivalry had forced many Jews to move from Germany and open up new markets in Eastern Europe. They had been invited to settle in the kingdom of Poland, which then covered a far greater area than the rump which survives at the present day: it included modern Lithuania, White Russia, the Ukraine, and other territories which are now within the Soviet Union. The Jews who settled in this area spoke a language, Yiddish, based on medieval dialects of Central and South-eastern Germany

with a considerable Hebrew and Aramaic vocabulary. Their communities have now been destroyed in a manner which in Herzl's lifetime was still inconceivable. To learn about their life we have to rely
on historians and on its literary recreation by Yiddish writers,
foremost among whom are the Singer brothers.

Kafka, however, did not learn about this world from books but
from people, and from fairly humble people at that. The Yiddish
actors could not afford to hire a theatre in Prague, and performed
instead in the sleazy Café Savoy. The quality of their performances
was perhaps not high. Although drama in Yiddish has a history that
goes back long before 1708, the date of the first printed Yiddish play,
the modern Yiddish theatre dates only from 1876, when Abraham
Goldfaden founded a troupe which performed in various Romanian
cities and then moved to Odessa.[35] Several similar troupes were formed
in the Jewish centres of Russia, and aroused such enthusiasm that in
1883 the Tsarist government issued an edict forbidding all theatrical
performances in Yiddish, in case they should lead to political unrest.
Most of the actors and playwrights then emigrated to the United
States, so that in Kafka's time the centre of Yiddish drama was New
York. Many of its playwrights were little more than hack writers.
Kafka saw several plays by the indefatigable Joseph Latayner, the
author of some 150 plays in all. On a higher level were the historical
dramas of Goldfaden and the realistic plays of Jakob Gordin. Kafka
records that Löwy spent an afternoon reading aloud to him from Gordin's adaptation of *Faust*, entitled *Got, mensh un tayvl* and said to be
Gordin's best play, and indeed one of the best in the Yiddish repertoire at that time. As for the acting, some idea of its quality can be
gained from a fascinating book, *The Spirit of the Ghetto*, by Hutchins
Hapgood. First published in 1902, this book describes Jewish life on
the Lower East Side of New York in intimate and sympathetic detail,
and pays particular attention to the Yiddish theatre. Hapgood assures
the reader that the players' realistic acting brings even the most melo-
dramatic or implausible plays to life:

The Yiddish players, even the poorer among them, act with remarkable
sincerity. Entirely lacking in self-consciousness, they attain almost from the
outset to a direct and forcible expressiveness. They, like the audience, rejoice
in what they deem the truth. In the general lack of really good plays they yet
succeed in introducing the note of realism. To be true to nature is their
strongest passion, and even in a conventional melodrama their sincerity, or
their characterization in the comic episodes, often redeems the play from utter
barrenness.[36]

These effects were probably achieved by somewhat unsubtle means. Alfred Döblin, who saw the famous Vilna troupe of Yiddish actors during his visit to Poland in 1924, found their acting exaggerated and sensational: 'Sie wollen Wirkung und glauben sie mit Aufdringlichkeit zu erreichen. Zu heftige Gesten, dicke Unterstreichungen; von der Bühne ins Publikum.'[37]

Still, it was not the quality of the plays or of the acting that enthralled Kafka. He criticizes both in his diary, without stinting in his admiration for the actors. Whatever their shortcomings, they embodied a living Jewish culture, in sharp contrast to the merely theoretical Zionism of the Bar Kochba. Moreover, unlike most of Kafka's acquaintances, the Yiddish actors were not self-conscious about being Jews. In their company, Kafka could feel that he was no longer being labelled a Jew by the more or less hostile Gentile world; he was not compelled to accept other people's definitions of him; he was able to be a Jew and revel in it. After one of his first visits in 1911, when he saw a performance of Latayner's play *Der meshumed* ('The Apostate') which included songs by one of the actresses, Flora Klug, he noted in his diary:

Bei manchen Liedern, der Ansprache 'jüdische Kinderlach', manchem Anblick dieser Frau, die auf dem Podium, weil sie Jüdin ist, uns Zuhörer, weil wir Juden sind, an sich zieht, ohne Verlangen oder Neugier nach Christen, ging mir ein Zittern über die Wangen. (T 81.)

Evidently the theatre fulfilled for Kafka the purpose that Schiller had claimed for it in 1784, in his lecture *Was kann eine gute stehende Schaubühne eigentlich wirken?*: that of harmonizing the beliefs and emotions of the audience and thus creating national solidarity. No doubt the content of the plays also helped, since some, like Goldfaden's *Bar Kochba* and *Sulamit*, dramatized episodes from Jewish history, while others were set in contemporary Eastern Europe and portrayed the triumph of faithful Jews over apostates and Gentiles.

Kafka's judgements on individual plays are rather curious. He preferred the technically inferior plays because in their *naïveté* and clumsiness they seemed to him to capture more of Jewish life than the more accomplished and sophisticated plays by Gordin. The latter tried too hard to be literature and made such concessions to the American Jewish public for which they were originally written that, as Kafka complained, one had as it were to crane one's neck to see over the heads of the New York theatre audience (T 117). Kafka valued the plays less as works of art than as expressions of Jewish life, and also because they aroused his sense of being Jewish without the embarrassment which he felt at political gatherings.

His contact with the Yiddish theatre gave Kafka a burning desire to find out all he could about Jewish history and culture. On 1 November 1911 he started reading Heinrich Graetz's *Geschichte der Juden*, the source from which many Jews with a largely secular upbringing had drawn their Jewish self-awareness.[38] But though Kafka read Graetz 'gierig und glücklich' (T 132), he had another source of information in his friend Jizchok Löwy. Löwy was the son of well-to-do orthodox parents in Warsaw and had studied the Talmud till the age of twenty. But long before then, unknown to his pious parents, he had become fascinated by the theatre, which he had been visiting surreptitiously since the age of fourteen. His very first visit to the Yiddish theatre made him resolve to become an actor and led to a breach with his parents, for whom the theatre was naturally *treyfe* (forbidden). On the basis of Löwy's somewhat incoherent stories Kafka began writing down an account of his life, which forms a curious counterpart to better-known fictional and semi-fictional narratives about people who try to escape from a constricting environment to the theatre with its opportunities for both genuine and vicarious self-realization. Besides the obvious examples, Goethe's *Wilhelm Meisters theatralische Sendung* and Moritz's *Anton Reiser*, one might think of Karl Emil Franzos's underrated novel *Der Pojaz*, which narrates the heroic efforts made by a poor, illegitimate, and sickly Jewish boy from a Galician village to become an actor. Since recollections of Löwy doubtless helped to inspire the 'Teater von Oklahama' episode of *Der Verschollene*, one could be tempted to add that novel to the list, interpreting Karl's journey westward as a search for the self-realization that industrial America has denied him, though, as the next chapter will show, this is only one of several strands in the story.

While Löwy may have helped indirectly to supply Kafka with literary images, he was of unquestionable importance in providing him with information about traditional Jewish communities in Eastern Europe. Between November 1911 and January 1912 Kafka recorded in his diary much curious information about customs and beliefs in such communities. He reports in particular detail Löwy's account of circumcision, including the precautions taken to ward off evil spirits (T 210–11). Since he wrote this on 25 December 1911, he must have been struck by the contrast between these elaborate rites and the perfunctory, half-understood ceremony he had witnessed at his nephew's circumcision on the previous day.

Löwy also introduced Kafka to Yiddish poetry and fiction. In his diary Kafka mentions Löwy's recitation of poems by Morris Rosenfeld, the New York writer famous as the 'poet of the sweat-shop', and of the one Yiddish poem written by the Hebrew poet Bialik (T 105). Löwy also read aloud prose pieces by the nineteenth-century short-story writers Perets and Sholem Aleichem. The only book that Kafka is known to have read for himself in Yiddish is Gordin's play *Di shkhite* ('The Slaughter'), which he presumably borrowed from Löwy. For a native speaker of German who had been taught the Hebrew alphabet at school, like Kafka, it would not be difficult to read Yiddish, though some of the vocabulary would be unfamiliar, as is shown by Kafka's mistranslation of Gordin's title (T 173). If he read no more, that was probably not because of linguistic difficulties but because books in Yiddish were then as hard to procure as they are now. Still, in 1916 he recommended to Felice some collections of stories by the Yiddish authors Perets and Sholem Ash in German translation, for use in the Berlin home where she was teaching refugee children (F 709, 713), and in one of these letters he mentions an unspecified book by Sholem Aleichem (F 711), which he may have read in Yiddish.

Though Kafka's first-hand acquaintance with Yiddish literature was very scanty, he acquired a fair knowledge of it through translations and secondary sources. In January 1912, when his enthusiasm for Jewish culture and history was at its height, he plunged into a 500-page history of Yiddish literature, written in French, which had recently been submitted as a doctoral thesis at the University of Paris.[39] Its author, Meyer Isser Pinès (1881–1942?), came from a well-to-do family in Mogilev in White Russia, and had received both a traditional Talmudic education at the Rozinay *yeshiva* and a Western education at universities in Switzerland and France; he helped to found the Jewish Territorial Organization, a breakaway movement from Zionism which tried unsuccessfully to acquire land for Jewish settlements in countries ranging from Mexico to Australia, and is thought to have died in one of Stalin's labour camps. His book has the merit of being the first comprehensive survey of Yiddish literature in a Western language, though its inaccuracies provoked outrage when a Yiddish translation of it appeared in 1911. However, it did provide Kafka with an overview of the development of Yiddish literature, and, since Pinès quotes copiously from many of the works discussed, and gives long summaries of others, the book also served Kafka as an anthology. He read it 'gierig, wie ich es mit solcher Gründlichkeit, Eile und Freude bei ähnlichen Büchern noch niemals getan habe' (T 242).

By one of the anomalies of textual history, the notes that Kafka took from Pinès are available only in the English translation of his diaries, having been omitted by Brod from his German edition.[40] From his notes it would appear that four aspects of Yiddish literature particularly interested Kafka. The first was the relation between literature and the life of the Jewish people. For example, the fate of Jewish conscripts compelled to serve in the Tsar's armies was recorded in popular songs, from which Kafka copied out some lines; and he notes also the existence of the *badkhen*, the singer and jester who performed at weddings. These illustrated the intimate relationship between literature and popular life, in contrast to the second main topic of Kafka's notes: the influence exerted on Yiddish literature by the *Haskalah*, the movement for Jewish enlightenment that had originated with Moses Mendelssohn. Though the *Maskilim*, or adherents of the *Haskalah*, disapproved of Yiddish, they had to employ it as the medium in which to spread their ideas among the people, and thus they involuntarily assisted the growth of Yiddish literature. Kafka noted that their immediate influence on literature was bad, since their ideas were propagated through the didactic and moralizing novels of Dik and Shomer, with their improbable plots and cardboard characters. Their efforts at enlightenment were discredited by the pogroms which were unleashed against the Russian Jews in 1881 and which showed that attempts at assimilation were futile. Though Kafka mainly records facts discreditable to the *Haskalah*, he does mention with apparent approval its exaltation of manual labour. Thirdly, Kafka shows interest in the relation between writers and their public. He notes that when Rosenfeld, at the age of 44, was afflicted with paralysis and threatened with blindness, his readers, despite their poverty, collected a sum of money to keep him from destitution, and that it was customary to celebrate the anniversaries of Yiddish writers, such as the fiftieth birthday of Sholem Aleichem. And, fourthly, Kafka notes down information from Pinès's final chapter, which deals with the Yiddish theatre, and copies out part of Gordin's complaint about the reluctance of talented authors to write for the theatre. Altogether, Kafka's notes from Pinès demonstrate his interest in the social context of literature, and in the possibility of an autonomous literature free from what seemed harmful external influences, such as the *Haskalah*.

Kafka's new-found interest in Yiddish literature had practical effects the following month, when he managed to persuade the Bar Kochba to sponsor an evening of recitations performed by Löwy. This took place on 18 February in the Jüdisches Rathaus and was introduced by Kafka with a speech on the Yiddish language. By championing Yiddish Kafka proved his independence of judgement, for Westernized Jews had looked down on Yiddish ever since Moses Mendelssohn's time. In 1782, when Mendelssohn was consulted by a lawyer in Breslau about revising the oath which Jews were required to take before testifying in a Christian court, he recommended that they should be allowed to take the oath in German or Hebrew, but on no account in Yiddish: 'Ich fürchte,' he wrote, 'dieser Jargon hat nicht wenig zur Unsittlichkeit des gemeinen Mannes beygetragen, und verspreche mir sehr gute Wirkung von dem unter meinen Brüdern seit einiger Zeit aufkommenden Gebrauch der reinen deutschen Mundart.'[41] Zionists also regarded Yiddish with disfavour, and considered it a debased and sub-standard version of German. Herzl called it the 'verstohlene Sprache von Gefangenen'[42] and assumed that the future Jewish state would be a federation on the Swiss model in which various European languages were spoken; the principal language, he thought, would be German. Other Zionists despised Yiddish because of its association with the Diaspora, and were intent on reviving Hebrew. In Kafka's day, however, the cause of Yiddish was being taken up by Nathan Birnbaum, who organized the conference at Czernowitz in 1908, the greatest landmark in the history of Yiddish studies. He addressed the Bar Kochba in January 1912, and Kafka, who was present (T 243), may have been encouraged by his talk to try to help in promoting interest in Yiddish.

In his *Rede über die jiddische Sprache* Kafka had two aims. One was to provide information, mostly drawn from Pinès, about the derivation of Yiddish from medieval German, and to mention various morphological forms which had been lost in modern standard German but survived in Yiddish. This was also, no doubt, a tactic for making Yiddish seem more respectable, and hence it also supported Kafka's second aim, which was to soothe the fear of Yiddish that he assumed his hearers would have. Though he discreetly refrained from saying why they might feel 'Angst vor dem Jargon' (H 422), one can easily guess. Yiddish was the language of people whose dress, customs, and religious practices made them appear alien; it was also associated with the poverty from which many of the parents of Kafka's contemporaries had emerged, and could arouse a fear of being sucked back into that environment. Kafka told his hearers that they would be able to understand Yiddish, not because they already knew some of the vocabulary—a Yiddish word like *toyt*, he insisted, was not identical with the corresponding German word *tot*—but rather because they possessed an intuitive affinity with it which would enable them 'Jargon fühlend zu verstehen' (H 426). That is, they already had a latent understanding of Yiddish and needed simply to stop repressing this faculty, as Westernized Jews usually did, and to let Yiddish work on them. With hindsight, one can detect Kafka's concealed ideological purpose: having himself begun recovering his Jewish consciousness at the Yiddish theatre, he wanted to expose his audience to Yiddish so that it would have the same effect on them. Language, as the medium in which people could become aware of their social allegiance, had for Kafka become a political matter.

Another product of Kafka's interest in Yiddish literature has been almost entirely overlooked by Kafka scholars. This is the series of notes on the character of minor literatures which Kafka wrote down in his diary on 25 December 1911, after two months of contact with the Yiddish theatre and conversation with Löwy. These notes are important evidence for Kafka's views about literature and its relation to society. He writes about it in general terms, and was not inspired solely by his acquaintance with Yiddish literature. He was also interested in Czech literature and conscious of its political importance as a vehicle of national feeling: two months earlier he had noted in his diary that Smetana's *The Bartered Bride*, though composed without any relevance to the struggle for independence, had subsequently become a symbol of Czech nationalism. He paid several visits to the Czech theatre to see plays by the dramatists Vojnovič and Vrchlický, though he thought them worthless and mentions no redeeming features (T 108, 195). In keeping with the range of his interests, Kafka's notes on minor literatures apply to the literature of any small nation which is trying to assert its identity and to resist the influence of a neighbour with greater cultural prestige and political power. If his remarks have any validity, therefore, they should also apply to present-day Welsh or Irish literature in their relation to English, though Czech literature had to assert itself principally against German, and Yiddish literature, in different places, had Polish, Russian, and German literature as its more powerful competitors. The notes are an extremely compressed and often obscure body of writing, which it would be very difficult to analyse if Kafka had not himself felt the need for clarity and appended to them a table listing their main points (T 210). In the summary that follows I shall use this table as a guide.

As his first point, Kafka stresses the intimate connection between a minor literature and the life of its nation. Unlike history, which surveys the main features of the nation's past from a superior vantage-point, literature is a 'Tagebuchführen einer Nation' (T 206) which records even petty events just as they happen. It preserves national self-awareness from disintegration, and fortifies its resistance to the hostile world outside. It focuses people's attention on the affairs of their own nation, and is the medium through which they become aware of foreign cultures. It does not smooth over the conflicts within the nation itself, but makes these conflicts easier to live with: for example, it presents the shortcomings of the national character in a manner which, though painful, frees people from embarrassment (Kafka was perhaps thinking of the tales in which Sholem Aleichem satirizes the Jewish citizens of Kasrilevke); it helps to incorporate discontented social groups into the nation's life; and it creates a medium in which the antagonism between fathers and sons assumes a more acceptable form and can be talked about. (Here we may cast our minds forward eight years to that passage in the *Brief an den Vater* in which Kafka claims that if his father had taken a genuine interest in Judaism, it might have provided common ground on which the two of them could have met (H 197).) Such a literature will itself be an object of national interest, and will generate lively discussion in newspapers and journals. Thus national feeling and literature can influence one another reciprocally. The insecure position of a nation which has to defend, if not its political independence, then at any rate its cultural integrity against the encroachments of powerful neighbours provides literature with a central role in society. In return, literature causes the 'Vergeistigung des großflächigen öffentlichen Lebens' (T 206) by increasing the cultural and intellectual level of people's lives in general.

Secondly, a minor literature is likely to have minor writers. This is not a drawback, for a commanding genius like Goethe (Kafka gives no examples, but this one comes readily to mind) is a mixed blessing for the literature he belongs to. Such a figure dwarfs all other writers. In his absence, there is no indisputable standard of literary merit, and hence plenty of scope for vigorous debate about the value of individual writers. Each writer has to establish his reputation on his own merits;

there is no towering genius whom others can simply imitate. (As illustrations, we may recall how English blank verse withered in Milton's shadow, or the host of now forgotten nonentities who imitated Goethe and were even encouraged by him to such an extent that, as Heine said, to have been praised by Goethe became discreditable.)[43] People entirely devoid of talent will therefore not dare to try their hand at writing, so all writers will have at least a modicum of talent. Since minor writers are less likely to be affected by foreign influences, the literature to which they belong is likely to retain its national integrity. Its writers will be valued for their national significance as well as for their intrinsic merit, and their reputations will therefore be secure from day-to-day fluctuations of taste. The history of such a literature will be a history of stable reputations, preserved in the memory of the people and not just in volumes written by literary historians: 'die Literatur ist weniger eine Angelegenheit der Literaturgeschichte als Angelegenheit des Volkes' (T 208). Here we may usefully recall both Kafka's distaste for the professorial attitude to Goethe and his interest in the esteem shown for Yiddish writers by their public.

The minor writers who make up a minor literature will be at liberty to treat minor themes. Kafka does not explain what he means by the 'Behandlung kleiner Themen' (T 209), and his assertion seems odd when one considers how often emergent literatures have tried to authenticate themselves by laying claim to a national epic: one thinks of the national significance that the *Nibelungenlied* acquired after its rediscovery in the eighteenth century, or of the supposed Czech medieval heroic poems which were forged in the early nineteenth century by the romantic nationalist Václav Hanka and exposed only in the 1880s. Kafka may have been imagining a literary environment specially congenial to himself. When he made these notes, some of the sketches later published in his first book, *Betrachtung* (1912), had already appeared in magazines. These short pieces illustrate the liking for small-scale art that helped Kafka to appreciate Kleist's anecdotes and Robert Walser's essays. A literary environment that favoured such miniature works would certainly have appealed to him.

Kafka's third main point concerns the relations between a minor literature and politics. The passage in which he discusses this is so dense and obscure that it had better be reproduced as well as explicated:

'Weil die zusammenhängenden Menschen fehlen, entfallen zusammenhängende literarische Aktionen. [. . .] Wenn auch die einzelne Angelegenheit oft mit Ruhe durchdacht wird, so kommt man doch nicht bis an ihre Grenzen, an denen sie mit gleichartigen Angelegenheiten zusammenhängt, am ehesten erreicht man die Grenze gegenüber der Politik, ja man strebt sogar danach, diese Grenze früher zu sehen, als sie da ist, und oft diese sich zusammenziehende Grenze überall zu finden. Die Enge des Raumes, ferner die Rücksicht auf Einfachheit und Gleichmäßigkeit, endlich auch die Erwägung, daß infolge der innern Selbständigkeit der Literatur die äußere Verbindung mit der Politik unschädlich ist, führen dazu, daß die Literatur sich dadurch im Lande verbreitet, daß sie sich an den politischen Schlagworten festhält. (T 209.)

Kafka seems to mean that a small nation would have no room for a cohesive literary society, consisting of a network of magazines, publishers and writers' gatherings. There would be no such 'zusammenhängende literarische Aktionen' and hence no self-contained literary *Bohème*. Instead, a minor literature would rely on politics for its support and dissemination; since politics was omnipresent, any topic dealt with in literature would very soon reveal its political significance, and one would be so much on the look-out for the political implications of literature that one might try to identify them prematurely. Literature would be associated with political slogans, which ensure that it attracts popular attention. Here we may recall Kafka's observation that *The Bartered Bride* had come to symbolize the Czech nationalist cause. Now one might suppose that the state of affairs Kafka envisages, in which every new work of literature is promptly scrutinized for its relevance to the nationalist movement or some other political cause, would damage literature by reducing it to propaganda. But Kafka seems not to think so. Rather he thinks that literature has an inner autonomy which cannot be affected by the external link between literature and politics, perhaps because he has in mind works like *The Bartered Bride* which are non-political in origin and are given a retrospective political significance which does not damage their integrity. He certainly does not mean that literature should be transformed into propaganda.

It should be clear by now that by a minor literature Kafka did not just mean a collection of books but was envisaging a society in which literature was intimately connected with popular and political life and had a central place in people's interest. What Kafka has compressed into these few pages of his diary is nothing less than an essay on the sociology of literature. At the same time, we may reasonably infer that Kafka was imagining a society to which he himself would have liked to belong. In such a society literature would no longer have the marginal status that it had in his home, where his parents regarded his writing and his reading with uncomprehending disapproval. Nor, on the other hand, would literature need the support of a self-enclosed *Bohème* such as Kafka found when he met Brod, Werfel, and other writers in the Café Arco. Instead, literature would permeate the life of the society, especially its political life, without sacrificing its artistic integrity. The problem of the artist's position in society would thus be overcome. Moreover, literature by its ubiquity would provide a shared medium in which conflicts between members of society, especially between fathers and sons, could be, if not resolved, at least expressed and rendered bearable.

All these are sufficiently compelling reasons for Kafka to be attracted by the idea of a minor literature. But a further reason can be gathered from his remark about the 'Mangel unwiderstehlicher nationaler Vorbilder' (T 207) in such a literature and from the fact that in December 1911 and January and February 1912 he was reading Goethe so avidly that he could not get down to his own writing. On 25 December, the day on which he made these notes, he also wrote: 'Goethe hält durch die Macht seiner Werke die Entwicklung der deutschen Sprache wahrscheinlich zurück' (T 212), and decided that subsequent German prose-writers had never managed to wrest themselves free of Goethe's influence. He felt that Goethe's achievement was so monumental that it blocked the further development of German literature. That implies, of course, that Kafka's own literary efforts had already been forestalled by Goethe, and that he would only be able to develop as a writer in a literary tradition without a Goethe.

The numerous references to Goethe in Kafka's diaries for these months, however, also bear out Brod's suggestion that Kafka felt himself to have an exceptionally intimate relationship to Goethe. Not only did Kafka feel that Goethe had set an unattainable standard of literary achievement; he contrasted his own difficulty in writing with Goethe's happy and unimpeded productivity. 'Meine Lust am Hervorbringen war grenzenlos,' runs a sentence from *Dichtung und Wahrheit* which Kafka copied into his diary on 8 February 1912 (T 248). Kafka carried the contrast still further by commenting on a full-length silhouette of Goethe which showed a perfect human body (T 247). When he made this comment, Kafka was overstrained, constantly tired, subject to occasional fainting fits; but he was also chronically self-conscious about his tall, gangling build, so we may justifiably assume that he was comparing Goethe's physique with his own. But this passage also implies an association between Goethe and Kafka's own father. Hermann Kafka was a big, burly man; when Kafka was a child his father took him to the swimming-baths, where they undressed in the same cubicle, and Kafka was ashamed of the contrast between his own skinny frame and his father's massive, powerful body (H 168). It is this contrast which he seems now to have transferred to Goethe, casting Goethe in the role of a literary parent; we remember that later in 1912 the interior of Goethe's house in Weimar made him think of dead ancestors. Just as Kafka's actual father intimidated him and hindered him in becoming an independent adult, so Goethe, his literary father, inhibited him by representing a standard of excellence which he could not hope to reach, let alone surpass. The trap in which Kafka found himself was particularly painful at this time, since he had recently made a half-hearted attempt to emulate his father's commercial success by becoming a sleeping partner in a small factory run by his brother-in-law. Knowing, however, that he could not rival his father, he normally preferred to escape from their conflict into literature. But there he found that instead of evading the conflict he had simply transferred it to a different arena, with Goethe as literary father blocking his future as a writer.

It might now be tempting to see Kafka the writer as engaged in an oedipal conflict with Goethe. Harold Bloom maintains that every major writer is engaged in such a conflict with a literary father-figure, and that literary works can be analysed as attempts to deny, elude, or overcome the predecessor's influence.[44] If applied to Kafka, however, this theory might prove not only as reductive as other Freudian approaches, but also distorting. Kafka may have felt his life to be dominated by his relationship with his father, but their conflict was not an oedipal one in any exact sense. The Oedipus complex, as Freud defines it, includes the unconscious desire to kill the father. One can no doubt see such desires being realized vicariously in Expressionist dramas of this time, like Sorge's *Der Bettler* (1912) and Hasenclever's *Der Sohn* (1914). In the former play, a son actually kills his father; in the latter, the son is about to do so when the father conveniently drops dead from heart failure. But, as the late Roy Pascal pointed out, Kafka treats this theme differently.[45] The sons in his stories, far from killing their fathers, do not even rebel against them. Georg Bendemann in *Das Urteil* submits to the death by drowning to which his father has condemned him, saying as he dies: 'Liebe Eltern, ich habe euch doch immer geliebt' (E 68); Gregor Samsa in *Die Verwandlung*, instead of trying to oppose his father, willingly retreats into his bedroom, stays there while it fills up with dirt and junk, and submissively dies after his family have decided they can no longer tolerate him; while in *In der Strafkolonie* the traveller finally escapes from the island where the Old Commandant is buried. It would be less misleading to say that Kafka is trying to imagine ways not of attacking but of eluding his father.

If literature represented for Kafka a means of escaping from his actual father, then a minor literature was a way of eluding his literary father and escaping from Goethe's masterful shadow. The only commentators to discuss Kafka's notes on minor literatures in any detail, Gilles Deleuze and Félix Guattari, reach a similar conclusion, but with emphasis on the importance of the Yiddish language for Kafka. They argue that for Kafka a minor literature had to be permeated by politics but could not contain any source of authority; instead, it had to be in a constant state of rebellion against authority. Kafka himself says that a small literature must maintain 'eine ununterbrochene nationale Kampfstellung' (T 88) towards its competitors. Deleuze and Guattari then claim, less plausibly, that Yiddish was the ideal vehicle of a minor literature, since it was not a separate language like Czech, but a dialect of German which could function as a subversive agent within German.[46] It is, however, hard to believe that Kafka wanted in any sense to subvert the German language. He was a linguistic purist who, before allowing any of his writings to be published, took pains to adjust their spelling, vocabulary, and punctuation to the High German standard. It is more likely that Yiddish offered Kafka a refuge from literary and family pressures.

Even so, this was hardly more than a theoretical possibility. Kafka could participate in Yiddish literature only passively, by attending plays and listening to Löwy's readings. His native language was the same as Goethe's, and he had to make the best of it. His close contact with Yiddish literature came to an end in February 1912, when the actors left Prague, though he continued to correspond with Löwy, whom he met for the last time in Budapest in 1917. Their respect and liking were mutual. A touching letter from Löwy to Kafka, dated 28 October 1913 and partially quoted by Brod, says: 'Sie waren doch der Einziger was war so gutt zu mir . . . der einzige was hat zu meiner Seele gesprochen, der einzige was hat mich halbe

Wegs verstanden.'[47] Löwy retained his admiration for Kafka all his life, if we can trust the evidence of the story 'A Friend of Kafka' by Isaac Bashevis Singer, who met Löwy in Warsaw in the 1930s and portrays him as 'Jacques Kohn'.[48]

The immediate effect of Kafka's encounter with the Yiddish theatre, as we have seen, was to set him thinking about the place of literature in society, to arouse his awareness of himself as a Jew and his interest in Jewish history and culture, and to prepare the way for his gradual (and probably never unqualified) acceptance of Zionism. Later in 1912 he wrote his first major work of fiction, *Das Urteil*. Did his new interest in Jewish culture contribute in any way to this literary breakthrough?

To talk about literary influences on *Das Urteil* is hazardous, because there were so many. We now know so much about Kafka's reading and how he used it that this story, in particular, appears like a collection of literary reminiscences, held together and formed into a strikingly original work of art by the centripetal force of Kafka's imagination.[49] Kafka himself mentions some of his reminiscences in the diary entry of 23 September 1912 where he described how he had written the story at a single sitting during the previous night: 'Gedanken an Freud natürlich, an einer Stelle an *Arnold Beer*, an einer andern an Wassermann, an einer an Werfels *Riesin*, natürlich auch an meine *Die städtische Welt*' (T 294).

Die städtische Welt is a narrative fragment which Kafka wrote in his diary in February 1911 (T 45–52) and which anticipates some formal features of *Das Urteil*. It consists largely of a dialogue between Oskar M., a student, and his father, who reproaches Oskar violently for his shiftlessness, while Oskar tries to appease him by talking mysteriously of a plan which cannot yet be revealed. Its dialogue form anticipates *Das Urteil*, but the dialogue in *Die städtische Welt* is poorly constructed, beginning too abruptly and then meandering on without real development. Like *Das Urteil*, *Die städtische Welt* also relies on another dramatic technique, the use of gesture as a means of indicating characters' thoughts. Sometimes the gesture is insignificant, as when Oskar's father gazes into a corner of the room, instead of looking his son in the face, but other gestures are incipiently symbolic, as when the father stands up, 'wodurch er ein Fenster verdeckte' (T 45). Nothing in the fragment explains its title: Kafka may have intended to work outwards from the familial confrontation to its urban setting, but he did not get that far.

The allusion to Brod's novel *Arnold Beer: Das Schicksal eines Juden* (1912) is of considerable importance for the content and meaning of *Das Urteil*. Kafka read this book with great enthusiasm (T 277, Br 94), and, as Karlheinz Fingerhut has recently demonstrated, derived from it the plot outline, the relationships among the characters, and numerous motifs in *Das Urteil*.[50] The piecemeal borrowings that Fingerhut catalogues are less important, however, than Kafka's response to the theme of Brod's novel. Brod's declared intention was to assist the understanding of the 'Jewish problem' by portraying various types of Jew in fiction. There was no single Jewish type, he insisted: 'Vielmehr scheint mir die Mannigfaltigkeit und das Umfassen vieler Gegensätze dem Judentum sehr wesentlich zu sein.'[51] He had made a start in *Jüdinnen* by contrasting the neurotic, cerebral Irene Popper with the simple country girl Olga Grosslicht. In *Arnold Beer* he sets out to depict a Jewish intellectual. Arnold, though a strong-willed and competitive young man, is in danger of becoming a hopeless dilettante. He attends university solely in order to stave off entering his father's business, and dabbles in everything from experimental physics to Sanskrit. Although his friends admire the diversity of his talents, Arnold comes to feel that he is wasting his life. Under the influence of a Zionist friend, he momentarily wonders if his situation is typical of young Jews. The answer, though not stated in the novel, must be that it is at least typical of young educated Jews in German and Austrian fiction of this period. Arnold's superficial brilliance and lack of real creative power are shared, for example, by Detlev Spinell in Thomas Mann's *Tristan* (1903),[52] Heinrich Bermann in Schnitzler's *Der Weg ins Freie* (1908), or the over-educated, under-employed young Jews described at the beginning of Herzl's novel *Altneuland* (1902).

Arnold finds a temporary outlet for his energies when he goes into a rather shady business with his school-friend Philipp Eisig, who, though clumsy and backward as a youth, has acquired drive and confidence from a visit to America. Soon, however, Arnold loses interest both in the business and in the German girl with whom he is having an affair, and wishes he could escape from both entanglements. His release comes unexpectedly when he learns that his 94-year-old grandmother is dying and pays her a visit. Though she is portrayed as intolerably cantankerous, her sheer vitality impresses Arnold and somehow transmits itself to him: 'beim Anblick dieser arbeitsamen wilden Greisin bekam er aufs Neue Lust, sich ins Leben zu stürzen, aus dem er mit vorschneller Erfahrung schon hatte entweichen wollen;

bekam Lust, wieder zu toben und zu schaffen, wie es in seiner Art lag.'[53] She is associated with the Jews of the Old Testament, whom Brod represents, in an extraordinary passage bearing the imprint of Nietzsche and Martin Buber, as ruthless, amoral people filled with primitive energy, 'eine Reihe von klotzstirnigen gewalttätigen aufdringlichen Ahnen'.[54] When Arnold happens to notice a picture with a classical subject, it leaves him cold: 'Was ging ihn dieses Bild an, die Griechen, die andere Welt, die fremde Kultur . . .'.[55] After taking leave of his grandmother, Arnold's new-found decisiveness enables him to abandon his friend and his girl-friend and set out for Berlin, where a post as a journalist awaits him. With his entry upon a new life, the novel ends.

The visit to his grandfather has restored Arnold's contact with his Jewish roots. Although it reflects Brod's commitment to the Bar Kochba's nationalism, it does not mean that Arnold is going to become a Zionist. The change in his character has occurred at an instinctive, unreflective level. He has been rescued from the chronic indecision of the Western Jew by a kind of injection of primitive vitality, administered by a representative of the Jewish past, whom he imagines as gigantic in stature: 'Das Bild der alten Frau im Bett, zu Riesengrößen aufwachsend, stellte sich wie ein Schatten überallhin, vor jedes Haus. Um wie viel wichtiger war sie, ja nichts auf der Welt erschien ihm jetzt in gleicher Weise wichtig.'[56]

In writing *Das Urteil*, Kafka has borrowed the hero's uneasy relationships with friend and girl-friend and the climactic visit to an aged and (apparently) bedridden relative whose charismatic authority produces the illusion of gigantic size. The motif of 'Riesengrößen' has coalesced with the image of the giantess in Werfel's dramatic sketch *Die Riesin*[57] to form the figure of Bendemann senior: '"Mein Vater ist noch immer ein Riese," sagte sich Georg' (E 57). The common ground of the two stories, however, extends beyond the motifs which Kafka borrowed and adapted. If Fingerhut is right in calling *Das Urteil* an 'Anti-*Beer*',[58] the two stories must be different answers to the same question; and the question, I would argue, is the *Judenfrage*, the problem of the position of Jews in Western society.

Kafka's interest in this topic is demonstrated by his draft review of *Jüdinnen*, which begins: 'Wir sind jetzt fast gewöhnt, in westeuropäischen Erzählungen, sobald sie nur einige Gruppen von Juden umfassen wollen, unter oder über der Darstellung gleich auch die Lösung der Judenfrage zu suchen und zu finden' (T 52). It goes on to criticize

Brod's novel for failing to offer a solution to this problem. *Das Urteil* may well have more to do with this problem, and less with Kafka's immediate situation, than its interpreters have usually acknowledged. While Georg Bendemann is condemned for wanting to succeed in practical life, Kafka's own ambitions were chiefly literary; and though Frieda Brandenfeld owes at least her initials to Felice Bauer, as Kafka later recognized (T 297), he was not yet engaged to Felice when he wrote the story; he had known her for only a month, and had written his first letter to her two days earlier. It would be more appropriate to see the Bendemanns not as correlatives to figures in Kafka's immediate experience but as recognizable Jewish types, though, in keeping with Brod's insistence on the diversity among Jews, Kafka has made Georg into a different type from the one represented by Arnold Beer. While Arnold hates the prospect of commerce, Georg has assumed control of his father's business and increased the turnover fivefold. Instead of an impractical dilettante, he is an only too practical businessman whose complacent materialism is implicitly condemned by his estrangement from his friend in Petersburg. The friend's commercial failure hints at the belief, developed later in *Der Prozeß* and elsewhere, that failure in one's worldly ambitions is the prerequisite for any spiritual achievement. Earlier in 1912 Kafka had attended a lecture in the Jüdisches Rathaus which argued that the commercial spirit was leading to the dissolution of traditional Jewish communities and the decline of the German Jews (T 246), and he had in his own father a striking illustration of how Jews who succeeded in business tended to lose touch with their religious tradition. A strictly biographical account of *Das Urteil* would therefore need to contradict the usual view by seeing Georg himself as partly modelled on Kafka's father.

All this confirms Ingo Seidler's claim that Georg represents 'das Urbild des emanzipierten, dem Glauben seiner Väter untreu und ganz weltlich und materialistisch gewordenen Juden'.[59] The confrontation between Georg and his father articulates the conflict experienced by many of Kafka's contemporaries between the traditions of the Jewish past as represented, however residually and unattractively, by their parents, and the new, secular, materialistic world to which assimilation had admitted them. The feature of the past that Kafka chooses to emphasize is its contact with absolute justice. Refusing to be covered up by his son, Bendemann senior becomes the embodiment of a justice from which there is no appeal. As the officer says in

In der Strafkolonie: 'Die Schuld ist immer zweifellos' (E 206). Like other twentieth-century Jewish writers, notably Isaac Bashevis Singer and Joseph Roth, Kafka is concerned with the estrangement of the modern world from the realm of absolute values;[60] but he differs from them in his readiness to turn his critical gaze in both directions and to ask, especially in *Der Prozeß* and *Das Schloß*, whether some degree of estrangement from the absolute may not be necessary if one is to go on living.

For Georg Bendemann, at any rate, the intervention of absolute justice proves fatal. *Das Urteil* turns into an anti-*Beer* when he fails to draw new strength from the past but instead submits helplessly to its authority. Though the story suggests that Georg's guilt is beyond question, its nature, nevertheless, is strangely shifting and elusive. At the beginning of their confrontation, Georg's father denounces him for a series of acts of impiety. He has tried to usurp his father's authority by taking charge of the family business. His uninformative letters to his friend in Russia are described as deceitful and treacherous; and since the friend is also called the representative of Georg's father, who says of him: 'Er wäre ein Sohn nach meinem Herzen' (E 63), Georg's conduct towards him seems to have been another act of family disloyalty. Finally, Georg's engagement is said to have dishonoured his mother's memory. These accusations make Georg appear a self-centred rebel against family piety. Yet they are neither intelligible in themselves, nor sufficient to account for the overwhelming sense of guilt that makes Georg accept his sentence and perform his own execution.

Of the many explanations offered by commentators, one of the most interesting has recently been put forward by Gerhard Neumann, who argues that the story expresses the double-bind latent in the Enlightenment conception of education for freedom.[61] An order like 'Be independent!' can only be obeyed if one shows one's independence by disobeying the person who issued it. Thus Georg was supposed to to show filial obedience by imitating his father and becoming a successful businessman, yet this means making himself independent of his father and so constitutes disobedience. Compellingly neat though Neumann's interpretation is, it does less than justice to the perplexing way in which Georg's guilt keeps changing its character.[62] If at first his guilt seems to consist in a series of impious actions, any or all of which could in theory have been avoided, it ends up located in a level of Georg's being so deep-seated that his consciousness can never penetrate to it. His father's last words before the death sentence are: 'Ein unschuldiges Kind warst du ja eigentlich, aber noch eigentlicher warst du ein teuflischer Mensch!' (E 67). Through their very failure to make sense, Georg's alleged crimes point to a guilt which is 'noch eigentlicher' and as absolute as the justice by which he is condemned. His guilt resides in what he is, not in what he has done. As elsewhere in Kafka's fiction, guilt precedes wrongdoing, not vice versa. Conscious reflection can therefore never save one from guilt, for one's guilt must always elude one's introspection, unless, like Georg, one becomes conscious of it in the instant before one's death. *Das Urteil* explores the moral aspect of a more general problem which, as subsequent chapters will show, is present in all Kafka's major fiction, the relation between being and consciousness. Since being is the fundamental, unconscious level of human existence, consciousness is by definition estranged from being. There is no Archimedean point from which consciousness can apprehend being; and even if there were, an aphorism of 1920 suggests that its discovery might be as fatal as the encounter with absolute justice was for Georg: 'Er hat den archimedischen Punkt gefunden, hat ihn aber gegen sich ausgenützt, offenbar hat er ihn nur unter dieser Bedingung finden dürfen' (H 418).

We can now see more clearly how and why *Das Urteil* diverges from its model *Arnold Beer*. Kafka's story abandons the customary standards of coherence in its character portrayal, its mode, and its theme. Like *Beer*, it leads to a climax at which the hero undergoes a change at a profound, non-rational level. Arnold is galvanized by innate though dormant racial energies, Georg by innate though unconscious guilt. But, while Brod is only too explicit about Arnold's motives, the guilt that Georg encounters in himself is inaccessible to consciousness and therefore cannot be made explicit in the story. The reader, denied a position of knowing superiority, has to re-enact Georg's discovery by inferring his real guilt from the incoherent charges pronounced by his father. To add to the reader's difficulties, the story shifts in midcourse from one literary mode to another. Georg's reflections at his window, which occupy the first few pages, contain some puzzles (why is he reluctant to write to his friend? why should such a friend be an obstacle to his engagement?) but nothing definitely incompatible with verisimilar realism. But by the time Bendemann senior leaps upright, the realistic mode has been discarded for one which relies on vivid, quasi-Expressionist images and pays no attention to verisimilitude. As the mode changes, so does the theme. Kafka begins with a social problem, the relation between a Jewish father and son, which he had already broached in *Die städtische Welt*. But as he penetrates further into this aspect of the *Judenfrage*, he finds that it is at bottom a moral problem with epistemological implications concerning the very nature of consciousness.

These changes of mode and theme are the more bewildering for being masked by a rapidly moving narrative which scarcely allows the reader a pause for reflection. Its pace, tautness, and concentration distinguish *Das Urteil* very markedly from the lyrical sketches in Kafka's first book, *Betrachtung* (1912), and from his earlier, fragmentary narratives *Beschreibung eines Kampfes* and *Hochzeitsvorbereitungen auf dem Lande*. As Gerhard Kurz has recently shown,[63] these loose, rambling works owe much to the dream-like early fiction of Hofmannsthal, whom Kafka greatly admired; but they have none of Hofmannsthal's intensity. Even in 1911, when he wrote *Die städtische Welt*, Kafka had not learnt how to tell a story. The narrative of *Das Urteil*, however, is triumphantly successful. From its opening exposition it gradually gathers pace until the peripeteia when Bendemann senior regains his strength; from then on we have an intense confrontation between Georg and his father, in which the story presses unremittingly towards its climax, the delivery and execution of the death-sentence on Georg. In describing it I have had to use dramatic terms, for the most striking qualities of *Das Urteil* are dramatic. *Die Verwandlung*, written two months later in November 1912, is likewise dramatic in structure. Its three main episodes resemble the three acts of a play. Each rises to a confrontation between Gregor and the rest of the family. The climax of the whole story is perhaps Gregor's third appearance, which drives away the three lodgers; Kafka then relaxes the tension with the family council and Gregor's peaceful death, and concludes with a lengthy epilogue. In these highly dramatic and concentrated stories, Kafka has achieved a synthesis of two literary forms and also of two cultures: he has combined the German *Novelle* with the Yiddish family drama. His own enjoyment of *Novellen* included the pleasure of reading them aloud. In his diary he comments on his own readings of Wilhelm Schäfer's *Beethoven und das Liebespaar* (T 191), Grillparzer's *Der arme Spielmann* (T 282), and Kleist's *Michael Kohlhaas* (T 341). By reading these stories aloud, Kafka made them into dramatic performances. This helped him to enlarge the tradition of the *Novelle* by combining it with elements of the Yiddish drama, to which he was indebted for content, characterization, and structure.

Kafka read and saw several plays by Gordin which are realistic family dramas. The play he read, *Di shkhite*, concerns a fragile girl whose parents force her into marriage with a brutal and dissipated man whom she finally kills. *Der vilde mensh*, whose action Kafka recounts at length in his diary and describes as very bold (T 117), centres on an idiot boy who develops an ambivalent attraction towards his stepmother, in which hatred of her for replacing his mother is mingled with sexual desire. The strength of his feelings drives him insane and he finally murders her. The play which most closely resembles *Das Urteil* is Gordin's *Got, mensh un tayvl*. Its protagonist is the merchant Hershele, who is tempted by Satan into divorcing his barren wife and marrying his young niece. Thereafter Hershele's business prospers, but his character goes from bad to worse. He neglects his new wife, boards out his aged father, and ruins his best friend Khatskel. The play ends with a confrontation between Hershele and the friend, in which the latter points out to Hershele how much suffering he has caused and thus arouses his conscience, with the result that Hershele hangs himself. The resemblances between Gordin's plot and that of *Das Urteil* are close, and have been examined in detail by Evelyn Torton Beck in her valuable book on Kafka and the Yiddish theatre.[64] The newly married Hershele resembles the newly engaged Georg. His treatment of his father resembles Georg's; Hershele, like Georg, even physically carries his father off to bed, and in making Georg address his father as 'Komödiant!' Kafka may have been recalling that the father in Gordin's play is a retired wedding-jester or *badkhen*. Georg's relationship to his friend in Russia resembles that between Hershele and Khatskel. The final confrontation in Kafka's story is between Georg and his father, not his friend, but the father turns out to have been in close contact with the friend. All these similarities put it beyond doubt that Kafka was inspired not only by Yiddish family tragedies in general, with their violent endings, but also by the details of *Got, mensh un tayvl* in particular.

As for characterization, I have already mentioned the expressive and often exaggerated acting of the Yiddish players. *Der vilde mensh* relies especially heavily on gesture because the idiot, unable to understand or articulate his emotions, can only convey them by dumb show. Similarly, the resumption of authority by Bendemann senior is given direct physical expression by his leaping on to the bed and towering over Georg. In *Die Verwandlung*, too, and in other stories by Kafka, the characters express their emotions by exaggerated gestures and movements. A whole paragraph describes the behaviour of the Managing Director of Gregor's firm as he retreats before the advancing insect:

Aber der Prokurist hatte sich schon bei den ersten Worten Gregors abgewendet, und nur über die zuckende Schulter hinweg sah er mit aufgeworfenen Lippen nach Gregor zurück. Und während Gregors Rede stand er keinen Augenblick still, sondern verzog sich, ohne Gregor aus den Augen zu lassen, gegen die Tür, aber ganz allmählich, als bestehe ein geheimes Verbot, das Zimmer zu verlassen. (E 89.)

The Managing Director is one of many Kafka characters who express themselves primarily through gesture. The 'as if' construction in the last clause shows that the narrator, instead of claiming any knowledge of their inner lives, or trying even to guess at the workings of their minds, is concerned to bring out the exact quality of their gestures. Kafka's characters always have a physical presence, like actors on a stage.

The third debt that Kafka's early stories owe to the Yiddish theatre, in their dramatic structure, has already been touched on. Like the Yiddish family tragedies, *Das Urteil* ends with the death of the protagonist. The next two stories Kafka wrote, *Die Verwandlung* and *In der Strafkolonie*, end less abruptly and therefore without the cathartic effect of *Das Urteil*; instead, the deaths of Gregor and of the officer are followed by epilogues, in the former case with a change of narrative perspective, which round off the stories at the cost of dissipating the force of their climaxes. That perhaps is why Kafka was dissatisfied with the conclusions of both these stories; he complains in his diary of the 'Unlesbares Ende' (T 351) of *Die Verwandlung*, and in a letter to his publisher he said of *In der Strafkolonie*: 'Zwei oder drei Seiten kurz vor ihrem Ende sind Machwerk' (Br 159).[65]

I have tried in this chapter to demonstrate the close connection between Kafka's exploration of Judaism and the beginning of his career as a major writer. He drew extensively and intricately on two cultures, the German culture in which he was brought up and the specifically Jewish culture which he encountered most memorably in the Yiddish theatre, to produce a story which is a synthesis of both. Indeed, it may be that the 'Jewish–German symbiosis' described by Felix Weltsch existed only on the night of 22–3 September 1912. In the following months, Kafka was to write *Die Verwandlung* and the greater part of *Der Verschollene*. Like *Das Urteil*, they show that Kafka's interests were divided between social and private themes. In *Das*

Urteil his concern with the society around him, particularly with Western Jewish society in a state of transition and internal conflict, leads him to the private, moral problem of guilt. In the other two stories written in 1912 he moves away from Jewish themes to examine modern industrial society and its effect on the life of the individual. At the same time he continues the exploration of guilt and associated themes that *Das Urteil* had initiated. The following chapter will show how these social and moral themes are developed and interrelated in *Der Verschollene* and *Die Verwandlung*.

2

The Urban World
Der Verschollene (1912–1914) and Die Verwandlung (1912)

'DURCH die Mitte des vergangenen Jahrhunderts', wrote the industrialist and politician Walther Rathenau in 1912, 'geht ein Schnitt. Jenseits liegt alte Zeit, altmodische Kultur, geschichtliche Vergangenheit, diesseits sind unsere Väter und wir, Neuzeit, Gegenwart.'[1] The caesura referred to was the one dividing modern industrial society from its pre-industrial past. Unlike most attempts to identify epoch-making historical changes, Rathenau's has some plausibility. Even in Britain, where the industrial revolution was comparatively gradual, we know from observers like Engels and Mayhew how drastically it changed the lives of those who participated, actively or passively, in the process. In the German-speaking countries industrialization began later and effected a correspondingly more abrupt change in the conditions under which people lived and worked. By the beginning of the century Germany had overtaken Britain as the greatest industrial power in Europe, and almost half its population was living in towns of over 5,000 people. In the Austro-Hungarian Monarchy industrial expansion took place more slowly; but although in 1910 the 'Austrian' half, where it was largely confined to centres in Lower Austria, Bohemia, and Moravia, was still predominantly agricultural, 26 per cent of the population was employed in industry or mining, and industrial growth combined with agricultural depression ensured a drift to the towns. Here too, though more slowly than in Germany, town life was becoming the norm.[2]

In addition, a new kind of town had come into existence, the *Großstadt* or giant city. By 1914 the populations of both Vienna and Berlin had passed the two million mark. The concentration of so many people in small areas was made possible by the rapid development of technology in the two preceding decades. By 1900 urban railways and tram-services had made movement within conurbations cheap and easy. The first motor-car was registered in Germany in 1892, and the first lorry bought in 1897; bicycles, telephones, and typewriters became widely used during the 1890s, and electricity was generated cheaply enough for normal use in factories and homes, while large-scale technology and methods of mass-production were spreading from America to Europe.[3] All these changes supported Rathenau's argument that modern man had created a new environment for himself. Rathenau goes on to describe the modern city with unmistakable exhilaration:

In ihrer Struktur und Mechanik sind alle größeren Städte der weißen Welt identisch. Im Mittelpunkt eines Spinnwebes von Schienen gelagert, schießen sie ihre versteinernden Straßenfäden über das Land. Sichtbare und unsichtbare Netze rollenden Verkehres durchziehen und unterwühlen die Straßenschluchten und pumpen täglich Menschenkörper von den Gliedern zum Herzen. Ein zweites, drittes, viertes Netz verteilt Feuchtigkeit, Wärme und Kraft, ein elektrisches Nervenbündel trägt die Schwingungen des Geistes. Nahrungs- und Reizstoffe gleiten auf Schienen und Wasserflächen herbei, verbrauchte Materie entströmt durch Kanäle.[4]

Rathenau's imagery deserves scrutiny as an example of how the imagination responds to technical change. First of all, the city is implicitly compared to a giant spider at the centre of a constantly widening web. This image gains its force from the symmetry of a spider's web and from the calculating cruelty that we tend anthropomorphically to attribute to the spider as it waits to suck its prey dry. The spider's insatiable demand for nourishment, and the word 'versteinernd', implying the callous annihilation of organic life, lead on to Rathenau's second main image, that of the city as a huge body, organized with the utmost complexity to consume food and excrete waste. No soul animates this body. It contains intellect only in material form, as oscillations passing along its nerves (i.e. telecommunications), just as energy is conveyed through other networks. Human beings are merely the blood corpuscles floating helplessly through the city's veins; and here we have an exact parallel with an image used by Georg Heym, the poet who has rightly been placed alongside Alfred Döblin as Germany's greatest 'Großstadtdichter':

> Wie Aderwerk gehn Straßen durch die Stadt.
> Unzählig Menschen schwemmen aus und ein,
> Und ewig stumpfer Ton von dumpfem Sein
> Eintönig kommt heraus in Stille matt.[5]

Heym's image conveys the insignificance of human beings in the great city and the pointlessness of their activities. Though they may believe themselves to be autonomous, they are really drifting in a circle round the city's bloodstream. And Rathenau's image of the city as a vast and greedy organism implies that the city as a whole also lacks a purpose, except to sustain its own existence.

Both Rathenau and Heym regard the city ambivalently. For Rathenau it is a monster, but filled with vitality, and he clearly enjoys describing its size and complexity. Heym, in poems like the cycle 'Verfluchung der Städte', relishes the corruption of the cities, with a deliberate Baudelairean perversity, at the same time as he denounces it, and he looks forward to their destruction with savage eagerness. Sheer size, sheer energy, can be exciting in themselves. The expansion of modern cities enabled spectators to savour this excitement. The dwarfing of the individual by his new urban environment was deplored by some, but celebrated by others. Döblin argues in his essay 'Der Geist des naturalistischen Zeitalters' (1924) that technology has transformed human life for the better. Even though the individual has no freedom except as part of a collective, humanity as a whole now possesses a formerly unimaginable freedom thanks to its technological achievements, and therefore has a more than adequate substitute for the religious beliefs of the past: 'Es wird so: der bestirnte Himmel über mir und die Eisenbahnschienen unter mir.'[6] Writers who reject urban civilization as fervently as Döblin welcomes it sometimes qualify their rejection in surprising ways. Few have rejected it more whole-heartedly than Rilke. His famous letter of November 1925 to Witold Hulewicz denounces the techniques of mass-production which denude material objects of their human associations and replace them with 'Schein-Dinge',[7] and in the seventh Duino Elegy he attacks this process of abstraction and counters it with the conserving powers of the imagination. But his imagination could also be excited by technology. The denunciations of machinery in the *Sonette an Orpheus* (i. 18 and ii. 10) should not make one overlook the beautiful Sonnet i. 23, which uses the image of a light aircraft to represent the perfect work of art. K. R. Mandelkow has referred to this poem, convincingly, as 'dem kühnsten Technikgedicht der deutschen Literatur'.[8]

Writers of Kafka's generation could not easily avoid confronting the new urban world, unless they took refuge in the stolid pieties of *Heimatdichtung*, but they could scarcely write about technological civilization without some ambivalence. Kafka's response resembles Rilke's in containing a large element of disapproval, but differs in that he knew considerably more about technology. Rilke's and Kafka's native

Bohemia was one of the principal industrial regions in the Austrian Empire, specializing in mining, textile production, and machine-manufacturing. Although Prague was not a *Großstadt*, by 1900 its population was approaching 400,000 and it was encircled by spreading working-class suburbs, whose existence Rilke acknowledges in his early poem 'Hinter Smichow' (1895).[9] Rilke, however, left Prague in 1896, whereas Kafka, though he often toyed with the same idea, stayed there, doing a job which forced the industrial environment on his attention. After ten months of ill-paid, time-consuming work for the Assicurazioni Generali, an insurance company with its head office in Trieste, he secured a post requiring shorter working hours (8 a.m. to 2 p.m. without a break), in August 1908, with the Arbeiter-Unfall-Versicherungs-Anstalt für das Königreich Böhmen in Prag. This and similar institutes had been set up in 1889 in response to the increasing expansion of industry and to the political pressure which the Austrian Social Democratic Party, founded in 1888, was beginning to exert on behalf of industrial workers. The Institute's efforts to compensate workers for industrial accidents were at first not very successful, because manufacturers were predictably reluctant to contribute, as they were legally required to do, towards the upkeep of the Institute, and because the installation of electricity in many smaller factories and workshops from the turn of the century onwards made their standards of safety difficult to assess. In 1908 the Institute acquired a new, young and vigorous director, Dr Robert Marschner, who is the 'Chef' so often referred to in Kafka's letters to Felice. Under Marschner's direction the Institute began to show a profit, and a new system was introduced which classified factories for their insurance contributions according to the degree of danger involved in their operations.

Though the six-hour working day in the Institute was shorter than in Kafka's previous job, the work was more demanding, since he had to master a large quantity of information about accident insurance and industrial processes. His contributions to the annual reports of the Institute, concerning insurance in the building trade, the insurance of private cars, and similar subjects, demonstrate his expert knowledge.[10] Particularly noteworthy is the essay 'Maßnahmen zur Unfallverhütung' which Kafka contributed to the 1910 report, since it describes in detail the operation of various models of planing-machine, and makes the hindsighted reader think of the meticulous account of the punishment-machine in *In der Strafkolonie* (1914). Not all Kafka's time was spent at his desk, however; he made numerous tours of inspection through the industrial regions of northern Bohemia, and occasionally had to attend public meetings in provincial towns in order to explain the Institute's new system of classification.[11] When in the office, Kafka often had to work after hours, though since he found time to write many letters in the office, and he and Marschner once amused themselves by reading Heine's poems together while subordinates and even clients gathered impatiently outside Marschner's door (F 103), the pressure cannot have been unremitting. One afternoon in the summer of 1909 he sent Max Brod this description of his work, written on official headed notepaper:

Denn was ich zu tun habe! In meinen vier Bezirkshauptmannschaften fallen— von meinen übrigen Arbeiten abgesehn—wie betrunken die Leute von den Gerüsten herunter, in die Maschinen hinein, alle Balken kippen um, alle Böschungen lockern sich, alle Leitern rutschen aus, was man hinauf gibt, das stürzt hinunter, was man herunter gibt, darüber stürzt man selbst. Und man bekommt Kopfschmerzen von diesen jungen Mädchen in den Porzellan- fabriken, die unaufhörlich mit Türmen von Geschirr sich auf die Treppe werfen. (Br 73.)

The humour of this letter does not mean that Kafka failed to take his duties seriously or was callous towards injured workers. His superiors' reports speak highly of his industry, devotion, and general usefulness.[12] Brod tells us how distressed Kafka was by mutilations suffered by workers, and how amazed he was at the docility with which they requested compensation;[13] and a diary entry of 10 October 1911, 'Einen sophistischen Artikel für und gegen die Anstalt in die Tetschen-Bodenbacher Zeitung geschrieben' (T 92), indicates the unease he felt at having to defend publicly an institute whose provision for accident victims he privately knew to be inadequate. His work forced him to become acquainted not only with the details of technology, but with some of its most obviously deplorable effects.

Further undesired contact with technology came through Kafka's family. To his father, a self-made man, Kafka seemed a failure. His university education had brought him no further than to an undistinguished administrative post, and he seemed to be stuck there; his first major promotion, to the rank of vice-secretary, came only in March 1913. There was an embarrassing contrast with the brilliant career of his cousin Bruno Kafka, an outstanding academic lawyer who took his doctorate in 1906 and became a lecturer and subsequently a professor at Prague University. Kafka, therefore, had little option but

to yield to family pressure and, in December 1911, become a partner,
along with his brother-in-law Karl Hermann, in a newly founded
asbestos-factory. Though Kafka was only a sleeping partner, his
family expected him to visit the factory after finishing work in the after-
noons, thus reducing still further the time and energy available for his
literary work, which, in his parents' eyes, was no more than an eccentric and unhealthy hobby. In October 1912, when he was hard at
work on *Der Verschollene*, his family's insistence that he should spend
more time at the factory drove him to contemplate suicide; the situation was saved by the intervention of Brod, who persuaded Kafka's
mother to tolerate her son's absence from the factory and conceal it
from her husband by means of white lies. The factory was never profit-
able. It ceased production on the outbreak of war in 1914, and went
into liquidation three years later.

While it still functioned, however, the factory employed twenty-five
workers and was fully mechanized. As his diary for 5 February 1912
explicitly shows, his visits there convinced Kafka of the dehumanizing nature of factory work:

Gestern in der Fabrik. Die Mädchen in ihren an und für sich unerträglich
schmutzigen und gelösten Kleidern, mit den wie beim Erwachen zerworfenen
Frisuren, mit dem vom unaufhörlichen Lärm der Transmissionen und von
der einzelnen, zwar automatischen, aber unberechenbar stockenden
Maschine festgehaltenen Gesichtsausdruck, sind nicht Menschen, man grüßt
sie nicht, man entschuldigt sich nicht, wenn man sie stößt, ruft man sie zu
einer kleinen Arbeit, so führen sie sie aus, kehren aber gleich zur Maschine
zurück, mit einer Kopfbewegung zeigt man ihnen, wo sie eingreifen sollen,
sie stehn in Unterröcken da, der kleinsten Macht sind sie überliefert und
haben nicht einmal genug ruhigen Verstand, um diese Macht mit Blicken
und Verbeugungen anzuerkennen und sich geneigt zu machen. (T 247–8.)

He expressed the same feelings in a letter to Felice a year later. Felice
worked in a Berlin firm that manufactured an early form of dictation-
machine called a *Parlograph*. She had originally been a typist, but her
efficiency had gained her a post in the management of the firm within
a few years. Although Kafka took a lively interest in her work, he
could not reconcile himself to the impersonality of the machine:

Eine Maschine mit ihrer stillen, ernsten Anforderung scheint mir auf die
Arbeitskraft einen viel stärkern, grausamern Zwang auszuüben, als ein
Mensch. Wie geringfügig, leicht zu beherrschen, wegzuschicken, nieder-
zuschreien, auszuschimpfen, zu befragen, anzustaunen ist ein lebendiger

Schreibmaschinist, der Diktierende ist der Herr, aber vor dem Parlographen ist er entwürdigt und ein Fabrikarbeiter, der mit seinem Gehirn eine schnurrende Maschine bedienen muß. (F 241.)

Kafka's argument is that even an employer who browbeats his secretary is in a direct human relationship with the latter, whereas the use of a *Parlograph* abolishes the human relationship altogether and makes one into the servant of the machine. Since the machine follows a regular rhythm and cannot respond to the vagaries of the user's personality, the latter is forced to become machine-like, as were the girls in the asbestos-factory.

But though Kafka was worried by many of the effects of technology, he was also fascinated, as Brod tells us, by its latest developments. Among these, Brod mentions the cinema[14] and the aeroplane. Kafka's fascination with the latter is evident from one of his first published works, 'Die Aeroplane in Brescia', which appeared in abridged form in a Prague newspaper, the *Deutsche Zeitung Bohemia*, on 28 September 1909. Earlier that year, on 25 July, Louis Blériot had made the first flight across the Channel, and in September an aircraft-display was held at Brescia in northern Italy, with a prize of 30,000 lire awarded to the aviator who could fly the greatest distance in the shortest time. The competition was a national event, attended by many Italian noblemen, and by prominent citizens such as the poet D'Annunzio and the composer Puccini. The crowd of more obscure spectators included Kafka, Brod, and the latter's brother Otto, who were on holiday at Riva on Lake Garda and had made an outing to the airfield to have their first sight of aeroplanes. Before they set off, Brod suggested to Kafka that they should each write an article about the event. This produced 'Die Aeroplane in Brescia', an accomplished piece of travel-writing, whose most noteworthy feature in the present context is the literary technique by which Kafka describes something so unfamiliar as an aeroplane. One way of bringing out the strangeness of the new phenomenon is to break it down into its separate components and describe each in an apparently factual manner, as in Kafka's picture of Blériot in the monoplane in which he had flown the Channel: 'Hier oben ist zwanzig Meter über der Erde ein Mensch in einem Holzgestell verfangen und wehrt sich gegen eine freiwillig übernommene, unsichtbare Gefahr.'[15] When another French aviator, Rougier, takes off, Kafka adopts a different technique, that of describing the unfamiliar in terms of familiar objects and thus making it seem recognizable at the first glance, but strange and even eccentric at the second: 'Er sitzt an seinen Hebeln wie ein Herr an einem Schreibtisch, zu dem man hinter seinem Rücken auf einer kleinen Leiter kommen kann.'[16] Here we can already discern the characteristic of Kafka's imagination that Edwin Muir pointed to in 1938: 'He sees everything solidly and ambiguously at the same time; and the more visually exact he succeeds in making things, the more questionable they become.'[17] This tendency is given free rein in the portrayal of technological civilization in *Der Verschollene*, most of which Kafka wrote in the autumn and winter of 1912–13.

Since technology and its effects were of both professional and private concern to Kafka, it is not surprising that technology is so prominent in his first novel. Almost at the outset the hero, Karl Rossmann, announces: 'Ich habe mich immer so für Technik interessiert' (V 11), and adds that his ambition is to become an engineer. Kafka told his publisher that the book portrayed 'das allermodernste New York' (Br 117), and was therefore disappointed to find, when its first chapter was published separately in May 1913 as *Der Heizer*, that its frontispiece was a steel engraving depicting the Brooklyn ferry and dating from 1838. He soon reconciled himself to the illustration, finding it so attractive that it could be mistaken for the work of Kubin (which may suggest that he wanted his New York to have a sinister air), but his remark is nevertheless valuable evidence of his intentions. Klaus Hermsdorf has shown how Kafka deliberately included the most recent technological advances in his book. The bridge over the East River, described in Kafka's manuscript as connecting New York with Boston (V 144, a mistake for Brooklyn), had been completed only in 1910; torches and electric ovens were still novelties; and the cars, typewriters, and telephones which are everyday objects in Kafka's America were not yet so common in Europe.[18]

It would seem beyond doubt that the presentation of the world's most advanced industrial and technological society, by a method between realism and fantasy, was a major part of Kafka's project. America is not just the setting but the theme of the novel, though not its only theme: we know that Kafka's title for his book was *Der Verschollene* (F 86, T 453), placing the focus on Karl Rossmann. The moral and psychological themes surrounding Karl are familiar from *Das Urteil* and *Die Verwandlung*, the other stories Kafka wrote in the autumn of 1912. Chief among them are his relationship with his parents, who have exiled him and for whom he keeps seeking emotional substitutes, and the apparent inevitability of guilt. Commentators have disputed whether America or Karl should be seen as central to the novel, and as a result critical judgements on it have been even more grossly irreconcilable than is usual in Kafka studies. In the first major book on Kafka, Wilhelm Emrich declared:

Der Roman gehört zu den hellsichtigsten dichterischen Enthüllungen der modernen Industriegesellschaft, die die Weltliteratur kennt. Der geheime ökonomische und psychologische Mechanismus dieser Gesellschaft und seine satanischen Konsequenzen werden hier schonungslos bloßgelegt.[19]

A few years later Politzer was to urge the opposite view, concentrating on the psychological drama in *Der Verschollene* and regretting that Kafka should have crammed the novel with extraneous detail which, since he had never been to America, had no foundation in his own experience:

The reality in *Der Verschollene* is secondhand material. Besides Dickens it is taken from Benjamin Franklin's *Autobiography* and, perhaps, from the beginning of Edgar Allan Poe's *The Narrative of Arthur Gordon Pym* and some chapters in Ferdinand Kürnberger's *Der Amerikamüde*. Because of the tenuous and derivative nature of this material Kafka was unable to come to grips with it. It crumbled under the touch that was eager to penetrate and transform it.[20]

The opposition between America and Karl, between Emrich's and Politzer's interpretations, is, I think, a false one. The critical problem here is not to decide whether America is theme or setting, but to discover how Kafka has interrelated the novel's two main themes: on the one hand, the human implications of industrial and technological society, and, on the other, the moral and psychological significance of Karl's adventures. Emrich reduces the novel to the expression of the former theme alone. Politzer's approach, however, is still more obviously in need of correction. Research done since the appearance of his book has largely invalidated his view of *Der Verschollene*. We now know a great deal about the sources of Kafka's information about America; I shall review them briefly, with due acknowledgements to the scholars whose labours have unearthed them, in order to gain an accurate perspective on the America depicted by Kafka.

The list of literary sources offered by Politzer is in large part speculative and misleading.[21] We do have Kafka's own admission that *Der Verschollene* was intended as a 'Dickens-Roman' (T 536), with *David Copperfield* as the principal model.[22] But there is no evidence that he knew either Poe's *Pym* or Kürnberger's *Amerikamüde*, though, as I shall argue later, he was probably conscious of the latter novel even if he had not read it. As for Franklin's *Autobiography*, Kafka certainly knew this book later, and gave his father a copy of it in 1919 (H 201), but he never mentions it during the period (1911–14) when he was working intermittently on *Der Verschollene*, so its influence must be considered dubious.[23]

Kafka's interest in contemporary America owed little to imaginative literature and a great deal to personal contacts and non-fictional accounts. Several of his relations had emigrated to America and made good there.[24] His cousin Otto (the son of Kafka's paternal uncle Philipp, a businessman in the Bohemian town of Kolín) had gone there in 1906, with no contacts and no knowledge of English, had got a job as porter in a corset-making company, and worked his way up to become its export-manager. Later he founded his own business, the Kafka Export Corporation, and married into an American family. Otto's youngest brother, Franz (known in America as Frank), joined him in New York in 1909, and, after attending a private school there, became a clerk in the Kafka Export Corporation. In *Der Verschollene* Kafka seems to have combined details of their careers with some recollections of their brother Robert Kafka, a highly successful lawyer in Prague, who at the age of fourteen had been seduced by his parents' forty-year-old cook and fathered her son. Another cousin, Emil Kafka, had emigrated to America in 1904 and worked for the Sears Roebuck department store in Chicago. He is the 'E. K. aus Chicago' mentioned in Kafka's diary for 9 December (T 447), and the meeting with him probably helped to suggest the student Mendel who works in Montly's department store in *Der Verschollene*.

These real-life examples of success in America must have strengthened Kafka's feeling of being a stay-at-home and a failure. There were other, remoter examples, such as Thomas Alva Edison, who visited Prague in September 1911 and, with 1,200 patents to his name, impressed people as the very incarnation of American drive and ingenuity. Kafka copied into his diary for 11 November part of a newspaper interview in which Edison attributed the industrial development of Bohemia to the energy of emigrants returning from America (T 155). As Johannes Urzidil explains, Edison was probably thinking of one of his own closest colleagues, a Prague Jew named Kolben who returned to his native city and became a prominent industrialist.[25] Since the Prague Jewish community was so small, Kafka would certainly have known of Kolben and found in him further grounds for self-reproach. The *Prager Tagblatt*, which Kafka read on most days, reported on American politics, and also gave much space to American technological developments in its Friday supplement 'Aus Technik und Industrie'.[26]

From all these sources Kafka was aware of America as a country where everything was on a vaster scale than in Europe and where anyone could become rich with sufficient determination. This view is present in *Der Verschollene*, but superimposed on it is another, darker view of America as a society licensing the most ruthless exploitation of the disadvantaged, and using machinery to carry to extremes the process of dehumanization which Kafka had observed on his factory visits. He knew, for example, about the difficulties faced by 'green-horns' or newly arrived immigrants: the Yiddish poems which Löwy recited on the occasion organized by Kafka in February 1912 included one by Rosenfeld describing the arrival of 'greenhorns' in New York.[27] The slums on the East Side where immigrants clustered are twice referred to in *Der Verschollene* (V 97, 196), and the story Therese tells about her mother's death vividly conveys the misery of immigrants unable to find work or even shelter for the night.

The single most important source for Kafka's critical view of America was the account by the journalist Arthur Holitscher of his travels in the United States and Canada. Lengthy extracts were published in 1911 and 1912 in the *Neue Rundschau*, to which Kafka subscribed, and the entire narrative was published in 1913 as a book, *Amerika heute und morgen*, of which Kafka owned a copy.[28] Since Kafka's debt to Holitscher has received detailed study by Wolfgang Jahn and Alfred Wirkner, it will be sufficient to mention here that Holitscher describes not only the enormous scale of American life, with impressive photographs, but also its widespread poverty, unemployment and the resulting terror, and the merciless exploitation of the industrial worker. In particular he describes the application of time-and-motion studies, such as the Taylor system, to increase the efficiency of workers. In his memoir of Kafka, Brod talks about the inhumanity of these methods,[29] and we can fairly assume that they were discussed by both Brod and Kafka, who had highly developed social consciences, and that Kafka read with particular interest those passages where Holitscher reports on the use of workers as mere machinery. Holitscher describes how workers were required to keep up the most rapid tempo possible, under the supervision of a 'speed-boss'. Anyone who could not stand this pace was fired, and anyone who could was sure to be worn out by the age of forty. Many factories, especially in the South, relied on the labour of children, who worked a twelve-hour day for a pittance and often went blind early from over-exposure to electric light. (Kafka himself disliked electric light, considering it 'sowohl zu grell als zu schwach', T 591.) Many workers, according to Holitscher, escaped from this servitude by abandoning their wives and families and taking to the roads as tramps. A high proportion of tramps were Jews, since Jewish immigrants tended to be physically frail and became exhausted by the sweat-shop even earlier than other workers. It is curious that, instead of acting on this hint, Kafka makes his tramps, Delamarche and Robinson, respectively a Frenchman (a nationality scarcely represented among immigrants to America) and an Irishman with a very un-Irish-sounding name.

The image of America presented by Holitscher dominates *Der Verschollene*. Its keynote is incessant work under unrelenting pressure. As a lift-boy, Karl works twelve-hour shifts and has to take naps standing up. He competes with other lift-boys for the hotel guests' custom and attention; when his lift is on the way down, he disobeys regulations by tugging the cable to make it descend more rapidly. Another lift-boy, Giacomo, is already exhausted by six months of this work, and the Head Cook's assurance that one learns to stand the pace of American life and eventually acquires strength is countered by Therese's account of the toil in the kitchens, where one kitchen-maid has recently collapsed from overwork. When Karl and Therese run errands in the town of Ramses, they do so in frantic haste. Even people going to the theatre in the evenings rush there in terror of arriving late.

Work is governed rigidly by the clock. The harbour officials in the captain's office have their eyes on a watch, and a watch is one of the presents Karl's uncle gives him. The crisis which brings about Karl's dismissal from the Hotel Occidental follows a schedule: Robinson turns up drunk just after 4 a.m.; during Karl's brief absence from his post new guests arrive off the 4.30 express train; Karl finds the Head Waiter at his early-morning coffee and notices that the office clock shows that it is after 5.15; when he telephones the Head Cook, the Head Waiter mentions that it is now 5.45, and later he tries to hasten Karl's condemnation by remarking that it is already 6.30. Watching the clock is part of the discipline to which Karl is subjected by his uncle, who disapproves of his staring idly out of the window and playing with his elaborate desk, and objects that the proposed visit to Pollunder will disrupt Karl's programme of study. Uncle Jakob has

adapted to American civilization by becoming a man of rigid principles, as inflexible as the machinery around him; human ties such as
his relationship with his nephew count for nothing in comparison.
Human beings are subordinated to machinery in other, more palp-
able ways. This aspect of American life is first brought home to Karl
when he looks through the windows of the captain's office at the activity in New York harbour:

Inzwischen gieng vor den Fenstern das Hafenleben weiter, ein flaches
Lastschiff mit einem Berg von Fässern, die wunderbar verstaut sein mußten,
daß sie nicht ins Rollen kamen, zog vorüber und erzeugte in dem Zimmer
fast Dunkelheit, kleine Motorboote, die Karl jetzt, wenn er Zeit gehabt
hätte, genau hätte ansehn können, rauschten nach den Zuckungen der
Hände eines am Steuer aufrecht stehenden Mannes schnurgerade dahin,
eigentümliche Schwimmkörper tauchten hie und da selbständig aus dem
ruhelosen Wasser, wurden gleich wieder überschwemmt und versanken vor
dem erstaunten Blick, Boote der Ozeandampfer wurden von heiß
arbeitenden Matrosen vorwärtsgerudert und waren voll von Passagieren, die
darin, so wie man sie hineingezwängt hatte still und erwartungsvoll saßen,
wenn es auch manche nicht unterlassen konnten die Köpfe nach den
wechselnden Scenerien zu drehn. Eine Bewegung ohne Ende, eine Unruhe,
übertragen von dem unruhigen Element auf die hilflosen Menschen und ihre
Werke. (V 26-7).

Karl, as a detached and astonished observer, is unable to make sense
of these goings-on, and Kafka describes them in an appropriately
perplexing way. Objects are depicted in isolation; some cannot even
be identified and are merely called 'eigentümliche Schwimmkörper',
yet they seem to operate independently of humans ('selbständig').
The boats move in straight lines ('schnurgerade') with inhuman efficiency; the barrels are packed with such precision that they cannot
roll about; people either work laboriously, like the sailors at the oars,
or use only a tiny portion of their bodies to work, like the steersman
who guides the motorboat with movements of his hand—a vivid
illustration of the extreme specialization of labour. The passengers
being rowed have been packed in just as tightly as the barrels in the
cargo-boat, and sit 'so wie man sie hineingezwängt hatte', able to
move only their heads; the curiosity that makes them do so seems
non-functional and inappropriate to this scene of rigid efficiency. The
incessant movement of the sea seems to have been transferred to the
helpless human beings and their works: in other words, technology
has escaped from human control and acquired the inscrutability of a

blind natural force. Similarly, the noise in the New York streets at evening is later compared to a whirlwind and seems 'nicht wie von Menschen verursacht sondern wie ein fremdes Element' (V 73).

Later Karl sees other examples of enslavement to machinery. The telephonist with headphones on, impervious to any other sound, is immobile except for his fingers holding the pencil with which he takes down messages, and even their movement is more machine-like than human, 'unmenschlich gleichmäßig und rasch' (V 66). The assistant porters who provide information in the hotel do not address inquirers personally;. they rattle off information without a pause and without even looking the guests in the face. Human relationships have been suspended in the interests of efficiency. Of the employees in Uncle Jakob's business we are told: 'Keiner grüßte, das Grüßen war abgeschafft' (V 67)—as was the case in Kafka's asbestos-factory.

The discipline of efficiency is enforced by ruthless oppression. On the first page of the novel the Statue of Liberty holds a sword instead of a torch. This can hardly be a mistake, and the most plausible interpretation of this detail seems to be the one offered by Hermsdorf: 'In dieser Umfunktionierung des Symbols der amerikanischen Freiheit zu einem Symbol der erbarmungslosen Gewalt scheint der ganze Gehalt des Romans zusammengefaßt und im Symbol vorweggenommen zu sein'.[30] No doubt it is for the same reason that Kafka represents the captain of the passenger liner as wearing a sword and medals, and gives the American harbour officials black uniforms, though Holitscher had emphasized the rarity of uniforms in America. Kafka's desire to present America as a hierarchical society accounts also for the Head Porter's demand that Karl should say good morning to him every time he passes him; when he wrote this, Kafka had presumably forgotten that earlier he had mentioned the abolition of such ceremonies in the name of efficiency. The symbolic function of such details can be illustrated from the lift-boy's uniform that Karl has to wear. Despite its splendid gold buttons and braiding, it is an unpleasant garment, 'denn besonders unter den Achseln war das Röckchen kalt, hart und dabei unaustrockbar naß von dem Schweiß der Liftjungen, die es vor ihm getragen hatten' (V 185); and, being too tight, it constricts Karl's breathing. This detail conveys that Karl has been squeezed into a ready-made slot in society with only the most perfunctory attempt to adapt it for his individual needs. The contrast between exterior splendour and inner discomfort expresses not only the discrepancy between appearance and reality in America but also that between the mechanical homogeneity of American society and the physical, creatural reality of the sweating, breathing human beings forced to inhabit it. The hotel itself is a rigid hierarchy, where lift-boys occupy the lowest place 'in der ungeheueren Stufenleiter der Dienerschaft' (V 213). If the Head Waiter represents Kafka's form of justice, in which guilt is always taken for granted, the Head Porter embodies arbitrary tyranny which does not even pretend to be the instrument of justice. While Uncle Jakob punished Karl on principle, the Head Porter does so out of undisguised sadism. He decides that Karl is a dubious character, simply 'weil es mir so beliebt' (V 262), and prepares to torture him with the gloating remark: 'Aber da Du nun einmal hier bist, will ich Dich genießen' (V 262). The most terrifying character in the book, he anticipates the brutality of the porter Benedikt Pfaff in Canetti's parable of violence, *Die Blendung*.

Normally, however, American workers are kept under control without open violence; the obstinately inquisitive policeman who interrogates Karl is a comic figure. Terror of unemployment can be relied on to keep people docile. The student who lives next door to Brunelda tells Karl that getting a job in Montly's department store was the greatest achievement of his life. Immigrants are even in danger of being sent straight back to Europe: 'Denn auf Mitleid durfte man hier nicht hoffen' (V 54–5). Kafka's social concern is also apparent from the attention he gives to workers' resistance against exploitation. When Pollunder drives Karl out to his country house, their route is impeded by metalworkers who are on strike and holding a demonstration. Later Karl hears about a strike by building-workers which affects the father of his friend Mack, the biggest building contractor in New York. The lift-boys in the Hotel Occidental have a union, which was built up mainly by the present Head Waiter. Yet when Karl is brought before him as a delinquent, the Head Waiter does not bother about Karl's rights as a union member. Workers on different rungs of the social ladder feel no solidarity.

The hardships of American life are not mitigated by humane culture. Hermsdorf aptly calls Kafka's America a 'Zivilisation ohne Kultur'.[31] The only book mentioned is a handbook of commercial correspondence which Karl studies when free from his duties as a lift-boy. His uncle does buy him a piano, but Karl's absurd hope that his piano-playing may have some direct influence on American conditions (V 60) emphasizes not only his *naïveté* but the irrelevance of culture to American civilization. In any case, the only kind of music tolerated in America seems to be the kind that accompanies political demonstrations and advertising campaigns. Elsewhere Kafka tends to associate music with inwardness, as in *Die Verwandlung*, where Gregor Samsa, cut off from the outside world by his transformation, acquires for the first time a feeling for music. But in *Der Verschollene* music has to conform to the relentless pace of all activities in America. When Karl plays a tune on the piano at Klara's bidding, he does so 'im ärgsten Marschtempo' (V 118).

Religion, too, seems to be more characteristic of Europe than of America. Johanna Brummer, back in Europe, prayed to a wooden crucifix; Karl brings a pocket Bible to America with him; and the stoker has a picture of the Virgin Mary. New York does contain a cathedral, which is as 'ungeheuer' (V 55) as most things in America, but it is only dimly visible through the smog, while the chapel in Pollunder's house is to be separated from the rest of the building.[32] Apparently religion is fading from American life.

But although Kafka shows American technology to be the unrestrained instrument of oppression and dehumanization, his negative attitude to it is qualified in two ways. First, he evidently enjoys describing the enormous scale of American things, as when he tells us that Uncle Jakob's town house includes a lift big enough to contain a furniture-van, or describes Karl's first sight of New York 'mit den hunderttausend Fenstern seiner Wolkenkratzer' (V 20). He exercises some restraint in describing the height of buildings: Uncle Jakob's house has six storeys, though there are three more floors underground (V 54), and the Hotel Occidental is variously said to have five or seven floors, though it has thirty lifts and forty lift-boys![33] To a limited extent Kafka shares Döblin's inclination to ignore the fates of individuals and concentrate on the entire civilization in which human beings are only minor components. However, Kafka is incapable of the god's-eye view of human suffering that Döblin takes in novels like *Wallenstein* (1920) or *Berge Meere und Giganten* (1924), and instead keeps returning to the human beings trapped in the machinery of American civilization.

Second, Kafka devotes a long and puzzling passage to describing what may represent a humane use of technology. This is the account of the desk in Uncle Jakob's house which is so elaborately constructed that the layout of its pigeon-holes can be altered in innumerable different ways by turning a handle at the side. Emrich maintains that this desk stands for the liberating possibilities of technology: 'Hier öffnet sich eine letzte, höchste utopische Hoffnung: Wenn alle Technik sich in zweckfreies Spiel zu verwandeln vermöchte, dann wäre die Menschheit wieder vom Bann monotoner Arbeitsversklavung befreit.'[34] One could perhaps support this contention by pointing out that the desk is compared to the peep-shows depicting Nativity scenes that Karl saw as a child in the Christmas market at home. The desk would then be America's nearest equivalent to the redemptive power of religion. But it is, I think, more relevant that both the desk and the peep-show appeal to the imagination, for Kafka seems to have smuggled in a private allusion to his own imaginative writing. Not only is the desk specifically a 'Schreibtisch', but the upright part containing the pigeon-holes is called the 'Aufsatz' (V 57), which may be a pun on another meaning of *Aufsatz*, 'essay'. The desk would then be a piece of technology which is not strictly functional, not oppressive, and also a symbol of the imaginative process, like the light aircraft in Rilke's sonnet. This may be the real, unstated reason why Uncle Jakob disapproves of the desk and warns Karl to use the handle as little as possible. Indulging the imagination is incompatible with the American demand for efficiency.

By now it should be clear that the technological and urban world of America was not just a stimulus to Kafka's fantasies and is much more than a mere backdrop to the novel. Technology, industry, and their effects on human life were of intense concern to Kafka and form a major theme of *Der Verschollene*. But we still have to ask how this theme is related to the other aspects of *Der Verschollene*, and indeed what kind of novel we have before us. There are three main critical problems which I shall try to answer. First, how is one to define the literary method Kafka employs, which I provisionally categorized earlier as somewhere between realism and fantasy? Second, what is the meaning of the 'Teater von Oklahama' episode, which has been variously understood as religious allegory, brutal realism, or ironic travesty? Third, what is the relation between the theme of technology and the novel's other main theme, the complex of moral and psychological problems that besets Karl?

Kafka's literary method is obviously not realism. As we have seen, he feels no obligation to describe America accurately, but is willing to distort empirical reality in order to convey an idea, as when he places a sword in the hand of the Statue of Liberty. Even in this early work Kafka displays a tendency towards allegory. Instead of allowing significance to emerge from a faithful depiction of the empirical world, he often reduces the empirical world to almost diagrammatic simplicity so that it may convey his theme. This happens, for example, when he describes the New York traffic:

Und morgen wie abend und in den Träumen der Nacht vollzog sich auf dieser Straße ein immer drängender Verkehr, der von oben gesehn sich als eine aus immer neuen Anfängen ineinandergestreute Mischung von verzerrten menschlichen Figuren und von Dächern der Fuhrwerke aller Art darstellte, von der aus sich noch eine neue vervielfältigte wildere Mischung von Lärm, Staub und Gerüchen erhob, und alles dieses wurde erfaßt und durchdrungen von einem mächtigen Licht, das immer wieder von der Menge der Gegenstände zerstreut, fortgetragen und wieder eifrig herbeigebracht wurde und das dem betörten Auge so körperlich erschien, als werde über dieser Straße eine alles bedeckende Glasscheibe jeden Augenblick immer wieder mit aller Kraft zerschlagen (V 55.)

As one follows or tries to follow the cumulative structure of this sentence, one shares something of Karl's confusion as well as feeling how the hubbub on the street increases in intensity till it becomes unendurable. The traffic is described, not from some notional objective standpoint, nor from that of the people actually driving, but from that of a bewildered observer who cannot make sense of the scene, registers the people only as 'verzerrten menschlichen Figuren' and is more acutely conscious of the noise and smells rising from the street. From the people and objects down below, Kafka transfers our attention to Karl's sensations and then to the light itself, which is no longer a neutral medium but has acquired the physical character of a pane of glass being repeatedly smashed. The scene observed, the medium of observation and the sensations of the observer appear to have been fused into a single experience. Its essential features are conveyed by the final simile, which compresses into one clause the unintelligibility of events in the street, the deafening noise, and the sense of violent and impersonal energy. H. C. Buch well says of this passage that it reminds one, 'schon in ihrem hektischen Rhythmus, der sich bemüht, die Simultaneität aller Vorgänge adäquat sprachlich widerzuspiegeln, an ein futuristisches Bild von Boccioni oder Carrà'.[35]

An even closer affinity is with Expressionism. Although Kafka disliked the stridency of many of his Expressionist contemporaries, he has been aptly described as a 'klassischer Expressionist'.[36] He shared with the Expressionists the aim of penetrating beneath the surface appearance of the world to reveal what he took to be its true nature, if necessary by abandoning conventional criteria of mimetic accuracy and psychological plausibility. A passage from Kasimir Edschmid's manifesto *Über den dichterischen Expressionismus* applies also to Kafka's literary method: 'Die Realität muß von uns geschaffen werden. Der Sinn des Gegenstands muß erwühlt sein. Begnügt darf sich nicht werden mit der geglaubten, gewähnten, notierten Tatsache, es muß das Bild der Welt rein und unverfälscht gespiegelt werden.'[37] Edschmid is significantly ambiguous about whether Expressionists are to uncover an existing reality which has been concealed, or to create a new reality in art, and the same ambiguity underlies Kafka's efforts (to adopt a phrase from *Das Urteil*) to burrow beneath the reality commonly accepted as 'eigentlich' and reveal what is 'noch eigentlicher' (E 67). A realism that professes to disclose the truth beneath the surface of the empirical world has in effect abandoned literary mimesis. What it portrays will be a product not of empirical observation but of a theory held by the writer. Hence the super-realism advocated by the Expressionists must logically lead to allegory. Whether Kafka exhibits anything more than a tendency towards allegory is a thorny problem which will be deferred until after the discussion of *Das Schloß* in Chapter 6 below. For the moment it will suffice to note that his tendency is apparent in his early works and is part of the common ground between him and the Expressionists.

If Kafka departs from realism in the direction of Expressionism, he seems in other passages from *Der Verschollene* to move in the opposite direction by heightening the realism of his descriptions till he approaches the most meticulous Naturalism. The novel is full of what Buch calls 'Momentaufnahmen',[38] snapshots, like this one when Karl and the stoker enter the captain's office:

An einem runden Tisch saßen drei Herren, der eine ein Schiffsofficier in blauer Schiffsuniform, die zwei andern, Beamte der Hafenbehörde, in schwarzen amerikanischen Uniformen. Auf dem Tisch lagen hochaufgeschichtet verschiedene Dokumente, welche der Officier zuerst mit der Feder in der Hand überflog, um sie dann den beiden andern zu reichen, die bald lasen, bald excerpierten, bald in ihre Aktentaschen einlegten, wenn nicht gerade der eine, der fast ununterbrochen ein kleines Geräusch mit den Zähnen vollführte, seinem Kollegen etwas in ein Protokoll diktierte. (V 20.)

Here we have a superficially exact description of the three men and their work. Nothing is said about their personalities. Instead, Kafka focuses attention on their functions, as revealed by their uniform and the task of studying documents in which they are occupied. But since he does not tell us what the documents are, or for what purpose the officials are using them, Kafka prevents us from making sense of the scene as a whole and thus makes us share the bewilderment of Karl, from whose viewpoint the men are described. The demands of narrative perspective do not, however, explain why Kafka inserts one non-functional detail, the noise that one of the officials makes with his teeth. The fact that Karl notices this noise does not seem to reveal anything about his character. Could the noise be a 'reality effect', a detail whose lack of symbolic or thematic motivation makes it seem a piece of sheer brute fact and thus serve to enhance the plausibility of the fiction?[39] If the official had first been presented as a recognizable human being—if his face had been described, for instance—then the noise he makes would have been interpreted as a personal quirk and thus made Kafka's fiction more convincing. But since the official is presented primarily in functional terms, this detail, instead of heightening the impression of reality, is isolated and given an inexplicable emphasis. Moreover, though it is something familiar, Kafka defamiliarizes it by avoiding conventional terms like *mit den Zähnen knirschen*. Consequently this detail remains unmotivated and its effect is grotesque, as Martin Walser notes when he lists it among examples of Kafka's reification of his characters.[40]

Kafka's minute description therefore does not serve realism, though one might have expected it to. As Malcolm Pasley has recently shown, Kafka took over this ideal of precise and accurate description from Flaubert, especially from the latter's early travel journals, and practised it in his own diaries.[41] But exact description is a curiously limited artistic ideal. As Lukács points out in his great essay 'Erzählen oder Beschreiben?' (1936), description had a very subordinate role in fiction until the nineteenth century. Even Jane Austen is extremely economical in her descriptions of people, landscapes, or interiors. The passage from ch. 27 of *Emma*, where Emma pauses to look up and down the main street of Highbury, feels almost incongruous. Subsequent novelists, like Balzac, George Eliot, or Fontane, had to provide more detailed descriptions so that their characters might be understood in relation to their milieux. But the descriptions provided by Flaubert and the Naturalists, while retaining this pretext, tend more and more to become ends in themselves. And once description is served from its function of explaining character and action, it loses its human significance. No principle enables the writer to select significant details, for if all the details are significant, none of them is. Consequently, in Lukács's words: 'Die falsche Gegenwärtigkeit des Beschreibens verwandelt den Roman in ein schillerndes Chaos.'[42] Accordingly, Kafka's passages of precise description do not help the reader to understand American life. If they are intended to convey Karl's incomprehension, or to show that technology has rendered human beings helpless, then one has to say that they are too numerous and that Kafka has laboured and obscured the point he wanted to make. While some passages, like the memorable descriptions of New York harbour and of the street traffic quoted above, do admirably serve Kafka's aim of presenting the de-humanizing effects of technology, others, like the scene in the captain's office just quoted, come close to being stylistic exercises pursued for their own sake. Kafka seems, then, to be alternating between two literary methods which not only differ but may even conflict. One is to portray the surface of American life by means of Flaubertian Naturalism; the other is to fracture that surface and expose the forces underlying it by a version of Expressionism.

In the 'Teater von Oklahoma' episode, written in 1914, Kafka seems to have adopted yet another mode, and interpretations of it can be divided into the transcendentalist, the ironic, and the realistic. The first of these is still the most popular. It can point to Kafka's cryptic remarks, reported by Brod, on how the novel was to end: 'Mit rätselhaften Worten deutete Kafka lächelnd an, daß sein junger Held in diesem "fast grenzenlosen" Theater Beruf, Freiheit, Rückhalt, ja sogar die Heimat und die Eltern wie durch paradiesischen Zauber wiederfinden würde.'[43] Much in the text does suggest that the theatre somehow transcends the world of the earlier chapters. Religious associations, suggesting entry into heaven, are supplied by the women dressed as angels and playing trumpets. In contrast to the extreme difficulty of finding employment elsewhere in America, the advertisement for the theatre declares: 'Wir sind das Teater, das jeden brauchen kann, jeden an seinem Ort!' (V 387), and it appeals to potential artists, for whom there is otherwise no place in this philistine society. When Karl finds his way to the smallest of the two hundred reception desks, the official in charge is suspicious of his credentials, but is overruled by the 'Schreiber', and Karl is admitted. (These two officials may represent a covert allusion to Kafka's own double existence as official and as writer.) Emrich argues that Karl's admission signifies his escape from the rule of soulless efficiency and economic pressure into a realm where all who want it have the chance of self-realization.[44] This interpretation relies heavily on the contrast between technology and nature supposedly indicated by the title of this chapter in Brod's edition, 'Das Naturtheater von Oklahoma'. However, the title was supplied by Brod, and the word 'Naturtheater' does not occur in Kafka's text, though of course he may have had in mind an open-air theatre like the one at Chautauqua described by Holitscher.[45]

Other transcendentalist interpreters have made much of the religious imagery. Gerhard Kurz, for example, has recently called the theatre a 'Fantasmagorie des Todes und der Verklärung, ein Theater des Paradieses und ein Theater des Jüngsten Gerichts'.[46] But it is hard to overlook the irony to whose these religious images are subjected. The women look ridiculous and play their trumpets incompetently, producing a confused jumble of sound; worse still, their place is taken every two hours by men dressed as devils, whose presence would seem to cancel out their angelic message. Wolfgang Jahn has therefore argued that Kafka introduces religious images only to travesty them and to show that they have lost whatever spiritual content they once possessed:

Allgemeine menschliche Einrichtungen wie Bote, Buch, Richter, Mahlzeit, Fürst, die als Allegorien im Neuen Testament ihren fest geprägten transzendenten Inhalt besitzen, erscheinen im Oklahoma-Kapitel so, als sei ein solcher Inhalt gar nicht vorhanden; sie erscheinen als Werbekomparsen, Geschäftsbuch, Personalchef, Massenspeisung und Staatspräsident, das heißt als buchstäbliche und darum lächerliche, in sich widersprüchliche Materialisationen geistlicher Bedeutungsinhalte.[47]

The realistic interpretation has been advanced most persuasively by Alfred Wirkner. He points out that Kafka had read in Holitscher and in the press grotesque descriptions of American advertising,[48] and argues that the Theatre of Oklahoma uses such methods as part of an enormous swindle which, like the Eden Land Corporation in *Martin Chuzzlewit*, is intended to exploit the *naïveté* of immigrants. He supports his argument by relating the name Clayton, the town where the theatre mounts its advertising campaign, to the Clayton Anti-Trust Bill, which was progressively watered down by amendments and finally discarded on 5 June 1914. Kafka wrote the theatre chapter between August and October 1914, and could well have read about the fate of the Clayton Bill in the press. The chapter would then show Karl innocently entering on his last and worst servitude, with all hope of liberation removed. Wirkner also offers an explanation for the false name Negro which Karl uses at the reception desk. It may be connected with an illustration in Holitscher's book, showing a negro being lynched, with the caption 'Idyll aus Oklahama'.[49] We know that Kafka paid attention to this picture, for in his manuscript he repeats Holitscher's misspelling of Oklahoma; so perhaps Karl is heading for a similar fate.[50] Alternatively, one could accept Binder's suggestion that Negro is an alias adopted by Karl in a previous job. The surviving fragments show Karl slipping into the American underworld; the 'Unternehmen Nr. 25' to which he brings Brunelda (V 383) sounds like a brothel, and, working there, Karl might well have adopted a false name.[51] This argument could fit in with the dismal end that Wirkner foresees for Karl and with Kafka's own remark that Karl was finally to have been 'strafweise umgebracht' (T 481), though the rider that Karl would be 'mehr zur Seite geschoben als niedergeschlagen' suggests a milder fate than lynching.[52]

Nevertheless, in seeing Kafka's religious imagery merely as an advertising stunt, Wirkner seems to be oversimplifying the text just as much as those commentators who see in it an unequivocal religious allegory. Jahn's ironic interpretation is more convincing than either of the others. It must be added, however, that Kafka's travesty of religious symbols does not necessarily mean that those symbols are vacuous or fraudulent. If a transcendent reality exists, all symbols that try to convey its nature must be more or less inadequate and ridiculous. The composition of the 'Teater von Oklahama' chapter overlaps with that of *Der Prozeß*, and the next chapter will argue that the shortcomings of the Court's agents cannot diminish the absolute authority of the Court, precisely because it is absolute. In *Der Verschollene*, similarly, the razzmatazz surrounding the theatre does not mean that it has no transcendent significance; yet this mistaken conclusion is drawn not only by commentators but also by characters in the book. Most people are put off by the unexpected and unattractive trumpet-playing, like the family Karl meets: 'Sie hatten wohl auch erwartet eine Arbeitsgelegenheit zu finden, dieses Trompetenblasen aber beirrte sie' (V 390). Karl is the first person to cross the podium and request admission, and his example encourages the others to follow him. The *naïveté* he has brought from Europe, which makes him expect fair dealing despite repeated disappointments, enables him to respond to the theatre's message and see behind its gaudy and tasteless façade.

If this interpretation is correct, the 'Teater von Oklahama' chapter is the first of several occasions in Kafka's work where a transcendent reality is manifested in shabby and repellent guise. His choice of Christian symbols for travesty may be meant to imply that Christianity is particularly misguided in the way it envisages transcendence.' Other symbols are treated more seriously, especially that of music. The trumpets are fine instruments which the women abuse by their incompetence, but when Karl takes the trumpet from Fanny and blows on it, she acknowledges his skill with the words: 'Du bist ein Künstler' (V 393). Since the Romantic period music has provided a symbol of an ideal which can never be more than imperfectly realized, as when the nightwatchman in 'Bonaventura''s *Nachtwachen* tells how his life began as 'eine Mozartsche Symphonie von schlechten Dorf-musikanten exekutiert'.[53] The ideal whose fulfilment the theatre offers is evidently more an artistic than a conventionally religious one.

The gap of almost two years separating the composition of the 'Teater von Oklahama' episode from that of the first six chapters helps to account for the change in mode to something resembling ironic allegory, which seems so incongruous when one reads through the surviving text. Within the first six chapters, however, there are further incongruities. It is not at all clear how the presentation of America is related to that of Karl's moral and psychological problems. The latter follows a scheme which Jahn has outlined: 'Ein Mensch hat innerhalb einer festen Daseinsordnung gelebt. Da verführt ihn jemand zu einer Handlung, die dieser Ordnung wider-spricht. Ohne Schuld schuldig, wird er von einer höchsten Autorität sofort und ohne Möglichkeit der Rechtfertigung ausgestoßen.'[54] This ground-plan underlies the novel's successive episodes. Karl is sent away from Europe for having been seduced by a servant-girl; he is expelled from his uncle's house for accepting Pollunder's invitation; he is dismissed from the Hotel Occidental for a momentary absence from his post; and we may assume that the series of events bringing him to 'Unternehmen Nr. 25' would have contained several more humiliations and expulsions. The problem is that this scheme has nothing to do with America. It could be enacted in any setting. And it is essentially narrative, while Kafka's other main preoccupation, the urban world of America, is conveyed mainly through description. His closest approach to realistic integration of milieu and event comes in Therese's account of her mother's death, but this is told as a

self-contained *récit*, like Olga's much longer story in *Das Schloß*, instead
of being incorporated into the narrative. Nor are the descriptions of
American technology integrated into the action of the novel. It is
typically seen from the viewpoint of a detached and ignorant observer,
as when Karl pauses on his journey with Delamarche and Robinson
to look back at New York and Brooklyn. 'Alles in beiden Riesenstädten
schien leer und nutzlos aufgestellt', we are told (V 144), but since we
are not carried into the midst of that life, the comment merely records
Karl's ill-informed impression.[55] The desk which is described at such
length has no part in the action, though Kafka could, for example,
have made Karl lose his uncle's favour by playing with it. Later,
Karl's work as a lift-boy is described in detail, but there is no necessary connection between the nature of his work and the events that
befall him. Robinson could still have turned up drunk and got Karl
into trouble, no matter what job he was doing. In short, Kafka has
not succeeded in integrating his two main themes. The novel falls
apart into description and action.

Still, this may be a premature judgement, and I want now to test it
by examining the means Kafka has used to structure his narrative.
Since he did not plan his stories beforehand, he needed to have some
structural model before his mind in order to organize his material and
keep the narrative from rambling. While *Das Urteil* and *Die Verwandlung* owe their cohesion in part to the example of the Yiddish
drama, *Der Verschollene* seems dependent rather on narrative models. I
use this deliberately vague term to comprehend a group of models
which are less specific than particular sources but more so than the
abstract patterns studied by structuralists. Some of the narrative
models Kafka employs are properly described as genres, and later I
shall draw on the current theory of literary genre in order to explain
his use of them. Altogether, four main narrative models seem to be
used in *Der Verschollene*, the first three of which can be discussed with
relative brevity.

The first of these narrative models should perhaps be called a
cultural myth, although Kafka has stood it on its head. It is the
characteristically American myth of progression from rags to riches,
from log cabin to White House. The internal tensions in this myth
can be illustrated from an anonymous article about America quoted
by Binder from the *Prager Tagblatt* of 7 March 1906:

Immer noch ist Amerika das fabelhafte Goldland, in dem man rasch Schätze
erwirbt und in dem man ebenso durch Arbeit wie durch Zufall einer

glücklichen Spekulation zu einem Vermögen gelangt, dessen Ziffern selbst
für vornehme Europäer etwas Ehrfurchtsgebietendes haben [. . .] immer
noch gibt es auch einen Onkel, der aus seiner kleinen Gemeinde in Europa
nach Amerika zieht, sich dort unkenntlich unter das Volk mischt, für seine
Angehörigen verschwindet und verschollt.[56]

America appears first as the land of opportunity and justice, in which
hard work is sure to be rewarded by wealth. But since experience
shows that this rarely happens, and since hard work is perhaps not
attractive enough to form part of a fantasy, a compensatory counter-
myth is generated in which one can become rich by sheer chance.
This version preserves equality of opportunity while eliminating the
notion of work. The uncle in America serves as evidence for the
possibility of acquiring wealth there, but since he has dropped out of
touch, this evidence has the advantage of being unverifiable. Kafka
has worked into his novel all these components of the myth, while
reversing it by sending Karl from riches to rags. Karl hopes to make
his fortune by honest toil and self-improvement, and uses his spare
time in the hotel for studying a book on commercial correspondence,
in the best Horatio Alger manner. But his eyes are opened by the
student Mendel, who works in a department store during the day,
reads all night, and hopes to catch up on sleep in a few years' time
after finishing his studies; yet Mendel rates his prospects low and
would sooner drop his studies than relinquish his job in Montly's.
Karl does have an example of the self-made man in his uncle, who is
not only wealthy but a Senator, and owes his success to imposing an
inhumanly rigid discipline on himself. Thus Kafka exposes the rags-
to-riches myth by showing that success in America is almost unattainable and its results repellent. But he also exploits it and related myths
as narrative devices. The myth of the rich uncle enables Kafka to get
Karl off the immigrant-ship and into a wealthy setting. After that, by
sending him from riches to rags, Kafka ensures that successive
episodes are not just a string of incidents but form a meaningful
sequence, with Karl's hopes of self-improvement diminishing at each
stage of his social descent. Though Kafka had never been to America,
Der Verschollene is as valid a satire on American ideals as Mark
Twain's *Connecticut Yankee* or Nathanael West's *A Cool Million*.

Kafka's second narrative model is that of a visit to America which
begins with high hopes and ends in disillusion. Its most obvious prototype is *Der Amerikamüde* (1855) by the Austrian journalist Ferdinand
Kürnberger. Kafka is likely to have known this book by reputation,

though if he ever began reading it one cannot imagine him getting far with it. Although not quite so absurd as Jeffrey L. Sammons makes out in his entertaining survey of German fiction set in America,[57] it is certainly a ham-fisted performance, with hundreds of pages taken up by conversation among faceless characters, and what action there is relying on improbable coincidences. Kürnberger had never been to America either, but based his novel on the experiences of the poet Nikolaus Lenau, who had emigrated to the United States in 1832 but returned, disappointed, within a year. In the novel Lenau passes under the name Moorfeld. Disillusion sets in at the start, when a lyrical description of New York harbour is ironically followed by a comment on the brokers' clerks, hoteliers, and employment agents who swarm aboard the passenger ship in order to entrap the immigrants. After moving in New York high society and among the German community, Moorfeld buys land in Ohio, finds it to be barely cultivable, is swindled out of it by his neighbours, and finally leaves for Europe just as a xenophobic mob is burning down the German quarter of New York. Despite some ludicrous trivia—he complains, for example, that American forests lack dignity because the trees are not all of the same species, and claims that New Yorkers' favourite Sunday recreation is setting fire to houses and then watching pitched battles with water-hoses between rival fire-brigades—Kürnberger does get in some well-aimed blows at the Americans' commercialism, and at their maltreatment both of immigrants and of their own Indian population. He maintains that commercialism is so powerful in America that even the most idealistic Europeans succumb to it; Moorfeld sees several German friends become cynical materialists, and feels that he is escaping in the nick of time.

Kürnberger's narrative scheme corresponds roughly to Kafka's. Arriving in New York harbour, Moorfeld shows his *naïveté* by uttering an ecstatic address to liberty; but he soon learns the true character of American life by a sojourn in New York society and by contact with German immigrants, as Karl first stays with his uncle and then makes friends with the Head Cook, who is from Vienna, and Therese, who is from Pomerania. Moorfeld then moves into the American hinterland, as Karl is doing when *Der Verschollene* breaks off. At each stage of his travels the ruthlessness and amorality of American life are more brutally brought home to him, so that the book also moves from relative civilization to barely concealed savagery. Similarly, Karl becomes increasingly exposed to physical dangers such as violence. After leading a sheltered life in his uncle's house, he is defeated in a wrestling match by Klara, is robbed by Delamarche and Robinson, just escapes being tortured by the Head Porter, is chased by policemen, and ends up as the *de facto* slave of Delamarche and Brunelda.

The third narrative model discernible in *Der Verschollene* is that of ironic or black comedy in which the hero is also the victim. Adorno implies the existence of this model when he remarks: 'Wie Unschuldige bei Sade—auch im amerikanischen Groteskfilm und in den "Funnies"—gerät das Kafkasche Subjekt, insbesondere der Auswanderer Karl Roßmann, aus einer verzweifelten und ausweglosen Situation in die nächste: die Stationen epischer Abenteuer werden zu solchen der Leidensgeschichte.'[58] If Sade's *Justine* can be read as a black comedy, as Adorno suggests, the humour lies not in the sadism itself but in the pig-headed innocence with which Justine blunders from one den of villains to another. Black comedy arouses a peculiarly contradictory response in the reader. The sympathy aroused by the hero's sufferings is immediately short-circuited by the hero's stupidity and inability to learn from experience, and usually also by the narrator's detachment. Kafka may have known Sade's work, though his remark to Janouch, 'Marquis de Sade [. . .] ist der eigentliche Patron unserer Zeit', is probably apocryphal.[59] But he had certainly read subtler works of black humour, notably Dostoyevsky's *The Double*.[60] The sufferings of Dostoyevsky's hero Golyadkin are not physical, but emotional and social: the tale mercilessly explores the experience of embarrassment, anticipating the treatment of shame in Dostoyevsky's mature novels. Not only does Golyadkin expose himself to disgrace by intruding into the party given by his superior, State Councillor Berendeyev, but a double appears who usurps his place in the office, achieves the social success denied to him, humiliates him publicly, and finally replaces him altogether while the real Golyadkin is carried off to the fate he dreads most—incarceration in a madhouse. Golyadkin inspires little sympathy. He is barely a character: we learn nothing about his past life, and only the functionally indispensable details about his present circumstances. He is rather an experimental subject who permits Dostoyevsky to depict the most hideous embarrassment conceivable and make the reader squirm vicariously without feeling pity.

Like Golyadkin, Karl is driven mercilessly from one embarrassing experience to another, serving as a surrogate victim for his creator's own self-tormenting fantasies of disgrace. The most painful of these incidents is his 'trial' before the Head Waiter, in which a minute offence—his deserting his post long enough to put the drunken Robinson to bed—generates clouds of suspicion, causes him to appear a hardened reprobate, and leads to his expulsion from the hotel. Even before the discovery of Robinson, Karl is accused by the Head Porter of showing disrespect and of spending every available night out on the town, and his absence from his post is alleged to have caused the Head Waiter 'schwere jetzt noch gar nicht übersehbare Unannehmlichkeiten' (V 231) which are never specified. These suspicions seem confirmed by the discovery of Robinson; Karl has to admit that he promised Robinson money, which sounds deeply nefarious, and the Head Waiter easily catches him out in contradictions that seem to inculpate him still more. Worse still, he loses the confidence of his friend the Head Cook, and has to endure her reproaches. Then he is handed over to the Head Porter, and until Karl's escape it looks as though moral humiliation is going to be followed by physical torture. But then Kafka stops the machinery and sets Karl temporarily free, for Karl is not a mere cipher like the heroes of other black comedies, such as Paul Pennyfeather in Waugh's *Decline and Fall*, or Lemuel Pitkin in West's *A Cool Million*. By retaining his innocence in corrupt America, he is something of a wise fool, and when Kafka chooses to foreground this aspect of Karl black comedy modulates into a different kind of comedy, defined by Northrop Frye as 'an ironic deadlock in which the hero is regarded as a fool or worse by the fictional society, and yet impresses the real audience has having something more valuable than his society has', as in Dostoyevsky's *Idiot* and Hašek's *Good Soldier Schweik*.[61] Further discussion of Karl's wise folly must be deferred, however, until we have identified Kafka's fourth narrative model.

At this point the discussion of genre can no longer be postponed. Politzer has given *Der Verschollene* the generic label *Bildungsroman*,[62] but the use of this term is beset with difficulties, some of which arise from misapprehensions about what a literary genre is. Often the word *Bildungsroman* is used narrowly to designate a small group of German novels centring on Wieland's *Agathon* (1767), Goethe's *Wilhelm Meisters Lehrjahre* (1796), and Stifter's *Der Nachsommer* (1857), but at other times it is used more broadly to cover any novel, not necessarily in German, which deals with a young man's entry into the adult world.[63] Each of these applications, however, is based on a fallacy.

The first is anachronistic, for the widespread use of the term dates only from 1870, when Dilthey wrote: 'Ich möchte die Romane, welche die Schule des Wilhelm Meister ausmachen (denn Rousseaus verwandte Kunstform wirkte auf sie nicht fort), Bildungsromane nennen.'[64] Since Goethe, Wieland, and Stifter did not use the word *Bildungsroman*, it serves to classify their novels retrospectively. The construction of literary taxonomies, however, is not the purpose of genre-study; Alastair Fowler has recently reminded us that 'in reality genre is much less of a pigeonhole than a pigeon, and genre theory has a different use altogether, being concerned with communication and interpretation'.[65] Genres, that is, are not timeless categories but are caught up in constant historical change, and the study of them aims to reconstruct the concepts that guided authors and the expectations that guided readers at specific historical moments. After Dilthey had given it currency, the term *Bildungsroman* entered literary history and formed an element in the intentions of certain novelists: both Thomas Mann and Günter Grass have stated explicitly that their intentions in writing *Felix Krull* and *Die Blechtrommel* were to parody or ironize the concept of the *Bildungsroman*, as defined by Dilthey.[66] There is, however, no sign that Kafka shared these intentions, and hence Jürgen Pütz's recent study of *Der Verschollene* in this light is forced to settle for the lame conclusion that it is neither a *Bildungsroman* nor an anti-*Bildungsroman* but 'in der Tradition des Bildungsromans eine Sonderstellung einnimmt'.[67]

If Dilthey's retrospective application of the term *Bildungsroman* to the novels of Goethe and his contemporaries represents the taxonomic fallacy, a more easily identifiable fallacy occurs when the term is applied liberally to any novel whose hero passes from youth to maturity. The error here is to suppose that the genre of a work is defined by its subject-matter. In any genre, however, subject-matter and formal features are interdependent, and the latter are likely to be more important than the former. Not every poem about a wedding is an epithalamium.

Generic study of the novel is notoriously difficult, for while the term 'novel' obviously comprehends many different types of fiction, the expectations associated with most types are implicit and hard to bring to consciousness. Distinct subgenres like science fiction or the detective novel are exceptional. Often a subgenre arises in a casual way when a novelist takes as his model a single work or group of works by a predecessor, and a third novelist then similarly modifies the work of the second. At the present day, for example, Grass's *Die Blechtrommel*, Márquez's *One Hundred Years of Solitude*, and Rushdie's *Midnight's Children* form a recognizable group which, if we wanted to, we could label the 'modernist family chronicle', tracing lines of descent from *Buddenbrooks* in one direction and *Tristram Shandy* in another. This is not a taxonomy, nor is it simply a statement about sources and influences; it is rather an attempt to define the changing relationship between the intentions of authors and the developing expectations of their readers. Someone who has never before read a book like *Midnight's Children* will be perplexed by it, but someone familiar with the two earlier novels will have an appropriate set of expectations with which to approach it.

In trying to reconstruct the generic intentions of novelists, we must not expect them always to use generic terms; more often we have to seek clues in their statements about previous writers of whose influence they are conscious. Kafka's diary contains such a statement about the genesis of *Der Verschollene*:

Dickens *Copperfield* (*Der Heizer* glatte Dickensnachahmung, noch mehr der geplante Roman). Koffergeschichte, der Beglückende und Bezaubernde, die niedrigen Arbeiten, die Geliebte auf dem Landgut, die schmutzigen Häuser u.a., vor allem aber die Methode. Meine Absicht war, wie ich jetzt sehe, einen Dickens-Roman zu schreiben, nur bereichert um die schärferen Lichter, die ich der Zeit entnommen, und die mattern, die ich aus mir selbst aufgesteckt hatte. (T 535–6.)

Though Kafka does not specify what he means by Dickens' method, his own novel certainly shares with *David Copperfield* the basic narrative structure which exposes the hero to diverse milieux and characters. Dickens had taken this over from the moribund picaresque novel, made it less episodic by integrating more of the characters into the plot, and given far more prominence to the hero's childhood and adolescence. He had portrayed childhood with great sensitivity, presenting the adult world through the child's innocent eye, and showing how David's personal relationships develop as he grows up: David searches for surrogate parents (Murdstone, Micawber; Peggotty, Aunt Betsey Trotwood), gradually learns to distinguish trustworthy from untrustworthy friends (Traddles, Steerforth), and makes his way by trial and error (marriage with Dora) towards a suitable emotional partner (Agnes). Kafka borrowed from Dickens not only the motifs listed in his diary, but also the episodic structure, the diversity of characters and settings, and the emphasis on childhood with its psychological and moral implications. But all these should not be seen as piecemeal borrowings from a specific source, rather as features of a type of novel, the 'Dickens-Roman', of which Kafka wanted to write another specimen. They are what Fowler calls the repertoire of a subgenre.[68] It does not matter how, or whether, we label this subgenre ('picaresque novel of childhood' might do), provided we realize that it exists not as an ahistorical category but as the unformulated assumptions of writers and readers in a certain historical period.

How Kafka develops the moral potential of this subgenre can now be briefly shown. Among Karl's most salient characteristics are his sense of justice and his loyalty to his parents. He never complains of the injustice with which, as the Kleistian opening sentence blandly informs us, he himself has been treated, but continues to dream of regaining his parents' affection. His notion of justice, however, differs from the one current in the adult world. For Karl, justice is the allocation of credit and blame; for the adults in charge, it is the administration of punishment. As in *In der Strafkolonie* and *Der Prozeß*, guilt is always taken for granted, and justice exists not to investigate misdemeanours but to punish them. Hence Karl's attempts to stand up for the stoker are ineffectual, for what seems to Karl a 'Sache der Gerechtigkeit' (V 46) is converted by his uncle into a 'Sache der Disciplin' (V 48).[69] This initial defeat does not lessen Karl's idealism. He behaves towards Delamarche and Robinson with naïve generosity: when they consume his salami, he refrains from asking for any because to do so would be petty, and although he reproaches them for stealing the photograph of his parents, he offers them the entire contents of his suitcase in return for it. Even in the worst situations, like his imprisonment in Brunelda's flat, he remains touchingly polite, reasonable and defenceless. Admittedly, some commentators have been more critical of him. Politzer complains that he subscribes to a narrow, conformist, petty-bourgeois morality: 'His thriftiness, mistrust of chance acquaintances, and general apprehensiveness bear witness to the narrowness of his upbringing.'[70] But these qualities would seem highly commendable in the cut-throat world of Kafka's America, and it is a pity that Karl is not better endowed with them. His fate shows that he is not mistrustful enough to survive. The widely held view of him as an innocent and ingenuous character seems broadly correct.

Guilt in Kafka's fiction tends to be psychological as well as moral. Instead of resulting from the hero's actions, it precedes them. A clear conscience does not guarantee freedom from a guilt so deep-seated that one cannot perceive it till made aware of it by others' accusations. This is the problem articulated in the narrative scheme outlined by Jahn, in which an innocent person incurs guilt and is expelled from the secure order in which he has previously lived. We can now begin putting flesh on the bare bones of this scheme. Karl repeatedly finds himself in an apparently secure environment, guarded by parents or parental substitutes (his real parents, Uncle Jakob, the Head Cook). He is charged with an offence which is either somebody else's fault or a triviality (he is seduced by Johanna Brummer, he disobeys his uncle's implied wishes by visiting Pollunder, he leaves his post at the lift) and receives the monstrously disproportionate punishment of expulsion without hope of return. Each of these incidents involves disobedience to parents. Not only Uncle Jakob but also Pollunder and Green are father-substitutes; the latter two illustrate the splitting of the image into a good and a bad half, but all three are versions of the father-type that is found throughout the fiction Kafka wrote in the autumn of 1912. This type is always gigantic. 'Mein Vater ist noch immer ein Riese,' reflects Georg Bendemann (E 59). Pursued by his father, Gregor Samsa is astonished by the 'Riesengröße seiner Stiefelsohlen' (E 116). The stoker is first introduced as 'ein riesiger Mann' (V 8); Pollunder and Green are both 'große dicke Herren' (V 68) and Karl is impressed by 'der riesigen Gestalt Greens' (V 79). The father-type may be either kindly or harsh. If the former, he is also weak: the stoker needs Karl's help to claim his rights, and Pollunder looks flabby, pale, and worried. The kindly father is presented with mildly homosexual overtones: the stoker and Karl lie side by side on the stoker's bed, and later they hold hands; Uncle Jakob squeezes and fondles Karl; Pollunder holds Karl's hand, puts an arm round him, and squeezes him. By contrast, the harsh father is terrifyingly strong. In *Das Urteil* and *Die Verwandlung* the fathers change abruptly from helpless old men into vigorous and frightening embodiments of authority, while in *Der Verschollene* the feeble Pollunder eventually retires and is replaced by Green, who then seems so much more enormous that Karl wonders whether he has devoured Pollunder. The harsh father is heterosexual in his tastes: Green, a bachelor whom Karl suspects of loose living, fondles Klara 'mit deutlicher Absicht' (V 84).

The standard father-type of Kafka's early fiction owes something, no doubt, to Hermann Kafka's physical bulk and terrifying rages, but he is also the product of Kafka's reading. He is already to be found in the person of Herr Benjamenta in Robert Walser's *Jakob von Gunten*, a book we know Kafka to have read, probably as early as 1909 (Br 75). Benjamenta runs a mysterious boarding-school which seems to have no other teachers except his sister. He is gigantic: 'Herr Benjamenta ist ein Riese, und wir Zöglinge sind Zwerge gegen diesen Riesen, der stets etwas mürrisch ist,' says the narrator, who also compares him to Samson and Goliath.[71] Benjamenta, too, is an ambivalent figure: he tries to strangle Jakob von Gunten, who only escapes by biting him in the finger, but soon afterwards he becomes unexpectedly tender towards Jakob and offers to kiss him; at the end the two are about to leave together for an unspecified destination. Benjamenta's huge bulk, and his alternation between brutality and a tenderness tinged with homosexuality, evidently coalesced with Kafka's own experience. Werfel's sad little sketch *Die Riesin*, describing a visit to a giantess named Penthesilea who is displayed in a circus, also contributed to Kafka's composite father-image. What seems to have lodged in Kafka's memory is the picture of the giantess standing on a podium and towering over the spectators, as Bendemann senior does when he stands on the bed, Herr Samsa when confronting the earthbound Gregor, and Green when he stands at the top of a staircase.

Karl's superiors at the Hotel Occidental also serve as surrogate parents. The motherly Head Cook protects him, while he is punished by those harsh father-figures the Head Waiter and the more brutal Head Porter. As he leaves the Head Waiter's office, Karl spots a hint of a sexual relationship between him and the Head Cook: 'Während er sich zum Abschied verbeugte, sah er flüchtig, wie der Oberkellner die Hand der Oberköchin wie im Geheimen umfaßte und mit ihr spielte' (V 253). There is a similar scene of implied betrayal in *Die Verwandlung*. After a family council has deemed Gregor a non-person, he retreats to his room for the last time and notices, looking back, how the alliance which his father and his sister have formed against him is represented by their positions: 'der Vater und die Schwester saßen nebeneinander, die Schwester hatte ihre Hand um des Vaters Hals gelegt' (E 135).

It is not simple disobedience, but a particular kind of misdemeanour, that brings about Karl's repeated disgrace: namely, a sexual misdemeanour, or even the mere possibility of one. He was originally sent to America because of his seduction by the maid-servant. By inviting Karl to his home to meet his daughter Klara, Pollunder seems to be offering Karl the opportunity for further sexual experience, and this may be the unstated reason for Uncle Jakob's disapproval of the visit. Before giving Karl his uncle's letter, Green asks him suspiciously: 'Was haben Sie denn bei Fräulein Klara getrieben?' (V 121). One of the grounds on which the hotel staff distrust Karl is that they think he is planning a nocturnal visit to Brunelda. Delamarche, who has a few paternal traits—he saves Karl from the police, and there is some physical contact when he strokes Karl's forehead as the latter, exhausted, is leaning against him—also keeps Karl away from women: he forbids Karl to look at three women from a neighbouring flat, hinting that they are prostitutes.

Ironically, Karl always finds sexual experience unpleasant. He recalls Johanna Brummer's seduction of him with repugnance. Klara proves aggressive, forces him on to a couch by 'Jiu-Jitsu' (V 91), and threatens to slap his face. When he next sees her, her nightdress is crumpled and her face flushed, indicating that she has been making love to Mack, who turns out to be in bed in the next room. This suggestion of voyeurism recurs when Karl and Robinson are confined to the balcony outside the room Delamarche shares with Brunelda, and when Robinson recounts how he was once fortunate enough to glimpse Brunelda in the nude. Throughout the novel, sexually active women are domineering, repulsive, and sometimes violent. The struggle between Klara and Karl was probably inspired by an incident in Sacher-Masoch's *Venus im Pelz*, a book which has left traces elsewhere in Kafka's fiction.[72] Its narrator, the masochist Severin, becomes the voluntary slave of Wanda von Dunajew, who tortures him physically and emotionally. After she has caused him agonies of jealousy by starting an affair with a handsome Greek, Severin's torments culminate in a scene in which Wanda first tells him that she is tired of the Greek's crudity and loves only him, then ties him up and prepares to whip him, whereupon the Greek emerges from behind the curtains of Wanda's four-poster bed and himself whips Severin. Karl's only female friend of his own age is Therese, who is eighteen but physically undeveloped. The implication is that friendship is possible only with women who do not challenge one by inviting sexual intimacy. In the contrast between Klara and Therese, we have Kafka's version of the then standard typological opposition between the *femme fatale* and

the *femme fragile*. The former is demonic, violent, and dangerous, like
Sacher-Masoch's Wanda and Wedekind's Lulu, while the latter is
sickly, sexually undeveloped, or both, like Hauptmann's Hannele or
Gabriele Klöterjahn in Thomas Mann's *Tristan*.[73]

The ground-plan of *Der Verschollene* can now be defined as follows:
Karl at first enjoys the approval and protection of parents or parental
figures; but sexual experience, or the mere possibility of it, causes
him to appear guilty and be condemned and expelled. Guilt is always
taken for granted. A clear conscience, and even a distaste for sexual
experience, are no defence. Nor could they be, for no matter what
Karl may consciously think and feel, sexual urges are inevitably present in his unreflecting physical being. He is being punished, therefore, not for what he does but for what he is. He is one of many Kafka
heroes who experience a disjunction between their consciousness and
their physical, appetitive, unconscious being. Kafka's longest fictional study of this disjunction is *Der Prozeß*, where Josef K.'s guilt
does not result from any of his actions but from his being the person
he is.

In *Der Verschollene*, however, Kafka has not yet learnt how to extract
the narrative potential from his theme of inevitable guilt. Instead, he
has written a series of episodes in which the basic situation repeats
itself mechanically. Karl himself has no chance to develop his personality, but remains trapped in the cycle of inculpation and expulsion.
Neither of the two main themes of *Der Verschollene*, in fact, contains
any narrative dynamism. The other, the portrayal of the technological and urban world of America, is simply that, a static portrayal,
only superficially connected to the novel's events. Kafka has
developed both themes with great skill, but has not managed to make
the two interact. Schiller's famous account of the dialectical development of the hero in *Wilhelm Meisters Lehrjahre*—'er tritt von einem
leeren und unbestimmten Ideal in ein bestimmtes tätiges Leben, aber
ohne die idealisierende Kraft dabei einzubüßen'[74]—would not apply
to Karl, for since his private moral experience and his American
environment are too unrelated even to come into conflict, no dialectical resolution could ever be reached. Kafka could only end the story
by intervening forcibly to change its mode, in the 'Teater von
Oklahama' chapter, into ironic allegory.

Not, of course, that *Der Verschollene* should be judged a failure. The
only literary crime, as Henry James said, is to bore the reader, and
Der Verschollene is probably the most continuously readable of Kafka's

longer works. It lacks the tragic intensity of *Der Prozeß*, but also the frequent *longueurs* of *Das Schloß*; and it contains some of Kafka's finest comic writing. However, the novel was hardly the most suitable form for a writer who, like Kafka, did not plan his work in advance, relied on the inspiration of the moment, and had difficulty in structuring any unit longer than an episode. With *Das Urteil* he had already shown that he could write a short, concentrated, and powerful story. If he was to write a longer work, he had two problems to overcome: he had to give it an overarching structure which would make it more than a series of episodes; and he had to create an organic relation, not merely an external one, between the moral and psychological issues that interested him and the setting in which he wished to depict them.

Die *Verwandlung*, written in November and December 1912, represents the solution to both these problems and is perhaps Kafka's most successful work. How he dealt with the problem of structure was touched on at the end of the last chapter. The Yiddish family dramas he saw gave him models of dramatic tension and concentration. The three sections of *Die Verwandlung* resemble the three acts of a play. As in *Der Verschollene*, each section varies the same basic situation, in which Gregor breaks out of his room, to his family's horror, and is driven back into it; but here the three sections mount to a dramatic climax. The third time Gregor emerges from his room, his family fear that he will deprive them of their livelihood by frightening away their lodgers; they therefore decide that the creature is no longer Gregor and that it must go, a decision in which Gregor acquiesces by dutifully dying. The story gains additional dramatic vigour from the fact that the Samsa family is a constellation of forces in which the most powerful member dominates the rest, and in each of the three sections the balance of power is different. At the outset Gregor supports the rest of the family, but after his metamorphosis power is transferred to his father and then to his sister, who convenes the family council and insists that the insect must disappear. By all these means, then, Kafka gives the story dramatic tension, conflict, and diversity.

Some of the story's intensity comes from Kafka's highly original narrative technique. Friedrich Beissner's path-breaking lecture *Der Erzähler Franz Kafka* first drew attention to Kafka's monoperspectival narration.[75] By confining the reader to the narrative perspective of the protagonist, Kafka obliges him to share the latter's bewilderment and induces in him a similar sense of confinement. Beissner's conclusions need qualification, however, for even in his early fiction Kafka reduces the stringency of his narrative viewpoint in various ways. Even though everything in *Das Urteil* is presented through the consciousness of Georg Bendemann, some hints in the text encourage the reader to detach himself from Georg in a critical spirit. Georg's willingness to write his friend off as a failure; his unexplained difficulty in informing his friend of his engagement; and his perceptible satisfaction in marrying a girl 'aus wohlhabender Familie' (E 56, 57)—all these have a distancing effect.[76] While *Der Verschollene* presents America through Karl's eyes, many of the descriptive passages might as well come from an independent narrator (e.g. V 140-1, 142-3), and occasionally the use of the 'als ob' construction shows that the narrator has stepped momentarily outside Karl's consciousness (V 11, 12). In neither of these stories is the narration as strictly monoperspectival as Beissner would claim. In *Die Verwandlung* the narrative perspective is established from the outside as dual:

Als Gregor Samsa eines Morgens aus unruhigen Träumen erwachte, fand er sich in seinem Bett zu einem ungeheueren Ungeziefer verwandelt. (E 71.)

Here the narrator immediately places the reader in a position superior to Gregor's by revealing a fact, Gregor's transformation, which Gregor himself fails to register. The rest of the first section then immerses us in Gregor's consciousness, and we participate uncomfortably in his efforts to manipulate his unwieldy body out of bed and open the bedroom door with his jaws. But at the same time we know that he is under an illusion, and we should laugh at his futile efforts if the narrative technique did not force us into a disturbing empathy with his struggles. Kafka's achievement as a narrator, here and elsewhere, is to make the reader share intimately in the hero's feelings, despite having superior knowledge. This, I think, is the real reason why his best work is both so compelling and so uncomfortable. He makes us experience what it is like to have one's knowledge contradicted by one's sensations, when the latter are more immediate and more powerful. This discrepancy between what one knows and what one feels is of course one of the commonest experiences in life, but it is not easy to convey in literature, where sympathetic identification with a character—a sense of solidarity with his or her sufferings, based on shared emotion—cannot well coincide with the ironic form of identification in which one comprehends the character's situation from the vantage-point of superior knowledge.[77] Yet Kafka has managed to combine the two. We cannot withhold our sympathy from Gregor's desperation, but neither can we forget the information about his metamorphosis that the narrator imparted to us at the outset and which Gregor did not register, for it is indispensable, both for the most basic understanding of the story, and to preserve the emotional distance that keeps his sufferings from becoming unbearably painful to read.

Besides solving the problem of narrative structure and devising an original form of narrative perspective, Kafka in *Die Verwandlung* has succeeded in integrating his presentation of the hero with that of the hero's social circumstances. In *Der Verschollene*, as we saw, information about America and its technological marvels was not properly worked into the story. The narrative stops to let Kafka describe New York harbour or Karl's desk, then it starts up again. But in *Die Verwandlung* we learn about Gregor's job as a commercial traveller, and about the pressures he is under from his family, through the medium of his own reflections as he lies in bed. For this technique Kafka was indebted to Dostoyevsky. Mark Spilka has shown how closely the opening of *Die Verwandlung* is modelled on that of *The Double*, where Golyadkin wakes up and remains in bed, as though uncertain 'whether what is happening around him is real and actual or only the continuation of his disordered dreams', but eventually recognizes his dingy room and 'the dull, dirty, grey autumn day'.[78] These motifs—the dreams, the sense of disorientation, the drab room, and the dismal weather—also accompany Gregor Samsa's awakening; the difference of course is that he is already transformed, though without realizing it, while it is some time before Golyadkin's double makes his appearance. But the motifs are less important than the method of characterization that Kafka has adopted from Dostoyevsky. A Dostoyevsky hero is normally presented through his own self-awareness. Hence we learn about Golyadkin's surroundings and situation from his own reflections. Even his physical appearance is mentioned only when he examines himself in the mirror. We do not apprehend his character as a stable nucleus, or even as an assemblage of traits; we infer his character from the way he perceives himself and his world.[79] Similarly with Gregor Samsa: we are shown his room as his gaze travels round it, and instead of seeing him at work, we are told about his job through his disgruntled meditation on it. Our interest is thus displaced from the work itself to the effect it has on Gregor's consciousness.

In *Die Verwandlung*, therefore, Kafka is continuing and deepening the exploration of the nature of modern work that we saw in *Der Verschollene*. But while *Der Verschollene* emphasized the external features of modern work—frantic haste, subjection to a time-table, rigid discipline, fear of unemployment—*Die Verwandlung* moves inwards into the consciousness of the worker. Its critique of modern work overlaps in many respects with that in *Der Verschollene*. Gregor's firm is as paternalistic as the Hotel Occidental. The 'Chef' is in the habit of sitting not behind his desk but on top of it, and addresses his employees from this elevated position; to add to their discomfort, his deafness obliges them to come very close in order to make themselves heard. Another oddity of Gregor's firm is its close surveillance of its employees. Gregor fears that if he reports sick he will be visited not only by the doctor but by his employer in person; and indeed his failure to catch the 5 a.m. train does bring him a visit from the Managing Director, ten minutes after the office has opened. Kafka places particular stress on Gregor's subjection to the clock. Having missed both the 5 a.m. and the 7 a.m. trains he resolves to catch the train at 8. On waking he notices that the time is 6.30, and the subsequent events follow a precise schedule: his mother knocks on his door at a quarter to seven; he decides to get out of bed by 7.15, but is terrified into haste by the arrival of the Managing Director at 7.10. *Die Verwandlung* is exactly contemporary with the famous essay 'Die Großstädte und das Geistesleben' in which Georg Simmel discusses, among many other topics, the necessity for modern urban life to be governed by a strict time-table:

Wenn alle Uhren in Berlin plötzlich in verschiedener Richtung falschgehen würden, auch nur um den Spielraum einer Stunde, so wäre sein ganzes wirtschaftliches und sonstiges Verkehrsleben auf lange hinaus zerrüttet. Dazu kommt, scheinbar noch äußerlicher, die Größe der Entfernungen, die alles Warten und Vergebenskommen zu einem gar nicht aufzubringenden Zeitaufwand machen. So ist die Technik des großstädtischen Lebens überhaupt nicht denkbar, ohne daß alle Tätigkeiten und Wechselbeziehungen aufs pünktlichste in ein festes, übersubjektives Zeitschema eingeordnet würden.[80]

Gregor's work is exhausting and uncongenial. He complains to himself about the constant travelling, his worry about catching trains, the bad food he has to eat, and the brief and superficial human contact to which he is confined. The work itself—displaying samples, soliciting orders—is barely mentioned and appears, by default, as a wholly unmemorable and unfulfilling activity. Yet it dominates his life, and his mother is quite correct in telling the Managing Director: 'Der Junge hat ja nichts im Kopf als das Geschäft' (E 80). His family provides no refuge, for since the collapse of his father's firm five years earlier, Gregor has had to support the entire family by his commissions. In addition, they have been lent money by his employer, and it will be another five or six years before the debt is paid off and Georg is able to give up his job. The pressures that harass him from all sides are vividly conveyed through the position of his bedroom. It has three doors, one opening into the living-room, one into his parents' bedroom, and one into his sister's room. When Gregor is late in rising, one member of the family taps at each door to urge him to go off to work.

Gregor's scanty leisure is spent at home, reading the newspaper, studying railway timetables, or doing fretwork. He has little chance to develop his emotional and sexual life. He does recall a brief encounter with a maid in a hotel, and he once unsuccessfully courted a cashier in a hat-shop; but at the time of his transformation his sexual life seems to be represented by the lady in furs, whose picture he has cut out of a magazine and hung on his bedroom wall, and who may have found her way into the story from *Venus im Pelz*, where the hero, on becoming Wanda's slave, assumes the name Gregor. He is so attached to this picture that when his mother and sister start clearing the furniture out of his room he tries to save it by crawling on to the wall and shielding it with his body. Like the bank cashier in Kaiser's play *Von morgens bis mitternachts* (also written in 1912), who leads a mechanical existence till the sight of an exotic, sensually exciting lady from Italy inspires him to embezzle money and escape, Gregor is a model employee, but his subservience to his firm, his family and the clock has stunted his development as a human being. He resembles the featureless workers described memorably by Auden in *New Year Letter*:

> All in their morning mirrors face
> A member of a governed race.
> Each recognizes what LEAR saw,
> And he and THURBER like to draw,
> The neuter outline that's the plan
> And icon of Industrial Man.[81]

Gregor's attitude to his work is of course rooted in Kafka's own experience, and is anticipated in earlier writings. Eduard Raban, the hero of *Hochzeitsvorbereitungen auf dem Lande* (written between 1907 and 1910), broods on his exhausting work: 'Man arbeitet so übertrieben im Amt, daß man dann sogar zu müde ist, um seine Ferien gut zu genießen' (H 8), and wishes that he could send his body out to attend to his duties while he himself lay in bed in the shape of a large beetle (H 12). Kafka complains in letters about his exhausting tours of inspection (Br 75, 77), and the plan for *Die Verwandlung* first occurred to him on the morning of 17 November 1912, as he was lying in bed feeling miserable about Felice's failure to write to him (F 102). But that does not, of course, explain why the antithesis to mechanical routine should be transformation into an insect. The image of the 'Ungeziefer' is extraordinarily rich in its implications, and no interpretation can or should hope to exhaust them. Biographical associations, however, do provide one approach to its meaning. In the *Brief an den Vater* (written in 1919), Kafka acknowledges the potential accusation that his conflict with his father was a 'Kampf des Ungeziefers' (H 222), but he also recalls that in 1911 his father described Jizchok Löwy as an 'Ungeziefer' (H 171, cf. T 139). Writing to Felice on 1 November 1912, Kafka says that only writing has given his life meaning: 'Schrieb ich aber nicht, dann lag ich auch schon auf dem Boden, wert hinausgekehrt zu werden' (F 65); in *Die Verwandlung*, the servant prods Gregor's corpse with her broom and later announces that it has been 'weggeschafft' (E 141). These passages suggest three of the meanings Kafka associated with the image of the insect: the rebellious son, the Galician Jew (regarded with revulsion by the Prague bourgeoisie), and the artist. All three types are outcasts from conventional Western society. Like other writers of his generation, Kafka was interested in social outsiders: we may think of the urban poor encountered by Josef K. in *Der Prozeß* and described sympathetically by Rilke in *Die Aufzeichnungen des Malte Laurids Brigge* (1910), or of the various outsiders (acrobat, negro, stoker, coolie) apostrophized by Werfel in 'An den Leser', the last poem in *Der Weltfreund* (1911).[82] One can see the transformation as the fulfilment of a fantasy about getting one's own back on an exploitative family by terrifying them, and also as an expression of Kafka's solidarity with the despised Galician Jews.[83] These associations, however, seem to have formed part of the genesis of the story but not to have been realized in the text itself, though awareness of them helps to sharpen the opposition between the conventional middle-class world of strictly regulated work and the new experiences to which Gregor's transformation admits him. These must now be explored further.

Gregor's failure, throughout the first section, to register his predicament consciously shows that even when trapped in the body of an insect he retains the mental habits of a travelling salesman. The need to go about his work and appease the Managing Director so obsesses him that he can spare no attention for the outward change that has come over him. Even after acknowledging it, he goes on worrying about how his family will cope without his earnings. Eventually, however, his transformation does show itself to be an ironic fulfilment of his wish to give up his job, and liberates him in some measure from the identity of dutiful son and model employee that society has imposed on him. If Elizabeth Rajec is correct in deriving the name 'Samsa' from the Czech *sám* 'oneself',[84] then Kafka may have been hinting that he himself was to be identified with Gregor, or that Gregor himself is in some way responsible for his own transformation. Some commentators have maintained that Gregor is thus abandoning the false, merely conventional world and encountering the bedrock of inner reality. Wilhelm Emrich, for instance, says: 'Die scheinbar phantastische Irrealität dieses "Ungeziefers", gerade sie ist höchste Realität, der niemand zu entrinnen vermag.'[85] However, the method of characterization that Kafka adopted from Dostoyevsky means that no amount of self-exploration can reach the bedrock, the fundamental being, that underlies consciousness. Being portrayed not from the outside but through his own self-awareness, a Dostoyevsky figure can only reveal that area of his personality that is present to his consciousness at any given time. The rest has to be inferred, and is as perplexing to the character as to the reader. Commenting on the inability of Dostoyevsky's characters to understand themselves, Lukács has observed that they keep subjecting themselves to experiments.[86] Raskolnikov, for example, commits murder in order to test whether he is a potential Napoleon. But their experiments are always inconclusive, for the self is undiscoverable. It always retreats before attempts to define it. No matter where the observer places himself, the self stays just beyond the horizon of consciousness.

In Kafka the self is equally elusive. As in the case of Georg Bendemann, one's 'eigentlich' identity always conceals another which is 'noch eigentlicher', but there is no superlative term. So

Gregor's transformation admits him to different aspects of his own being, none of which can be called fundamental. He may not have a self, but he has selves. The multiplicity of the self was a commonplace of Kafka's time. Ernst Mach in *Die Analyse der Empfindungen* (1886) argued that consciousness was only a sequence of sensations, and the continuous self that received them was no more than a fiction. The influence of Freud, starting from the widely read *Studien über Hysterie* (1895), helped to discredit the notion of the unified self. Schnitzler's Heinrich Bermann is uttering a contemporary topos when he says:

Es kommt immer nur darauf an, wie tief wir in uns hineinschauen. Und wenn die Lichter in allen Stockwerken angezündet sind, sind wir doch alles auf einmal: schuldig und unschuldig, Feiglinge und Helden, Narren und Weise.[87]

Kafka, however, is more radical than Schnitzler in his presentation of the divided self. For Schnitzler, the recesses of the self can be explored by sufficiently resolute introspection; but for Kafka, as for Dostoyevsky, self-scrutiny is by definition impossible. In *Die Verwandlung* Kafka shows the self-estrangement of the protagonist in the most drastic terms: Gregor 'fand sich', we are told, transformed into an insect; he actually sees his new body with its many helpless little legs (E 71); but the sight is too unfamiliar to impinge on his consciousness, and he decides to go back to sleep and forget his 'Narrheiten'. Once he has accepted his transformation, a discrepancy remains between his self-awareness and his physical being, as when he devours the rotten cheese: ' "Sollte ich jetzt weniger Feingefühl haben?" dachte er und saugte schon gierig an dem Käse' (E 98).

As this quotation indicates, much of Gregor's new experience is physical. He has to learn how to manage with an insect's body. Kafka describes how Gregor gets out of bed, and how he opens the door, with the severely factual concentration of Defoe recounting how Robinson Crusoe adjusts to life on the desert island. Gregor's body has become unfamiliar to him. He is like somebody who has recovered from paralysis and is learning to walk again, or like Kleist's Màrquise von O. who finds her body displaying unaccountable signs of pregnancy.[88] Like the Marquise, Gregor has to be alienated from his body to become freshly conscious of it. This awareness is often painful, for his new body is vulnerable: he hurts his head falling out of bed, injures his jaw in turning the key and emits 'eine braune Flüssigkeit' (E 86 —Kafka could have written 'Blut', but the word 'Flüssigkeit' stresses how alien Gregor's new body is and makes it seem more like a machine), and an apple thrown by his father lodges in his back, making him faint with agony, and festers. On the other hand, some of his wounds heal rapidly, and he has acquired new abilities such as crawling on the ceiling. As F. D. Luke has shown in a classic article,[89] his new condition is in many ways infantile, and lets him enjoy childish pleasures like playing with his food and crawling about in dirt, which he does 'mit wachsendem Vergnügen' (E 126). So Kafka uses the transformation to show how Gregor's physical being comes increasingly to dominate his identity. But since Gregor retains his identity until his death, even after his family have declared him a non-person, the lasting implication of the story is that personal identity is independent of the body. Though Kafka shows how the animal side of Gregor's nature asserts itself, he is much less interested than his contemporaries Rilke and Gottfried Benn in exploring what it is like to be an animal; he tends to use animals rather as images for aspects of humanity. Gregor's animal body is a vivid illustration of one of Kafka's favourite themes, the split between being and consciousness.

Gregor's transformation serves many other functions. As a travelling salesman his life was ruled by the clock, but once he is confined to his room he loses track of time. His seclusion seems to last for several months, and at one point he surmises that Christmas must be past, but it is not until after his death that we get another reference to the date, and are told that it is now the end of March. Thus his metamorphosis liberates him from the impersonal time recorded by the clock into the private, timeless world of fantasies and memories. It also arouses the artist in him. Before his transformation he had no interest in music, though he was planning to finance his sister's study at the Conservatory. Afterwards, as though in compensation for his lost power of speech, he acquires an appreciation of music. When his sister plays the violin, the lodgers listen with ill-concealed boredom, but Gregor is enraptured:

War er ein Tier, da ihn Musik so ergriff? Ihm war, als zeige sich ihm der Weg zu der ersehnten unbekannten Nahrung. (E 130.)

Music is, firstly, a substitute for language. Like many of his contemporaries, Kafka shared the scepticism about language propagated by Fritz Mauthner's *Beiträge zu einer Kritik der Sprache* (1901–2).[90] The first sentence quoted above, as Fingerhut points out, is ambiguous, since it could invite either 'yes' or 'no' as an answer.[91] If 'yes' is implied, then Kafka is suggesting that in approaching the animal level Gregor is leaving behind the systematically misleading form of communication used among human beings and is learning to respond to a different, more immediate one. The scholarly dog in *Forschungen eines Hundes* is similarly overwhelmed by music. But both Gregor and the dog have to starve in order to hear the music. Music is a substitute not only for language but also for food. F. D. Luke has best formulated the implications:

Has he become less, or more than human—merely infantile, or mature in a different dimension of maturity? Or is not illness a kind of holiness, and anguished primitive fantasy the substance of art and religion, and may not the energy of savage instinct serve the loftiest aims?[92]

It should also be noticed, though, that the music intensifies Gregor's love for his sister, and seems to promise an escape from his isolation. He spins an extraordinary and repellent fantasy of begging her to enter his room with her violin and then keeping her there for the rest of his life. His hideous shape will frighten off outsiders; 'die Schwester aber sollte nicht gezwungen, sondern freiwillig bei ihm bleiben' (E 130)—a poignant insight into the double-bind latent in possessive love. He then imagines kissing her throat (as Josef K. in *Der Prozeß* kisses Fraulein Bürstner's throat). The suggestion is horrifying, not only because of its Beauty and the Beast overtones but because Gregor may well be a blood-sucking insect (cf. Kafka's comparison of himself to a blood-sucking 'Ungeziefer' in H 222); it also emphasizes Gregor's isolation, since he can still have fantasies of human affection. Ironically, the sister soon afterwards decides that he must go, and Gregor shows his devotion by obligingly dying: 'Seine Meinung darüber, daß er verschwinden müsse, war womöglich noch entschiedener als die seiner Schwester' (E 136).

While his transformation allows Gregor to explore his inner potential, therefore, it leaves him helplessly dependent on his family, both physically and emotionally. When he was supporting them, they soon came to take his support for granted; and once they have to fend for themselves, it turns out that they have some savings which Gregor did not know about. Still, they all have to go out to work, and curiously enough they seem to benefit from it. Herr Samsa, previously a valetudinarian, regains his vigour. Grete, the spoiled child of the family, takes a job as a shop-assistant, and becomes a forceful character. The former breadwinner Gregor becomes the only member of the family who is dependent on the others. As the economic relations within the family are reversed, an accompanying change occurs within their power-relations, symbolized by the fact that while the others increase in strength, Gregor pines away. During the story power passes from Gregor's father to his sister. At the outset Herr Samsa still has some authority, while Grete, a weak and timid girl, is Gregor's principal ally. Gradually she becomes his main adversary, a change which Kafka indicates by the recurring motif of the fist. When Gregor's family first appear, they are knocking on each of the three doors of his bedroom. Grete only moans softly, but their father's knock is 'schwach, aber mit der Faust' (E 75). On Gregor's first appearance in insect form, we are told: 'Der Vater ballte mit feindseligem Ausdruck die Faust' (E 87). But on his second emergence, it is his sister who raises her fist to threaten him: ' "Du, Gregor!" rief die Schwester mit erhobener Faust' (E 114). When she insists on being Gregor's sole guardian, she beats on the table with her fists; and after his third break-out she opens the family council by rapping on the table with her hand. Thus Kafka shows the family to be an unstable system of power-relations. Instead of providing a refuge from the pressures of the outside world, the family is traversed by the same political and economic forces as society at large. But one should not get carried away, like the Marxist critic Hermsdorf, into saying that the Samsas' conduct reveals 'die kleinbürgerliche Familie in der ganzen Gräßlichkeit ihrer wirklichen Erscheinung.'[93] To talk in such terms is to evade Kafka's insight. It is not only the petty-bourgeois family that suffers from self-interest, possessiveness, and the desire to dominate. It is difficult to imagine any system of emotional relationships that is not vitiated in some measure by these impurities. Nor does Kafka permit power-relations to be reinterpreted as economic relations. Gregor's sister, not his father, ends up taking charge of the family. Kafka conceives power rather as personal will, a form of charisma, almost something magical. It appears in a mysterious light in *Der Prozeß*, for example when K. says cryptically: 'Die Frauen haben eine große Macht' (P 253) and the doorkeeper warns the man from the country: 'Merke aber: ich bin mächtig' (P 256). Kafka's understanding of power derives from the charismatic authority exercised by his father and described thus in the *Brief an den Vater*:

In Deinem Lehnstuhl regiertest Du die Welt. [. . .] Du bekamst für mich das Rätselhafte, das alle Tyrannen haben, deren Recht auf ihrer Person, nicht auf dem Denken begründet ist. (H 169.)

Furthermore, the analysis of Gregor's work and its effect on him is certainly unsparing, but would not be easily accommodated in a conventional Marxist view. Gregor's work could be called alienated labour: it offers no intrinsic satisfaction, and the profits go to his firm and his family. But it is unsatisfactory partly because of its abstract nature. He shows samples and takes orders. He is an economic middleman, as is Karl Rossmann's uncle on a vaster scale (V 66). His work is not creative but administrative, and in this respect it is typically modern, corresponding to the description of modern work given by Rathenau in *Zur Kritik der Zeit*. Modern urban man, Rathenau says, belongs to a huge range of social categories, as citizen, voter, taxpayer, parishioner, employer or employee, houseowner, shareholder, possessor of a bank account, and so on; and he has to keep up with these countless responsibilities by organizing his life in accordance with the ruling principle of modern society, that of mechanization. Similarly, his work is likely to be primarily administrative, and to demand efficiency rather than imagination. His satisfaction comes not from the content of his work but from the speed with which he can dispose of it: 'Mag ihm die Arbeit eine Freude sein, so ist nicht mehr die Freude des Schaffens, sondern des Erledigens.'[94] Here Rathenau has given an admirable description of the thin, abstract satisfaction that administrative work affords. It is difficult to imagine how such work could be made intrinsically fulfilling, but harder still to imagine how the complexity of modern society could survive without it. Gregor's circumstances, no doubt, are peculiarly oppressive; but his central problem—a job which engages only a minute portion of his personality—springs from the nature of modern civilization.

This chapter and the previous one have tried to show how much the fiction Kafka produced in his first great creative period, the autumn of 1912, reflects his concern with specific problems of modern society. He was concerned about the position of Jews like himself, whose values differed sharply from those of their less assimilated parents and who therefore could scarcely avoid conflict; and, as his wish to describe 'das allermodernste New York' shows, he wanted to explore the nature of life in the contemporary urban and industrialized world, especially the nature of modern work and its effects on the worker. But he also wanted to explore a group of psychological and moral problems, arising from family relationships, and closely connected with his own experience. In *Der Verschollene* he did not quite succeed in integrating these two main themes, but in *Die Verwandlung* he brought them into a triumphant synthesis: we learn about Gregor's work and environment as they are refracted in his consciousness, and then explore previously unsuspected layers of his inner life, seeing meanwhile how his relationship with his family changes. However, the synthesis of his two main themes that Kafka had achieved in *Die Verwandlung* was an unstable one. For the future, he had to choose between exploring one or the other. He could move out again into another depiction of the urban world, or press on inwards to a closer examination of the moral and psychological problems of the individual. The latter was the obvious option. It permitted Kafka to articulate further what was basically a single problem, though it could be divided into moral and psychological aspects. Seen morally, it was the relationship between guilt and innocence, explored in *Das Urteil* and *Der Verschollene*. Could someone be guilty as a result of what he was, not what he had done? Could one be fundamentally 'ein teuflischer Mensch', like Georg Bendemann, so that one's best intended actions were certain to be exposed as devilish; or, like Karl Rossmann, an innocent child, yet constantly getting into scrapes where one not only appeared to be guilty but perhaps revealed an innate guilt that was always cancelling out one's good intentions? Seen psychologically, this appeared as a conflict between one's consciousness of innocence and one's actual guilt. It was one version of the split between consciousness and being. Before his transformation, Gregor has a consciousness obsessed with his work and separate from his physical being. This estrangement persists afterwards, when he cannot realize that he is trapped in the body of an insect. Supposing consciousness is always like this, so that no matter how much of the unconscious you expose, your true being always retreats further and eludes your introspective gaze? After two years of comparative literary sterility, Kafka was to address this problem in *Der Prozeß* and make it the pivot of a profoundly tragic novel. Only then, after pressing to the limits of his theme, was he able to re-emerge and again contemplate the society around him; and when he did so, it was no longer with the concessions to realism evident in *Der Verschollene*, but in the mode of sober fantasy that dominates the shorter fiction written between 1914 and 1917. These stories will be discussed in Ch. 4, but first we must turn to the unsparing exploration of the individual's moral and psychological problems that Kafka undertakes in *Der Prozeß*.

3

The Intricate Ways of Guilt
Der Prozeß (1914)

Der Prozeß is the most familiar and the most controversial of Kafka's novels. It is the one best known to the reading public, and its opening incident, the unexplained arrest of Josef K., is fixed in many people's minds as the quintessence of the 'Kafkaesque'. Scholars concerned with the novel, however, show no sign of approaching a consensus. Instead, the current tendency is to respond to the diversity of interpretations by arguing, as Theo Elm has recently done, that Der Prozeß is a 'Leerform', a form without content, or a riddle without an answer, designed to provoke and then frustrate the reader's desire for an intelligible meaning.[1] Although it is easy to understand the attraction of soaring like this above the critical battlefield, I believe such arguments to be wrong; and in opposing them I shall be relying especially on an older interpretation of Der Prozeß, Ingeborg Henel's magisterial article of 1963,[2] which has been prevented from receiving the attention it deserves by the sheer volume of subsequent criticism.

First, however, it must be acknowledged that there are substantial obstacles of a practical sort to the understanding of this novel. Like Kafka's other novels, it was left incomplete. But the textual situation here is more complicated than with Der Verschollene and Das Schloß. Kafka wrote the novel between August 1914 and January 1915 in a series of notebooks. He then divided up his manuscript and placed each chapter in a separate envelope. In 1920 he made a present of the manuscript, in this form, to Max Brod; it is now in the possession of Brod's legatee in Israel, and there is, at the moment of writing, no prospect of the manuscript's being made available for critical editing. Anything one says about Der Prozeß, as about the majority of Kafka's works, must therefore be provisional.

Without access to the manuscript, there is limited scope for argument about Brod's transcription of the text, though the afterword to the revised second edition, where Brod tells us that in correcting Kafka's punctuation he has been guided by his recollection of Kafka's speech rhythms, and that he has preserved Kafka's word-order and verbal repetitions 'an vielen Orten' (!), does not inspire confidence. Eric Marson has compared the first and second editions in minute detail and discovered 1,778 textual variations between them.[3] One can only hope that the second edition does approximate to what Kafka wrote, though my own experience of collating Brod's editions of *Das Schloß* and *Der Verschollene* with the Critical Edition suggests that Brod's text contains roughly one substantive error per page. However, the main textual controversy over *Der Prozeß* concerns the ordering of the chapters. There are nine completed chapters and seven incomplete ones, besides the self-contained episode 'Ein Traum' which appeared in Kafka's *Landarzt* collection in 1919. Brod omitted the incomplete chapters from his edition, and included them only as an appendix in the second edition. Except for ch. 8, recounting K's visit to the Advocate in order to dismiss him, they have not been included in either of the English translations.[4] But Kafka did not discard them; he simply stopped and failed to resume work on them, and these incomplete chapters should therefore be regarded as integral parts of the novel. Consequently, *Der Prozeß* is unfinished in a different sense from Kafka's other novels. *Das Schloß* breaks off before the end; *Der Verschollene* consists of a torso and several fragments, with no ending; whereas *Der Prozeß* does have a final chapter, but also has large gaps in the narrative.

It is perhaps impossible to determine with any certainty at which points in the narrative the incomplete chapters belong. Even the completed chapters have not proved easy to arrange. Since Kafka did not number them, there are two possible criteria: (1) the order in which they were composed, (2) the internal coherence of the narrative. The fact that Kafka divided the manuscript up suggests that he may have wished to arrange the chapters in a different order from that of composition, so that arguments from internal coherence deserve considerable attention. Those advanced by Herman Uyttersprot in the 1950s found little acceptance, but the discussion has since been reopened by Eric Marson and Hartmut Binder.[5] Of the rearrangements they suggest, two seem to me compelling, and I shall take them for granted in the rest of this chapter. Firstly, the present ch. 4, 'Die Freundin des Fräulein Bürstner', should follow directly on ch. 1. It takes place on a Sunday five days after K.'s arrest (P 94), whereas in ch. 2, 'Erste Untersuchung', K. states that he was arrested 'vor etwa zehn Tagen' (P 57).[6] Secondly, the present ch. 5, 'Der Prügler', should follow ch. 2, because it shows how rapidly the Court has responded to K's complaint against the two guards by having them punished (cf. P 57–8 and 104) and because it introduces a change of scene between chs. 2 and 3, both of which are set in the Court premises.[7] I shall assume, therefore, that the first five completed chapters of *Der Prozeß* are (i) 'Verhaftung'; (ii) 'Die Freundin des Fräulein Bürstner'; (iii) 'Erste Untersuchung'; (iv) 'Der Prügler'; (v) 'Im leeren Sitzungssaal'. This arrangement has the advantage of bringing into prominence the present ch. 3, whose final episode, as I shall argue, is a crucial turning-point in the Court's dealings with Josef K.

There is another, less obvious difficulty which must be faced before interpretation of *Der Prozeß* can begin. This is the problem of genre, which has already been introduced in the discussion of *Der Verschollene*. In reading any new work of literature, one has to make a preliminary assumption about what kind of work it is—in other words, about its genre. In accordance with the well-known model of the hermeneutic circle, one makes an assumption about the character of the work as a whole, which enables one to make sense of the constituent parts; but acquaintance with the parts may oblige one to revise one's initial assumption and substitute a more accurate generic term. (For example, if one begins reading *Der Prozeß* on the assumption that it is a verisimilar novel, one will be forced by the 'Prügler' chapter to correct that assumption and associate it rather with contemporary fantasies by Kubin and Meyrink.)[8] There is no evading this process, for literary experience is both cumulative and systematic. It is cumulative because one's previous reading helps one to locate and define each new work one encounters, and systematic because one subsumes each new work within a category of which it is either a conformist or a deviant representative. Genre-categories, as I argued in the last chapter, are, however, not timeless or ahistorical: they exist as the expectations of readers and the intentions of authors at a given point in history. They are not always explicitly formulated, and to bring them to the surface can be a difficult task, especially as a rich or complex work of literature may combine elements of several genres in differing degrees of prominence. To reconstruct the genres of past works is indispensable, however, since one cannot read any work except on the basis of a—usually unconscious—assumption about the kind it belongs to, and since assigning a work to the wrong genre will obscure one's understanding of it. Much contemporary Kafka criticism, in fact, proceeds on a generic assumption which I believe to be false: it assigns a novel like *Der Prozeß* to the genre of mystificatory fiction represented by Beckett and Robbe-Grillet, and concludes that Kafka intended only to urge upon the reader the ultimate absence of meaning both in his own writings and in the surrounding world.[9]

Instead, I would argue that *Der Prozeß* belongs to a genre of which the greatest exemplar is Dostoyevsky's *Crime and Punishment*, and which may be called the metaphysical (or religious) crime novel. This genre has its antecedents in the Gothic and psychological fiction of the eighteenth century, and its members include Conrad's *The Secret Agent* (1907) and Greene's *Brighton Rock* (1938). The genealogical relationships among these novels are not in doubt. The one that immediately concerns us, that of *Der Prozeß* to *Crime and Punishment*, is well established. As early as September 1913 Kafka placed Dostoyevsky (along with Kleist, Grillparzer, and Flaubert) in the group of writers whom he called 'meine eigentlichen Blutsverwandten' (F 460), largely because of his knowledge of Dostoyevsky's biography; but he had already read *The Double*, and in 1914 he also read *The Brothers Karamazov*, about which he argued with Brod in December of that year (T 450–1), and *Crime and Punishment*. The latter was in Kafka's private library, and its influence on *Der Prozeß* is so apparent that, as W. J. Dodd has said, Kafka must have been prompted by 'a profound need to respond to Dostoyevsky's novel'.[10] His response took the form of writing a novel in the same genre, just as he had responded to Dickens by writing a 'Dickens-Roman', *Der Verschollene*. Here, as often, genre-study overlaps with source-study, but it serves to make us aware that the various debts of structure, theme, and motif that Kafka owed to *Crime and Punishment* were not isolated borrowings which could just as well have come from twenty different sources; instead, he found them already interrelated as features of a genre. For example, the dramatic structure and the squalid urban setting of *Der Prozeß*, which might seem unconnected, were already related as features of the metaphysical crime novel.

The relationships among members of a literary genre have been compared to family relationships.[11] All have features drawn from a common pool—the generic repertoire—but there is no one feature that must be present in all members of the genre. The following seem to be the main items in the repertoire of the metaphysical crime novel:

(1) The primary interest is not in the ingenuity of the detective (as in Poe's *Purloined Letter* and the modern whodunnit), nor in the

psychology of the criminal, important though that is (as in Schiller's *Der Verbrecher aus verlorener Ehre* and Godwin's *Caleb Williams*), but in the metaphysical or religious theme arising out of the criminal's deed. Dostoyevsky's Raskolnikov first commits murder, then tries to understand his own motives, and is finally induced by Sonya to abandon his Napoleonic egoism and start on the path of spiritual regeneration; while Greene makes a not dissimilar use of Pinkie and Rose to illustrate extremes of evil and good. In *Der Prozeß* Kafka outdoes Dostoyevsky by having the culprit known but not the crime, so that the reader is forced to ask what Josef K. is guilty of and what the Law is under which he is found guilty.

(2) The structure of these novels is dramatic. They usually develop as a series of dramatic confrontations moving towards a climax. Konstantin Mochulsky described *Crime and Punishment* as 'a tragedy in five acts with a prologue and an epilogue', and compared Dostoyevsky's descriptive passages to stage directions.[12] *Der Prozeß* likewise consists of confrontations. In the very first chapter, K. is confronted in turn with the guards, the Inspector, Frau Grubach, and Fräulein Bürstner. Kafka has an unfortunate tendency, however, to dissipate the dramatic tension of a scene by over-elaborating the mystifying monologues which his characters deliver, a tendency which in some of his later fiction gets entirely out of hand.

(3) In keeping with their dramatic character, the action of these novels usually covers a short span of time. Chapters 4–12 of *The Secret Agent* occupy a single day. The time-span of *Der Prozeß* is precisely stated as running from K.'s thirtieth birthday to the eve of his thirty-first, and the first five chapters cover only two and a half weeks.

(4) The narrative stance is usually detached and ironic. Dostoyevsky treats the misery of the Marmeladov family with grotesque humour. Conrad's irony applies even to the murder of Verloc by his wife. Like Conrad, Greene as narrator appears to stand back and let a seemingly inevitable train of events work itself out; but he clearly favours the spiritually aware central characters, Rose and Pinkie, and implies that although they are largely passive victims of the plot, they do have the freedom to make decisions governing their ultimate salvation or damnation. In *Der Prozeß* there is virtually no narrative voice other than Josef K.'s, though by means to be discussed below Kafka provides for the reader's partial distancing from K.

(5) The setting is urban, with emphasis on slums and squalor, rendered in naturalistic detail. Kafka's description of the slum

tenement where K. attends the first hearing may well be indebted to
Dostoyevsky's description of the police-office to which Raskolnikov is
summoned:

The staircase was steep and narrow and smelt of dishwater. All the kitchens of
all the flats on all four floors opened on to the staircase, and as all the doors
stood open almost the whole day, it was terribly stuffy. Up and down these
stairs moved porters with books under their arms, messengers, and various
visitors of both sexes. The door into the office also stood wide open. He went
in and stopped in the ante-room. Several peasants were always standing there
waiting. Here also it was extremely stuffy and in addition the nostrils were
assailed by the sickly odour of new paint which had been mixed with rancid
oil. He waited a little and then decided to move forward into the next room.
All the rooms were very small and low-ceilinged.[13]

By the early nineteenth century the modern city had become the
obvious setting for a crime novel. It offered as much danger and
mystery as any exotic setting. Balzac's Vautrin compares Paris to an
American forest inhabited by warring Indian tribes.[14] The slum
quarters, above all, might be full of dangers. Conrad's Professor,
who always carries a bomb in his pocket, and is trying to invent the
perfect detonator, lives in 'a shabby street, littered with straw and
dirty paper, where out of school hours a troop of assorted children ran
and squabbled with a shrill, joyless, rowdy clamour'.[15] Josef K. is
forced to penetrate similar settings, likewise populated by crowds of
children, and to discover that almost all the attics in the city are
occupied by Court premises.

(6) Without necessarily sacrificing their realistic authenticity, settings tend also to become symbolic. Donald Fanger has discussed in
detail the symbolic relation between Raskolnikov's obsessive brood-
ings and his cramped, airless room, and shown how the labyrinthine
alleys and staircases of the Petersburg slums embody the diverse and
often unacknowledged relations among the people living there and
between the private and public aspects of Raskolnikov's own life.[16]
By relinquishing verisimilitude, Kafka manages to describe similar
scenes with great symbolic intensity: the crowded slums, the attics,
the lumber-room in the bank where the guards are punished, all suggest aspects of K.'s inner world.[17] Greene takes a step into allegory
when Pinkie visits Paradise Piece, the slum where he spent his childhood, and finds that it has been demolished.

(7) Despite the naturalistic settings, ordinary social relationships
play only a subordinate role in these novels. What takes precedence is

the hero's relation to a large organization which he only dimly understands: the police in *Crime and Punishment*, the Court in *Der Prozeß*, the Church in *Brighton Rock*; while Conrad shows terrorists, diplomats and police to be linked at so many points as to form practically a single body, though without a head to direct it.

To recognize these features as generic rather than as Kafka's single-handed creation enables us to integrate *Der Prozeß* into our experience of literature and to do so with some historical accuracy. It can restrain us from making over-hasty connections between the work and the world, as Peter Demetz does when he attributes the rarity of natural description in the works of Kafka and other Prague German writers to their supposed confinement to an urban ghetto;[18] we can now see that the urban setting of *Der Prozeß* is first and foremost a generic feature. It also shows that diverse aspects of *Der Prozeß*—dramatic structure, metaphysical theme, urban setting—are not intrinsically separate, as critical analysis makes them appear, but, being features of the one genre, already stand in an intelligible relationship to one another. However, while the resemblances between *Der Prozeß* and its immediate predecessor, *Crime and Punishment*, are striking, so are the differences, and two of the ways in which Kafka modified the generic pattern must now be mentioned.

If *Crime und Punishment* represents in part an accommodation of the Gothic novel to the norms of verisimilitude, Kafka undoes Dostoyevsky's work by reintroducing elements of Gothic fantasy at the expense of plausibility. As will be shown more fully below, the Gothic mode pervades *Der Prozeß* inasmuch as we can never be sure how far K.'s antagonist, the Court, exists independently of his own mind. But Kafka also makes an excursion into Gothic in the 'Prügler' chapter, adopting the motif, familiar from tales of terror, of the mysterious locked or abandoned room. The lumber-room where K. finds the two guards being punished by the Flogger has two obvious contemporary analogues. The first, still within the bounds of verisimilitude, is the attic room in Musil's *Die Verwirrungen des Jünglings Törleß* (1906), where the schoolboys practise sadistic tortures; the second is the supposedly haunted room in which Pernath, the protagonist of Meyrink's *Der Golem* (1915), becomes identical with the Golem. The room is connected by a labyrinth of underground passages to a room next to Pernath's own, and symbolizes the insanity in his past, which he has repressed but not overcome. Its heavy psychological significance has been described by Thomas Anz in terms which also apply to the lumber-room episode in *Der Prozeß*:

Die grauenvolle Begegnung mit dem Golem ist Bild der Begegnung mit sich selbst, mit einer vom Bewußtsein abgespaltenen Dimension der eigenen Existenz, die zwar einer lebensgeschichtlich vergangenen Episode angehört, in der aber immer noch 'die Triebfeder' des 'Denkens und Handelns' verborgen liegt.[19]

The people in the lumber-room likewise belong to an area of K.'s life which he has hitherto dismissed as marginal and which he thinks he has under control. Not only is the room like a forgotten corner of his brain where his secret fantasies are being acted out, but the candle which lights it, contrasting with the electric light outside, makes the room resemble a survival from the primitive past. The scene in the room (like primal scenes and other memories stored in the unconscious) is, in another sense, timeless: when K. reopens the door twenty-four hours later, the Flogger and the guards are still there.

Besides the introduction of fantasy, Kafka also modifies the genre by extending the narrative technique which he had first used in *Die Verwandlung*. There, as we saw in the last chapter, he established an initial distance between the reader and Gregor, by telling the reader of the transformation which Gregor himself failed to register; thereafter the reader was brought close to Gregor's thoughts and sensations by the monoperspectival narration, while remaining ironically distanced from Gregor by superior knowledge. The narrative method in *Der Prozeß* is slightly different. The famous opening sentence— 'Jemand mußte Josef K. verleumdet haben, denn ohne daß er etwas Böses getan hätte, wurde er eines Morgens verhaftet' (P 9)—betrays the hand of the narrator only in the placing of the conclusion before the premiss; otherwise it is evidently stated from Josef K.'s perspective and is the first of his many attempts to exculpate himself.[20] Thereafter, until the very last chapter, the independent narrative voice is so largely absent that Beissner's account of Kafka's monoperspectival narrative technique is still, up to a point, an accurate description.[20] It needs to be qualified, however, by Ingeborg Henel's observation that the reader does not identify with the hero but rather is offered a perspective congruent with that of the hero.[21] Hence the reader can participate in Josef K.'s sensations while retaining intellectual detachment. This detachment is indeed, as Beissner says, not urged on the reader by any narratorial interventions; instead, the reader becomes gradually distanced from Josef K. by observing his constant display of arrogance, self-righteousness, self-contradiction,

and obtuseness. Kafka has once again achieved a precarious combination of sympathetic with ironic identification. The narrative
voice does appear at the beginning of most chapters, but only to
give us some neutral information about K.'s habits (e.g. 'In diesem
Frühjahr . . .', P 27) or his present situation (e.g. 'An einem Winter-
vormittag . . .', P 137). Towards the end of the novel these pieces of
information become more concise, so that K.'s mental world appears
to be becoming more constricted, and the final chapter begins with
information inaccessible to K. about the conduct of his executioners
before they knock at his door.[23] The world is closing in on K.; he is
now hopelessly confined to his own mental set, and the narrator's
brief departure from K.'s perspective, without giving the reader any
other characters to identify with instead (for the executioners are
practically automata), ensures the reader's detachment both from K.
and from his executioners. All three seem to be playing out their roles
in a prearranged drama.

Given that Kafka adapted the genre of the metaphysical crime
novel, what did he want to express through it? There is still some
need to contest a narrowly biographical view of the novel. Binder, for
example, has recently maintained that *Der Prozeß* is a 'Darstellung
autobiographischer Probleme des Autors' in which Kafka tried to
come to terms with the breakdown of his relationship with Felice
Bauer.[24] Since close connections unquestionably do exist between
Kafka's interpretation of his own experience and his fiction, this view
cannot be dismissed out of hand. The most obvious connections are
the guilt he felt about the termination of his engagement to Felice and
his use in this context of the imagery of trial and punishment. Kafka
and Felice had become officially engaged in 1914, at a ceremony held
in the Bauers' home in Berlin at Whitsun (30 May–1 June). Immediately after his return from Berlin, Kafka, who had been reading
Dostoyevsky's account of penal servitude in Siberia, wrote in his
diary: 'War gebunden wie ein Verbrecher' (T 384). Two years later
he recalled: 'die Verlobungsexpedition mit meinen Eltern war für
mich eine Folterung Schritt für Schritt' (Br 139). Though he loved
Felice, he dreaded the prospect of a settled bourgeois life in which he
would never be able to resign his job and would lack the solitude
necessary for writing. Felice, however, was determined on a model
bourgeois existence. She wanted to have a wedding ceremony in the
synagogue, much against Kafka's will (F 620), and took him on an
expedition to buy furniture, massive pieces which reminded Kafka of

tombstones (F 650). His efforts to make her appreciate the things he valued, like literature and athletics, seem to have been ineffectual ('Vergiß übrigens nicht, daß zu Deiner Ausstattung in viel höherem Maße als Möbel und Wäsche das Schwimmen gehört', he wrote during their engagement (F 590)). The couple could hardly have been less compatible, and their engagement was severed, on Felice's initiative, in a distressing scene in Berlin which Kafka later called a 'Gerichtshof' (T 407).[25]

Now it is clear that these events helped to inspire *Der Prozeß*, and that there is a connection between Kafka himself and Josef K., and between Felice Bauer and Fräulein Bürstner. But the link need not be more than an onomastic one. *Der Prozeß* is in no sense a *roman à clef*. I should even hesitate to follow Walter Sokel in calling it a punishment-fantasy.[26] Such biographical and psychoanalytical interpretations tend to ignore the fact that for Kafka writing was a way of objectifying problems, gaining detachment from them and seeing them in perspective: 'Hinausspringen aus der Totschlägerreihe, Tat-Beobachtung' (T 563). To objectify a problem in art is to generalize it; and once that is accomplished, the particular circumstances which made the artist scrutinize the problem are no longer of direct relevance. In Josef K., Kafka has not depicted himself; he has depicted a type of character, very different from himself, and explored how such a character reacts to a wholly unprecedented situation.

Another tendency in the interpretation of *Der Prozeß* has been to see it as a prophecy of totalitarian dictatorships in general and of Nazism in particular. This was why Brecht valued Kafka's writings:

in ihm findet sich in merkwürdigen verkleidungen vieles vorgeahnte, was zur zeit des erscheinens der bücher nur wenigen zugänglich war, die faschistische diktatur steckte den bürgerlichen demokratien sozusagen in den knochen und kafka schilderte mit großartiger fantasie . . . die kommenden konzentrationslager, die kommende rechtsunsicherheit, die kommende verabsolutierung des staatsapparats, das dumpfe, von unzulänglichen kräften gelenkte leben der vielen einzelnen, alles erschien wie in einem alpdruck und mit der wirrheit und unzulänglichkeit des alpdrucks.[27]

Undoubtedly the mysterious apparatus of justice in *Der Prozeß*, the arrival of the guards in K.'s flat while he is still in bed, the Court's assumption that since K. has been arrested he must be guilty, and the practice of rearresting those released after an 'illusory acquittal', along with many other details, do bear a chilling resemblance to the workings of police states around the world and, especially, to the

travesty of law under Nazism.[28] But, precisely because this interpretation seems at first glance so persuasive, it is necessary to apply
all one's common sense to the question *how* Kafka, who died in 1924,
could have foreseen political developments that occurred after his
death.

Two types of explanation have been suggested. One is that Kafka
was an exceptionally acute observer of his own society and perceived,
as Brecht claims, the fascist tendencies already present in democracy;
or, as J. P. Stern argues, the insecure position of Jews like himself,
who enjoyed legal equality but not social acceptance, enabled him to
anticipate their future victimization; or, in Ernst Fischer's version,
the insurance office where he worked prefigured the eventual domin-
ation of the entire capitalist West by a tyrannical bureaucracy.[29] Most
present-day readers will, I imagine, regard Brecht's and Fischer's
social analyses with some scepticism; while Stern, though without
their dogmatic presuppositions, does seem to exaggerate the insecurity
felt by assimilated Jews in Austria before the First World War. If,
however, we reject these explanations of Kafka's apparent foresight,
the alternative is the Marxist belief that great writers have a prophetic
faculty which, Lukács tells us, is not just correct political foresight but
rather the artist's 'unconscious possession of a perspective independent of, and reaching beyond, his understanding of the contemporary
scene'.[30] This sounds like a restatement of the Romantic view of the
poet as seer; in which case it is surely no more than a mystification.

I do not see, therefore, on what basis *Der Prozeß* could reasonably be
interpreted as a prophecy. Nor are there any statements in Kafka's
diaries or letters at this time that would encourage us to interpret the
novel as an analysis of contemporary society. Kafka was of course
aware of the existence of police-states: from newspaper reports, and
from the life of Dostoyevsky, he knew about the oppression practised
in Tsarist Russia, though one must add that the Tsarist police-state
seems half-hearted and amateurish compared with its successor.
From accounts of Dostoyevsky's life in Siberia, in particular, Kafka
has borrowed the imagery of injustice and imprisonment, but he has
applied it to a different theme, rather as he did when he imagined
himself being tried and convicted for his conduct towards Felice. One
could perhaps describe his procedure by saying that he has taken
expressions like 'the moral law' literally. Suppose the moral law were
not an abstract imperative but a law which one could be arrested and
tried for breaking? Suppose it had an entire legal system, with its own

courts, lawyers, and policemen, even its prison chaplain and its professional executioners; and suppose that these functionaries, though
in the service of something absolute, were themselves human, fallible,
and prone to misbehaviour? It was by some such analogy that the
imaginary world of *Der Prozeß* came into being. Directly political
readings of it, therefore, confuse the vehicle of the dominant
metaphor (the Court) with its tenor, and assume that legal and
political matters supply the theme as well as the imagery of the novel.
The contrary interpretation—that the primary concern of *Der Prozeß*
is with the moral accountability of the individual—needs, however,
to be defended at length. First, it must be shown that Josef K., far
from being victimized, is morally at fault.

There is a widespread view that Josef K. is a deliberately non-
descript character with 'as little body and soul as the monolinear
figures Kafka drew on the margins of his manuscripts'.[31] However,
he has a number of distinct characteristics, appropriate to his position
as manager of a large bank. His life follows a routine, which starts being disrupted when, for the first time ever, the cook fails to appear
with his breakfast. He begins work early, sometimes at 7 a.m., and
usually continues until 9 p.m., after which he joins older colleagues at
a *Stammtisch*. His weekly visits to his girl-friend Elsa are merely part of
his working routine: when he refuses to obey a Court summons and
goes to visit Elsa instead, we are told: 'die Gedanken an die Bank
begannen ihn wieder, wie in früheren Zeiten, ganz zu erfüllen' (P 276).
He feels more at home in the bank than he does in his lodgings, and is
sure that he would have been able to cope with his arrest if it had
occurred in the bank. He neglects family relationships. Though he
promised to visit his mother regularly on his birthday, he has failed to
do so for the last two years, and is content to learn at second hand that
her health is improving, or at least that she is complaining less
('wenigstens klagte sie weniger', P 277). Nor has he paid any attention to his cousin Erna, who is at a boarding-school in the city.

The relationships that interest K. are professional ones. These are
strictly hierarchical. He goes on outings with the director of the
bank, and considers the society of his *Stammtisch* 'außerordentlich
achtungswürdig' (P 282) because it consists of highly placed judges
and lawyers, including his influential friend Staatsanwalt Hasterer.[32]
Junior officials are tolerated at the *Stammtisch*, but may only speak
when spoken to, and the high officials delight in putting them on the
spot with embarrassing questions. Accordingly, K. reacts to his arrest

in hierarchical terms, dismissing his guards as ignorant subordinates, looking forward to clearing the matter up by a conversation with an equal ('einem mir ebenbürtigen Menschen', P 15), but promptly taking offence when reproved by the Inspector: 'K. starrte den Aufseher an. Schulmäßige Lehren bekam er hier von einem vielleicht jüngeren Menschen?' (P 22). When unexpectedly confronted with the three junior employees from the bank, Rabensteiner, Kullich, and Kaminer,[33] he refuses to acknowledge them as colleagues. He attaches importance not only to rank but to its visible symbols, enjoys having a servant and two telephones at his disposal, and pooh-poohs his arrest on the grounds that the Inspector and the guards are not in uniform.

In his dealings with other people, K. is aggressive and calculating. On learning that he cannot have his breakfast, he leaps out of bed and resolves to call his landlady to account. Towards the end of his interview with the Inspector, he believes that he has the upper hand, steps menacingly close to the Inspector, and becomes openly insulting. The sentence 'Er spielte mit ihnen' (P 24) indicates K.'s groundless belief that he is in control. He tries, though unsuccessfully, to manipulate the Inspector by offering him his hand, in the hope that the matter of his arrest can be dismissed by a handshake.[34] He relies on his intellect in a manner that recalls Georg Bendemann's futile resolve 'alles vollkommen genau zu beobachten' (E 64). After failing to notice the disappearance of the Inspector and the guards, K. reproaches himself for inattention and resolves 'sich in dieser Hinsicht genauer zu beobachten' (P 27); even when being led to execution he still trusts in his 'ruhig einteilenden Verstand' (P 269). He could serve as a case study in the 'instrumental rationality', the use of rational means to achieve irrational ends, which, according to the sociologists of the Frankfurt School, modern society has inherited from the Enlightenment.[35]

But, though K. may be an unscrupulous operator, that is not how he sees himself. Rather, he thinks of himself as disinclined to learn from experience or to provide for the future: 'Er neigte stets dazu, alles möglichst leicht zu nehmen, das Schlimmste erst beim Eintritt des Schlimmsten zu glauben, keine Vorsorge für die Zukunft zu treffen, selbst wenn alles drohte' (P 12). This, it had better be emphasized, is K.'s description of himself, not the narrator's account of K.[36] It is repeatedly disproved by K.'s increasing worry about the progress of his trial, and also, as Binder has pointed out, by the fact that the name of K.'s job, 'Prokurist', is an etymological doublet of 'Vorsorge', so that K. is professionally committed to 'Vorsorge für die Zukunft'.[37]

Neither does K. realize how far his calculating rationality has estranged him from the physical, sexual, animal side of his being. His obsession with Fräulein Bürstner suggests that those weekly visits to Elsa do not satisfy all his needs. One reason why his arrest disconcerts K. so much is that the guards concern themselves with the intimate, physical area of his life—eating, sleeping, and his sexual fantasies. They consume his breakfast; they examine his nightshirt, tell him to put on a much plainer one, and confiscate the rest of his linen; and the desk where the Inspector sits to inform him of his arrest is Fräulein Bürstner's bedside table. The guards' insistent bodily presence makes it difficult for K. to compose his thoughts rationally. Although K. prefers to keep other people at arm's length (except when he wants to intimidate or manipulate them), the guards cross the frontier of his person by butting against him: 'in Gegenwart dieser Leute konnte er aber nicht einmal nachdenken, immer wieder stieß der Bauch des zweiten Wächters—es konnten ja nur Wächter sein—förmlich freundschaftlich an ihn' (P 12).[38]

Josef K., therefore, is a character of a distinct and recognizable type. Calculating, egoistic, aggressive, authoritarian, self-deceived, and repressed, he is somebody who, willingly or not, has discarded large tracts of his personality in order to fit into the organization which employs him. Without a family to support, Gregor Samsa might have grown into such a person. Both have allowed their personalities to be impoverished by yielding to the pressure to conform which critics of modern industrial society have so often condemned. One of these critics, Nietzsche, begins his essay 'Schopenhauer als Erzieher' by denouncing the timidity and laziness which makes the great majority of people conform to a standard pattern. Only artists, says Nietzsche, dare to remind people that they are unique individuals:

Die Künstler allein hassen dieses lässige Einhergehen in erborgten Manieren und übergehängten Meinungen und enthüllen das Geheimnis, das böse Gewissen von jedermann, den Satz, daß jeder Mensch ein einmaliges Wunder ist; sie wagen es, uns den Menschen zu zeigen, wie er bis in jede Muskelbewegung er selbst, er allein ist, noch mehr, daß er in dieser strengen Konsequenz seiner Einzigkeit schön und betrachtenswert ist, neu und unglaublich wie jedes Werk der Natur und durchaus nicht langweilig.[39]

Whether or not Kafka knew these sentiments, he would certainly have agreed with them. In a long notebook entry, written perhaps in 1916, he complains that although every individual is unique, the goal of education, at home as well as in school, is to erase that uniqueness so that the child can fit into life more comfortably (H 227–32). Josef K. has undergone this process so effectively that he has no regrets about it. As the Marxist critic Sánchez Vázquez has said: 'K. has reached such an extreme of alienation that he no longer experiences his life as fragmented or torn. He no longer notices a conflict or schism between his private and public life because he no longer has a private life. His entire being consists of his role as functionary.'[40] Like Thomas Mann's Aschenbach, he has become estranged from his own nature, and the subsequent narrative tells how he is gradually destroyed by forces which he never understands and whose power comes from the fact that they are not wholly external, but, as in Aschenbach's Dionysiac dream, 'ihr Schauplatz war vielmehr seine Seele selbst'.[41]

However, although the social criticism that we saw in *Der Verschollene* and *Die Verwandlung* is still present in *Der Prozeß*, it does not point to the source of K.'s guilt. The crime for which he is arrested is not that of being a bank-manager. Nor, despite his resemblance to Aschenbach, is his trial a well-meaning psychotherapeutic exercise designed to cure his repressions. The Court has been attracted to K. by a more deep-seated deficiency in him, which he reveals when he says that he does not know the law under which he has been arrested. The guard Franz puts in the comment: 'Sieh, Willem, er gibt zu, er kenne das Gesetz nicht, und behauptet gleichzeitig, schuldlos zu sein' (P 15). This means that ignorance of the law is incompatible with innocence under the law. Now there is no known legal system to which this applies. Nobody is ever tried simply for not knowing the law. But there is another kind of law which can be transgressed by sheer ignorance of it, and that is the moral law. In an adult human being, moral ignorance is itself a moral offence.[42] There is therefore nothing paradoxical or absurd in Franz's comment. It only seems absurd from the standpoint of K., whose first thought is that he lives in a 'Rechtsstaat' (P 12) in which all the laws are in force, and who does not realize that the personal documents (first his bicycle-licence, then his birth-certificate) which he offers the guards are irrelevant to their mission. However the reader, as was argued earlier, is not confined to K.'s standpoint, but enjoys a perspective congruent with but superior to K.'s, from which it is possible to sympathize with his perplexity while comprehending his situation as he himself cannot.[43]

The essential idea with which *Der Prozeß* begins—that K.'s ignorance of the moral law constitutes his guilt under this law—is compellingly neat and simple, but profoundly disturbing in its consequences. It has the elegant construction of a trap from which there is no escape. Somebody arrested on these grounds is *ipso facto* guilty. If he claims that he is innocent, he merely demonstrates his guilt. That is why the Court is impervious to evidence ('für Beweisgründe unzugänglich', P 184) and why K.'s uncle quotes the pertinent proverb: 'Einen solchen Prozeß haben, heißt ihn schon verloren haben' (P 119). An accused man can never acknowledge his guilt, because his guilt consists in the belief that he is innocent. This is the type of logical *huis clos* to which Kafka often recurs, as in this aphorism dating from 1920:

> Die Erbsünde, das alte Unrecht, das der Mensch begangen hat, besteht in dem Vorwurf, den der Mensch macht und von dem er nicht abläßt, daß ihm ein Unrecht geschehen ist, daß an ihm die Erbsünde begangen wurde. (B 295–6.)

This paradox is close to *Der Prozeß* in structure and theme. Man can be freed from original sin if he realizes that he himself committed the original sin. Similarly, Josef K.'s conviction of his innocence cuts him off from the possibility of becoming innocent. To escape from this closed circle, he would have to lift himself by his own moral bootstraps, or, to quote Kafka's reminiscence of Baron Münchhausen, 'an den eigenen Haaren sich aus dem Sumpf gezogen haben' (H 71). An aphorism of 1917 announces starkly: 'Du bist die Aufgabe. Kein Schüler weit und breit' (H 83).

This, however, is not a complete account of Josef K.'s situation. If it were, the novel's implied morality would be a sublimated form of sadism. Nor would it have any potential for narrative development: Kafka would simply be exhibiting the same situation over and over again, as in *Der Verschollene*. Wilhelm Emrich and Ingeborg Henel have shown[44] that the ground-plan of *Der Prozeß* can best be understood with the help of a difficult passage Kafka wrote in his notebook in January 1918:

> Seit dem Sündenfall sind wir in der Fähigkeit zur Erkenntnis des Guten und Bösen im Wesentlichen gleich; trotzdem suchen wir gerade hier unsere besonderen Vorzüge. Aber erst jenseits dieser Erkenntnis beginnen die wahren Verschiedenheiten. Der gegenteilige Schein wird durch folgendes

hervorgerufen: Niemand kann sich mit der Erkenntnis allein begnügen, sondern muß sich bestreben, ihr gemäß zu handeln. Dazu aber ist ihm die Kraft nicht mitgegeben, er muß daher sich zerstören, selbst auf die Gefahr hin, sogar dadurch die notwendige Kraft nicht zu erhalten, aber es bleibt ihm nichts anderes übrig, als dieser letzte Versuch. (Das ist auch der Sinn der Todesdrohung beim Verbot des Essens vom Baume der Erkenntnis; vielleicht ist das auch der ursprüngliche Sinn des natürlichen Todes.) Vor diesem Versuch nun fürchtet er sich; lieber will er die Erkenntnis des Guten und Bösen rückgängig machen (die Bezeichnung 'Sündenfall' geht auf diese Angst zurück); aber das Geschehene kann nicht rückgängig gemacht, sondern nur getrübt werden. Zu diesem Zweck entstehen die Motivationen. Die ganze Welt ist ihrer voll, ja die ganze sichtbare Welt ist vielleicht nichts anderes als eine Motivation des einen Augenblick lang ruhenwollenden Menschen. Ein Versuch, die Tatsache der Erkenntnis zu fälschen, die Erkenntnis erst zum Ziel zu machen. (H 102-3.)

To understand this, one must realize how sharp a distinction Kafka is drawing between moral awareness and moral conduct. Since the Fall, mankind has possessed an innate, intuitive moral awareness. We do not need to find out what is good and what is evil; all of us already know. But the knowledge of good and evil is not like knowing, say, history or arithmetic. By its very nature, the knowledge of good and evil is not an object for passive contemplation, but urgently demands to be transformed into moral action. One must try to lead a good life at all costs—but since no human being is strong enough to do so, the cost must be that one will destroy oneself in the attempt. Yet this makes the moral imperative no less inflexible. Kafka writes as a moral rigorist, for whom only the most uncompromising morality is good enough.

Since the moral life is suicidally difficult, people do not attempt it. But since they cannot get rid of their moral awareness, they try to obscure their knowledge of good and evil by devising 'Motivationen'. That is, they assign motives and causes to their actions and invent excuses for their failure to behave morally; they pretend to be uncertain about how they should behave, and therefore make moral knowledge the object of their enquiries, although, since they already possess it, it ought instead to be the starting-point of their actions. A striking example of such behaviour is K.'s attempt to compose a submission for the Court in which he surveys all the more important actions of his life and explains his motives for each of them (P 137).[45] More generally, it may help us to understand Kafka's meaning if we recall Tolstoy's *The Death of Iván Ilých*, and especially the thoughts that pass throughout Ivan Ilyich's mind as he lies on his death-bed:

It occurred to him that his scarcely perceptible attempts to struggle against what was considered good by the most highly placed people, those scarcely noticeable impulses which he had immediately suppressed, might have been the real thing, and all the rest false. And his professional duties and the whole arrangement of his life and of his family, and all his social and official interests, might have been false.

Previously a contented, mediocre, worldly character like Josef K., Ivan Ilyich now concludes that all that he has lived for was 'a terrible and huge deception which had hidden both life and death.'[46]

Kafka is similarly concerned with a character entangled in deception. Josef K. may be morally ignorant at the very beginning of the novel, but the first effect of his arrest is to arouse in him the knowledge of good and evil, symbolized by his eating 'einen schönen Apfel' (P 17). The reflection that follows corresponds to another aphorism of 1917, beginning: 'Ein erstes Zeichen beginnender Erkenntnis ist der Wunsch zu sterben' (H 81). K. wonders why the guards have left him alone in his room, where he has many means of committing suicide. This thought suggests that K. is on the verge of acknowledging his guilt. It comes to him, we are told, 'aus dem Gedankengang der Wächter' (P 17): it is not part of his accustomed way of thinking. But simultaneously his habitual mentality reasserts itself and he begins suppressing and dismissing his momentary insight, reflecting that the very notion of suicide is senseless and that the guards clearly do not understand what they are talking about. On a few later occasions his repressed awareness of guilt comes close to the surface. When the guards tell him to put on a black coat, he says, without knowing why he says it: 'Es ist doch noch nicht die Hauptverhandlung' (P 18). That evening he betrays himself again by telling his landlady: 'wenn Sie die Pension rein erhalten wollen, müssen Sie zuerst mir kündigen' (P 33). The Court has begun arousing him from his previous moral indifference into the beginnings of self-awareness, though his self-awareness appears only in occasional flashes and his almost unlimited powers of repression are already coming into play. Nonetheless, what the Court has done is to release him from the logical trap in which he was unwittingly caught at the moment of his arrest. At that point, being guilty by definition under a law he did not understand, he was logically incapable even of acknowledging his guilt, let alone ridding himself of it. But now that the Court has made him a potentially moral being, the escape from his guilt is no longer a logical contradiction; it is merely superhumanly difficult. The difference may seem slight, but is in fact infinite. The first task was logically impossible; K.'s present task is merely physically impossible. Hence the ironic consolation offered by the 1917 aphorism: 'Das Mißverhältnis der Welt scheint tröstlicherweise nur ein zahlenmäßiges zu sein' (H 88).

The results of failing in this task, and of becoming entangled in 'Motivationen', are displayed to K. on his second visit to the Court premises. A mean-looking wooden staircase admits him to the Court offices, situated in an attic and connected by a long corridor in which accused persons are seated. Uncharacteristically, K. acknowledges these people as his 'Kollegen' (P 81), but their demeanour does not resemble his. Instead of sharing his self-assurance, they sit or stand with bent backs or bowed heads, like beggars, and are so timid that they can scarcely reply to a question; yet, like K. himself, they evidently come from 'den höheren Klassen' (P 80), and have not always been in the habit of behaving so humbly. One of them, the elderly man whom K. accosts, is waiting for an answer to the 'Beweisanträge' he has presented to the Court (P 82). He is already enmeshed in legal proceedings of the sort whose futility is amply demonstrated in the course of the novel. What this passage shows, in addition, is that in submitting to the Court and its labyrinthine procedures, one allows oneself to be shamefully humiliated.[47]

After K.'s arrest, the action of *Der Prozeß* falls, as Marson has shown in detail, into three phases. In the first (chs. 1–5), the Court is in close contact with K. Its emissaries visit his home and his office, and he pays two visits to its premises. In the second phase (chs. 6–8), the Court has withdrawn; K. no longer deals directly with its representatives, but with intermediaries like the Advocate and Titorelli, and is aware of the Court only as a vast, shadowy, inaccessible organization. In chs. 9 and 10 the Court again approaches K. in order to deliver to him, through the Chaplain, a final warning which he does not heed, and then to have him executed. In the first of these phases, the Court behaves towards K. with great civility and compliance. The Inspector does no more than inform him of his arrest, assures him that, instead of being taken into custody, he will be able to continue leading his accustomed life, and even supplies three of his junior colleagues to accompany him to the bank and make his late arrival less conspicuous. His first hearing is arranged for Sunday, so as not

to disturb his working life; when he complains of the guards'
behaviour, they are duly punished; and after he ends the hearing by
shouting 'Ihr Lumpen, [. . .] ich schenke euch alle Verhöre' (P 63),
the Court, to his surprise, seems to take him at his word and does not
summon him again. At the same time, the Court's very compliance is
deeply unsettling. The Sunday summons does affect his career, inasmuch as it obliges K. to refuse a social invitation from the Deputy
Director which would have served K.'s ambitions; while the
discovery of the guards and the Flogger in a lumber-room in the bank
understandably appals K. It is unsettling, too, that the Court seems
to respond even to K.'s unspoken thoughts. Since his summons to the
first hearing does not specify any time, K. decides to try to be there
by 9 a.m., and on arriving at five past ten he is duly reprimanded for
being an hour and five minutes past the time he set himself.[42] He conceals his mission by asking for the fictitious 'Tischler Lanz', but is
apparently understood by the woman who shows him into the courtroom. Later, in ch. 9, K. goes to the cathedral to show an Italian
visitor round; the Italian does not turn up, but K. is called by name
by the Chaplain, as though his appointment with the Italian had
somehow been arranged in collusion with the Court.

Since the Court is so responsive to K.'s wishes, one is tempted to
see it as no more than a projection of K.'s mind, a system of 'Motivationen', which he unconsciously devises in order to avoid facing up to
his own guilt.[49] In the tirade which he delivers at the first hearing, K.
declares himself to be one of many victims of an immense organization which employs judges, secretaries, gendarmes, and perhaps even
hangmen, which is corrupt through and through, and whose sole purpose is to arrest innocent people and subject them to meaningless
trials. These assertions go far beyond K.'s knowledge; they are a
paranoid fantasy with only the slightest basis in his experience. But
later we do learn of a vast, impenetrable hierarchy of officials, and we
may wonder whether it has come into being to fulfil K.'s expectations. On this reading, the hierarchical structure of the Court would
mirror the hierarchy K. is used to in the bank; the rapacious sexuality
of the Examining Magistrate, and the squalor of the Court premises,
would reflect the discreditable aspects of K.'s own mind. This is an
inviting interpretation, not least because it reminds one that Kafka is
adapting one of the most alarming devices of Gothic fiction: the creation of a being who is a projection of the hero's mind and yet terrifying, alien, and uncontrollable. The mindless *Doppelgänger* who

pursues Medardus in Hoffmann's *Elixiere des Teufels*, or Stevenson's Mr. Hyde, who tends to appear whenever his creator, Dr. Jekyll, has relaxed his conscious self-control by falling asleep, are obvious examples. When Kafka most strikingly adopts the Gothic mode, in the Flogger episode, the horror of the incident is certainly intensified by the reader's suspicion that, in opening the lumber-room door, K. is looking into a concealed corner of his own mind—especially as the lumber-room, like the Freudian unconscious, seems to be outside time, since the Flogger and the guards are still there twenty-four hours later.

The argument that the Court is an emanation from K.'s mind should not be pressed too far, however, for it risks becoming un-falsifiable and therefore vacuous. Anything whatever could, after all, be explained as a projection of K.'s unconscious. The terror of the Court seems rather to reside in its ambiguity, in its being both inside and outside K.'s mind. In some theories, that is also true of moral values. The ethical theory put forward by Franz Brentano, with which Kafka is likely to have been familiar, maintains that moral values are neither subjective nor arbitrary; they are innate in the human mind, and they are also objective and absolute.[50] Accordingly, Kafka's Court is concerned, not with any particular set of laws, but with absolute good and evil. Whether the Court is a projection of K.'s mind or exists independently of him is therefore irrelevant, and Kafka is free to exploit the ambiguity for maximum effect, for in either case the Court is the limited embodiment of absolute justice, and K. makes the mistake of letting the sometimes grotesquely inappropriate character of the Court blind him to the absolute nature of what it embodies. This discrepancy between the absolute and its (necessarily) inadequate embodiment comes out most clearly when pictures are mentioned. On his second visit to the Court premises, K. sees on the Magistrate's desk some books which he thinks are law-books but which turn out to be pornography, with salacious but badly drawn illustrations. It is possible that by 1914 Kafka had already read the auto-biography of Salomon Maimon, including the digest of the teaching of Maimonides which Maimon provides in an appendix. Here Maimon-ides says that the mysteries of religion are sometimes symbolized in forms that seem inappropriate, offensive, or even obscene to the pro-fane eye. He illustrates this by a remarkable story from the Talmud:

Nach dieser Erzählung fanden die Feinde, die sich des Tempels bemäch-tigt hatten, im Allerheiligsten das Bildnis zweier Personen von beiden

Geschlechtern in dem Vereinigungsakt begriffen—und entweihten dieses
Heiligtum durch eine krasse Auslegung seines inneren Sinnes.—Dieses
Bildnis sollte eine lebhafte sinnliche Vorstellung von der Vereinigung der
Nation mit der Gottheit sein und mußte nur zur Verhütung des Mißbrauchs
dem Auge des gemeinen Volks, das nur beim Zeichen stehn bleibt, nicht aber
in den inneren Sinn dringt, entzogen werden.[51]

While one would not necessarily want to attach any specific meaning
to the picture K. sees, this passage does strengthen the likelihood that
any interpretation K. puts on pictures will be wide of the mark. On
two occasions he is shown pictures of judges, once by Leni and once
by Titorelli, and both times he is told that the pictures do not match
reality. The judge in the first picture, seated majestically on a throne,
is said to be in reality a tiny man, who sits on a kitchen chair covered
by an old horse-blanket (P 132); while the other judge was painted by
Titorelli, not from the life, but in accordance with a fixed system
of conventions (P 176). Though these paintings rely on 'Erfindung'
(P 132, 176), they are not therefore to be dismissed as false. While
they lack mimetic faithfulness (like the photograph of Elsa that K.
showed Leni), they may still symbolize accurately the office held by
the judges, even though they misrepresent the judges' appearance.

K., however, relies on appearances, and readily assumes that a
Court with shabby offices in garrets and with officials who miscon-
duct themselves cannot be taken seriously. Of the two mutually
contradictory ways in which he reacts to his arrest, one is therefore
bullying self-assertion, while the other is paranoid suspicion. Talking
to his landlady, he first pretends to accept her view that his arrest is
'etwas Gelehrtes', then, in a passage of self-contradictory pseudo-
argument typical of Kafka's characters, whittles away at her opinion
till it turns into its opposite:

Es ist gar nichts Dummes, was Sie gesagt haben, Frau Grubach, wenigstens
bin auch ich zum Teil Ihrer Meinung, nur urteile ich über das Ganze noch
schärfer als Sie und halte es einfach nicht einmal fur etwas Gelehrtes, sondern
überhaupt für nichts. (P 30.)

At the first hearing which K. attends, he makes no effort to learn
about the Court or the reason for his arrest, but responds to the
Magistrate's disconcerting question ('Sie sind Zimmermaler?', P 54)
with a long tirade (P 55–63), after which the Magistrate quietly informs him that through his conduct he has sacrificed the potential
advantages of his hearing. On his next visit, K. indulges in fantasies

of reforming the Court, of punishing the Magistrate by taking his mistress (the wife of the court servant) away from him, and of humiliating the student Berthold in front of Elsa's bed. His fantasies have something in common with Lear's 'I will do such things—What they shall be, I know not, but they shall be The terror of the earth.'

At the same time K. keeps betraying his insecurity. His concern over the 'Unordnung' (P 28, 34) caused by his arrest turns at one point into a plan to punish Frau Grubach (whom he supposes to be in some way involved) by allying himself with Fräulein Bürstner and giving notice jointly with her; at another point, he questions suspiciously a boy whom he finds smoking a pipe in the entrance to the building where he lives, but who turns out only to be the son of the *Hausmeister*. In a deleted passage K. notices a soldier outside, springs to the conclusion that he is already under guard, then abandons this notion on realizing that the soldier is simply waiting for a girl-friend (P 305–6).

His arrest, then, immediately undermines K.'s 'ruhig einteilenden Verstand' by bringing out the latent irrationality in his character. This is most apparent in the scene with Fräulein Bürstner. Feeling obliged to account for the disorder in her room (though it amounts only to the disarrangement of the photographs on her bedside table), he waits up for her and insists on re-enacting his confrontation with the Inspector. His culminating cry of 'Josef K.!' causes Frau Grubach's nephew, who is sleeping next door, to rap on the wall.[52] The rapping seems to unleash K.'s already obvious sexual desire for Fräulein Bürstner, and before long he is kissing her over her whole face, 'wie ein durstiges Tier mit der Zunge über das endlich gefundene Quellwasser hinjagt', and finally on the throat. The emotional implications are complex.[53] On the most obvious level, he is taking advantage of her weariness, and his ludicrous proposal that she should clear her reputation by putting it about that K. attacked her clearly expresses his desires. He is also using sex as a way of manipulating her and enlisting her help in his trial. Further, the image of the thirsty animal alludes to the normally suppressed animal side of K.'s nature, suggests his desperate need for sexual contact, hints at the aggression he is releasing, but also, through the image of 'Quellwasser', conveys his unconscious search for the purity which he feels to be lacking in himself. The repellently vampire-like image of his kissing her throat enhances the suggestion of aggressiveness and implies a desire to strengthen himself at her expense by sucking her blood. Altogether, this passage has a strange mingling of brutality and poignancy which recurs in the description of K.'s and Frieda's love-making in *Das Schloß*.

The turning-point in K.'s dealings with the Court comes in his second visit, two and a half weeks after his arrest, when he encounters a friendly and informative female Court employee and an official called the 'Auskunftgeber' ('Information Officer'). The girl asks him: 'Was wünscht der Herr?' (P 84), but K. cannot think what question to ask. As he stands pondering, we are told, 'wirklich sahen ihn das Mädchen und der Gerichtsdiener derartig an, als ob in der nächsten Minute irgendeine große Verwandlung mit ihm geschehen müsse, die sie zu beobachten nicht versäumen wollten' (P 85).[54] But no transformation occurs; instead, K. feels increasingly unwell, and the girl gives him a seat and explains to him that the sun beating on the roof immediately overhead causes the stuffy atmosphere, which is intolerable till one gets used to it.[55] She continues with a long account of the function of the Information Officer, including the fact that 'Er weiß auf alle Fragen eine Antwort, Sie können ihn, wenn Sie einmal Lust dazu haben, daraufhin erproben' (P 88); but K. is in no fit state to attend to these explanations, and, as the Information Officer mockingly but correctly remarks, he only wants to be guided out of the Court premises into the fresh air. Supported by the two officials, he manages to stagger to the exit, and is promptly restored by the air outside.

The symbolism of this episode is so rich and so economical that any explication must seem inadequate.[50] But one can briefly point out that here K. is presented with a unique opportunity to ask about the nature of the Court and the source of his guilt. What would happen if he did, we cannot tell, but it might be a 'Verwandlung', a transfor- mation into a consciously moral being able to acknowledge and thus be freed from his own guilt. But that does not occur. Instead, K. starts to feel faint, as though the proximity of truth were too much for him to bear. This anticipates the Bürgel episode in *Das Schloß*, in which, by an improbable chance, K. blunders into the room of an official competent to deal with his case, but is too sleepy to attend to and profit from Bürgel's explanations. Similarly, the girl's explana- tions fall on inattentive ears, and the Information Officer points out that K. cannot stand the atmosphere—'Dem Herrn ist nur hier nicht wohl, nicht im allgemeinen' (P 88)—and recommends leading him out of the courtroom altogether. The other occasion when K. feels overcome by a stuffy atmosphere is in Titorelli's room, when, once again, he comes uncomfortably close to the truth—namely, that only a 'wirklicher Freispruch', recorded solely in legends, would enable him to escape from the Court.

The episode of the Information Officer, then, shows K. receiving and squandering an opportunity to break out of his 'closed-circuit thinking', as Marson calls it,[59] and inquire into the reason for his arrest. But it can still be interpreted in two different ways. One may understand the scene as symbolizing K.'s obtuseness, even when offered every possible assistance by the essentially benevolent Court. That appears to be Marson's view. But there is another, less comforting interpretation, suggested both by the notebook entry quoted on pp. 102–3 above and by the analogy with the Bürgel episode. Granted that K. has the chance to penetrate the barrier of motivations which he has laboriously built up between himself and the truth: what if human beings are simply not strong enough to use such a chance? What if fallen man is so used to a world of untruth and motivations that he is unable to leave it, and if the atmosphere surrounding the truth is for him unbreathable? Another aphorism asks: 'Kannst du denn etwas anderes kennen als Betrug? Wird einmal der Betrug vernichtet, darfst du ja nicht hinsehen oder wirst zur Salzsäule' (H 119), recalling Lot's wife and her longing glance back at Sodom even as it was being destroyed. And Bürgel says in *Das Schloß*: 'Die Leibeskräfte reichen nur bis zu einer gewissen Grenze, wer kann dafür, daß gerade diese Grenze auch sonst bedeutungsvoll ist' (S 425). This perhaps explains why the Information Officer keeps bursting into ironic laughter and never actually tenders any information. He will not do so without being asked, and he knows that accused people who approach him will be too weak to take advantage of their opportunity.

If this reading is correct, then the first section of *Der Prozeß* reaches a climax which is deeply and disturbingly ironic. Assuming that it was not K.'s obtuseness but his sheer human limitations that prevented him from questioning the Information Officer and learning about his guilt, the conclusion must be that the weak and limited nature of humanity, though not itself a cause of guilt, makes it impossible for human beings to face and acknowledge their guilt. Not only, therefore, is man too weak to lead a good life; he is too weak even to acknowledge his innate awareness of good and evil and admit the necessity for leading a good life. Instead, his very weakness compels him to devote his energies to piling up motivations between himself and the truth. Man has moral autonomy, but is unable to use it. As Gershom Scholem pointed out in a letter to Walter Benjamin, the problem in *Der Prozeß* is not the absence of revealed religion, but the impossibility of living by it: 'Die *Unvollziehbarkeit* des Geoffenbarten ist der Punkt, an dem aufs Allergenaueste eine richtig verstandene Theologie [. . .] und das was den Schlüssel zu Kafkas Welt gibt, in-einanderfallen.'[58] What is worse, man's weakness in no way palliates his guilt, as K. tries to claim when he tells the Chaplain: 'Wie kann denn ein Mensch überhaupt schuldig sein. Wir sind hier doch alle Menschen, einer wie der andere' (P 253). The Chaplain agrees with the literal (and platitudinous) sense of K.'s statement, but rejects its implications: 'Das ist richtig [. . .], aber so pflegen die Schuldigen zu reden' (P 253). This is a new formulation of K.'s familiar dilemma: by protesting his innocence, he confirms his guilt.

Accordingly, K.'s failure to question the Information Officer gives rise to two developments which occupy the second phase of the action. First, K. becomes preoccupied with 'Motivationen', efforts to pro-mote his lawsuit which are in fact evasions of the only real way of escaping from it. Second, the Court takes on a different aspect. From being approachable and compliant, it becomes remote and inacces-sible. K. is told by the Advocate: 'Die Rangordnung und Steigerung des Gerichtes sei unendlich und selbst für den Eingeweihten nicht absehbar' (P 144). We are also reminded increasingly of the Court's punitive function. As in *Der Verschollene* and *In der Strafkolonie*, justice becomes identical with the infliction of punishment.

K. still consciously refuses to entertain the thought of guilt or to regard his trial as anything other than 'ein großes Geschäft' (P 152) such as he has often negotiated on behalf of the bank. But his trial comes to obsess him, eating away at the very powers of rational and efficient organization on which he relies, and distracting him from his career. Instead of dealing with clients, he sits in his office, brooding on the trial or staring out of the window, a sign of his inability to focus his thoughts. He no longer comes into direct confrontation with the Court. Instead, he consults with intermediaries, the Advocate and Titorelli, and even his contact with them has in turn to be mediated by his uncle and the Manufacturer respectively. However, the two intermediaries are direct opposites, as is conveyed by their living on opposite sides of the town (P 121, 169) and by the symbolism of light and darkness which pervades the novel: the Advocate lives in 'einem dunklen Haus' (P 121) with a gas jet above the door which hisses noisily but affords little light, whereas Titorelli's door has a skylight above it and is thus 'verhältnismäßig hell beleuchtet' (P 171). Correspondingly, the Advocate can offer K. only the illusion of help, whereas Titorelli is a more forthcoming version of the Information Officer, with potentially valuable knowledge from which K. does not and perhaps cannot profit. A brief account of these two figures will bear out the contrast between them.

Although the Advocate makes great claims for his influence with the Court, it is apparent from his long-winded speeches that he cannot in fact help K. The Court tolerates defence counsel, but does not provide for them in any way. All the documents of the Court, including the charges, are kept secret both from the accused and from his counsel; the submission prepared by the Advocate can therefore contain nothing relevant to the case, unless by accident. The Advocate is not even permitted to accompany the accused to hearings. Instead, he waits outside the door until the client emerges, questions the client about the hearing and, on the basis of the client's fragmentary report, tries to construct a defence. There is no mystery about why the Court discourages defence counsel: 'Man will die Verteidigung möglichst ausschalten, alles soll auf den Angeklagten selbst gestellt sein' (P 141): the accused is supposed to confront the Court without any intermediary. From this state of affairs, however, the Advocate draws the perverse conclusion that an intermediary is indispensable, though his mediation cannot consist of following legal procedures, for he does not know what his client is accused of and therefore can have no idea what procedures to follow. It consists rather in cultivating personal contacts with Court officials, about which the Advocate boasts in a manner that promptly undermines their importance: 'Wirklichen Wert aber haben nur ehrliche persönliche Beziehungen, und zwar mit höheren Beamten, womit natürlich nur höhere Beamten der unteren Grade gemeint sind' (P 142). Since, as we later learn, the Advocate and his like are only small fry compared to the immeasurably loftier 'großen Advokaten' (P 214), these contacts must in fact be worthless. Instead of the direct recourse to Court officials that was available earlier, K. is now offered the prospect of an agonizingly slow climb up endless ladders of intrigue and pettifoggery.

Given that the Advocate cannot really help K., what is he trying to achieve? It looks as though the Advocate's aim is to exploit the obtuseness and cowardice of his clients for his own self-aggrandizement.

This motive becomes perceptible in ch. 8, after K. has told the Advocate that he wants to dispense with his services. After reproaching K. for having insufficient trust in him, the Advocate summons another client, the merchant Block, and subjects him to elaborate humiliation. Block kneels beside the Advocate's bed and kisses his hand; he declares that his allegiance is solely to the Advocate (though in reality he employs five other advocates and is negotiating with a sixth); he addresses him submissively as 'mein Advokat' (P 231); and the maid Leni is called upon to testify to Block's good behaviour. It appears that Block has spent the entire day kneeling on the bed in the maid's room, studying certain legal writings with great assiduity but probably with little understanding, especially since the tiny room opens into an air shaft and admits hardly any light. K. is horrified at Block's degradation: 'Das war kein Klient mehr, das war der Hund des Advokaten' (P 233); and with good reason, for in all likelihood this is an object-lesson intended to impress upon K. the power which the Advocate wields.[59] Though the Advocate professes to be the servant of his clients, and to carry them to the verdict on his shoulders, his real aim is to enslave them: as he warns the rebellious K., 'es ist oft besser, in Ketten, als frei zu sein' (P 227).

It is tempting to see in the Advocate a satirical reference to a particular kind of intermediary. As early as 1947, André Németh compared him both to a priest and to a psychoanalyst.[60] The former suggestion carries more conviction. Emrich, though inclined to see him in more general and rather vague terms as embodying all the contemporary forces that offer to do one's thinking for one, nevertheless points out that his name, Huld, means 'grace', that Leni's name suggests Mary Magdalen, that the Advocate's submissions on Block's behalf (called 'Schriften', which can also mean 'scriptures') contain 'sehr viel Latein' (P 212), and that the answers Block provides when interrogated are 'wie eine Litanei' (P 213).[61] Marson finds a travesty of prayer and penance in Block's studies, and a parody of Catholic ritual in the scene where he kneels beside the Advocate's bed.[62] One might add that the written submissions, which contain invocations of the Court, flattery of particular officials, and self-abasement on the part of the Advocate, sound rather like invocations of saints. Kafka appears to be expressing here a distrust, not only of Catholicism, but by extension of all religions which offer to ease the individual's lot by mediating between him and the absolute, instead of forcing him back on his own spiritual resources. The clearest evidence of Kafka's opinion is a little story about a community of scoundrels, which he wrote in October 1917 and which is short enough to be quoted entire:

Es war einmal eine Gemeinschaft von Schurken, das heißt, es waren keine Schurken, sondern gewöhnliche Menschen. Sie hielten immer zusammen. Wenn zum Beispiel einer von ihnen jemanden, einen Fremden, außerhalb ihrer Gemeinschaft Stehenden, auf etwas schurkenmäßige Weise unglücklich gemacht hatte,—das heißt wieder nichts Schurkenmäßiges, sondern so wie es gewöhnlich, wie es üblich ist,—und er dann vor der Gemeinschaft beichtete, untersuchten sie es, beurteilten es, legten Bußen auf, verziehen und dergleichen. Es war nicht schlecht gemeint, die Interessen der einzelnen und der Gemeinschaft wurden streng gewahrt und dem Beichtenden wurde das Komplement gereicht, dessen Grundfarbe er gezeigt hatte: 'Wie? Darum machst du dir Kummer? Du hast doch das Selbstverständliche getan, so gehandelt, wie du mußtest. Alles andere wäre unbegreiflich. Du bist nur überreizt. Werde doch wieder verständig.' So hielten sie immer zusammen, auch nach ihrem Tode gaben sie die Gemeinschaft nicht auf, sondern stiegen im Reigen zum Himmel. Im Ganzen war es ein Anblick reinster Kinderunschuld, wie sie flogen. Da aber vor dem Himmel alles in seine Elemente zerschlagen wird, stürzten sie ab, wahre Felsblöcke. (H 80-1.)[63]

These scoundrels, like Josef K., practise an easy-going morality and follow the way of the world. But they are also united in a community which offers ready forgiveness of sins in return for confession and penance, and which outlasts death. Face to face with the absolute, however, their 'Kinderunschuld' turns out to be moral ignorance, as illusory as the professed innocence of Josef K., and they plunge back to earth; instead of having souls, they are made of the same material as the earth itself.

It may be possible to find a still more specific source for Kafka's Advocate in Dostoyevsky's Grand Inquisitor. As we saw earlier, he was reading *The Brothers Karamazov* in the winter of 1914. In Ivan Karamazov's tale about the Inquisitor, Dostoyevsky represents the Catholic clergy as exploiting their claim to mediate between God and man in order to divert to themselves the worship due to Christ. They have decided that Christ's moral demands on humanity are excessive, since human beings are too weak to endure moral freedom and to obey Christ's commandments. The Church has therefore resolved to correct Christ's work by persuading the faithful to surrender their unwelcome freedom and acknowledge their weakness. In return for their obedience, it allows them to be happy and even to sin, so long as they humbly confess their faults. It enforces obedience by means of miracle, mystery, and authority, and its clergy, having taken the curse of freedom upon themselves, are worshipped like gods. Kafka's Advocate has similar ambitions. He expects K. to surrender to him the entire responsibility for conducting his case, warns him against freedom, and expects abject obedience from his clients. His illness seems to result from his labours on behalf of his clients, and may have been suggested by the phrase Alyosha Karamazov uses after hearing Ivan's poem, 'Dein leidender Inquisitor';[64] in the context 'leidend' refers to moral suffering, but since its usual meaning is 'physically sick', it may have inspired Kafka to create a figure who was physically as well as morally 'leidend', especially as the Advocate's ailment is 'Herzleiden' (P 122), suggesting perverted love for his clients. The form that Block's humiliation takes may have been inspired by the Grand Inquisitor's comparison of mankind to an animal which will eventually be humbled: 'Dann aber wird das Tier zu uns herankriechen, und es wird uns die Füße lecken, und sie mit den blutigen Tränen seiner Augen netzen.'[65]

The arguments put forward by the Grand Inquisitor are directly relevant to *Der Prozeß*, for, as I have already argued, Kafka's novel is a sceptical exploration of human autonomy and its limits. K.'s dismissal of the Advocate would be a reassertion of his autonomy, though not necessarily a successful one, for the chapter in which he undertakes it is unfinished, and it has already been stated (P 148) that a client must remain faithful to his Advocate no matter what happens. However, K. promptly relinquishes his autonomy by resolving to compose a submission for the Court which will recount and justify all the more important actions of his life. In ch. 9 he tells the Chaplain that he is still at work on his submission (P 252).

By now it should be clear that, although the theme of *Der Prozeß* is ultimately religious, the novel is not written from the standpoint of any particular religion. A letter to Felice, written in February 1913, provides important evidence for the nature of Kafka's religious beliefs:

Wie ist Deine Frömmigkeit? Du gehst in den Tempel; aber in der letzten Zeit bist Du wohl nicht hingegangen. Und was hält Dich, der Gedanke an das Judentum oder an Gott? Fühlst Du—was die Hauptsache ist—ununterbrochene Beziehungen zwischen Dir und einer beruhigend fernen, womöglich unendlichen Höhe oder Tiefe? (F 289.)

Here Kafka distinguishes between a particular religion (Judaism) and the ultimate object of religion, which he evidently thinks of as something absolute, impersonal, and non-anthropomorphic. His use of the word 'Gott' seems metaphorical only. In the Zürau aphorisms he draws a similar distinction between the notion of a personal god and his own preferred concept of 'das Unzerstörbare' (H 90–1), and in 1920, criticizing the account of Greek religion in Brod's *Heidentum, Christentum, Judentum*, he speaks of the Greek pantheon as the means by which the Greeks shielded themselves from 'das entscheidend Göttliche':

Sie konnten das entscheidend Göttliche gar nicht weit genug von sich entfernt denken, die ganze Götterwelt war nur ein Mittel, das Entscheidende sich vom irdischen Leib zu halten, Luft zum menschlichen Atem zu haben. (Br 279.)

No particular religion, therefore, seemed to Kafka to have privileged access to the absolute. Although the claims of the Catholic Church to mediate between man and the absolute caused him to treat Catholic imagery with some irony in all three of his novels, he felt that in principle religious symbols were equivalent to one another and hence interchangeable, so that in ch. 9 of *Der Prozeß* the cathedral and its furnishings are able to serve as symbols pointing to the absolute. Marthe Robert has commented on how eclectic Kafka's interest in religion was:[66] he read avidly in both Jewish and Christian writings—the Old Testament and Maimonides, but also the Gospels, St Augustine, Pascal, Kierkegaard, Tolstoy, and the biography of Erdmuthe, wife of the founder of the Moravian Brethren, a book from which he sent Felice edifying quotations.[67]

It will therefore be best to speak of *Der Prozeß* as implicitly contrasting the absolute with the limited and relative world of 'Motivationen' in which K. is entrapped. From this world there is one genuine possibility of escape, and K. learns of it from Titorelli, though he draws no comfort from the information. There are, Titorelli says, three ways of escape from the trial, viz. genuine acquittal, apparent acquittal, and deferment ('Verschleppung'). He continues:

Die wirkliche Freisprechung ist natürlich das Beste, nur habe ich nicht den geringsten Einfluß auf diese Art der Lösung. Es gibt meiner Meinung nach überhaupt keine einzelne Person, die auf die wirkliche Freisprechung Einfluß hätte. Hier entscheidet wahrscheinlich nur die Unschuld des Angeklagten. Da Sie unschuldig sind, wäre es wirklich möglich, daß Sie sich allein auf Ihre Unschuld verlassen. Dann brauchen Sie aber weder mich noch irgendeine andere Hilfe. (P 184.)

This is essentially the same advice as K. received from the Inspector in ch. 1: 'denken Sie weniger an uns und an das, was mit Ihnen geschehen wird, denken Sie lieber mehr an sich' (P 21). The accused must not seek help from others but rely on his own resources. The cryptic and apparently senseless question that Titorelli first puts to K. —'Wollen Sie Bilder kaufen oder sich selbst malen lassen?' (P 174)— perhaps points in the same direction, inviting K. to contemplate himself rather than the ready-made categories in which he customarily thinks. Rigorous self-examination would be the only way of breaking down the wall of motivations separating him from his repressed moral awareness. However, when K. enquires further, he is discouraged to learn that instances of genuine acquittal are recorded only in legends, accessible to faith rather than proof: 'man kann sie glauben, nachweisbar sind sie aber nicht' (P 186). As befits a bank-manager, K. is not interested in anything that cannot be proved, and although Titorelli hints that the legends are well worth hearing, K. loses interest the moment he learns that they cannot be used as evidence in court. To profit from these legends, K. would have to break free from his accustomed habits of thought and somehow lift himself from the rational, functional world he occupies into a realm of imagination and intuition. But functional thinking is so ingrained in him that to depart from it, however briefly, he would have to become a different character. By ch. 9, his scepticism will have been eroded so far that he is prepared to listen to a legend told by the Chaplain, but even then his mental habits cause him to miss the point.

Since a genuine acquittal is out of the question, the alternatives are an illusory acquittal, which renders one liable to be rearrested at any time, or the deferment of a verdict by dragging out the proceedings in one's case for as long as possible. Neither of these appeals to K., for, as he correctly perceives, they ensure that one will not be condemned but also one will never be genuinely acquitted. They make it possible for one to lead a long life in the shadow of the Court; that is, they keep one entangled in the world of motivations. Since Titorelli's three suggestions are either unattainable or unacceptable, they are in K.'s eyes equivalent, and their equivalence is symbolized by the three identical pictures, entitled 'Heidelandschaft', which Titorelli presses on K., all depicting a lurid sun setting behind a heath. K. buys the pictures, but on returning to his office he locks them in the bottom drawer of his desk, to conceal them from the Deputy Director. Since he is also anxious that the Deputy Director shall not find out about his trial, this action confirms the significance of the pictures.[63]

The value that Titorelli could have had for K. is indicated in a deleted passage of the unfinished chapter 'Das Haus'. Here K., lying on his couch, has a day-dream in which Titorelli takes his hand and carries him off:

> Gleich waren sie im Gerichtsgebäude und eilten über die Treppen, aber nicht nur aufwärts, sondern auf und ab, ohne jeden Aufwand von Mühe, leicht wie ein leichtes Boot im Wasser. Und gerade, als K. seine Füße beobachtete und zu dem Schlusse kam, daß diese schöne Art der Bewegung seinem bisherigen niedrigen Leben nicht mehr angehören könne, gerade jetzt, uber seinem gesenkten Kopf, erfolgte die Verwandlung. Das Licht, das bisher von hinten eingefallen war, wechselte und strömte plötzlich blendend von vorn. K. sah auf, Titorelli nickte ihm zu und drehte ihn um. Wieder war K. auf dem Korridor des Gerichtsgebäudes, aber alles war ruhiger und einfacher. Es gab keine auffallenden Einzelheiten, K. umfaßte alles mit einem Blick, machte sich von Titorelli los und ging seines Weges. (P 294–5.)

This fantasy-experience stands out from K.'s normal existence by the dream-like ease and rapidity with which he and Titorelli move, and by the 'Verwandlung' (cf. P 85) affecting the light. Since the nature of this light is not explained, it may be identical with the light emanating from the Law in the legend of the door-keeper. Previously it has been shining behind K., suggesting that in his misdirected concern with his trial he has been moving further and further from the only real source of illumination. Now, all of a sudden, it is in front of him; he looks up, but Titorelli immediately turns him round and sends him back to his previous life. Bearing in mind that Titorelli's artistic calling may give him a privileged access to truth, we can see the relevance of the following aphorism, written in January 1918:

> Die Kunst fliegt um die Wahrheit, aber mit der entschiedenen Absicht, sich nicht zu verbrennen. Ihre Fähigkeit besteht darin, in der dunklen Leere einen Ort zu finden, wo der Strahl des Lichts, ohne daß dies vorher zu erkennen gewesen wäre, kräftig aufgefangen werden kann. (H 104.)

Titorelli has brought K. as close to the truth as is possible, but ordinary people cannot endure its light for more than an instant, and so K. must return to ordinary life. Here, none of the details of his life have changed, but its entire atmosphere is somehow 'ruhiger und einfacher'. The transformation that Kafka imagines is in one sense total, in another sense slight, for since it is a transformation of consciousness, it will leave the surrounding world looking much as it did before. The effect of such an experience is described in the following aphorism: ' "Dann aber kehrte er zu seiner Arbeit zurück, so wie wenn nichts geschehen wäre." Das ist eine Bemerkung, die uns aus einer unklaren Fülle alter Erzählungen geläufig ist, obwohl sie vielleicht in keiner vorkommt' (H 123). It may also be appropriate to quote a profoundly suggestive Hasidic saying about the next world: 'Alles wird sein wie hier—nur ein ganz klein wenig anders.'[69] Both sayings assume that the difference between the unredeemed and the redeemed worlds will be slight, perhaps indefinable, and yet crucial.

Kafka decided to omit this episode of illumination, however. It would have interfered with the logic of the novel, which points increasingly to K.'s condemnation. Some of the clearest signs are in a painting which K. sees in Titorelli's studio. It shows a judge, with a bushy black beard, gripping the arms of his throne and about to rise in a menacing fashion. As Malcolm Pasley has shown, this painting was suggested to Kafka by Freud's recently published essay on the Moses of Michelangelo.[70] It is an appropriate prototype, for Moses in this sculpture is holding the Tables of the Law and is about to denounce the Israelites for worshipping the golden calf. The judge's threatening posture seems directed at Josef K.'s incorrigible worldliness. It also draws attention to his prospect of being sentenced and punished, as does the figure which K. gradually makes out on the back of the throne. This is an allegorical figure representing justice, but the wings on her heels show that she is also the goddess of victory, and, as K. peers more closely, she comes to resemble the goddess of the hunt. The implication is plain: the justice embodied in the Court is going to defeat K. and to hunt him down. And yet its relentless pursuit does not spring from malice or vindictiveness, but is the exercise of pure justice untempered by mercy. We have already seen an example of the Court's justice in the brutal punishment administered to the guards, which, as the Flogger said, was 'ebenso gerecht als unvermeidlich' (P 104), and another aphorism, written in November 1917, indicates what is in store for K.: 'Noch spielen die Jagdhunde im Hof, aber das Wild entgeht ihnen nicht, so sehr es jetzt schon durch die Wälder jagt' (H 89). Given that K. is objectively guilty, then he deserves punishment, even if—and this is the most chilling aspect of Kafka's meditations—he was from the outset unable to obey the law. Absolute justice, being absolute, can make no concession to human frailty. This is shown by the story about the community of scoundrels, and also, even more starkly, by an aphorism written about a month later:

Die Krähen behaupten, eine einzige Krähe könnte den Himmel zerstören. Das ist zweifellos, beweist aber nichts gegen den Himmel, denn Himmel bedeuten [*sic*] eben: Unmöglichkeit von Krähen. (H 86.)

So long as the two orders, the absolute and the relative, remain separate, the merely relative beings, like the scoundrels, the crows, or Josef K., can indulge in fantasies of omnipotence. K. imagines that so long as he stays at home he can kick any of the Court officials aside (P 75). Such notions cannot be disproved, because they cannot become anything more than fantasies. When the two orders do meet, the relative one is certain to be destroyed by the absolute. K.'s execution is therefore the inevitable end to the novel.

Before his execution, however, K. receives a final warning. His missed appointment with the Italian business client proves to be a summons from the prison chaplain employed by the Court. Before the Chaplain calls to him (in a manner that parallels the Inspector's call in ch. 1), K. looks round the cathedral, and Kafka's imagery of light and darkness reappears, charged with significance. K., who used to belong, albeit only for business reasons, to an art conservation · society, examines the altar-pieces in the cathedral, but since the day is heavily overcast and the cathedral lit only by three candles on the high altar, he has to use his pocket-torch. He spends a long time looking at a painting of the burial of Christ. Since his torch has too narrow a focus for him to see the picture as a whole, he has to examine it square inch by square inch, and the light fixed above the painting hinders his view instead of aiding it: 'Störend schwebte das ewige Licht davor' (P 246). Here Kafka has portrayed, with great economy, the incompatibility of two opposed orders: the narrow rationality of Josef K., symbolized by the light of his pocket torch which prevents him from seeing the religious paintings properly, and the absolute order symbolized by the eternal light which interferes with the light from the pocket-torch and is also represented by the candles on the high altar which are extinguished in the course of the chapter, leaving the cathedral in almost total darkness. There can be no communication between Josef K.'s mental world and the absolute. If the two come into contact, Josef K. will only misinterpret what he sees or hears. The religious paintings mean as little to him as the legends which Titorelli offered to tell him.

Kafka's imagery here can probably be traced to a specific source, one of the best-known passages in Nietzsche. Section 125 of *Die fröhliche Wissenschaft* tells of a madman who lights a lantern in the morning and declares that mankind has killed God and that since then the earth has broken free from its orbit and is rushing into ever-increasing cold and darkness:

Ist es nicht kälter geworden? Kommt nicht immerfort die Nacht und mehr Nacht? Müssen nicht Laternen am Vormittage angezündet werden? Hören wir noch nichts von dem Lärm der Totengräber, welche Gott begraben?[71]

Kafka has taken over from this passage the motifs of gathering darkness, the need for artificial light by day (K.'s pocket-torch), and the burial of God. Later, Nietzsche's madman extinguishes his lantern, and the small lamp which the Chaplain gives K. also goes out, symbolizing K.'s inability to learn from his warning. The madman's question, 'Was sind denn diese Kirchen noch, wenn sie nicht die Grüfte und Grabmäler Gottes sind?'[72] may also have helped to suggest the setting of ch. 9, for, along with Kafka's other borrowings, it enables him to express the widening gulf between the two orders of reality, the absolute and the human. The remainder of the chapter shows K.'s incapacity to shake off his concern with motivations and to switch his thoughts to an understanding of the absolutes of good and evil which he is called upon to face.

How firmly K. is locked in his 'mind-forged manacles' first becomes apparent from his opening dialogue with the Chaplain. K. persists in claiming that people are prejudiced against him, that he needs help from others, especially women, that the Court is thoroughly corrupt, and that the Chaplain himself may not understand the nature of the Court. The more he reveals his benighted state of mind, the more the darkness deepens. Finally the Chaplain is provoked, more or less involuntarily, into the cry: 'Siehst du denn nicht zwei Schritte weit?' (P 254). Evidently K.'s blindness, his misunderstanding of the Court and of his own situation, is as grave as ever. After a charged silence, the Chaplain descends and offers K. his hand, a gesture of human solidarity which, in the first chapter, K. had unsuccessfully tried to extort from the Inspector. Now, however, K. is glad to receive such a gesture, and it strengthens his confidence in the Chaplain. But this confidence is itself a delusion, and to convey the nature of this delusion, the Chaplain tells K. the legend of the man from the country. This legend is deservedly famous, so need not be repeated here. It is perhaps the supreme moment in Kafka's writing, thanks to its Old Testament plainness and economy, and to the final peripeteia, which wholly transforms the reader's understanding of it. This peripeteia—the doorkeeper's information to the dying man that the door was all along intended for him and for him only—is an essential part of the story's meaning, for the story embodies, for the reader, precisely that transformation of consciousness, that escape from one's mental set into a new understanding of the world, which Josef K. needs in order to escape from his trial but which he cannot achieve. Nor can the man from the country achieve it: the information is the very last thing he hears before his death.

What is the delusion which the story is supposed to illustrate? K. characteristically leaps to the conclusion that the man has been deluded by the doorkeeper, just as he himself, in his own opinion, has been victimized by the Court. The subsequent disputation, which the more informed among Kafka's earliest readers recognized as Talmudic in style,[73] surveys various interpretations of the story, but the Chaplain never tells Josef K. the correct one, leaving him to work that out for himself. Far from deceiving the man, the doorkeeper has even exceeded his duties in being friendly to him; but the doorkeeper may himself be misinformed about the interior of the Law. There is room for dispute, too, about the relation between the man and the doorkeeper: on the one hand, the man is free, while the doorkeeper is a servant of the Law and hence subordinate also to the man; on the other, the doorkeeper's association with the Law, on however humble a level, can be seen as infinitely superior to the man's unattached freedom. Applied to the case of Josef K., this means that he was deluded in overestimating the solidarity between himself and the Chaplain. The Chaplain is, after all, a servant of the Court, while Josef K. is still a free man, potentially able to escape from the Court by his own decision. Like the man from the country, however, K. relies on other people, and believes their accounts of the vast hierarchy formed by the Court, just as the man believes the doorkeeper's account of the hierarchy of ever more terrifying doorkeepers. Both allow their antagonists to entrap them in double-binds. The doorkeeper formulates a double-bind in the order 'Wenn es dich so lockt, versuche es doch, trotz meinem Verbot hineinzugehen' (P 256). This is the only order—the only sentence in the imperative mood—which the doorkeeper addresses to the man. His other remarks are simply statements: that the man may not yet enter the Law, and that within there are terrifying doorkeepers. Understandably, these statements have for the man the force of commands, while the only command the doorkeeper does give him sounds merely rhetorical (equivalent to saying 'You'd better not'). The double-bind expressed in it could be summed up in the two words 'Disobey me'. Josef K. is also in a double-bind, since he can only demonstrate his innocence by acknowledging his guilt. The escape could only consist in a transformation of consciousness of which both the man from the country and Josef K. prove incapable. Both remain enslaved to the world of motivations, the systems of authority which they in effect create in order to avoid facing their own moral autonomy. The discussion between K. and the Chaplain merely confirms K.'s confinement in his own mental set; by its end, we are told, 'Die Lampe in seiner [K.'s] Hand war längst erloschen' (P 264), and in a deleted passage K.'s mental confusion is symbolized by the smoke that comes from the lamp before it goes out (P 310).

By its position in the novel, the legend of the doorkeeper recalls Dostoyevsky's story of the Grand Inquisitor. Both are inserted in their respective novels as narratives told by one character to another. Each interrupts the action of the novel in order to reveal the novel's deepest theme. And in both, the theme must be inferred by the reader without being explicitly stated in the text. Ivan's narrative is intended to put the case against God for creating a world full of evil, and to justify as persuasively as possible the Grand Inquisitor's project of correcting Christ's work by ensuring mankind's happiness at the expense of its freedom. But, as Mochulsky says, Ivan's assault on Christianity constitutes a 'proof by the contrary'; by replying to the Inquisitor only with a silent kiss, Christ implicitly demonstrates that his plans for humanity can only be degrading, and testifies to the ideal of spiritual freedom.[74] Hence Alyosha's surprised response: 'Dein Poem ist ein Lob Jesu, aber keine Schmähung'.[75] The meaning of the story cannot be stated within the story itself; it must be inferred by the reader. But while Dostoyevsky helps the reader by providing him with Alyosha as a surrogate, Kafka gives him no such aid. Although Josef K. needs to respond to his trial by becoming conscious of his moral autonomy, nobody gives him such instructions; with the help only of hints, he is supposed to work out the solution by himself. The legend of the doorkeeper is the most detailed of the hints he receives, but even here he receives no explicit instructions; he is supposed to gather for himself the nature of the man's delusion. K. fails, but the reader need not share in his failure. As we have seen, the narrative technique of *Der Prozeß* gives the reader a perspective congruent to K.'s but superior to it, so that while the reader can sympathize with K.'s desperate situation, he can also see the escape-route which is invisible from K.'s standpoint. Like the spectator at Brechtian theatre, the reader of *Der Prozeß* occupies a higher level of understanding than the fictional protagonist, and should respond similarly: 'Das Leid dieses Menschen erschüttert mich, weil es doch einen Ausweg für ihn gäbe.'[76] Since the 'Ausweg' is not stated in the novel, the reader has to infer it, but he is placed in a position where, unlike Josef K., he can do so; it is deeply ironic that so many recent critics have concluded that the reader of *Der Prozeß* is supposed merely to re-enact the perplexity of Josef K. To escape from his perplexity, K. would have to transform his consciousness, to make an imaginative leap into the position already occupied by the reader; he would need to become the reader as well as the hero of his own story.

There is another, more covert way in which the legend of the doorkeeper represents a mental world different from Josef K.'s. It is the only part of the novel to contain a cluster of unequivocal allusions to Judaism. It would be surprising if the intense interest in Jewish culture that Kafka developed in 1911–12 had been submerged altogether by 1914, but, despite some tantalizing suggestions, it is difficult to see Jewish imagery as governing the novel as a whole. It has been pointed out that Josef K.'s first hearing occurs ten days after his arrest and that in the Jewish calendar the ten days between New Year's Day (Rosh Hashanah) and the Day of Atonement (Yom Kippur) are supposed to give man time to repent of his sins before being called to account at a Court of Judgement.[77] Tempting though this identification is, the fact that K.'s arrest takes place in spring, while the Jewish New Year begins in autumn, makes one reluctant to accept any systematic allegory here. Again, the Court premises recall the Talmud schools described to Kafka by Löwy, which were always 'in einem alten unbrauchbaren Gebäude untergebracht' (T 236) and intolerably hot and smelly; K. imagines the people at his first hearing discussing him 'nach Art der Studierenden' (P 63), a phrase suggesting Talmud students, and they themselves, like Eastern Jews, all have long beards which are both 'steif und schütter' (P 62).[78] But if these really are Jewish allusions, then they seem at most to be casual and unsystematic.

The legend of the doorkeeper, however, is a much clearer case. The Law to which the man from the country seeks access immediately suggests the Torah, while the light emanating from it, which the man perceives only when on the point of death, may have a source in the Cabbala. The collection of essays, *Vom Judentum*, published by the Bar Kochba in 1913, and owned by Kafka, included some extracts from the Zohar, the main Cabbalistic text. One of these, 'Das Licht des Urquells', says that God concealed the primal light from the eyes of sinful mankind and will reveal it again only when the diverse worlds, into which the creation has disintegrated, are again united.[79] This may have suggested to Kafka the radiance which the dying man sees streaming from the Law.

The phrase 'Mann von Lande' itself represents a calque on the Hebrew *'am ha-'arets*. This phrase was originally applied to the rural population of Palestine who did not understand the intricacies of the Law as it had been systematized by the rabbis; Kafka had already encountered the phrase in his reading.[80] He also knew the Yiddish derivative *amorets*, which had come to mean 'ignoramus', and which he uses in his diary ('Amhorez', T 177). This underpins the contrast between the elaborateness of the Law and the simplicity of the man from the country with a hint that he could rely on his simplicity and ignore the authority of the Law. As for the doorkeeper, he has often been identified as an Eastern Jew, most emphatically by Giuliano Baioni, who mentions the following distinguishing features of Eastern Jews as relevant:

Caratteristiche comuni agli ebrei orientali ortodossi erano infatti i riccioli rituali alle tempie, la lunga barba divisa in due parti che Kafka nella sua parabola chiama 'barba tartarica', la pelliccia e il berretto di pelo.[81]

This is somewhat exaggerated: the doorkeeper has a fur coat, but no fur cap, nor is he said to have side-locks ('riccioli rituali'), as Baioni seems to think. But his fur coat, his long beard, and his 'große Spitznase' (P 256) all make him resemble an Eastern Jew, and so does his post as doorkeeper. Although the knowledge of Jewish ways that Kafka had acquired by 1914 must not be overestimated, he could well have heard from Löwy about the courts maintained by Hasidic *Wunderrabbis* or *tsaddikim*. These charismatic figures, about whom more will be said in the next chapter, were credited with miraculous powers, and therefore held court to great numbers of petitioners. To deal with them the *tsaddik* employed a doorkeeper or *gabbai* who would ask each petitioner his name, his occupation, and his place of origin, then take his money and admit him to the *tsaddik's* presence. Not only the *tsaddik* but also the *gabbai* expected to be paid, and the visitor often had to deal with several of these intermediaries. They were notorious for their corruption. In one of his sketches of life in Eastern Europe, Karl Emil Franzos describes the 'Gaboim' who stood guard outside the door of the famous *tsaddik* of Sadagora. On having their palms adequately greased, the doorkeepers would admit one to an ante-room where two more of their number would be awaiting payment. After satisfying them, the visitor would arrive outside the *tsaddik*'s own room, which also had guardians: 'An der Thüre dieses Allerheiligsten stehen neue Pförtner, die natürlich abermals ihren Zoll fordern.'[82] In 1916 Kafka himself used the word 'Gabim' to describe the attendants of the *tsaddik* of Belz, and mentioned their bad reputation (Br 144). Such people resemble the doorkeepers in *Der Prozeß* so closely as to make it likely that as early as 1914 Kafka knew about the *gabbaim*, most probably from Löwy, and modelled his doorkeeper on Hasidic prototypes. It is entirely in keeping with the world of *Der Prozeß* that religious mysteries should be guarded by somebody who is humanly limited and indeed venal.[83] If the doorkeeper is based on a *gabbai*, then he is even more closely analogous to the corrupt officials whom K. encounters.

The legend of the doorkeeper seems, then, to be a window opening on to the world of Jewish culture which Kafka himself had begun to explore. But every aspect of its significance is lost on Josef K., and nothing remains but his execution. It would be foolish to try to palliate the horror of the last chapter. Even granting that the Court embodies absolute justice, still the punishment it inflicts is appalling. The executioners are grotesque; K. can scarcely communicate with them. By making fussy preparations, and disputing with remarkably inappropriate politeness as to who shall plunge the butcher's knife into K.'s breast, they deprive his death even of dignity. He knows that he should take the knife and commit suicide—a last gesture of autonomy, which would be no more than a bitter travesty of the autonomy he should have exercised long before. But he relinquishes even this shred of dignity and dies like a dog, in a manner recalling the degradation of Block into the 'Hund des Advokaten' (P 233).

Since K. dies without comprehending his own guilt, one might be tempted to say that his death is not even tragic, as no anagnorisis precedes it. But K. does acquire, when it is too late to be of use, something which he previously lacked: a sense of the humanity he shares with other people. Even in ch. 9 the Court had worn down his arrogance enough for him to value the sense of human solidarity expressed in the Chaplain's handshake, though he failed to realize how great was the gulf dividing him, a free man, from a servant of the Law. Now, as he is led to execution, he does, even if only partially, realize his shortcomings: 'Ich wollte immer mit zwanzig Händen in die Welt hineinfahren und überdies zu einem nicht zu billigenden Zweck. Das war unrichtig' (P 269). Just before his death, the sight of a human figure silhouetted in the lighted window of a neighbouring house reawakens his will to live:

Seine Blicke fielen auf das letzte Stockwerk des an den Steinbruch angrenzenden Hauses. Wie ein Licht aufzuckt, so fuhren die Fensterflügel eines Fensters dort auseinander, ein Mensch, schwach und dünn in der Ferne und Höhe, beugte sich mit einem Ruck weit vor und streckte die Arme noch weiter aus. Wer war es? Ein Freund? Ein guter Mensch? Einer, der teilnahm? Einer, der helfen wollte? War es ein einzelner? Waren es alle? War noch Hilfe? Gab es Einwände, die man vergessen hatte? Gewiß gab es solche. Die Logik ist zwar unerschütterlich, aber einem Menschen, der leben will, widersteht sie nicht. (P 271-2.)

The logic is that of absolute justice, which has sentenced K. on grounds which are irrefutable, irreproachably objective, and wholly inhuman. The brief and belated awakening of K.'s human sympathies reminds one of the end of *Dantons Tod* where, just before Danton's death on the scaffold, his human feelings break through the cynicism with which he has largely repressed them, and while other revolutionaries are uttering their rhetorical last words, he says to the executioner who is roughly separating him from his friend Hérault: 'Kannst du verhindern, daß unsere Köpfe sich auf dem Boden des Korbes küssen?'[84]

Danton's final words, as an assertion of human feeling, are also an act of rebellion against the impersonal mechanism of the Revolution which has condemned him. Josef K.'s flicker of rebellion owes something to the attempt at metaphysical revolt against God's world made by Ivan Karamazov. In the chapter entitled, in the translation Kafka read, 'Empörung', Ivan describes to Alyosha his own insatiable vitality, and expresses a premonition that his energy will last till his thirtieth year and then be overcome by superior force:

Ich habe mich oftmals gefragt: Gibt es wohl in der Welt eine Verzweiflung, die diesen rasenden, wütenden und vielleicht unanständigen Lebensdurst in mir besiegen könnte?—und ich bin zu der Überzeugung gekommen, daß es wahrscheinlich keine solche Verzweiflung gibt, das heißt wiederum nur bis zu meinem dreißigsten Jahre, dann werde ich selbst nicht mehr wollen . . . so scheint es mir wenigstens.[85]

Josef K.'s final thoughts echo another remark made by Ivan a few sentences later: 'Leben will man, Aljoscha, und ich lebe, wenn auch wider die Logik.' Despite the views of some critics, *Der Prozeß* does not unequivocally advocate submission to an inhuman order of things.[86] Instead, the sheer brute energy which, at the beginning of the novel, K. directed towards his career and his womanizing, is now seen as potentially valuable, because it belongs to the irreducible core of his humanity. The law which hunts K. down is absolute and hence abstract, and its instruments partake in some measure of its abstract quality. 'Den Beamten fehlt der Zusammenhang mit der Bevölkerung', we were told in ch. 6; '[. . .] sie haben, weil sie fortwährend, Tag und Nacht, in ihr Gesetz eingezwängt sind, nicht den richtigen Sinn für menschliche Beziehungen' (P 143). But here, in a belated access of humanism, Kafka is suggesting that in the vital core of humanity there lies the potential for a rebellion against this abstract order, a rebellion which would resemble Ivan Karamazov's. The tragedy of *Der Prozeß* consists, however, in the fact that Josef K.'s sense of shared humanity awakens only in the last minute of his life.

For Kafka's future development, however, this brief outburst of humanism is of great importance, for it points to a way out of the various traps in which K. found himself that was never considered in the body of the novel. At the outset, K. was trapped because his failure to understand his own guilt confirmed his guilt and prevented his escaping from it. The intervention of the Court produced an ironic alleviation of his situation: instead of being logically inescapable, it became one from which there was indeed an escape in theory, which just happened to be superhumanly difficult in fact. The reason why it was so difficult was that the individual was thrown back on his own spiritual resources and forced to begin breaking down his own wall of motivations in order to confront his own moral autonomy. No individual could possibly have the strength to accomplish this. But what if the individual did not have to rely on his own resources? What if a permanent possibility of escape lay in the existence of other people? By becoming conscious of human solidarity, a solidarity which did not have to be created but was already latent in the fact of being human, one might somehow go on living in the shadow of the absolute; perhaps, indeed, the absolute would assume a different aspect if one faced it as a member of a community and not as an isolated individual. The aphorisms Kafka composed at Zürau in the winter of 1917–18 develop these ideas. They express the moral rigorism that underlies *Der Prozeß*, but they also explore the implications of belonging to a community, and eventually arrive at a dialectical synthesis of the two. But before going on to examine this profound and intensely difficult body of writing, we must see how Kafka's awareness of human solidarity developed in actual fact, through his contact with the Zionist movement and with Jews from Eastern Europe, and how this awareness is reflected in his writings of 1914–17.

4

Responsibility
The Shorter Fiction, 1914–1917

THE outbreak of the First World War was recorded by Kafka only with the diary entry: 'Deutschland hat Rußland den Krieg erklärt.— Nachmittag Schwimmschule' (T 418). At this time he was too pre-occupied with the collapse of his engagement to pay much attention to politics. The 'Gerichtshof' in the Hotel Askanischer Hof in Berlin had taken place on 23 July 1914, the day on which Austria, provoked by the assassination of Archduke Franz Ferdinand and his consort the previous month, had delivered her ultimatum to Serbia. After its deliberately unacceptable terms had been rejected, Austria declared war on Serbia on 28 July; Russia then came in on Serbia's side and Germany on that of Austria. Meanwhile, on 26 July, Kafka returned to Prague, absorbed in his private misery, and wrote in his diary on 28 July: 'Wenn ich mich nicht in einer Arbeit rette, bin ich verloren' (T 411). On the following day Josef K. makes his first appearance (T 414), and during the succeeding six months Kafka faced his own sense of guilt and explored the nature of guilt and the possibility of expiation by writing *Der Prozeß*.

However, the war could not be ignored. Kafka's brothers-in-law, Josef Pollak and Karl Hermann, were both called up. The former returned on leave from the front in November, rendered almost hysterical by his experiences, including a seemingly providential hair's-breadth escape from death (T 442); he later got sciatica and was sent to the Bohemian resort of Teplitz [Teplice] for treatment (F 632–3). The latter served in the Carpathians. Both survived the war. Kafka himself, like Max Brod, was declared unfit for service except in the militia, but was exempted even from this by being deemed indispensable as an official of the Arbeiter-Unfall-Versicherungs-Anstalt. Kafka was not relieved by his exemption, for, as he repeatedly told Felice, he had hoped to be called up (F 633, 638). He could of course have volunteered for active service, and he accounts for his failure to do so in cryptic terms: 'Mich freiwillig zu melden, hindert mich manches Entscheidende, zum Teil allerdings auch das, was mich überall hindert' (F 633).

Why was Kafka so anxious to serve and yet so reluctant to volunteer? Simple-minded patriotism, at any rate, was not among his motives: he records his dislike of the patriotic demonstrations, engineered by commercial interests, which in the early stages of the war were held daily (T 420–1). Despite his aversion to vulgar jingoism, however, his trip through Germany in July 1914 had given him the naïve notion that the strength, simplicity, and courage of the German people would guarantee their victory.[1] In December 1914 he expressed irritation at the incompetent leadership of the Austrian forces on the southern front (T 449). Nevertheless, his motives for wanting to be conscripted were mainly private. He seems to have fancied that military service would have freed him from his unfulfilling job and his sense of failure, and would have resolved the conflict between his literary vocation and his emotional commitment to Felice, by separating him from both. He hoped, in other words, that an intervention from outside would sweep away his present set of problems, even if it substituted physical hardship. But his failure to volunteer implies some awareness of the unrealism of these hopes. The element of fantasy in them emerges with especial clarity from a notebook entry of February 1917 in which Kafka describes his satisfaction at wearing a pair of army boots which he had originally bought on the assumption that he would be called up: 'In den schweren Stiefeln, die ich heute zum erstenmal angezogen habe (sie waren ursprünglich für den Militärdienst bestimmt), steckt ein anderer Mensch' (H 63).

Kafka's fantasy of joining the army draws attention to a persistent feature of his imaginative life: his fascination with great leaders, particularly Napoleon.[2] His interest in Napoleon can be traced back to September 1911, when he saw in the Galerie des Batailles at Versailles a picture of Napoleon bivouacking on the battlefield of Wagram (T 619). In October 1911 he read a collection of anecdotes about Napoleon (T 103–4), and in November he attended a lecture entitled 'La légende de Napoléon', during which he had a vision of Napoleon entering the hall and dwarfing the entire audience (T 156–9). In 1915 he became absorbed in reading about Napoleon's Russian campaign and made lengthy excerpts from books on the subject, which are printed only in the English translation of his diaries.[3] This fascination with Napoleon is no doubt related to Kafka's admiration for writers like Goethe, Hebbel, Balzac, and Dickens, whose energy and over-flowing creativity contrasted starkly with his own irresolute character and his difficulties in writing.[4] Besides energy and decision, Napoleon had the additional advantage of being a man of action instead of a writer. There are also hints of a more personal identification with Napoleon. Kafka quotes Napoleon's complaint about the prospect of dying childless, refers to his lack of friends (F 221), and shows interest in his supposedly deficient sexual life (F 271).[5] Moreover, he keeps drawing deliberately far-fetched comparisons between Napoleon's career and his own life. Writing to Brod from Zürau in September 1917, he talks about the failure of his engagement to Felice and describes the self-knowledge which his recently diagnosed tuberculosis has brought him as

Erkenntnis der ersten Stufe. Der ersten Stufe jener Treppe, auf deren Höhe mir als Lohn und Sinn meines menschlichen (dann allerdings nahezu napoleonischen) Daseins das Ehebett ruhig, aufgeschlagen wird. Es wird nicht aufgeschlagen werden und ich komme, so ist es bestimmt, nicht über Korsika hinaus. (Br 161.)

Four years later, after the end of his affair with Milena Jesenská, he castigates himself in similar terms for being too feeble even to answer a letter from her:

So kommt zu dem Leid noch die Schande, es ist etwa so wie wenn Napoleon zu dem Dämon, der ihn nach Rußland rief, gesagt hätte: 'Ich kann jetzt nicht, ich muß noch die Abendmilch trinken' und wenn er dann, als der Dämon noch fragte: 'Wird denn das lange dauern?' gesagt hätte: 'Ja, ich muß sie fletschern'. (Br 318.)[6]

This comparison was clearly habitual with Kafka, and at times it becomes ludicrous, as when he claims that a two days' visit to Berlin was for him a feat comparable to Napoleon's invasion of Russia (Br 447, cf. M 32, O 40). At other times, however, it conveys Kafka's feeling that one's inner struggles may be just as great whether they are enacted on the great stage of world history or the tiny stage of domestic life. After mentioning to Milena the letter he had written to his father surveying their relationship, he adds: 'einer kämpft eben bei Marathon, der andere im Speisezimmer, der Kriegsgott und die Siegesgöttin sind überall' (M 165). The same thought is expressed in one of the Zürau aphorisms: 'Sein Ermatten ist das des Gladiators nach dem Kampf, seine Arbeit war das Weißtünchen eines Winkels in einer Beamtenstube' (H 86).

These last quotations show that, even when Napoleon is not explicitly invoked, Kafka likes describing his own life in military imagery. 'Kampf' is among his favourite words from *Beschreibung eines Kampfes* onwards, that mystifying story which he may have begun writing as early as 1902.[7] In 1920 he says that he now feels for Felice 'die Liebe eines unglücklichen Feldherrn zu der Stadt, die er nicht erobern konnte' (Br 285). His life is a 'stehendes Marschieren' (T 560), his writing is at best 'Ansturm gegen die Grenze' (T 553), at worst 'eine mit Nägeln aufgekratzte Deckung im Weltkrieg' (Br 374). Besides Napoleon, other commanders and leaders become prominent in his diaries and letters: Alexander the Great (H 87), Moses (T 545, 565), Abraham (Br 333); in 1922 Kafka represents himself as a military commander, a 'Feldherr' (T 572–3). But the other side of the coin is also visible: he likes to imagine himself as an unimportant person who accidentally gets caught up in earth-shaking events, like the anonymous Greek who stumbles into world history by getting involved in the siege of Troy (Br 313–14), or the obscure soldier, already a veteran, who trembles at the sight of a toy gun but suddenly finds himself 'einberufen zu dem großen welterlösenden Kampf' (M 36).

Within this complex of images, there are two noteworthy developments. One is the tendency for the figure of the military commander to merge with that of the national leader. Both are combined in the 'Feldherr' who has to guide the masses over the mountains:

Du führst die Massen, großer langer Feldherr, führe die Verzweifelten durch die unter dem Schnee für niemanden sonst auffindbaren Paßstraßen des Gebirges. (T 572.)

Kafka wrote this as he was beginning work on *Das Schloß*, so that the image of the commander not only has political implications but represents his own relationship to society. It is therefore also the culmination of the second development in Kafka's military imagery: the tendency for these images to change from being self-deprecating comparisons emphasizing the failures in Kafka's personal life to vehicles for Kafka's growing sense of responsibility towards society. In a detailed study of this development, Malcolm Pasley has drawn attention to the ambiguity of the word *Verantwortung*, which was Kafka's original title for the collection of stories published in 1919 as *Ein Landarzt: Kleine Erzählungen*, some of which are to be discussed in this chapter.[8] *Verantwortung* can mean both 'accountability' for one's shortcomings, the theme of Kafka's guilt-laden earlier fiction, and a 'responsibility' which one is obliged to bear; it thus sums up neatly the shift in Kafka's understanding of his own relationship to society. The image of the military leader is not the only one through which Kafka expresses his feeling of responsibility. Another is that of the watchman or guardian. It occurs as early as 1914, in ch. 9 of *Der Prozeß*, where K. is examining an altar picture showing the burial of Christ. What chiefly holds K.'s attention, however, is a minor figure in the picture, a knight leaning on his sword at one side of the canvas, as though commanded to keep guard. This figure can be interpreted on more than one level. Since, as I argued in the previous chapter, the subject of the picture is related to the theme of the decline of religion which is symbolized in the following pages of *Der Prozeß* by the extinction of the lights in the cathedral, the knight who watches this process without intervening seems like a representative in the text of Kafka the author. The sentence 'Es war erstaunlich, daß er so stehenblieb und sich nicht näherte' (P 246) would apply also to Kafka's impassive narrative method. If so, the immediately following sentence, 'Vielleicht war er dazu bestimmt, Wache zu stehen', would express Kafka's conception of his task as a writer: to observe or record events with some undefined responsibility which precludes active intervention.

Another guardian-figure occurs two years later in the hero of Kafka's only surviving play, the fragment *Der Gruftwächter*.[9] For the past thirty years the hero has been guarding the tomb of Duke Friedrich. Though the courtiers think his task is merely nominal, 'wirkliche Bewachung unwirklicher, dem Menschlichen entrückter Dinge' (B 303), it appears in fact to be important and strenuous. The guardian of the tomb stands at the 'Grenze zwischen dem Menschlichen und dem Anderen' (B 303), as though protecting humanity against obscure and perhaps supernatural perils. At night, he explains, all the buried nobles emerge from the vault, led by Duke Friedrich, who wrestles with the guardian, while the others stand round in a ring and mock and humiliate him by cutting open his trousers and playing with his shirt-tail. The guardian always wins the fight, though it leaves him in a state of collapse.

These nocturnal struggles first of all suggest Kafka's own writing. He describes his letters to Felice as 'Nachrichten aus der Unterwelt' (F 443), while in his diaries he complains that his creative ability fluctuates too much to be relied upon and that therefore his writing is 'leider kein Tod, aber die ewigen Qualen des Sterbens' (T 420). The ghosts' feeling the guardian's shirt-tail is clearly a euphemism for sex-ual titillation and may be associated with the unleashing of shameful fantasies in writing: Kafka also calls his writing a 'Hinabgehen zu den dunklen Mächten, diese Entfesselung von Natur aus gebundener Geister' (Br 384). The guardian, however, also implies a more than private conception of the writer's task. One cannot be sure what is meant by saying that he occupies the border between mankind and 'dem Anderen',[10] but the tomb from which ghosts emerge is associated with other images Kafka uses in 1914–17: the old, dark building where the Old Commandant is buried in *In der Strafkolonie*, and the pigsty from which the stable-boy and the supernatural horses emerge in *Ein Landarzt*. These images imply, first, the sheer power of the past over the present, 'die Macht der früheren Zeiten' (E 235); authority-figures like Duke Friedrich and the Old Commandant may be dead, but have not lost their power. They also imply a close link between obscenity, primitive vitality, and creativity; the last is emphasized in a diary entry where Kafka, deploring his inability to write, consoles himself with images from *Ein Landarzt*: 'es kann erfahrungsgemäß aus Nichts etwas kommen, aus dem verfallenen Schweinestall der Kutscher mit den Pferden kriechen' (T 563). A provisional conclusion might be that the writer's creative gift puts him in contact with the forces which society has denied or repressed, and that his task is to control the 'return of the repressed' by diverting into literature those primitive energies which would otherwise destroy him and perhaps society as well.

The responsibility for defending society against primitive forces is the theme of *Ein altes Blatt*, which Kafka wrote in March 1917. It is set in a semi-mythical China, a country which appealed so much to Kafka's imagination that in May 1916 he declared: 'im Grunde bin ich ja Chinese' (F 657). The capital has been invaded by nomads from the north, who camp in the central square, covering it with filth.[11] Both they and their horses eat raw flesh, and once devoured a live ox. One cannot communicate with them, for they seem to have no articulate language: they shriek like jackdaws and make terrifying but meaningless grimaces. Unable to oppose them, the Emperor has withdrawn into the interior of his palace, while the imperial guards cower behind barred windows. The lower middle classes, the trades-men and shopkeepers who used to go about their business without bothering about public affairs, suddenly find that the defence of their country has been neglected and that, since traditional authority-figures are impotent, the task of saving it from the nomads has fallen to them. But the responsibility is more than they can bear, and has, they feel, only been assigned to them by mistake: 'Ein Mißverständnis ist es; und wir gehen daran zugrunde' (E 158).

More emphatically than in *Der Gruftwächter*, authority is in decline and at the mercy of anarchic, barely human assailants. How contemporary events inspired the story is unusually obvious: the opening sentence, 'Es ist, als wäre viel vernachlässigt worden in der Verteidigung unseres Vaterlandes' (E 155), was a natural reflection in the third year of the war. Even before the war, however, Kafka had felt that the Austrian Empire was in decay: in April 1914 he called Vienna 'dieses absterbende Riesendorf' (F 545); and in 1921, writing from the sanatorium at Matliary, he compared his situation as an invalid to the decline of the Empire before the war:

Sie [meine augenblickliche innere Situation] erinnert ein wenig an das alte Österreich. Es ging ja manchmal ganz gut, man lag am Abend auf dem Kanapee im schön geheizten Zimmer, das Thermometer im Mund, den Milchtopf neben sich und genoß irgendeinen Frieden, aber es war nur irgendeiner, der eigene war es nicht. Eine Kleinigkeit nur, ich weiß nicht, die Frage des Trautenauer Kreisgerichtes war nötig und der Thron in Wien fing zu schwanken an. (Br 288–9.)[12]

More generally, as Claude David has shown, Kafka's fiction is pervaded by a pessimistic interpretation of history as a process of decline.[13] Hence we learn in *Ein Hungerkünstler* that the golden age of starvation-artists lies in the past, or in *Forschungen eines Hundes* that the ancestors of the dog community possessed a truth that their ancestors have lost. It would be hard to say how far Kafka's sense of decline comes from the intellectual ambience of the *fin de siècle* and how much from observing the society around him (so far as the two can be separated), but the latter, a consciousness of political decay in the Austrian Empire, seems to have found its way into *Ein altes Blatt*. The upsurge of primitive energies represented by the nomads comes from a different area of Kafka's imagination. Himself a dedicated vegetarian, probably to the detriment of his health,[14] he often associates flesh-eating with brutality and menace, and opposes it to the asceticism of his artist-figures: one thinks of the lodgers in *Die Verwandlung* who gorge themselves while Gregor is starving, and of the cannibal whom Kafka originally intended to contrast with his starvation-artist and whom he replaced with a panther.[15] In the context of

Ein altes Blatt, however, the nomads' flesh-eating acquires social implications, suggesting the violent, irrational energies that break out in a time of social crisis. Kafka retained a good command of Greek from his schooldays and could have known that Euripides in *The Bacchae* treats this topic by describing how the Maenads tear live cattle to pieces.[16] Certainly he shows a keen awareness of how vulnerable civilization is to the primitive energies which it attempts to keep under control.

From *Ein altes Blatt* it seems that if one acknowledges one's responsibility to society one may be faced with tasks that far exceed one's powers. Would it not be better, then, to opt out and deny one's responsibility altogether? This is the possibility explored in *Der neue Advokat,* a story dating from January 1917 which illustrates Kafka's habit of contrasting a heroic past with a mediocre present and of elaborating this basic distinction by superimposing different temporal levels upon one another. The war-horse of Alexander the Great has survived into the present, where he is somewhat out of place, but he has been treated with generosity and admitted to the legal profession with the title 'Dr Bucephalus': 'Mit erstaunlicher Einsicht sagt man sich, daß Bucephalus bei der heutigen Gesellschaftsordnung in einer schwierigen Lage ist und daß er deshalb, sowie auch wegen seiner weltgeschichtlichen Bedeutung, jedenfalls Entgegenkommen verdient' (E 145). As Kafka's use of officialese brilliantly conveys, the present is a dull world, run by grey bureaucrats. Not only does it lack any great figure like Alexander, it has inherited only his worse qualities: 'Zu morden verstehen zwar manche; auch an der Geschicklichkeit, mit der Lanze über den Bankettisch hinweg den Freund zu treffen, fehlt es nicht' (E 145)—an allusion to Alexander's stabbing of his friend Cleitos at a drunken banquet.[17] Given the degeneracy of the present, it may be the wisest course to retreat into private life, as Bucephalus does, and devote oneself to studying the books that have come down to us from the past.

Kafka's technique of superimposition serves to blur and complicate what might otherwise have been too pat a contrast. For much of the story we are in the contemporary world with lawyers, the 'Barreau' (i.e. the French Bar Association), and horse-racing. In the second paragraph, however, we seem to be in Macedonia after the death of Alexander, and with nobody else who could lead to freedom the people who find Macedonia too confining. Besides this, Kafka practises another kind of superimposition which causes other historical figures to loom up behind Alexander. Now that there is no Alexander, we are told, 'niemand, niemand kann nach Indien führen' (E 145): this recalls Kafka's fascination with Napoleon, who also planned to conquer India, while the emphasis on leadership rather than warfare, with the king's sword mentioned only as pointing the way, makes Alexander resemble a national leader who can guide his people out of captivity—a suggestion of Moses. The gates of India, unattainable even in Alexander's time, though their direction was known, imply less a geographical location than a spiritual goal. Nobody can point the way there now; many people hold swords, though they can only brandish them uselessly—a hint at the dispersal and weakening of authority in modern states. The present lacks authority, but requires not so much a political leader (Alexander) as a spiritual one (Moses).

By his methods of indirection and suggestion, Kafka conveys in these stories a diagrammatic picture of the condition of the world. Traditional authority is impotent, society is in decline: at best it lacks heroes, at worst it is threatened by primitive violence and anarchy. A spiritual leader is required, but none is available; instead, the task of defending the community has fallen to frail and humble people who are unequal to it, and the best course may indeed be to retire into a studious and secluded life.

If, however, one did acknowledge one's responsibility towards society, an obvious way to try to carry it out would be through political activity, and this accordingly seems a suitable point to survey the evidence for Kafka's interest in actual political movements. Despite the diary entry quoted at the beginning of this chapter, he seems normally to have taken a degree of interest in politics that one would expect of an educated man. His school friend Hugo Bergmann tells us that as a sixth-former he followed the progress of the Boer War and sided enthusiastically with the Boers.[18] We learn further that at the age of sixteen Kafka developed sympathies with socialism, and took to wearing a red carnation in his button-hole. At a meeting of the *Altstädter Kollegentag*, the German nationalist student society to which the pupils at the Altstädter Gymnasium belonged, Kafka and Bergmann were thrown out for refusing to join in singing *Die Wacht am Rhein*.[19] This is not enough to suggest a strong or specific commitment to socialism. Nor can one be deduced from his later habit of listening to public speeches by Czech politicians, for it was not only socialist orators like Soukup and Klofáč, but also Masaryk's liberal-democratic Realist Party, that attracted him.[20] If the books he most admired included Lily Braun's *Memoiren einer Sozialistin*, that was because of the author's social conscience, her selflessness, and her determined opposition to the hypocrisy of her class (Br 282, F 638). His programme for an ascetic, all-male community of propertyless workers ('Die besitzlose Arbeiterschaft', H 126–7) may well, as Eduard Goldstücker argues, be indebted to pre-Marxist utopian socialism, but it is obviously not a blueprint for a new socialist society, especially since it specifies that the workers may be employed in capitalist factories.[21]

Kafka has, however, been persistently connected with a Prague anarchist group, the *Klub mladých* ('Club of the Young'), whose members are said to have included the writers Stanislav Kostka Neumann and Jaroslav Hašek. The main evidence for this is a detailed account by the anarchist Michal Mareš, published in Wagenbach's biography, which says that Kafka often came to the group's meetings, though he never said anything, and also attended such events as a commemoration of the Paris Commune, an anti-war demonstration, and a demonstration against the execution of the French workers' leader Liabeuf in 1912.[22] Brod first heard of Kafka's involvement from another member of the group, Michal Kácha, around 1930.[23] These reports must be treated with scepticism. Both Mareš and Kácha are said by acquaintances to have been unreliable informants.[24] Since the club had been broken up by the police in October 1910 and had to meet secretly thereafter, it is hard to imagine its members tolerating a visitor who always remained silent and who, for all they knew, might have been a spy. Though Kafka did know Mareš, he says they had only a nodding acquaintance ('eine Gassenbekanntschaft', M 306, cf. 137). Finally, if Kafka did attend these gatherings, it is extremely unlikely that Brod should have known nothing of them. On all these grounds Kafka's attendance at anarchist meetings looks very like a legend, as does his alleged friendship with Jaroslav Hašek.[25] Hašek was probably not a member of the *Klub mladých* at all, for he seems to have had little connection with the Anarchist movement after his imprisonment for street violence in 1907, and the party he founded in 1911, the 'Party for Moderate Progress within the Bounds of the Law', whose meetings Kafka and Brod are alleged to have attended, appears to have been a practical joke and not, as Mareš claimed, a cover for an anarchist organization. In any case one can scarcely imagine two less congenial people than Kafka and the drunken ne'er-do-well Hašek.

There do not seem, therefore, to be any reliable grounds for connecting Kafka with socialist or anarchist politics. If one is inquiring into Kafka's political leanings, it is, in fact, misleading to think in terms of the usual antithesis between left and right. The appropriate context would be the ideology which Michael Löwy has labelled 'romantic anti-capitalism' and summed up as follows:

In romantic ideology, opposition to the Enlightenment, the French Revolution and the Napoleonic Code combined with an anti-capitalist rejection of the bourgeois social universe, of economic liberalism and even industrialization. Faced with the development of capitalism, which progressively reduces man to an abstract, calculable quantity and establishes a rigorously quantitative system of reasoning, romanticism passionately defended the concrete, qualitative and intuitive forms of living and thinking, and the personal and concrete human relations which still lived on among the pre-capitalist layers (peasantry, petty bourgeoisie, nobility).[26]

Romantic anti-capitalism (to adopt Löwy's term, though 'anti-industrialism' might be more accurate) had many different versions, some of which will be examined more closely later in this chapter, but as a general ideology it transcended the opposition of left and right. As Löwy shows, its assumptions were shared by conservatives like the Thomas Mann of *Betrachtungen eines Unpolitischen* (1918), liberals like Max Weber and Georg Simmel, and even by those who, like Lukács and Bloch, would respond to the First World War and its aftermath by committing themselves to the Marxist form of anti-capitalism. The one political movement with which Kafka can definitely be associated, Zionism, cannot be classified overall as left-wing or right-wing, but romantic anti-capitalism forms the thread running through the diverse manifestations of Zionism with which Kafka came in contact. We saw in Ch. 1 that he attended a number of meetings, cultural rather than directly political, organized by the Bar Kochba, but held himself aloof from the committed Zionists and indeed went through a phase which he later called 'Antizionismus'. One of the aims of the present chapter is to follow Kafka's gradual rapprochement with Zionism from 1915 onwards, though it must be admitted from the outset that he always remained on the sidelines of the movement and shunned practical involvement with it, however great his theoretical sympathy became. First, however, I want to look more closely at the ideology of the Bar Kochba in the years before the First World War, and especially at the influence exerted over it by Martin Buber, in order to suggest that somewhat more of the Bar Kochba's beliefs rubbed off on Kafka than his word 'Antizionismus' might imply.

The members of the Bar Kochba were educated middle-class Jews who, like Kafka, had been brought up in almost complete ignorance of Judaism by parents who were anxious to assimilate fully to Western society. When Brod and Kafka first made contact with the Bar Kochba, its main ideological preceptor was not Theodor Herzl, whose detailed plans for a Jewish state perhaps did not provide enough emotional sustenance, but Ahad Ha'am, the proponent of cultural Zionism. Ahad Ha'am argued that since Palestine was too small to accommodate more than a fraction of the world's Jews, it should constitute a spiritual rather than a political centre. In the words of some of his followers, he was not advocating a Jewish national state but a Jewish Vatican. The Jews remaining in the Diaspora should concentrate on developing their Jewish self-awareness, which would include learning Hebrew.[27] Accordingly, the main concern of the Bar Kochba, as proclaimed in the first issue of their journal *Selbstwehr*, was with the 'Belebung der jüdischen Idee',[28] i.e. consciousness-raising, and for some years they took relatively little interest in the Palestinian settlements.

Alongside Ahad Ha'am's stress on Jewish consciousness, however, there were other, more strictly political lines of thought in early Zionism. One that eventually impinged on the Bar Kochba, and hence on Kafka, originated with Max Nordau, a close friend of Herzl and author of *Entartung* (1892), a polemical critique of contemporary Western culture. In a speech to the First Zionist Congress in Basle in 1897, Nordau took his hearers aback by claiming that the traditional Jewish ghetto, the physical concentration and cultural isolation of Jews whether in a city or a village, had not been the degrading confinement that Western Jews usually thought it; on the contrary, it had provided the Jews with an indispensable refuge in which they could develop their full human potential:

So lebten die Ghettojuden in sittlicher Hinsicht ein Volleben. Ihre äußere Lage war unsicher, oft schwer gefährdet, innerlich aber gelangten sie zur allseitigen Ausgestaltung ihrer Eigenart und sie hatten nichts Fragmentarisches an sich. Sie waren harmonische Menschen, denen keins der Elemente des Normaldaseins eines Gesellschaftsmenschen fehlte.[29]

On the contrary, Nordau went on, it was the emancipated Western Jew who was fragmented, unable to return to the shelter of the ghetto or to find acceptance in Gentile society, and condemned to a life of insecurity and self-distrust. At the time this must have sounded like wilful paradox-mongering, but in Nordau's wake other Zionists were able to discover in the Jewish communities of Eastern Europe a social cohesion and an unabashed acceptance of being Jewish which could serve as models for a future Jewish community. In 1912 Kafka attended a meeting of the Bar Kochba which was addressed by Nathan Birnbaum, the great champion of Yiddish, who spoke passionately on behalf of the Eastern Jews: 'Die Ostjuden sind ganze, lebensfrohe und lebenskräftige Menschen', he declared.[30] The collection of essays entitled *Vom Judentum*, which the Bar Kochba issued in 1913 and of which Kafka owned a copy, included a contribution by Adolf Böhm restating Nordau's praise of the ghetto and emphasizing the interpenetration of all aspects of its life by religion:

Im Ghetto war das Gemeinschaftsleben ein vollständiges, es umfaßte nicht nur Religion, sondern auch Sitte, Recht, Sprache, Familienleben, in vollständiger Einheit. [. . .] Das 'Judentum' war keine bloße Konfession, nicht allein Individualreligion, sondern umfaßte die Gesamtheit aller durch Gesetz und Tradition geheiligten Formen des Gemeinschaftslebens in ihrer bestimmten Eigenart.[31]

This version of romantic anti-capitalism, with its ideal of a close-knit, actively religious community best represented by the Eastern Jews, was formulated most influentially by Martin Buber. Though Buber's work as a religious philosopher still lay in the future, he was already well known in several different guises: he had been prominent in the Zionist movement since 1898, he had nourished the current interest in mysticism by publishing an anthology of mystical testimonies, *Ekstatische Konfessionen*, and his retellings of Eastern Jewish tales had begun to make Western Europe aware of the Jewish communities further east and their religious traditions. He addressed the Bar Kochba three times in 1909 and 1910, and the third speech probably had Kafka in its audience. These speeches had a lasting influence on some at least of his hearers through their exposition of Buber's conception of Jewish nationhood.

Buber's nationalism is rooted in his mysticism, which he sets out in the introduction to *Ekstatische Konfessionen*. The individual, Buber assumes, is normally more or less estranged from his social environment. In mystical experience one accepts the consequences of this estrangement by withdrawing into the depths of the self. Though in one sense a state of utter solitude, in another sense this is an experience of union. The self escapes from the prison of individuality and is united with the 'Weltich' and hence with the rest of mankind.[32] God, for the early Buber, is simply a convenient fiction on to which one projects this experience. This, as it were, secular mysticism probably derives from Schopenhauer, who maintains that the individual will has direct access to the *Ding an sich* through being itself a portion of the *Ding an sich*, and from the concept of Dionysiac ecstasy that Nietzsche unfolds in the opening pages of *Die Geburt der Tragödie*.[33]

Since there is no question of union with a transcendent God, Buber's mysticism only needed to be transposed into social terms to reappear as romantic nationalism. The estrangement of the individual from society, which Buber takes for granted, assumes much more concrete form as the estrangement of the Western Jew from Gentile society and as the estrangement of the would-be Zionist from the Jews around him who are trying desperately but ineffectually to assimilate to their Gentile environment. Lacking any help from outside, each individual, alone and unaided, must discover his Jewishness within himself. Buber quotes a famous remark by the journalist Moritz Heimann: 'Was ein auf die einsamste, unzugänglichste Insel verschlagener Jude noch als "Judenfrage" erkennt, das einzig ist sie.'[33] If the Jew makes a mystical descent into the depths of his own being, he will find there a latent Jewish identity which will release him from isolation and unite him with his people, for at this mystical, intuitive level there is no longer any distinction between the individual and the race. One should come to feel: 'Meine Seele ist nicht bei meinem Volke, sondern mein Volk *ist* meine Seele.'[35]

What holds a people together is nothing so superficial as economic or religious association: it is the blood. 'Ein Volk wird zusammengehalten durch primäre Elemente: das Blut, das Schicksal—soweit es auf der Entwicklung des Blutes beruht—und die kulturschöpferische Kraft—soweit sie durch die aus dem Blute entstandene Eigenart bedingt wird.'[36] These ties of blood are normally intuitive, below the threshold of consciousness, but even for somebody cut off from his people they can provide a feeling of organic unity, not only with compatriots in the present, but with past and future generations. The Bar Kochba not only lapped up this teaching but found a memorable expression of it in Richard Beer-Hofmann's poem 'Schlaflied für Mirjam' (1897) which evokes the mutual estrangement of people in modern society and contrasts it, in the final stanza, with the intuitive unity of the individual and his nation:

> Schläfst du, Mirjam?—Mirjam, mein Kind,
> Ufer nur sind wir, und tief in uns rinnt
> Blut von Gewesenen—zu Kommenden rollts,
> Blut unsrer Väter, voll Unruh und Stolz.
> *In* uns sind *Alle.* Wer fühlt sich allein?
> Du bist ihr Leben—ihr Leben ist dein—
> Mirjam, mein Leben, mein Kind—schlaf ein![37]

To realize oneself fully, however, one needs roots in an actual community, which must avoid the destructive effects of modern life by maintaining its ties with the primeval past. The Jews' national awakening cannot, therefore, be fully accomplished until they return from exile and regain contact with the soil of Palestine:

> Die schöpferische Größe unserer Urzeit ist einst aus diesem Boden erwacht; seine Säfte haben sie genährt, sie wuchs im Schatten seiner Berge, und wenn sie ermattete, legte sie sich an sein Herz und wurde wieder stark.[38]

They must also adopt Hebrew, their ancient language. Once their geographical and linguistic ties with the remote past have been re-established, creativity and culture will again be possible.

About the actual organization of the Jewish community, Buber is hazy. He has none of the engaging delight in planning the details of a new society that Herzl shows in *Der Judenstaat*, his diaries, and his utopian novel *Altneuland*. In a memorial address, Buber deplored Herzl's tendency to get bogged down in political minutiae instead of realizing that the Jewish problem centred on the intuitive relationship between the individual and the *Volk*. He does assume, however, that the new community will be agrarian, based on contact with the soil and the natural rhythm of the seasons. As for its social structure, he envisages a creative élite whom he calls 'die Schaffenden', a term borrowed from Nietzsche's *Zarathustra*; these will be neither intellectuals nor artists, though they will combine the best qualities of both, and it appears that some will exercise their creativity as leaders and become 'Schaffende, die ihr Werk aus Menschenseelen, aus Völkern und Kulturen bilden'.[39]

Buber's social thinking is clearly remote from present-day democratic politics. So is his language. His favourite words include 'Blut', 'Boden', 'Volkstum', and 'Wurzelhaftigkeit', all of which have been banished, for good reasons, from the modern political vocabulary.

He also has a fondness for words beginning with the prefix 'Ur-'. The essay 'Mein Weg zum Chassidismus' (1917) alone contains 'Urmenschliches', 'Urjüdisches', 'Uraltes', and 'Urkünftiges'.[40] The main topics of his Zionist writings do not really form any coherent programme, and to understand them properly one has to realize that Buber is using the clichés of romantic anti-capitalism, with passionate conviction, to demolish a currently accepted stereotype of the Jew and put an alternative image in its place. He agrees with Nordau in disapproving of the modern Western Jew, but goes even further by insisting that the Western Jew is degenerate and deeply sick.[41] The typical product of the Diaspora is the Jewish intellectual: a passive, morbidly introspective character, a 'Problematiker' who is entirely inept in practical life.[42] Such a person has no true creativity, though he may be capable of a brilliant but specious 'Scheinproduktivität'.[43] This stereotype of the Jew is widespread among anti-Semites (and not only anti-Semites): German literature of the nineteenth and early twentieth century is full of portraits of the uncreative, over-rational Jew who has lost touch with his instincts, who can adapt to any environment because he has no firm identity to lose, but whose adoption of Western culture is shallow and unconvincing. Wagner asserts in *Das Judentum in der Musik* that Jews are incapable of authentic passion and therefore cannot sing.[44] Nietzsche in *Der Antichrist* charges the Jews with 'die radikale *Fälschung* aller Natur, aller Natürlichkeit'.[44] Treitschke declared that the peasants in the Black Forest stories of Berthold Auerbach, a fully assimilated Jew, must be artificial creations, because a Jew could have no genuine rapport with tillers of the soil.[45] The type that Buber particularly denounces, the over-complicated intellectual, appears repeatedly in fiction; one example is the decadent Edward Nieberding in Wassermann's *Die Juden von Zirndorf* (1897), who tells a woman that he will not be able to love her properly until she is married to someone else and therefore inaccessible.[47] It is a bitter irony that this image of the rational, adaptable Jew had itself been propagated by eighteenth-century Jewish publicists, foremost among them Moses Mendelssohn, to demonstrate that the Jews were not enslaved to ritual and superstition but fully capable of serving the ideals of the Enlightenment.[48] The reaction against the Enlightenment—a reaction in which Buber, who described the Enlightenment as the expression of 'eines blutlosen Menschheitsideals',[49] fully shared—meant that the rational Jew fell into disfavour, and Buber therefore took it upon himself to show that the Jews had reserves of irrationality as profound as the Germans had.

Buber's Zionist writings are indebted to certain specific strains within romantic anti-capitalism. They presuppose the antithesis of *Gemeinschaft* and *Gesellschaft* which, as George Mosse has said, was a commonplace of German thinking around the turn of the century.[50] This antithesis has an impeccably academic origin in the writings of the sociologist Ferdinand Tönnies, who contrasted *Gemeinschaft*, a traditional community based on blood-relationships and inherited customs, with *Gesellschaft*, an atomistic society whose members were held together only by rational self-interest.[51] Tönnies, who came from a country village in Schleswig-Holstein and witnessed the rapid industrialization of Germany with disquiet, betrays a distinct bias towards *Gemeinschaft*. His antithesis proved serviceable to the current of thought, deriving from Herder and the German Romantics, which attacked bourgeois liberalism and capitalism in the name of the *Volk*, imagined as an innately creative, intuitive, tradition-conscious organic community consisting mainly of peasants and craftsmen. No doubt *völkisch* thinking was regressive and unrealistic, notably in refusing to admit that industrial society could not simply be dismantled, but it provided wrong answers to a real problem. The intemperate polemics of Paul de Lagarde, for instance, include some well-aimed shots against the dehumanizing effects of industry: 'die industrie unserer tage braucht menschen überhaupt nur da, wo sie maschinen nicht anstellen kann, und sie braucht die menschen möglichst als maschinen, das heißt, sie entkleidet sie ihres charakters als menschen.'[52] Buber's vision of sturdy peasants tilling the soil of Palestine is simply a transposition to Asia of Lagarde's vision of North German farmers.[53] The influence of *völkisch* thought helps to account, too, for Buber's ready identification with the German national spirit, and for the enthusiasm with which, like the majority of German and Austrian intellectuals, he gave his support to the First World War. In December 1914 he told an audience of Berlin Zionists that participation in the war was already freeing the Jews from their rootlessness and admitting them to the community of the blood, and that it would regenerate the Jewish people: 'Sie werden ihre Einheit als Juden fühlen und erkennen lernen. Sie werden ihr Gemeinschafts-erlebnis vertiefen und aus ihm ihr Judentum neu aufbauen.'[54] These sentiments, which scandalized many Zionists, were a Jewish variant of the 'ideas of 1914' which, as T. J. Reed has said, were 'the common coin of the majority of self-respecting intellectuals'.[55]

Buber's *völkisch* thought would have commanded far less authority, however, if he had not been able to point to the living embodiment of his ideals in contemporary Eastern Europe. He found a model for his image of the Jewish *Volk* in communities dominated by Hasidism, the eighteenth-century 'revivalist' movement within Judaism which in his day was still widespread among the Eastern Jews. Since Hasidism was to be of great importance to Kafka, we must give the movement some attention.[56] Its founder, Israel ben Eliezer, was born around 1700 near Kamenets-Podolsk in what is now the south-western Ukraine. After working at various unskilled trades he became a *ba'al shem*, the usual term for an itinerant medicine-man. Besides curing physical illnesses, Israel also drove out evil spirits and distributed magic amulets. He came to rely increasingly on religious faith as the means of his cures, but, as the historian Simon Dubnow pointed out, he resembled Jesus of Nazareth in establishing a solid reputation as a miraculous healer before coming forward with a religious message.[56] Some time in the early 1740s Israel settled in the Ukrainian town of Medzhibozh, surrounded by followers, to whom he conveyed his teaching in the form of parables and aphorisms. His foremost adherents included Dov Ber, the Great Maggid (Preacher) of Mezhirich, who led the Hasidic movement after his death. Israel is generally known simply as the Ba'al Shem or the Ba'al Shem Tov ('Man of the Good Name'), which is often reduced to the acronym Besht. After his death in 1760 several collections of his sayings were published, the principal one being the two-volume *Keter Shem Tov* ('Crown of the Good Name', 1784 and 1795). His life is told in the *Shibkhe ha-Besht* ('Praises of the Besht', 1815). As historical sources, these books are, of course, no more trustworthy than the Gospels.

The teaching of the Ba'al Shem will be discussed further in the next two chapters, but its central themes appear to have been the following. His main doctrine, sometimes loosely called pantheism, was in fact panentheism: the Creator, though not identical with the creation (as in pantheism), was present in its midst, and the created world was a mere garment which the devout could penetrate in order to enjoy *devekut*, or communion with God. Since God was omnipresent, man should be confident and joyful, and allow *devekut* to permeate his entire life. Where the Cabbala had reserved *devekut* as the reward for extreme spiritual distinction, Hasidism made it freely available to all, thus annulling the division between the sacred and the profane. Man could be united with God, not only in ecstatic prayer, but even in the most mundane details of daily life. Hence the remark by one Hasidic saint: 'I did not go to the Maggid of Mesericz to learn Torah from him but to watch him tie his bootlaces.'[58] The study of the Torah, central to orthodox Judaism, was demoted to minor status and declared to be valuable only if done in a spirit of devotion.

After the death of the Ba'al Shem Hasidism was carried by his followers to much of Eastern Europe, provoking fierce but largely unsuccessful resistance by the orthodox. The movement was maintained by a spiritual élite, the *tsaddikim* or 'just men'. Unlike an orthodox rabbi, who is simply a learned man, the *tsaddik* was thought of as a mediator between God and mankind. They were credited with miraculous powers, including that of intercession with God, and exercised a charismatic authority over their followers. Their office soon became hereditary, and since they were in a position to acquire great material wealth, it is not surprising that by the middle of the nineteenth century Hasidism had declined a long way from the ideals of its founder.

Buber first encountered Hasidism when, in his childhood, he spent his summers on an estate in the Bukovina, near the small town of Sadagora, which was the seat of a famous dynasty of *tsaddikim*. The dynasty had been founded by Israel Ruzhin Friedmann, the great-grandson of the Maggid of Mezhirich, who had moved to Sadagora, on Austrian territory, after getting embroiled with the Russian police. He held court in a luxurious palace surrounded by a park; this estate had been bought for him by his followers, who kept him and his descendants so generously that they were richer than the local landowners. The *tsaddik* Buber encountered would have been Israel, the grandson of the founder of the dynasty.[59] Despite the *tsaddik*'s vulgar ostentation, his authority over his followers made a powerful impression on Buber, who later described the spectacle thus:

Der Palast des Rebbe, in seiner effektvollen Pracht, stieß mich ab. Das Bethaus der Chassidim mit seinen verzückten Betern befremdete mich. Aber als ich den Rebbe durch die Reihen der Harrenden schreiten sah, empfand ich: 'Führer', und als ich die Chassidim mit der Thora tanzen sah, empfand ich: 'Gemeinde'. Damals ging mir eine Ahnung davon auf, daß gemeinsame Ehrfurcht und gemeinsame Seelenfreude die Grundlagen der echten Menschengemeinschaft sind.[60]

In his early twenties Buber temporarily dropped his Zionist activities and spent four years in an intensive study of Hasidism. Its first products were two collections of Hasidic tales, *Die Geschichten des Rabbi Nachman* (1906) and *Die Legende des Baalschem* (1908). These aroused intense interest among Germans of Jewish descent who were otherwise estranged from their origins, like Walther Rathenau and Hugo von Hofmannsthal. Georg Lukács was so taken with them that he dreamed that he might be descended from the Ba'al Shem. They made Arnold Zweig return to Jewish problems after being put off by Zionist rhetoric, and enabled the publisher Salman Schocken to feel himself a Jew for the first time.[61] This, surely, was the response Buber hoped for. The tales demonstrated that the Jews, as well as the Germans, had a creative *Volksseele*, whose products were a Jewish counterpart to the Grimms' fairy-tales. They helped to provide an alternative image of the Jew, one which Western Jews were only too glad to identify with. Such strong prepossessions are necessary to account for the success of the tales, for Buber had retold them in a precious style which is very remote from most conceptions of the primitive and which one reader at least, Kafka, found 'unerträglich' (F 260). Though Buber toned down his stylistic excesses in subsequent editions, his legends bear much the same relation to the world of Hasidism as Lady Gregory's *Cuchulain of Muirthemne* does to the early Irish heroic tale.

Not only the style but also the substance of Buber's presentation of Hasidism, in these and later works, has been criticized as misleading. Gershom Scholem has pointed out that in addition to the legends and sayings of the *tsaddikim*, Hasidism possesses an equally large body of sermons, biblical commentaries, and treatises on religious topics, which Buber almost entirely ignores.[62] Moreover, the legends date mostly from the nineteenth century, while the more theoretical writings were composed during the flowering of Hasidism between 1770 and 1815 and therefore give far more reliable information about the movement. Buber, for his part, always maintained that the legends, as creative products, were true in a 'deeper' sense than mere intellectual compositions. In the preface to *Die Legende des Baalschem* he claimed that the ties of blood linking him to the original writers ensured that he had transmitted them authentically.[63] But if one casts a colder eye on Buber's work, one can see that he depicted Hasidism as the mirror-image of Western society. Hasidic communities appealed to him for several obvious reasons. Firstly, they were permeated by religion, while Western society was secular. Secondly, they were organic, while the West had succumbed to the mechanizing influence of *Gesellschaft*. Thirdly, the charismatic authority exercised by a *tsaddik* represented the ideal of leadership that Buber attributed to his creative élite. Fourthly, the Hasidic tradition of teaching in parables seemed to be a mythopoeic force, in contrast to the arid intellectualism of the West and especially of the Western Jews. And finally, the Hasidim seemed to Buber to retain a primitive vitality, an unreflective openness to immediate experience, which had largely vanished from the over-sophisticated West.

Buber's compound of mysticism, *völkisch* thought, and primitivism met with an enthusiastic response from the Bar Kochba. The strongest impression was made by his third address to them, 'Die Erneuerung des Judentums', in which Buber described the principal traits of the Jewish character and exhorted his audience to develop these traits and thus acquire a 'positives Volksbewußtsein'.[64] Though some of his hearers were electrified by this speech, others were left cold, and Kafka seems to have been among the latter, if this is the occasion he is referring to when he says of Buber, in a letter to Felice, 'ich habe ihn schon gehört, er macht auf mich einen öden Eindruck' (F 252). We must remember, however, that his contact with Buber's ideas was indirect as well as direct, for they were a constant topic of conversation among his Zionist friends. The intellectual temper of the Bar Kochba can be gathered from the collection of essays, *Vom Judentum*, which the society issued in 1913, and of which Kafka owned a copy. Among the contributors were six members of the Bar Kochba, a number of prominent Zionists including Buber, Birnbaum, and Moses Calvary, and some sympathizers from outside the movement, such as Jakob Wassermann and Karl Wolfskehl. The prevailing tone is distinctly radical, recalling that of contemporary Expressionist manifestos. In his introduction, Hans Kohn proclaims the revolt of youth against a mechanized and capitalist civilization which has lost its sense of purpose and allowed its materialism to suppress spiritual values. He and other contributors follow the economist Werner Sombart in considering this system largely the creation of the Jews:

Kalt und leer, rastlos und sinnlos, ohne Erhebung und Weihe schwingt das Leben zwischen seinen Polen, zwischen Gott und dem zweckverfangenen Ich, immer gottferner, seelenloser, mutloser. Die Juden haben diese Mechanisierung mit herbeigeführt; durch die Notwendigkeit der Geschichte waren sie es in erster Linie, die, da sie ihren Gott verloren, ihre Seele mißachtet hatten, das Netz der Unfreiheit und Bedingtheit immer dichter spannten.[65]

Accordingly, the human type produced by civilization is best represented by the modern Western Jew, who is typically a shallow materialist with no sense of community. In his place, the Bar Kochba proclaim a new kind of Jew and 'ein rein völkisches Judentum'.[65] This ideal is akin to the Expressionist conception of the New Man who, like Eustache de Saint-Pierre in Kaiser's *Die Bürger von Calais* (1914), is prepared to subordinate and even sacrifice himself to the community. The new community envisaged by the Bar Kochba is on the Buber model, united by ties of blood; it has nothing to do with biological theories of race, however, but is based on a mystical sense of union. Rejecting the arid rationalism often ascribed to the Jews, the writers are anxious to regain access to the irrational, mythopoeic, creative depths of the Jewish soul, and agree that these faculties can only flourish in a restored Jewish community. They set youth against age, mysticism against rationalism, the Orient against the Occident, and *Gemeinschaft* against *Gesellschaft*.

Kafka's response to the Zionism of Buber and the Bar Kochba can, I think, be found in *In der Strafkolonie*, which he wrote in October 1914. This may seem a surprising claim, for the story bears a particularly obvious relation to Kafka's own private fantasies. He made no secret of his taste for dwelling on and exaggerating his own sufferings: 'Die Lust, Schmerzliches möglichst zu verstärken, haben Sie nicht?' he asks Grete Bloch with mild surprise, in a letter which also expresses interest in the details of an attack of toothache suffered by Felice (F 478). He also confesses his fondness for fantasizing about still worse sufferings. 'Ja, das Foltern ist mir äußerst wichtig,' he tells Milena, 'ich beschäftige mich mit nichts anderem als mit Gefoltert-werden und Foltern' (M 290). It is appropriate that he once agreed to be the model for a painting by the artist Ernst Ascher, showing St Sebastian being shot to death with arrows (T 242).[67] In his diaries he imagines throwing himself through a pane of glass or having a butcher's knife cutting slices from his body (T 213, 305), and one can understand why his favourite poem was Justinus Kerner's 'Der Wanderer in der Sägemühle', in which a pine-tree speaks to the traveller as the saw cuts into it:

> Die Tanne war wie lebend,
> In Trauermelodie
> Durch alle Fasern bebend,
> Sang *diese* Worte sie:
>
> 'Du trittst zur rechten Stunde,
> O Wanderer! hier ein,

Du bist's, für den die Wunde
Mir dringt in's Herz hinein.'[68]

But while the relation between Kafka's masochistic fantasies and the punishment-machine is beyond question, Kafka himself suggests some wider implications. In reply to a complaint from his publisher, Kurt Wolff, that the story was too painful, Kafka wrote:

Zur Erklärung dieser letzten Erzählung füge ich nur hinzu, daß nicht nur sie peinlich ist, daß vielmehr unsere allgemeine und meine besondere Zeit gleichfalls sehr peinlich war und ist und meine besondere sogar noch länger peinlich als die allgemeine. (Br 150.)

The analogy that Kafka mentions between his own experience and that of his society can be confirmed if we glance at one of the less respectable literary sources which nourished his fantasies. He appears to have read Octave Mirbeau's *Le Jardin des supplices* (1899), whose narrator, investigating penitentiaries in the Far East, visits a torture-garden presided over by a genial torturer who deplores the decline in professional standards brought about by the crude techniques of mass-murder which technologically-minded Westerners have introduced 'unter dem Vorwand der Zivilisation'.[69] Here Kafka's private obsession with torture encounters another of the great commonplaces of his age, the antithesis between *Kultur* and *Zivilisation*. The latter term was used to describe the rational and technical features of modern society which helped to make it a *Gesellschaft* in Tönnies's sense. A neat formulation of the antithesis can be found in *Betrachtungen eines Unpolitischen*, where Thomas Mann writes: 'Deutschtum, das ist Kultur, Seele, Freiheit, Kunst und *nicht* Zivilisation, Gesellschaft, Stimmrecht, Literatur.'[70]

In der Strafkolonie turns on the antithesis of *Gemeinschaft* and *Gesellschaft*. The traveller from Europe finds the penal settlement in a state of transition between an old and a new order. In the past, the colony was administered by the Old Commandant, a figure who was at once soldier, judge, engineer, and draughtsman, and who invented the punishment-machine. Under his regime, punishments were carried out in the presence of the entire population of the colony, children included. They witnessed the twelve-hour ceremony with awe and with assurance that absolute justice was being enacted before their eyes: 'alle wußten: Jetzt geschieht Gerechtigkeit' (E 218). Now that the New Commandant has taken over, the punishment-machine has only one devotee left, the officer, and since he can no longer obtain spare parts the machine is breaking down. Though the New Commandant has not prohibited the use of the machine, he and his throng of admiring ladies try to temper its severity by visiting the condemned man and feeding him with sweets (which the prisoner is unable to keep down, since his diet hitherto has consisted of rotten fish). Most of the New Commandant's attention, however, is given to building extensions to the harbour.

The basic contrast is clear. On the one hand, the closely knit community of the past, united by the focus of a ceremony which administered absolute justice in an atmosphere of religious awe; on the other, present-day society, in which religious practices are conceded a marginal place but no longer give meaning even to the voluntary deaths of their adherents (the officer, who submits himself to the machine, experiences no transfiguration but is merely mangled), and in which a half-hearted and ineffectual humanitarianism accompanies an inhuman devotion to large-scale technological schemes. Kafka's *Gemeinschaft*, like Buber's, is dominated by religion. It is now customary to point out that the Old Commandant suggests Jehovah; that the message which the machine inscribes on the prisoner's body recalls the Ten Commandments by being termed a 'Gebot' (E 205); and that the squiggles and curlicues around it may be meant to suggest the minutely detailed commentaries with which Talmudists had surrounded the Torah. Malcolm Pasley, who first drew attention to some of these hints, also points out how deeply Kafka is indebted to Nietzsche's critique of religion in *Zur Genealogie der Moral*. The central image probably comes from Nietzsche's description of the religious exploitation of suffering as 'Heils-Maschinerie' and his account of cruelty as an integral part of religion, an occasion for public festivities, and an indispensable means of imprinting moral commands on the unreceptive memory of the human animal.[71] Kafka's officer says that death on the machine leads to an understanding of one's offence about the sixth hour (a possible allusion to the crucifixion of Jesus: cf. Mark 15: 33), when 'Verstand geht dem Blödesten auf' (E 212). Extreme suffering, then, does give meaning to death and leads to an understanding that is perhaps attainable by no other means. Despite its harshness, the organic and authoritarian community in which such an institution can flourish may be preferable to a society in which religious values have declined and nothing but an obsession with technology ('Hafenbauten, immer wieder Hafenbauten!'—E 224) has taken their place.

It will be evident that I cannot accept Roy Pascal's view that the only principle represented by the Old Commandant and his acolyte is 'punishment of the most savage sort', and that the traveller recognizes in the execution 'a disturbing *parody* of religious faith'.[72] Such an interpretation is a refusal of Kafka's suggestion that cruelty may be essential to religion and that religion may yet be superior to modern humanitarianism. Nor am I convinced that the officer is an unreliable witness, or that the reactions of the traveller, in particular his failure to live up to his humane ideals, are central to the story. Neither the officer nor the traveller is presented as untrustworthy; indeed, as Ingeborg Henel has observed, the latter's reliability is underlined by the narrator's statement: 'er war im Grunde ehrlich und hatte keine Furcht' (E 225).[73] Pascal seems to be foisting his own liberal views on to Kafka, both here and in his conjecture that the traveller embodies Kafka's own uncertainty about the First World War.[74] Kafka's attitude to the war, as outlined at the beginning of this chapter, makes such a speculation highly unlikely. But Pascal does provide a distinguished illustration of a difficult problem in the interpretation of Kafka. Given the apparent openness of his stories, and his abstention from authoritative narratorial pronouncements, it is tempting to remake Kafka in our own image and ignore how ready he was to explore beliefs that are seldom voiced nowadays and that we must find deeply disturbing. A striking example is the officer's conviction that punishment by the machine is not inhuman but rather 'das menschlichste und menschenwürdigste' (E 221) of legal procedures. The infliction of pain, no doubt, is inhumane, but is it necessarily inhuman? May it not, under some circumstances, be a recognition of human dignity? And if pain really were the royal road to spiritual insight, what could possibly justify its abolition? One thinks here of Thomas Mann's Naphta and his insistence on the human value of pain, illness, and punishment. If any of the sanatoria Kafka stayed in had contained a similar pair to Naphta and Settembrini, and he had been privileged, like Hans Castorp, to listen to their arguments, I suspect that he would have sided with Naphta.[75]

In exploring these themes, Kafka started from the assumptions about society which Buber transmitted to the Bar Kochba. Although he was not attracted by their nationalism, he shared their assumption of an antithesis between religious *Gemeinschaft* and secular, utilitarian *Gesellschaft*, and was inclined to think more favourably of the former. At this stage, however, the *völkisch* enthusiasm of the Bar Kochba was still rather theoretical. It was soon to acquire substance as a result of the First World War. In the first winter of the war, Russian armies overran Galicia and reached the passes of the Carpathians, obliging many thousands of civilians to flee westwards. Most of these were Jews. In the past, Eastern Jews had rarely been seen in Prague, but by mid January 1915 fifteen thousand Galician refugees had arrived there, and committees were hastily set up to appeal for charitable funds for their support. A Prague Zionist, Dr Alfred Engel, set up a school in which over two thousand refugee children were taught.[76] Among the teachers was Max Brod, who also took a keen interest in all aspects of Galician Jewish life, visiting rabbis and learning folk-songs. Teaching Homer to Galician schoolgirls, he felt that he was in contact with a living community of people whose fresh spontaneity gave them an intuitive understanding of Homer. 'Ich habe ein Volk, eine Gemeinschaft vor mir, nicht zersiebte Individuen,' he wrote. 'Ein Volk, das im höchsten Sinne geistig und dabei dennoch volkstümlich, also ungekünstelt, unverbraucht ist.'[77] Other Zionists elsewhere in Europe were making similar discoveries. Most of them, unlike Brod, had had no contact with Eastern Jews before encountering them as refugees or finding them *in situ* in traditional Jewish communities on the Eastern front. The experience proved to them that cohesive Jewish communities did exist and could serve as a model for a future Jewish state. Walter Preuss, who later emigrated to Palestine, recorded his impressions of Eastern Jews as follows:

In Tomaszow, einer hübschen Stadt von 40 000 Einwohnern, malerisch an der Pilica gelegen, lebten fast nur Juden. Hier, in Tomaszow, ging mir zuerst auf, wie anders als wir Westjuden es uns hochmütig vorgestellt hatten, die jüdische Wirklichkeit in Polen aussah, wieviel natürlicher die soziale Gliederung war als in Deutschland, wo die Judenheit nur noch aus Bourgeoisie und Intellektuellen bestand, wieviel jüdischer und traditionsverbundener sie noch war.[78]

Similar experiences convinced Sammy Gronemann, a Zionist lawyer from Berlin who was also to settle in Palestine, that the Lithuanian Jews possessed a 'Kultur' far superior to the 'Zivilisation' of the German occupying forces.[79] There were some dissentient voices, of course. The refugees in Prague, who were mostly poor village Jews, often made a bad impression. A series of discussion evenings was organized in the hope of bringing Eastern and Western Jews together, but the debates were banal and unproductive; Kafka describes one in unenthusiastic terms (T 465–6). Kafka himself, who sometimes visited Brod's Homer classes (T 468), writes about the Eastern Jews with sympathy (T 443) and seems to have admired above all 'das selbstverständliche jüdische Leben' (T 468): like the Yiddish actors he had mixed with four years earlier, the Eastern Jews were in no way self-conscious about being Jews.

The enthusiasm of Prague Zionists for the Eastern Jews could not remain at its intense pitch for very long. In a letter to Buber of 11 May 1915, Hugo Bergmann argued that contact with the Eastern Jews had actually made the task of forming a Jewish national community seem more difficult, for it had shown Zionists that they were inseparably attached to German culture and could not simply step out of their skins and fit into an Eastern Jewish community. What they needed was a Jewish community which would allow them to retain their identity as Germans.[80] Since no such community existed, the next task was to create it, and Bergmann pursued this topic in April 1916 in the first issue of Buber's monthly *Der Jude*. Hitherto, he complained, Zionism had been too abstract, lacking the discipline which practical responsibilities would have imposed. Only in Palestine were Zionists grappling with concrete problems like land reclamation and the labour supply. Could Western Jews do anything similar? 'Es kommt eben auf den Versuch an, ob nicht auch im Westen ehrliche Volksarbeit und ein wirkliches Volksleben möglich ist.'[81]

Bergmann's article illustrates an ideological shift in the Zionist movement in Prague and elsewhere, resulting from the impact of the Eastern Jews and the awakening of a real sense of community. Before the war, as we have seen, the ideology which the Bar Kochba derived from Buber was a Jewish counterpart to German nationalist and *völkisch* ideas. Once these doctrines had been absorbed, and Zionists had been sobered by military service and the task of caring for refugees, a humanistic socialism came to dominate the movement.[82] Buber, Gershom Scholem, and Arnold Zweig all shared this new mood. The last argues, in the romanticizing but moving essay 'Das ostjüdische Antlitz' (1920), that traditional Jewish society is essentially Socialist in being based on co-operation rather than competition, and expects young Jewish intellectuals from Eastern Europe to create an organic socialism which will be superior to the mechanistic doctrines inherited from Marx.[83]

These new ideals were put into practice most successfully by the medical student Siegfried Lehmann, who in May 1916 set up the

Jüdisches Volksheim in the slum quarter of eastern Berlin where Jewish immigrants congregated. It was run by young Jewish students and professional people, and included a nursery school, youth clubs, workshops, and settlements in the countryside; 200 to 250 children from the neighbourhood attended it daily. Though not explicitly Zionist in its aims, it seems to have produced a real sense of community among all those involved, and it provided a model for similar centres in Vienna and Prague.[84] Kafka was enthusiastic about it and pressured the initially reluctant Felice into working there, insisting on its importance and on the selfless idealism of its organizers (F 673).

There were, however, some initial difficulties. Lehmann, an ardent follower of Buber, wanted the Volksheim to concentrate on developing a national consciousness, combining the aesthetic sense of the Western Jews with the religious inwardness of the Eastern Jews.[85] When Gershom Scholem attended an evening discussion among the organizers of the Volksheim, he found them seated (the girls, among them Felice Bauer, arranged in picturesque attitudes on the floor) listening to Lehmann reading Werfel's poems aloud. This and similar aesthetic indulgences struck Scholem as trivial, and in a heated argument on a later occasion he proposed that they should instead devote themselves to learning Hebrew.[86] When Felice reported this discussion to Kafka, who was constantly demanding news about the Volksheim, he admitted that Scholem's suggestion appealed to him just because it was so extreme and impractical (F 703–4). Though the proposal was not well received, the Volksheim seems thereafter to have tended away from Lehmann's rather bookish efforts to construct a new culture and towards the practical goals advocated by other contributors to *Der Jude*. This new practicality is most clearly spelt out in another article, bluntly entitled 'Arbeit', in the opening number of *Der Jude*. Its author, A. D. Gordon, was a pioneer in Palestine and the leader of the party *Ha-poel Ha-tsa'ir* ('The Young Worker'). He sharply attacked Diaspora culture for its abstractness, its estrangement from nature, and its contempt for work, dismissing the Western Jew as a parasite:

Charakteristisch genug ist der Satz: 'Solange Israel den Willen Gottes tut, arbeiten andere für es.' Das ist nicht bloß ein Wort. Dieser Gedanke ist—bewußt oder unbewußt—in uns zu einem instinktiven Gefühl, einer zweiten Natur geworden.[87]

Instead, he continued, the Jews needed a conception of culture which comprehended the whole of life and gave an honoured place to manual and technical work. As the prospects of constructing a new society in Palestine became more realistic, attacks on the Western Jew sharpened. Lehmann's brother Alfred, a helper in the Volksheim and a writer for whom Kafka had considerable though qualified respect (F 712), delivered an attack on the urbanized Western Jews in which it is difficult to tell whether the word 'Boden' is literal or metaphorical:

Die Juden in Westeuropa verloren die ureigene volkliche Bindung und konnten, soweit sie sich noch jüdisch fühlen, eine lückenlose neue Bindung mit den sie umgebenden Völkern, sollte es ehrlich zugehen, noch nicht eingehen. *Sie* bauen, zum Geist erwachend, nicht auf einem Boden weiter, der von Menschen ihrer besonderen Art in der Vergangenheit bestellt wurde.[88]

These polemics must have touched Kafka on more than one exposed nerve. First, they appealed to his sense of responsibility and made him aware that he was fulfilling it only vicariously, by inducing Felice to help in the Volksheim and by reading and recommending the biographies of self-sacrificing figures like the Socialist Lily Braun and the Pietist Erdmuthe Countess Zinzendorf (see e.g. F 638, 677). It is true that his job presented him with obviously beneficial tasks: at the end of 1916 the Anstalt placed him in charge of dealing with shell-shocked soldiers, and he helped to raise money with which a unit caring for such sufferers was opened in May 1917. But such tasks had nothing specifically Jewish about them, and Kafka was not only acutely aware of being a Jew but felt that he represented precisely the type of degenerate Western Jewish intellectual against which the polemics of Buber, Lehmann, Gordon, and many other Zionists were aimed.

Kafka's sense of 'Jewish self-hatred' deserves close attention.[89] It is best understood with the aid of a long letter Kafka sent Brod in 1921 commenting on Karl Kraus's play *Literatur oder Man wird doch da sehn.* Kraus's play is an attack on Werfel, who had included a polemic against Kraus in his play *Spiegelmensch* (1920).[90] The strategy of Kraus's counter-attack is to parody the inflated pseudo-Goethean verse of *Spiegelmensch* and to insinuate that the only other language available to Werfel is the *Mauscheldeutsch* of his imperfectly assimilated forefathers. To Kafka, the play seemed to convey with deadly accuracy the situation of Jewish writers using German. Their adoption of German was always a misappropriation, 'die laute oder stillschweigende oder auch selbstquälerische Anmaßung eines fremden

Besitzes' (Br 336), and the resulting literature could at best be a 'Zigeunerliteratur' (Br 338) without a linguistic home. Kraus himself exemplified this problem, as Kafka once said in conversation with Brod: 'Karl Kraus sperrt die jüdischen Autoren in seine Hölle, gibt gut acht auf sie, hält strenge Zucht. Er vergißt nur, daß er in diese Hölle mit hineingehört.'[91] But these remarks are, of course, directed against Kafka himself, and show that by 1921 he had fully accepted the Zionist argument that Jews could not lead an adequate life in Western Europe. In his discussion of Kraus he is projecting on to literature his understanding of the social position of Western Jews. Rejecting psychoanalytic explanations, he prefers to formulate the problem in social terms:

Besser als die Psychoanalyse gefällt mir in diesem Fall die Erkenntnis, daß dieser Vaterkomplex, von dem sich mancher geistig nährt, nicht den unschuldigen Vater, sondern das Judentum des Vaters betrifft. Weg vom Judentum, meist mit unklarer Zustimmung der Väter (diese Unklarheit war das Empörende), wollten die meisten, die deutsch zu schreiben anfingen, sie wollten es, aber mit den Hinterbeinchen klebten sie noch am Judentum des Vaters und mit den Vorderbeinchen fanden sie keinen neuen Boden. Die Verzweiflung darüber war ihre Inspiration. (Br 337.)

Kafka's use of the word 'Boden' shows how thoroughly this piece of disguised self-analysis concurs with the standard Zionist account of the Western Jew. The metaphor of 'Boden', and its literal application to the soil of Palestine, had been repeated constantly since Nordau had described the Western Jew to the First Zionist Congress in these terms: 'Er hat keinen Boden unter den Füßen und er hat keinen Anschluß an eine Gesamtheit, in die er sich als willkommenes, vollberechtigtes Mitglied einfügen konnte.'[92]

Kafka, however, never set foot on the soil of Palestine, and it is doubtful how serious he was about wanting to emigrate there. As he admits, his own inspiration came from his uncomfortable situation as a Western Jew, suspended between the ghetto of the past and the Israel of the future. His upbringing had made him acutely conscious of the diversity of social types among Western Jews, depending on the degree of their assimilation to Gentile society. This emerges, for example, from his description of the writer Ernst Weiss, written in June 1913:

Vorvorgestern mit Weiß, Verfasser der *Galeere*. Jüdischer Arzt, Jude von der Art, die dem Typus des westeuropäischen Juden am nächsten ist und dem man sich deshalb gleich nahe fühlt. Der ungeheuere Vorteil der Christen, die im allgemeinen Verkehr die gleichen Gefühle der Nähe immerfort haben und genießen, zum Beispiel christlicher Tscheche unter christlichen Tschechen. (T 306–7.)

Evidently Gentiles seemed to Kafka to form a homogeneous body with automatic solidarity. It was not that they lacked national and class distinctions, but that they could not, like Jews, be classified according to their degree of assimilation. Kafka and his contemporaries felt compelled to classify Jewish acquaintances by this standard, as when Kafka felt obliged to dissociate himself from the embarrassingly under-assimilated Jew with whom he shared a railway compartment in 1911 (T 589). At the other extreme, he was disgusted by Jews who were baptized and largely assimilated but unable to conceal their origins, like the rich tourists he encountered in Merano in 1920, who provoked the comment: 'was für abscheuliche jüdische Kräfte können bis ans Bersten in einem getauften Juden leben, erst in den christlichen Kindern der christlichen Mütter glättet es sich' (Br 269). The habit of dissociating oneself from such fellow-Jews made Kafka occasionally indulge in rather distasteful anti-Jewish jokes: in a letter to Brod, written from Zürau in October 1917, Kafka jocularly describes the goats which he has just been feeding as 'vollkommen jüdische Typen, meistens Ärzte, doch gibt es auch Annäherungen an Advokaten, polnische Juden und vereinzelt auch junge Mädchen' (Br 176). The Jews he felt at home with were assimilated, educated people like Ernst Weiss or the helpers in the Volksheim, whom he described to Felice as being in 'dem Zustand des gebildeten Westjuden unserer Zeit, Berlinerischer Färbung und, auch das sei zugegeben, dem vielleicht besten Typus dieser Art' (F 697). Alternatively he could feel at ease with completely unassimilated Eastern Jews like the Yiddish actors, who had never begun to worry about how far they resembled Gentiles.

Kafka not only adopted the Zionist image of the Western Jew, but, in keeping with his self-tormenting character, applied it to himself with extreme severity. In his letters to Milena he dwells on how the Jews' insecure position in Western society has made them constitutionally timorous, and portrays himself as a typical specimen:

Wir kennen doch beide ausgiebig charakteristische Exemplare von Westjuden, ich bin, soviel ich weiß, der westjüdischeste von ihnen, das bedeutet, übertrieben ausgedrückt, daß mir keine ruhige Sekunde geschenkt ist, nichts ist mir geschenkt, alles muß erworben werden, nicht nur die Gegenwart und Zukunft, auch noch die Vergangenheit. (M 294.)

This recalls a little notebook entry dating from earlier in 1920:

Alles, selbst das Gewöhnlichste, etwa das Bedientwerden in einem Restaurant, muß er sich erst mit Hilfe der Polizei erzwingen. Das nimmt dem Leben alle Behaglichkeit. (H 419.)

Perhaps here, and certainly in the letter, Kafka is (half-consciously) stylizing himself to fit a standard image of the Jew. His affair with Milena, who was a Gentile, seems to have called forth all his 'Jewish self-hatred', as when he tells her that in his opinion a Gentile girl who marries a Jew requires more courage than Joan of Arc (M 25), or when, writing to Brod about Milena, he refers to himself wryly as 'der krumme Westjude' (Br 317). The most notorious expression of his 'Jewish self-hatred' is the outburst:

manchmal möchte ich sie eben als Juden (mich eingeschlossen) alle etwa in die Schublade des Wäschekastens dort stopfen, dann warten, dann die Schublade ein wenig herausziehn, um nachzusehn, ob sie schon alle erstickt sind, wenn nicht, die Lade wieder hineinschieben und es so fortsetzen bis zum Ende. (M 61.)

The masochism implicit in 'mich eingeschlossen', and the repulsive thoroughness with which Kafka imagines the process, illustrate his tendency to use his letters to Milena (like the earlier correspondence with Felice) to release his own neurotic obsessions rather than to respond to the individuality of his correspondent. From the seven hundred closely printed pages of the *Briefe an Felice*, in particular, one can construct only the sketchiest picture of Felice's personality. Kafka's letters to women he was not sexually involved with, like Minze Eisner, or to male friends like Max Brod and Robert Klopstock, are detached, humorous, reflective, and full of interest in the world around him. Some, like the letters to Minze, are irresistibly charming. The letters to Felice and Milena, on the other hand, display the self-torturing side of Kafka's personality. This means that apparently anti-Semitic utterances like the one quoted above, while undoubtedly revealing, should be read as outbursts whose chief target is Kafka himself, and certainly not as expressing his considered attitude to the Jewish problem.

One must therefore give all the more weight to Kafka's complex and tortured response to Hans Blüher's pamphlet *Secessio Judaica*, which he read in June 1922. He began drafting a review (T 582–3), but could not complete it because he felt himself not enough of a

Talmudist for the subtle task of separating Blüher's insights from his errors (cf. Br 380). The fragmentary review, in a cautious and even convoluted style, accepts at face value Blüher's claim to be an 'Antisemit' but not a 'Judenfeind', that is, to condemn the Jews on purely intellectual grounds without feeling any animus against them. In retrospect, this distinction looks spurious, and Blüher's work is indeed a very repellent little tract. Blüher writes as an enemy of the Weimar Republic, blaming its existence on the Jews, and declaring that the German Reich must be restored and the Jews extirpated. Their sole function in history was to prepare for the birth of Christ. Since they killed him, their guilt has rendered them sick, not just as individuals but as a people: 'Daher ist jeder Jude in der Substanz krank: was bei keinem anderen Volke vorkommt.'[93] Their effect on other nations has always been destructive, and at present their influence is corrupting the Germans by such means as socialism and Freudian psychology. Intermarriage between Jews and Germans must stop, since the two races cannot mix: 'Die Liebe der jüdischen Männer zu deutschen Frauen mag unantastbar sein, aber die Ehe zwischen ihnen geht gegen das deutsche Blutgesetz.'[94] In saying this, Blüher claims to be dispassionately stating an objective fact. The superior Jews have already recognized the necessity of a Jewish secession from Germany, and Zionism represents their best hope, for it may enable them to take root in the soil and find a historical future. Otherwise their prospects are gloomy: Blüher notes with approval the increase in anti-Semitism, the vogue of the swastika, and the Jews' alarm at these developments: 'Der psychische Hauptvorgang des Judentums ist die Angst.' He ends by foreseeing a 'Weltpogrom'.[95]

It would not take hindsight to be horrified by this book. Kafka must, however, have agreed with much of it. He knew that Blüher was right in pointing to an increase in anti-Semitism: he had witnessed anti-Semitic riots in Prague in November 1920 (M 288), read anti-Semitic tirades in the Czech press (M 291), and knew about the recently published *Protocols of the Elders of Zion* (Br 273).[96] The suppression of the Munich Soviet, which was largely led by Jews (Eugen Leviné, Gustav Landauer, Ernst Toller, Erich Mühsam), had already made him feel that Jews and Germans were incompatible (Br 274). He agreed that the Western Jew, besides being timorous, was sick (Br 417), that intermarriage was at least problematic, that Jews needed to regain contact with the soil, and that their best hope lay in Zionism. Though he did not of course share Blüher's German nationalism or his racialism, he did accept a large part of his diagnosis of the state of the Western Jews.

Long before he came across Blüher, however, Kafka had already reached a similar diagnosis and given it fictional expression in two stories which were published in *Der Jude* in October and November 1917 under the heading 'Zwei Tiergeschichten'. These stories, *Schakale und Araber* and *Ein Bericht für eine Akademie*, are both satires on the Western Jew from a Zionist standpoint, and were understood thus by contemporaries: in January 1918 Brod declared that *Ein Bericht* was the most brilliant satire ever written on Jewish assimilation.[97]

More recently, Jens Tismar has demonstrated, with examples from Hebbel, Grillparzer, and Stifter, that the jackal was an accepted image for the Diaspora Jew, who was seen as incapable of manual labour and confined to a parasitic existence at the expense of his host society, and has argued that Gordon's denunciation of the Western Jew as parasite in the opening number of *Der Jude* helped to prompt Kafka's use of the image in *Schakale und Araber*.[98] Kafka's jackals inhabit an Arab country, but detest the filthiness of the Arabs and, in particular, their habit of slaughtering animals instead of letting them die naturally: 'ruhig soll alles Getier krepieren; ungestört soll es von uns leergetrunken und bis auf die Knochen gereinigt werden. Reinheit, nichts als Reinheit wollen wir' (E 163). This appears to allude to the requirement that animals killed by a Jewish slaughterer should be allowed to bleed to death, and to the provisions for ritual purity in the Torah. The jackals further resemble Jews in following 'unserer alten Lehre' (E 161) and in having Messianic notions. They carry around with them a rusty pair of scissors which they present to every traveller, entreating him to cut the Arabs' throats with it and thus 'den Streit beenden, der die Welt entzweit' (E 163). This is a sceptical reference to the Messianic tradition which, as we shall see in Ch. 6, Kafka was to investigate much more deeply in *Das Schloß*. It fits in with the presentation of the jackals as parasites: they want some improvement in their condition, but are incapable of the self-reliance advocated by Gordon and expect a Messianic intervention to solve their problems.

Ein Bericht für eine Akademie is a more sharply focused satire with richly suggestive thematic implications, and has received a corresponding variety of interpretations. Walter Sokel has interpreted it, on a very general level, as portraying the process of civilization, in which the primitive, 'natural' instincts have to be sublimated into artificial social behaviour.[99] Like Nietzsche and Freud, Kafka stresses the pain involved in this process, starting with the two wounds that the ape received from his captors, one on the cheek and the other below the thigh. One might also recall Schiller's contention that civilization, in requiring human potential to be narrowed and specialized, has inflicted a wound on mankind: 'Die Kultur selbst war es, welche der neuern Menschheit diese Wunde schlug.'[100] Recently this *kulturgeschichtlich* interpretation has been taken further by Margot Norris. After describing how Nietzsche interpreted Darwin's idea of protective adaptation as a strategy serving the weak in their conflict with the strong, she argues that Kafka, in his account of the ape's adaptation to humanity, 'directly links animal mimicry and theatrical performance as evolutionary strategies in the struggle for survival'.[101]

What Norris overlooks, however, is that among Kafka's contemporaries the Darwinian term 'mimicry' was frequently applied to the process by which Jews assimilated to their host society, shedding their Jewish traits and assuming the manners of their environment in a form of protective camouflage which, it was hoped, would eventually become second nature. At the beginning of his diaries Herzl recalls how in 1893 he still believed that anti-Semitism would spur the Jews into merging with their environment by mimicry:

Erzogen wird man nur durch Härten. Es wird die Darwinsche Mimikry eintreten. Die Juden werden sich anpassen. Sie sind wie Seehunde, die der Weltzufall ins Wasser warf. Sie nahmen Gestalt und Eigenschaften von Fischen an, was sie doch nicht sind. Kommen sie nun wieder auf festes Land und dürfen da ein paar Generationen bleiben, so werden sie wieder aus ihren Flossen Füße machen.[102]

In his address to the First Zionist Congress, Nordau described scornfully the efforts of the emancipated Jew to fit into Western society by means of 'Mimicry'.[103] This gives us a historical context for Kafka's use of evolutionary imagery, and enables us to begin to recover the contemporary thrust of his satire. The interpretation I am about to develop need not conflict with the implied reflections on the history of culture which Sokel and Norris have found in the story, any more than with Gerhard Neumann's ingenious poetological reading of the story as a self-reflexive meditation on the possibility of mimesis.[103] These interpretations do not conflict because they do not intersect: they start from unrelated premises and deal with different aspects of the story. I cannot, however, accept those interpretations that see the ape as achieving some kind of triumph. Sokel, for example, has also placed the ape among Kafka's artist-figures, and argued that, unlike most of them, he does achieve a partially successful compromise with his public.[105] Such a reading misplaces the emphasis of the story and fails to notice its irony.

Kafka's satirical intention was picked up not only by his original readers but also by later interpreters, among them William C. Rubinstein, who suggested that Rotpeter represented an assimilated Jew and that his learning to drink schnaps symbolized Holy Communion and hence his conversion to Christianity.[106] Evelyn Torton Beck took up Rubinstein's interpretation in her book on Kafka and the Yiddish theatre, arguing that the ape was modelled on the figure of Berele, a converted Jew in one of the plays Kafka saw in the Café Savoy.[107] This is not a very plausible source, since Berele is driven into apostasy by the intolerance of the Hasidim, while Rotpeter is forcibly separated from his tribe by the Hagenbeck expedition. Nonetheless, I think this approach is correct and needs to be worked out in more detail. One might begin by relating the ape's original home on the Gold Coast not only to the myth of the Golden Age but to the primitive vitality which Western Zionists ascribed to the Eastern Jews. The ape's wound implies that, by contrast, the Jew in Western society is lamed or disabled. This is again a Zionist commonplace, but Kafka's satire goes further in hinting that the second wound, which the ape received 'unterhalb der Hüfte' (H 186), actually emasculated him. The ape interrupts his narrative at this point to reply to the journalistic charge that he still betrays his simian origins by taking his trousers down in public: 'Ich, ich darf meine Hosen ausziehen, vor wem es mir beliebt; man wird dort nichts finden als einen wohlgepflegten Pelz und die Narbe nach einem—wählen wir hier zu einem bestimmten Zweck ein bestimmtes Wort, das aber nicht mißverstanden werden wolle—die Narbe nach einem frevelhaften Schuß. Alles liegt offen zutage; nichts ist zu verbergen' (E 186). By the elaborate pedantry with which he insists that he has nothing to hide, the ape arouses the suspicion that something has been shot away, and that not too much should be made of his intimacy with the female chimpanzee of whom he later says, very vaguely, 'ich lasse es mir nach Affenart bei ihr wohlgehen' (E 196).

After his capture, the ape is put in a cage too narrow for him to stand upright or sit down, and he has to squat with his face to the wall, in a position suggesting that of the unassimilated Jew in Europe before emancipation: confined to a ghetto and refusing contact with the Gentile world outside. Thereafter he learns the rudiments of human behaviour—smoking and drinking schnaps—from the sailors, who give him the name Rotpeter, suggested by the red scar on his cheek. Though he finds the name repulsive and inappropriate, he has to accept it, and this not only conveys his helpless submission to his captors but also alludes to the recent history of Western Jews. One of the earliest stages in the emancipation of the German and Austrian Jews was legislation compelling them to assume family names instead of patronymics. Joseph II issued the first such edict in 1787. Attractive-sounding names like Rosenthal, Goldstein, or Demant had to be paid for, while poor Jews were often given ridiculous or offensive names. Walking through the Warsaw ghetto in 1924, Alfred Döblin noted the following names above shops: 'Waiselfisch, Klopfherd, Blumenkranz, Brandwain, Farsztandig, Goldkopf, Gelbfisch, Gutbesztand.'[108] Kafka himself mentions in his travel diaries a Bohemian Jew named Puderbeutel (T 676), and would have known of the Prague coal-dealer named Notdurft who eventually changed his name to Northof.[109]

On arriving at Hamburg, Rotpeter has to choose between the zoo and the music-hall. Since the zoo would be just another kind of ghetto, he opts for the music-hall and works feverishly to qualify himself for a theatrical career by attaining 'die Durchschnittsbildung eines Europäers' (E 195). He becomes a celebrity, and, in his own opinion, he has become human. But of course the reason for his fame is precisely that he is not human—he is an ape who has learnt to imitate a human being with astonishing faithfulness. Although his efforts have gained him admission to human society, he has not been accepted as a human being but rather as an alien with extraordinary imitative skill. The greater his fame, the further he is from real membership of humanity. This expresses Kafka's views about the situation of the Jew. The Jew can enter Western society only by adapting himself to its customs. If he can act his part skilfully enough, he will be allowed to mix with Gentiles, and he may imagine that his mimicry has been completely successful. But to the non-Jews around him it remains obvious that he is an actor, and they appreciate the act without being taken in by it. There is a Jewish figure of this type, Polledi, in Brod's first novel, *Schloß Nornepygge* (1908). Though he comes of a poor ghetto family, Polledi is accepted socially because he can adapt himself to any surroundings and because cultivated society welcomes him as a clown. In other words, he is tolerated as an entertainer, and in fact his talent for mimicry is so great that one of his most popular party tricks is to imitate Kainz and other actors— that is, to imitate imitators.[110]

Rotpeter and Polledi represent an image of the Western Jew common to Zionists and anti-Semites: the Jew is seen as lacking in 'depth', with no profound emotions, no imaginative resources, no traditional loyalties; he can slip into any disguise, simply because he himself is so shallow. What he does have is a ruthless determination to make his way in society by any available means. Houston Stewart Chamberlain claims that the distinguishing feature of the Jew is an abnormally developed will, and cites the example of a Jewish scholar who, unable to make money in his profession, became a soap-manufacturer until foreign competition put him out of business, after which he became a playwright and amassed a fortune. He owed his success not to any commercial or literary talent but to sheer force of will.[111] Wagner, in *Das Judentum in der Musik*, sketches a portrait of the educated Jew which would fit Rotpeter almost perfectly:

Der gebildete Jude hat sich die undenklichste Mühe gegeben, alle auffälligen Merkmale seiner niederen Glaubensgenossen von sich abzustreifen: in vielen Fällen hat er es selbst für zweckmäßig gehalten, durch die christliche Taufe auf die Verwischung aller Spuren seiner Abkunft hinzuwirken. Dieser Eifer hat den gebildeten Juden aber nie die erhofften Früchte gewinnen lassen wollen: er hat nur dazu geführt, ihn vollends zu vereinsamen, und ihn zum herzlosesten aller Menschen in einem Grade zu machen, daß wir selbst die frühere Sympathie für das tragische Geschick seines Stammes verlieren mußten. Für den Zusammenhang mit seinen ehemaligen Leidensgenossen, den er übermütig zerriß, blieb es ihm unmöglich, einen neuen Zusammenhang mit der Gesellschaft zu finden, zu welcher er sich aufschwang.[112]

In order to lose his simian characteristics, Rotpeter has made just such exertions as Wagner describes; and his attitude to other apes is as callous as the attitude to other Jews which Wagner ascribes to the assimilant. He refers with hostility to the trained 'Affentier' Peter who has recently 'krepiert' (significant choice of word!) in order to stress the gulf that supposedly separates them (E 186). He is almost as callous towards the half-trained female chimpanzee with whom he spends his nights: during the day he cannot stand the sight of her, obviously because she reminds him of what he really is. She and Peter are merely trained, but Rotpeter speaks of himself in human terms as having studied ('ich lernte', E 194) and calls his instructors teachers rather than trainers. Here we can recognize the painful sensitivity with which assimilated Jews reacted to the embarrassing behaviour of the less assimilated.

It is certainly disturbing to find Kafka using so deliberately offensive an image as that of the ape to represent the Western Jew, especially as we cannot play down *Ein Bericht* as an unpremeditated outburst. To gain the appropriate perspective on the story, and on *Schakale und Araber*, we need to realize that they belong to a group of works by Jewish writers who use animal imagery, often degrading in its implications, to express their ambivalent feelings about the Jewish people. One example is well known, Heine's poem 'Prinzessin Sabbat', which tells of a prince named Israel who has been transformed into a dog and lives in squalor during the week but is temporarily restored to human shape on the Sabbath:

> Hund mit hündischen Gedanken,
> Kötert er die ganze Woche
> Durch des Lebens Kot und Kehricht,
> Gassenbuben zum Gespötte.
>
> Aber jeden Freitag Abend,
> In der Dämmrungstunde, plötzlich
> Weicht der Zauber, und der Hund
> Wird aufs neu' ein menschlich Wesen.
>
> Mensch mit menschlichen Gefühlen,
> Mit erhobnem Haupt und Herzen,
> Festlich, reinlich schier gekleidet,
> Tritt er in des Vaters Halle.[113]

In the present context it is worth stressing the contrast Heine draws between the dog's canine thoughts and his human feelings. During the week, we gather, the Jew has to employ his intellect in the struggle to make a living, so that the determination and rationality for which H. S. Chamberlain later censured the Jews are forced on him by his circumstances. But it is his emotions that make him truly human, though he can only indulge them on the Sabbath. Thus Heine is anticipating by some sixty years the Zionists' polemic against the stereotype of the rational Jew. His defence of the Jews is qualified, though, by the bitter little phrase 'reinlich schier gekleidet' ('dressed almost cleanly'): by this hint that even on the Sabbath the Jew cannot be completely clean, Heine reveals his own ambivalence towards his fellow-Jews. As S. S. Prawer has recently said: 'It is a portrait from the outside, an unassimilated Jew partially seen by a Europeanized observer.'[114]

'Prinzessin Sabbat' helped to inspire the allegorical novel *Di kliatshe* (1873) by the classic Yiddish writer Mendele Moykher Sforim.[115] This great satire has two targets: the misery in which the Jews in the Russian Pale of Settlement are kept by their oppressors, and the bookish ineffectuality of the *Maskilim* who try to improve their condition through educational projects instead of social reforms. Its protagonist, Ishrulik, is a clever boy who resolves to escape from the Jews' misery by studying at university. The chapter in which he makes this resolution is headed 'Ishrulik vil veren a mentsh' ('Ishrulik wants to become a human being'), with a double-edged irony: Mendele means that the Jews' condition is unworthy of human beings, but Ishrulik means that his fellow-Jews are subhuman and that he must make his way in Gentile society if he is to enter humanity. He is as callous a social climber as Rotpeter. As befits an educated man, however, he belongs to the Society for the Prevention of Cruelty to Animals, so when he finds some boys tormenting a skinny, broken-down mare, he makes a—characteristically ineffectual—intervention. When left alone with Ishrulik, the mare speaks to him, citing the precedent of Balaam's ass to reduce his astonishment, and reveals that she is a prince who has been transformed into a mare by sorcery and has roamed the world ever since, acquiring the sobriquet 'di eyvige kliatshe' (as it were, 'The Wandering Mare'), and suffering incessant exploitation and maltreatment at the hands of the righteous. In giving this satiric account of the Jewish fate in the Diaspora, Mendele is not trying, any more than Heine or Kafka, to paint a flattering picture of the Jews: his word *kliatshe*, 'mare', could also be translated 'nag'. However, he shows clearly that if the Jews are wretched, it is their Gentile persecutors who have made them so.

The genre of the Jewish animal fable still survives, a recent and brilliant example being 'The Evolution of the Jews', a story narrated in the first person by a Yiddish-speaking giraffe, in Clive Sinclair's *Hearts of Gold* (1979). All four works, by Heine, Mendele, Kafka and Sinclair, express their authors' ambivalent feelings towards the Jews, though with some obvious differences in the direction of the satire: Mendele's mare and Heine's dog represent the ghetto Jew, while Kafka's ape stands for the supposedly assimilated Jew of the same type as Mendele's Ishrulik. The three prose works all use self-betraying first-person narrative, a stand-by of satirists which is also employed in the animal stories by Hoffmann which were among Kafka's sources.[116] Like the dog, the mare, and the giraffe, the ape who delivers his report to the academy is the repository for complex and ambivalent feelings which make it implausible that Kafka should ever have been a straightforwardly uncritical partisan of Zionism.

Kafka's distanced and undogmatic attitude to Zionism is apparent in his remark to Felice, in his letter of 12 September 1916:

Wie Du mit dem Zionismus zurechtkommst, das ist Deine Sache, jede Auseinandersetzung (Gleichgiltigkeit wird also ausgeschlossen) zwischen Dir und ihm, wird mich freuen. Jetzt läßt sich darüber noch nicht sprechen, solltest Du aber Zionistin einmal Dich fühlen [. . .] und dann erkennen, daß ich kein Zionist bin—so würde es sich bei einer Prüfung wohl ergeben—dann fürchte ich mich nicht und auch Du mußt Dich nicht fürchten, Zionismus ist nicht etwas, was Menschen trennt, die es gut meinen. (F 697–8.)

Evidently Kafka regarded the Zionist movement as capacious enough to accommodate people with many different aims, provided they were basically in agreement. Zionism formed a medium in which the individual could enjoy a vital relationship with a larger community, even if his position were as marginal as Kafka's. What separated him from the majority of Zionists was his conviction that the new community that Zionism was trying to create must have a religious foundation. Practical endeavours, such as the work in the Volksheim which he urged upon Felice, struck him as valuable not only for their immediate results but for their spiritual effects. Encouraging Felice in her work, he wrote:

Es ist, soviel ich sehe, der absolut einzige Weg oder die Schwelle des Weges, der zu einer geistigen Befreiung führen kann. Und zwar früher für die Helfer, als für die, welchen geholfen wird. (F 696–7.)

This explains why he was so eager to hear about a lecture delivered by Lehmann on 'Das Problem der jüdisch-religiösen Erziehung',[117] which seemed to him the central issue, the 'Kernfrage' (F 694), which Zionists would never be able to avoid for long. It also helps to explain the strong and characteristically eclectic interest in religion which he displays at this period. In the summer of 1916 he studied the Old Testament, making notes from it in his diary and adding the Delphic comment: 'Nur das Alte Testament sieht—nichts darüber noch sagen' (T 504). At the same time he was reading an anthropological study of primitive religion, *Das Werden des Gottesglaubens* by Nathan Söderblom, a prominent theologian of the time, and noting down the ways in which African and Australian tribes had imagined the founders of their religions (T 500–1).

More about Kafka's highly individual attitude to Zionism, and the relation he perceived between religion and society, can be inferred from *Beim Bau der chinesischen Mauer*, which was written in March or April 1917 and inaugurates a series of works in which Kafka examines the position of his hero, or his narrator, on the fringes of a community, and reflects on the sources of social cohesion. The elaborately structured society of *Das Schloß*, the 'Hundeschaft' of *Forschungen eines Hundes*, and the 'Volk der Mäuse' in which Josefine enjoys such an ambiguous position, are the most salient examples of communities in Kafka's later works. Like the *kulturgeschichtlich* implications of *Ein Bericht*, Kafka's reflections in *Beim Bau der chinesischen Mauer* have a bearing which goes beyond the specific subject of his story, but I wish to argue that, as one would expect at this period, he is concerned in *Beim Bau* not only with society in general but with Jewish societies in particular. Like the narrator-dog in *Forschungen eines Hundes*, the narrator of *Beim Bau* is sufficiently detached from his society to question the very principles on which it is founded. However, since he also recognizes that such questioning risks undermining the foundations of social cohesion, he never presses his inquiries to a conclusion. His meditation falls into two parts, in each of which he examines one of the institutions that keep Chinese society united: first, the building of the Great Wall, and then the belief in the Emperor. Each of these institutions proves on inquiry to be based on a paradox.

The narrator is apparently the only person to wonder what is the purpose of the wall and why it has been constructed piecemeal, in scattered sections which were gradually linked up. The wall is officially supposed to protect China from incursions by the northern nomads; yet China is so vast that most of it, including the south-eastern region where the narrator lives, could never be reached by invaders, and in any case the system of piecemeal construction means that the wall can afford no protection until it is complete. The narrator surmises, therefore, that this system was intended to give the builders a ready sense of achievement. Groups of some twenty workers were set to building a five-hundred-metre stretch of wall which, after five years, could be linked up to an adjacent section. While still flushed with satisfaction, the builders were promptly sent off to begin constructing another segment in another region. Their commitment to the 'Volkswerk' (B 70) gave both the builders and the rest of the population a feeling of national solidarity:

Jeder Landmann war ein Bruder, für den man eine Schutzmauer baute, und der mit allem, was er hatte und war, sein Leben lang dafür dankte. Einheit! Einheit! Brust an Brust, ein Reigen des Volkes, Blut, nicht mehr eingesperrt im kärglichen Kreislauf des Körpers, sondern süß rollend und doch wiederkehrend durch das unendliche China. (B 71.)

The ideal of work recalls Gordon's article 'Arbeit', while words like 'Blut', 'Volk' and 'Einheit' belong to the customary rhetoric of *Der Jude*. Kafka seems to imply that communal activities like those demanded by Gordon are less important in themselves than as means of fostering a sense of national unity, which can be served just as well by impractical projects like the piecemeal construction of the wall. There is a sinister suggestion, too, that the wall was intended to serve as the foundation of a new Tower of Babel: that is, national sentiment could be abused for despotic or sacrilegious purposes. But even if the wall's real purpose is not its ostensible one, that does not mean that it is a mere deception, invented to generate a spurious sense of community, like the permanent warfare in Orwell's *Nineteen Eighty-Four*. For the narrator then reveals that the wall was planned by an unknown 'Führerschaft' (B 72), and conjectures that these leaders have no mortal existence but that both they and the project for building the wall have existed from time immemorial. Although he cautiously refrains from speculating any further, the suggestion he leaves is that the physical building of the wall corresponds to a mysterious, timeless reality. The practical value of the project is dubious, perhaps illusory, but its real purpose is to arouse a sense of nationhood whose basis is ultimately religious. It is noteworthy that the narrator describes the meaning behind the system of piecemeal building as 'eine Kernfrage des ganzen Mauerbaues' (B 71), for, as we have seen, Kafka considered the relation between nationalism and religion the 'Kernfrage' which Zionism had to face (F 694). *Beim Bau der chinesischen Mauer* explores this question and indicates that although Kafka was disinclined to accept nationalist rhetoric at its face value, he did subscribe to the ideal of a *Gemeinschaft* founded on religion.

From the significance of the Great Wall the narrator passes to the question of the Emperor. So vast is the Empire that nobody in the narrator's province has visited Peking or even knows which Emperor is on the throne. People cannot distinguish between history and legend, and even the orthography used in the next province strikes them as archaic. No message from the Emperor can ever reach a subject; instead, one must invent the message for oneself: 'Du aber sitzt an Deinem Fenster und erträumst sie Dir, wenn der Abend kommt' (B 79). People's faith in the existence of the Emperor is therefore weak, but the paradox is that, since this faith is equally weak in every one of China's five hundred provinces, its very weakness helps to unite the Chinese people: it is 'geradezu der Boden, auf dem wir leben' (B 83), and to criticize this state of affairs would shake the very foundations of their society.

In both parts of the story there are a number of veiled allusions to the Jewish people. The most obvious one comes at the beginning, where we learn that the wall is the work of two great armies of labourers, 'des Ost- und des Westheeres' (B 67), a clear reference to the Eastern and Western Jews ('Ost- und Westjuden'). The Chinese are imagined as a religious people of exceptional moral purity ('Sittenreinheit', B 82), which suggests the ideals of Judaism. The 'Führerschaft' whose plans for building the wall have been in existence 'seit jeher' (B 76) may have been suggested to Kafka by the Jewish legend, known to him from his reading, which compares the Lord to an architect and the Torah to the plans he followed in building the world, and which says that, since no writing materials existed before the creation, the Torah was inscribed on the arm of the Lord.[118] What clinches the matter, however, is the image of the wall itself. From his reading in Jewish history Kafka had learnt that the rabbis who insisted on the authority of the oral tradition, codified as the Talmud, as an indispensable supplement to the Torah, did so partly in order to keep out foreign influences during the Hellenistic period, and that their watchword was: 'Machet einen Zaun um die Thora!'[119] The Talmud was intended as such a protective fence. Kafka knew also that Jewish communities in Eastern Europe were surrounded by literal barriers. Since orthodox Jews were forbidden to carry burdens outside their dwellings on the Sabbath, each town or village was surrounded by a wire, called an *ayruv*, so that the whole town could be legally defined as a single dwelling. Löwy informed Kafka that the pious Jews of Warsaw had bribed the telecommunications engineers to link up the telephone and telegraph wires around the city to form a complete circle which constituted an *ayruv*, so that for the orthodox Jew the whole of Warsaw was legally a single house (T 178). This supports Clement Greenberg's suggestion that the Great Wall is intended as an allusion to the Talmud and that the story is, among other things, a criticism of the Jews for cutting themselves off from history.[120] The image of the Great Wall of China would readily suggest itself for this purpose. In German the word 'Chinese' can mean 'somebody who is cut off or behind the times', as when Nietzsche refers to Kant as 'der große Chinese von Königsberg'.[121] Otto Weininger, in *Geschlecht und Charakter*, had already drawn a comparison between the Jews and the Chinese.[122] Later the image of the Great Wall was independently applied to the Torah and the Talmud by Arnold Zweig in 'Das ostjüdische Antlitz': referring to the orthodox Jews' meticulous observance of the law, he says: 'Jede seelische Vorsichtsregel ist hier erlaubt, wo es gilt, das Gebäude, die chinesische Mauer um das Volk, zu stützen.'[123]

These allusions and analogues strongly imply that Kafka is criticizing the Jews' remoteness from history. They lead 'ein Leben, das unter keinem gegenwärtigen Gesetze steht und nur der Weisung und Warnung gehorcht, die aus alten Zeiten zu uns herüberreicht' (B 82). But Kafka complicates matters not only by the obliquity of his allusions but by employing the technique of superimposing different historical epochs on one another which we observed earlier in *Der neue Advokat*. If the references just discussed evoke the compilation of the Talmud, which took place in the post-exilic centuries, the repeated emphasis on the vastness of China and on the huge expanses separating one region from another seems to apply rather to Jewish life in the Diaspora. In saying that the general uncertainty about the Emperor's existence forms the 'Boden' on which the Chinese live, Kafka appears to be picking up the metaphorical use of the word 'Boden' in the vocabulary of Zionism, which has already been amply illustrated, and hinting that the very insecurity of life in the Diaspora is the Jews' substitute for a truly firm foundation to their lives. At the same time, the initial reference to the Eastern and Western armies of labourers suggests the co-operation of Eastern and Western Jews in the Zionist movement. Confusing though this technique of superimposition is, it corresponds to Kafka's theme in that it forces the reader to experience the blurring of the past and the present which is supposed to dominate the minds of the Chinese. The story evokes huge, dim vistas of time as well as of space. This atmosphere of uncertainty is strengthened even by the pronouns used, for the narrator speaks sometimes of 'wir', sometimes of 'man', rarely of 'ich', and the legend about the message from the Emperor is addressed to an unspecified 'du'.

Beim Bau der chinesischen Mauer appears, therefore, to be a sustained meditation on the sources of social cohesion, with particular reference to the history of the Jews. Insofar as it approaches any conclusion, its message is that the bases of society are religious, perhaps mystical, at any rate beyond the reach of the rational investigator. This perhaps helps to explain why Kafka kept himself aloof from the strictly political activities of the Prague Zionists and told Felice cryptically that Zionism was 'nur der Eingang zu dem Wichtigern' (F 675). What was more important for him was the rediscovery of a possible religious basis for a community. Accordingly, just as in 1911–12 he has disregarded the theorizings of the Bar Kochba and instead immersed himself in the living culture of the Eastern Jews, so during the war years he remained at a distance from politics and found out all he could about the religious life of the Eastern Jews and especially about Hasidism.

Kafka's main guide in this exploration was Jiří (Georg) Langer, whose importance in Kafka's life has hitherto been largely over-looked.[124] They were introduced by their common friend Brod early in 1915, though Kafka had already had dealings with Langer's brother František, who later became an important Czech dramatist, and who published some translations from *Betrachtung* in 1914 (Br 127). The Langers were an entirely assimilated, Czech-speaking Jewish family in Prague, and Jiří's upbringing was as secular as Kafka's. In his teens, however, he had become fascinated by Judaism. He learnt Hebrew, studied the Talmud, and in 1913, at the age of nineteen, he went off to Belz, a small town in Galicia which had been the seat of a dynasty of Hasidic *tsaddikim* for almost a century. Belz was one of the chief centres of Hasidism: Langer himself calls it the Jewish Rome.[125] The Belzer Rabbi was excep-tionally conservative, and the Hasidim of Belz were famous for their ritual strictness and their long, curling ear-locks. Langer joined the court of their current leader, Issachar Dov Rokeah, where he learnt to speak Yiddish, studied the Talmud in the *bet ha-midrash* ('study house') with the Hasidim, and took part in the ritual dances. When he returned home after a few months in Belz, he was wearing ear-locks and a kaftan, to his family's horror, and carried his obedience to Hasidic customs so far that he refused to look any woman, even his mother, in the face. By the time he met Kafka, Langer had relaxed his rigour somewhat, though he still dressed as a Hasid: he is presumably the person referred to in Kafka's diary as 'G. im Kaftan' and 'der Westjude, der sich den Chassidim assimiliert hat' (T 468). Langer had been called up for military service, but was discharged in

1915 because his adherence to orthodox Jewish ways made him refuse obstinately to do any work on a Saturday. After that he spent much of the war in the company of the Belzer Rabbi, who had been forced to flee to Hungary by the Russian invasion. Langer was learned not only in the Talmud and in Hasidic tradition, but also in the Cabbala; after the war he taught at the Jewish College in Prague and immersed himself in the study of Freudian psychoanalysis, the outcome of which was a curious book entitled *Die Erotik der Kabbala* (1923) and papers in *Imago* on the psychoanalytical significance of the *mezuzah* and the phylactery. He also produced, in 1929, a volume of Hebrew poetry which was the first Hebrew book to be published in Prague for a century, and, in 1937, a collection of Hasidic legends, written in Czech and later translated into English as *Nine Gates*. In 1939 he managed to escape from the Nazis by boat down the Danube and thence to Palestine, but the hardships of the journey permanently injured his health, and he died in Tel Aviv in 1943.

The reminiscences of Kafka which Langer published in Israel in 1941, and which have been retrieved and made available by Anne Oppenheimer, confirm that the two were close friends. After Kafka had mastered Hebrew they used to hold their conversations in that language: 'We always spoke Hebrew in the last time we had together. He, who always repeated and vowed that he was not a Zionist, studied our language in his middle age, and studied it devotedly. And unlike the other Prague Zionists, he was soon speaking Hebrew fluently.'[126] Langer adds the engaging detail that Kafka was always delighted to find that Hebrew had a word for some twentieth-century object such as an aeroplane. It is likely, though, that some of their conversation was about more esoteric matters, for Kafka records in his diary some Hasidic legends and traditions which he had heard from Langer (T 482–4). These probably represent only a fraction of what he learnt from Langer, for it may be doubted whether there was anybody in Prague, and more than a handful of people in Western Europe, who knew as much as Langer about Hasidism and the Cabbala.

Besides giving Kafka information, Langer brought him and Brod into contact with Hasidic *tsaddikim*. One of these was the Grodeker Rabbi, a refugee from Galicia, who was living with his followers in the working-class Prague suburb of Žižkov. Life seemed to be imitating art, for Kafka, Brod, and Langer, like Josef K. on his visit to Titorelli, had to make their way through swarms of children on the pavement and the stairs and along a badly lit corridor to the room where the Rabbi and his circle were praying. The Rabbi looked unkempt and none too clean, yet impressed Kafka by his 'väterliche[s] Wesen' (T 478), suggesting that—like Langer, perhaps—Kafka looked to such figures for a more endurable paternal authority than he himself had experienced. On the way home, however, Kafka remarked coolly: 'Genau genommen war es etwa so wie bei einem wilden afrikanischen Volksstamm. Krasser Aberglauben.'[125]

A similarly ambivalent response is discernible in the long letter to Brod in which Kafka describes Langer's spiritual master, the Belzer Rabbi, who was staying with his attendants in Marienbad, where Kafka and Felice had been spending a holiday, in July 1916. Kafka stayed on for another ten days after Felice's departure, and sent her an excited postcard announcing the Rabbi's presence and describing him as 'den höchsten Kurgast von Marienbad' (F 666). The letter to Brod begins with the prudent admission that Kafka cannot convey the spiritual truth embodied by the Rabbi, but can only describe the superficial details he has been able to observe: 'Mehr als Kleinigkeiten kann man mit bloßem Auge dort, wo Wahrheit ist, nicht sehn' (Br 142). This is presumably intended to forestall Brod from reacting to the account of the Rabbi in the same way as Josef K. reacted to the unappealing functionaries of the Court. After this warning, there follows a minute account of an evening walk through Marienbad undertaken by the Rabbi with about ten followers, among them Kafka and Langer, during which the Rabbi asks numerous naïve-sounding questions about the buildings they pass and his acolytes supply him officiously with information. Though Kafka insists that the Rabbi does not make at all a ridiculous impression, the letter certainly treats the antics of his followers with tongue-in-cheek irony. The Rabbi was a big, broad-shouldered man, aged 62 at this time, blind in one eye and with the long side-locks characteristic of Belz. The impression he made on Kafka was one of dignity, even majesty, and Kafka assures Brod that his questions are of the kind that heads of state ask to put their subjects at their ease (Br 145). The letter unfortunately breaks off before the end of the description, but there is enough to indicate that Kafka's attitude to the Rabbi, though less extravagantly expressed, was remarkably similar to Buber's response to the sight of the *tsaddik* of Sadagora.

Kafka's interest in Hasidism did not make him want to participate in Jewish religious practice: his early upbringing, as we saw in Ch. 1,

had estranged him much too thoroughly from the half-hearted ceremonies of Western Judaism. He seldom went to the synagogue except
to attend weddings, and these ceremonies seemed to him 'nichts als
Märchennachahmung' (Br 137, cf. F 255). 'Es fällt mir nicht ein, in
den Tempel zu gehn', he told Felice in September 1916 (F 700). A
year earlier, the sight of Eastern Jews on their way to attend the evening service on Yom Kippur had briefly made him feel that it was
suicidal not to accompany them (T 479), but his one voluntary visit to
the synagogue recorded from this period was to hear a lecture on the
Mishnah (T 488). His attraction to Hasidism was part of a more
general interest in Jewish tradition, and, as one would expect from
the character of his own writing, he paid special attention to the folk-
tales of the Eastern Jews. Although Hasidic legends transmitted to the
West by Buber had repelled Kafka by the mannered style in which
Buber had retold them, he admired Buber's later, more plainly narrated collection *Der große Maggid und seine Nachfolge* (1922). His
discovery of the Jewish folk-tale, however, occurred during the war
years. In November 1916 we find him recommending Perets's
Volkstümliche Erzählungen (1913) to Felice as a good book to read to the
children in the Volksheim (F 713). Besides Perets's stories, which are
Kunstmärchen rather than authentic folk-tales, he read the legends
retold by Micha Josef bin Gorion and the *Sagen polnischer Juden*
translated from Yiddish by Alexander Eliasberg. He also read the
Hasidic tales published in the Jewish press, about which he wrote to
Brod in September 1917: 'die chassidischen Geschichten im
Jüdischen Echo sind vielleicht nicht die besten, aber alle diese
Geschichten sind, ich verstehe es nicht, das einzige Jüdische, in
welchem ich mich, unabhängig von meiner Verfassung, gleich und
immer zuhause fühle' (Br 172-3). As Anne Oppenheimer has shown,
the themes of these short, simply told anecdotes are close to those of the
aphorisms Kafka wrote during the winter of 1917–18.[128] They turn on
the discrepancy between the physical and the spiritual worlds, showing that the apparent evil of the former must be accepted as a
necessary part of the divine plan being carried out within the latter
and beyond the comprehension of mankind. Motifs from all these
groups of stories appear in Kafka's fiction of this period. He also
drew on Jewish traditions closer to home, for early in 1916 we find in
the diaries two attempts at a story about the Golem, the man made
out of clay by the Exalted Rabbi Löw of Prague (T 497–8.).[129] But
the main product of his interest in Hasidic and other traditions at this

time is the story *Ein Landarzt*, written in January or February 1917.

Ein Landarzt, one of Kafka's richest and most perplexing stories, focuses most obviously on the problem of responsibility. The country doctor is torn between professional and private obligations. He is urgently required by a patient ten miles away, but he also becomes gradually conscious of a different kind of duty to his maidservant, 'dieses schöne Mädchen, das jahrelang, von mir kaum beachtet, in meinem Hause lebte' (E 150). Kafka uses word-play to equate the two obligations: the patient's wound is pink ('rosa'), and Rosa is the name of the maidservant. The choice between his conflicting responsibilities is forced on the doctor by the mysterious horses who emerge from a disused pigsty in his courtyard to replace his own horse which has just died, and carry him off instantaneously to his patient. Along with them a stable-boy also appears from the pigsty, a brutal character who promptly assaults Rosa, leaving teeth-marks in her cheek, and stays behind to complete his conquest. One can see this figure as a projection of the doctor's physical nature, since only his behaviour makes the doctor aware that Rosa is sexually attractive; her name is not even mentioned until the stable-boy uses it. But no sooner has he realized this than the horses sweep him away, leaving Rosa un-protected.

On reaching his patient, the doctor can find nothing wrong with him till a neigh from the horses which is somehow 'höhern Orts angeordnet' (E 150) draws his attention to a huge wound, swarming with worms, in or near the boy's right thigh. This seems to be more than a physical wound, for it is called a 'Blume' and a 'schöne Wunde', and the doctor implies that many people long for such a wound but never receive one: 'Viele bieten ihre Seite an und hören kaum die Hacke im Forst, geschweige denn, daß sie ihnen näher kommt' (E 152). Like the wound inflicted on Gregor Samsa by the apple which festers in his back, it incapacitates the victim for ordinary human life but may conceivably admit him to some other form of existence. Not that the boy welcomes his wound: he wants to be saved, but the doctor is unequal to the task. The wound appears to be a metaphysical one requiring abilities different from those of the doctor, who is no 'Weltverbesserer' (E 149); he serves his patients conscientiously, but he cannot take the place of the priest whose authority no one (including the priest himself) believes in any longer:

So sind die Leute in meiner Gegend. Immer das Unmögliche vom Arzt verlangen. Den alten Glauben haben sie verloren; der Pfarrer sitzt zu Hause

und zerzupft die Meßgewänder, eines nach dem andern; aber der Arzt soll
alles leisten mit seiner zarten chirurgischen Hand. (E 151.)

Here the story opens out to reveal a theory of cultural decline familiar
not only from Kafka but from many other writers. There is a striking
parallel in Ibsen's *The Wild Duck*, where the pastor is a drunkard and
the only substitute for the lost spiritual sustenance is provided by Dr
Relling, who strengthens the other characters' self-respect by means
of the life-lie. In Kafka's story, too, the doctor is being called upon to
fill the church's role in supplying the community with spiritual
strength. However, being only a doctor, he fails in his mission. The
villagers place him in the boy's bed, but he eventually sneaks away in
the hope of returning home as rapidly as he came, only to find that
the horses no longer move with miraculous speed but drag his cart
through the snow as wearily as old men. Facing the prospect of freez-
ing to death in the snowy waste, he alleges that the summons was
itself faulty, a 'Fehlläuten der Nachtglocke' (E 153).

The role of the spiritual healer, which the doctor cannot fill, has its
sources in two figures encountered by Kafka in his reading: the
Christian saint and the Hasidic *tsaddik*. The doctor has a saintly
prototype in the *Légende de St Julien l'Hospitalier* by Flaubert, one of
Kafka's favourite authors, in which the saint's culminating act of self-
sacrifice is to get into bed with a leper who, fortunately, turns into
Jesus Christ and carries Julien heavenwards in his arms.[130] By contrast, the doctor is a failed saint; and he is also a failed *tsaddik*. The
analogy between the *tsaddik* and a physician occurs frequently in
Kafka's reading; he would, for example, certainly have known the
articles by S. A. Horodetzky, 'Vom Gemeinschaftsleben der
Chassidim', which had appeared in *Der Jude* a month or two before
Kafka wrote this story, and in which Horodetzky illustrates the
spiritual authority of a *tsaddik* by quoting the words of a pupil of the
Ba'al Shem:

Ein treuer Arzt, der seinen Patienten liebt und ihm volle Heilung bringen
will, muß vorerst die Wunden und kranken Glieder bloßlegen. Erst dann
kann er mit der Heilung beginnen. Ebenso ist es mit der Zurechtweisung.
Wer dem Gebote: Liebe deinen Nächsten wie dich selbst, nachleben will,
muß die kranken Stellen, die Gebrechen der Seele aufdecken, um eine
Heilung für sie zu finden.[131]

The analogy between the physician and the spiritual guide was important in Hasidism: indeed, the two were often identified, and the

Ba'al Shem and his successors were credited with both physical and spiritual healing powers. One of the stories in Eliasberg's *Sagen polnischer Juden*, 'Von der Macht des Arztes', speaks of the physician's spiritual power and says that every physician is accompanied by an angel.[132] Kafka's doctor lacks this dimension: he is a conscientious employee of the state, an 'Amtsarzt' who is 'vom Bezirk angestellt' E 153, 149), but no more, and his deficiency is indicated by the words 'retten' and 'Rettung', which Kafka elsewhere uses with the meaning 'salvation' (T 320, Br 340, H 83). The patient's question 'Wirst du mich retten?' (E 151) superficially refers to a physical cure, but it is also an inquiry about the doctor's spiritual powers to which the doctor immediately supplies a mental negative. Left alone with the patient, he decides: 'Aber jetzt war es Zeit, an meine Rettung zu denken' (E 153), using the word only in its physical sense, and he seizes his clothes and makes his escape.

Other motifs in the story are also Hasidic. That of the miraculous journey occurs in two of Eliasberg's stories: 'Auferweckung einer toten Braut', in which the Ba'al Shem travels from his home to Berlin in a single night, and 'Rasche Reise nach Wien', in which a rabbi makes an even faster journey—from Mogilev in White Russia to Vienna in two hours.[133] Uncontrollable horses appear in 'Der zerstörte Sabbat' in Buber's *Legende des Baalschem*.[134] All these Hasidic borrowings contribute to the story's atmosphere of concentrated mystery, as do the darkness of the setting and the robust physicality of the unearthly intruders. This is Kafka's closest approach to the world of Isaac Bashevis Singer, who also has an intense and eclectic interest in Jewish tradition. The demons who populate Singer's supernatural stories, and occasionally narrate them (as in 'The Destruction of Kreshev' and 'The Last Demon'), similarly belong to a world in which earthly realities are continuous with the unearthly.

Ein Landarzt also resembles Singer's stories in its headlong pace. Kafka maintains the tempo by letting the first-person narrator adopt the present tense after about a page, and the story remains almost entirely in the present, apart from the few sentences describing the doctor's departure from his patient's house. As Dorrit Cohn has shown, this means that the doctor's reflections (e.g. 'So sind die Leute in meiner Gegend [. . .]', E 151), which belong properly to the time at which he is telling the story, are absorbed into the rapid flow of the narrative.[135] Kafka's use of tenses is even more ambiguous than Cohn remarks, however, for when the narrative re-enters the present tense in the closing sentences, Kafka blurs the distinction between past, present, and future in a way that recalls the technique of superimposition which we observed in *Der neue Advokat* and *Beim Bau der chinesischen Mauer*:

Niemals komme ich so nach Hause; meine blühende Praxis ist verloren; ein Nachfolger bestiehlt mich, aber ohne Nutzen, denn er kann mich nicht ersetzen; in meinem Hause wütet der ekle Pferdeknecht; Rosa ist sein Opfer; ich will es nicht ausdenken. Nackt, dem Froste dieses unglückseligsten Zeitalters ausgesetzt, mit irdischem Wagen, unirdischen Pferden, treibe ich alter Mann mich umher. (E 153.)

The resumption of the present tense means that these sentences seem both to continue narrating events in what would normally be the past, and also to belong to the fictional present in which the narrator tells the story. Moreover, the first clause, 'Niemals komme ich so nach Hause', almost certainly has a future meaning (i.e. 'I shall never get home at this rate'), so that in the rest of the sentence the doctor could either be foretelling what is likely to happen, or describing what is happening in the present. Nor can we tell whether the present-tense verbs are active or stative—that is, whether they refer to actions which are links in a chain of events (as in the main narrative), or to states which could continue indefinitely. If the latter, then the doctor's exposure to the frost has become a permanent state of affairs, as the metaphor in 'Froste dieses unglückseligsten Zeitalters' also implies. Having been summoned away from his mundane existence and given a task too great for his strength, the doctor is now abandoned to the spiritual winter from which his devotion to routine had previously sheltered him.

In *Ein Landarzt*, then, Kafka drew on Western and Hasidic sources to express the responsibility which had fallen to ill-equipped individuals in an age of religious decline. The story presents the problem vividly, but supplies no solutions; nor do any of the other stories which were published as *Ein Landarzt: Kleine Erzählungen* in 1919 and which were originally to have borne the title *Verantwortung*. His fiction of the war years left Kafka with a number of unanswered questions, of which two are salient. How was it possible to reconstitute society on a religious basis? And how was the isolated individual to carry out his unavoidable responsibilities towards the rest of the community? The last winter of the war gave him an opportunity to think these problems through in the seclusion of Zürau, and the literary medium in which he did so was not, for the most part, fiction, but principally the philosophical aphorism. The large body of aphoristic writing which Kafka composed in Zürau, and which has hitherto received far too little attention from Kafka scholars, must be the subject of the next chapter.

5

Reflections from a Damaged Life
The Zürau Aphorisms, 1917–1918

EARLY on the morning of 13 August 1917 Kafka woke up and found himself spitting blood. It was a haemorrhage, the first sign of what was diagnosed a few weeks later as pulmonary tuberculosis. Kafka seems to have taken the news very calmly; he mentioned in a letter to his sister Ottla that since the haemorrhage he had been sleeping well and his almost unbearable headaches had disappeared (O 40). His employers granted him extended sick-leave, and on 12 September he left Prague for the village of Zürau (now Siřem) in north-western Bohemia, where Ottla was living and working on a farm belonging to the family of their brother-in-law Karl Hermann. He stayed there until April the following year, except for a brief visit to Prague at the end of October and a longer one over the Christmas and New Year period.

The immediate effect of tuberculosis was to make Kafka feel healthier. During his first weeks in Zürau he rapidly put on weight and felt his illness 'mehr als Schutzengel denn als Teufel' (Br 168). He spent as much time in the fresh air as the weather permitted, lying in the autumn sun, working in Ottla's vegetable garden, or going for walks in which he was only slightly hampered by shortness of breath. Writing to Milena in 1920, he looked back to the Zürau period as the happiest of his life (M 36), and this is confirmed by the long, lively, humorous letters he sent to his friends in Prague. There were of course drawbacks to life in the country: noise, to which Kafka was acutely sensitive, persisted there—the farm animals emitted 'das gesammelte Geschrei der Arche Noah' (Br 160–1), and the only piano in the district happened to be in the house opposite—and his bedroom was infested by mice; but he enjoyed the company of his favourite sister and activities like gardening, feeding the goats, digging potatoes, or picking rose-hips, and took some part in village life by visiting neighbours and attending a funeral, a church service, and a fair. A local versifier who wrote couplets about every inhabitant of Zürau also supplied one for Kafka, who found it, apart from its faulty rhyme, reassuring:

> Der Doktor ist ein guter Mon
> Gott wird sich seiner erborm. (Br 234.)

Not the least reason for Kafka's comparative happiness, however, was the termination once and for all of his engagement to Felice. She came to see him in Zürau on 21 September and visited him again in Prague at Christmas, when they finally broke off their engagement and with it the correspondence which had probably given more torment than happiness to them both over the previous five years.

Thus tuberculosis gave Kafka the sharp break with his earlier life that he had hoped conscription would provide. Released from the combined pressures of his job and his emotional life, he at last had the leisure for self-examination, as he told himself in his first diary-entry after the haemorrhage:

15. September. Du hast, soweit diese Möglichkeit überhaupt besteht, die Möglichkeit, einen Anfang zu machen. Verschwende sie nicht. Du wirst den Schmutz, der aus dir aufschwemmt, nicht vermeiden können, wenn du eindringen willst. Wälze dich aber nicht darin. Ist die Lungenwunde nur ein Sinnbild, wie du behauptest, Sinnbild der Wunde, deren Entzündung F. und deren Tiefe Rechtfertigung heißt, ist dies so, dann sind auch die ärztlichen Ratschläge (Licht, Luft, Sonne, Ruhe) Sinnbild. Fasse dieses Sinnbild an. (T 529.)

Here Kafka shows himself aware of the dangers of self-scrutiny. Disgust with oneself can be perversely pleasurable, a wallowing in one's own filth. The correspondence with Felice amply documents Kafka's inclination to this kind of masochism, as in the letter of 16 June 1913, where a proposal of marriage is followed by a lengthy recital of his shortcomings (F 399–403). He had also become aware by now that such behaviour was a form of vanity. In so far as his writing expressed his personal situation, it was a way of indulging his own 'Gemeinheiten', displaying them to the world under the guise of art, and thus securing a privileged position as 'der einzige Sünder, der nicht gebraten wird' (F 755–6). The discovery that self-incrimination by writing was really a form of vanity struck Kafka as so important that, besides communicating it to Felice, he transcribed it in his diary (T 534–5) and in a letter to Brod (Br 178).

Instead, Kafka's writing could no longer be merely personal. Its starting-point must still be his damaged life, the wound which, as he later told Milena, had first found literary expression in *Das Urteil*: 'damals brach die Wunde zum erstenmal auf in einer langen Nacht' (M 235). But probing the wound was now a form of moral and spiritual exploration with 'Rechtfertigung' as its goal. What Kafka means by this word we shall see presently. His use of it accompanies a far-reaching change in his artistic aims, announced when he rejects *Ein Landarzt* (and by implication the whole of his earlier fiction) and formulates a new purpose: 'die Welt ins Reine, Wahre, Unveränderliche heben' (T 534). Here Kafka is abandoning an expressive view of art in favour of a mimetic one, with the rider that his art will imitate the world only to transmute it: the result will not be a copy of the existing world, but a purified and timeless version of it. This purpose was to be realized in *Das Schloß*, as the next chapter will show, but in preparation for it Kafka almost entirely gave up writing fiction and concentrated instead on a different literary form, the aphorism. In Zürau his creative and intellectual powers were at full stretch, enabling him to condense his ethical and metaphysical speculations into a large number of concise, vivid, and pregnant aphorisms. These are to be found in two small octavo notebooks, interspersed with brief notes on day-to-day life in Zürau and with a few short narratives, such as those to which Max Brod gave the titles 'Das Schweigen der Sirenen', 'Die Wahrheit über Sancho Pansa' and 'Eine alltägliche Verwirrung',[1] which are really compact illustrations of the themes normally treated in aphoristic form. Kafka's aphorisms have generally been neglected by his critics, or, at best, treated as marginal glosses on his fiction. It would be juster, I believe, to see them as central to Kafka's work, and to see Kafka, accordingly, as a different kind of writer: rather than being primarily a novelist, he belongs with that unclassifiable group of writers who adopt various literary genres but specialize in the aphorism, among them Lichtenberg, Novalis, Nietzsche, and Kraus.

The purpose that the aphorisms were to serve became clear only during their composition. Writing to Brod in November 1917, Kafka still emphasizes his own egregious failure in every area of his life, speaks tentatively of the new 'Ausweg' (Br 195) which has opened up, and is certain only that he must keep his vision clear to notice further developments. By his visit to Prague in December, his conception of his task had crystallized enough for him to tell Brod: 'Was ich zu tun habe, kann ich nur allein tun. Über die letzten Dinge klar werden. Der Westjude ist darüber nicht klar und hat daher kein Recht zu heiraten.'[2] Two months later, a notebook-entry of 25 February shows that by then the nature of the responsibility entrusted to him had become apparent:

Es ist nicht Trägheit, böser Wille, Ungeschicklichkeit—wenn auch von alledem etwas dabei ist, weil 'das Ungeziefer aus dem Nichts geboren wird'— welche mir alles mißlingen oder nicht einmal mißlingen lassen: Familienleben, Freundschaft, Ehe, Beruf, Literatur, sondern es ist der Mangel des Bodens, der Luft, des Gebotes. Diese zu schaffen ist meine Aufgabe, nicht damit ich dann das Versäumte etwa nachholen kann, sondern damit ich nichts versäumt habe, denn die Aufgabe ist so gut wie eine andere. Es ist sogar die ursprünglichste Aufgabe oder zumindest ihr Abglanz, so wie man beim Ersteigen einer luftdünnen Höhe plötzlich in den Schein der fernen Sonne treten kann. Es ist das auch keine ausnahmsweise Aufgabe, sie ist gewiß schon oft gestellt worden. Ob allerdings in solchem Ausmaß, weiß ich nicht. Ich habe von den Erfordernissen des Lebens gar nichts mitgebracht, so viel ich weiß, sondern nur die allgemeine menschliche Schwäche. Mit dieser—in dieser Hinsicht ist es eine riesenhafte Kraft—habe ich das Negative meiner Zeit, die mir ja sehr nahe ist, die ich nie zu bekämpfen, sondern gewissermaßen zu vertreten das Recht habe, kräftig aufgenommen. An dem geringen Positiven sowie an dem äußersten, zum Positiven umkippenden Negativen, hatte ich keinen ererbten Anteil. Ich bin nicht von der allerdings schon schwer sinkenden Hand des Christentums ins Leben geführt worden wie Kierkegaard und habe nicht den letzten Zipfel des davonfliegenden jüdischen Gebetmantels noch gefangen wie die Zionisten. Ich bin Ende oder Anfang. (H 120–1.)

Though Kafka still cannot resist cataloguing his failures, he now attributes them much less to his personal inadequacy than to his unfavourable environment. Both his remark to Brod and the imagery of the passage just quoted show that he is referring to the situation of the modern Western Jew as analysed by the Zionists. The word 'Boden', as we have seen, was used constantly by Zionists, and some-times by Kafka, to denote the sustaining, organic community that Western Jews lacked; 'Luft' was employed in a similar sense;[3] while the word 'Gebot' recalls Kafka's belief that religion was the 'Kern-frage' that Zionism must face (F 694) and his presentation in *In der Strafkolonie* of the Old Commandant's regime which did at least, though at a perhaps unacceptable price, supply certainty about religious absolutes. Suspended between the sheltering community of his forefathers and the still distant organic community of the future, the

Western Jew lacks religious guidance and is therefore in a state of confusion about the last things, the ultimate and absolute truths of religion. In this state he is not qualified to perform what are, in Kafka's eyes, the religious tasks of marrying and bringing up a family. As a hypertrophic specimen of the Western Jews ('der westjüdischeste von ihnen', as he later told Milena, M 294), Kafka lacks religious guidance to an extreme degree. Unlike Kierkegaard and the Zionists, he has not been supplied by his upbringing with any attachment to the surviving remnants of Christianity or Judaism. Living in an age when religious traditions are on the point of petering out altogether, he represents his age in its negative aspect. In his very weakness, however, lies his strength. Being wholly deprived of the shelter of a religious community, he has to start building one from scratch, and such a task, though not unique in kind, may well be unique in its magnitude. This task is to be accomplished through the aphorisms: in them Kafka ponders the last things of religion in order to establish the principles on which the new community of the future must be founded.

At first sight this may seem an almost ludicrously unrealistic notion. But 1917 was a year of political disaster and political opportunity: Russia was in revolution, and Austria-Hungary, under the new Emperor Karl, who had ascended the throne in November 1916, was in an obviously precarious condition; amid all this destruction the work of a movement dedicated to construction, like Zionism, might have incalculable consequences, especially after the Balfour Declaration of November 1917 committed the British government to establishing a national home for the Jews in Palestine. The opportunities for creating a new society were real, and if, as Kafka believed, society could only be constituted on a religious basis, then a religious thinker had a genuine task before him. Kafka was strengthened in this conviction by reading the essay 'Luther und der Protestantismus', by the theologian Ernst Troeltsch, in the October 1917 issue of *Die neue Rundschau*. Here Troeltsch argues that Protestantism was both destructive and creative. It destroyed the unified Church of the Middle Ages, and thus formed a transition to the largely secular, pluralistic, unmanageably complex world of the present. But it also ensured the survival of a religious community in a secular world by relying not on apostolic succession but on the revelation of the word of God in Scripture. It thus placed Christianity in the keeping of an invisible church, a community of believers united by their allegiance to Scripture, from which a visible religious community can be rebuilt in future: 'Die

Heilsanstalt hat sich in das Wunder der Schrift zusammengezogen und wächst aus ihr wieder hervor.'[3] This community will not be a clerical organization like the medieval Church, nor a political structure, and hence Troeltsch refers to it circumspectly as a 'Heilsanstalt'. Kafka borrowed this word in commenting on Brod's novel *Das große Wagnis*, in which a group of idealists founds a short-lived free society, called Liberia, in the no-man's-land between the trenches on the Western Front. The novel ought, Kafka felt, to end positively with 'die Aufrichtung einer Kirche, einer Heilanstalt, also etwas, was fast zweifellos kommen wird und sich schon im Tempo unseres Zerfallens um uns aufbaut' (Br 218). Since such a community must come, there could be few more urgent tasks than helping to work out the principles on which it should be based.

The aphorisms in which Kafka addresses this task circle round two central problems, both of which had preoccupied him for years and had already found expression in his fiction. They are closely related, and both take the form of apparent contradictions which have somehow to be reconciled. The first is the split between being and consciousness discussed above in connection with *Der Prozeß*, where Josef K.'s guilt consists initially in his conviction of innocence, so that for him to acknowledge his guilt is logically impossible. Once the Court has implanted the knowledge of good and evil in K., his task becomes the moral one of excavating his guilt from under the mountain of self-justifications which his consciousness has piled on top of it. Though this task defeats K., it is possible that self-knowledge and redemption might result from the most rigorous self-examination. This, however, promptly leads to the second contradiction that concerns Kafka. Such self-scrutiny could only be pursued in isolation from one's fellow men. But in isolating oneself in order to work out one's own salvation, one would be ignoring one's responsibilities towards one's fellow men and forfeiting one's salvation. The problem is therefore to work out a conception of community which preserves the spiritual integrity of the individual.

In meditating on these problems, Kafka was helped by his extensive reading. In Zürau he read the Old Testament, Kierkegaard, Schopenhauer, Tolstoy's diaries, and many autobiographical works; among the latter he singles out for praise the autobiography of Salomon Maimon, which he describes as 'eine äußerst grelle Selbstdarstellung eines zwischen Ost- und Westjudentum gespenstisch hinlaufenden Menschen' (Br 203) and in which he probably discerned analogies to his own position outside any established community. His friend Oskar Baum gave him two newly published books by Martin Buber, probably *Die Rede, die Lehre und das Lied* and *Ereignisse und Begegnungen*, both of which appeared late in 1917;[5] Kafka's attitude to them is somewhat problematic, since he calls them 'abscheuliche, widerwärtige Bücher' (Br 224), a response certainly justified by their repellently precious style, yet, as we shall see, at least one of Buber's leading ideas seems to have contributed to Kafka's thinking. Other influences can be detected, and those of Schopenhauer and Tolstoy in particular have received minute study,[6] but it is worth stressing that 'influence' with Kafka is never a matter of passively absorbing materials: he is a remarkably independent thinker who criticizes and modifies what he reads, and works his material into a system of thought which is highly individual in its content and expression and unusual in its subtlety and intricacy. With this proviso, it will be best to look now at two of the major influences on Kafka's thought at this time, before examining his ideas in detail. One of these is Kierkegaard; the other is Jewish mysticism.

Kafka had already read a selection from Kierkegaard's journals, entitled *Buch des Richters*, in 1913, and had found consoling resemblances between his own relationship to Felice and Kierkegaard's short-lived engagement to Regina Olsen (T 318). At some time before November 1917 he read *Furcht und Zittern*, and Baum, who visited Zürau in January 1918, encouraged him to read more of Kierkegaard's religious and philosophical works. By the beginning of March he had read *Entweder-Oder*, *Der Augenblick* and *Wiederholung*, besides a selection from Kierkegaard's papers entitled *Sören Kierkegaard und sein Verhältnis zu 'ihr'*, and a biography by O. P. Monrad. Of all these, the deepest impression seems to have come from *Furcht und Zittern*, especially the concept of the 'movement of faith' and the contrast between the 'knight of infinity' and the 'knight of faith' (Br 238). The 'knight of infinity' is the tragic hero who resists his own inclinations and instead submits to a universal principle. Though he may suffer distress and even death as a result, he has the consolation of knowing that he has acted in accordance with something universal and can win through, like Milton's Samson, to 'calm of mind, all passion spent'. Kierkegaard's example of the tragic hero is Aeschylus's Agamemnon who is compelled by the gods to offer up his daughter Iphigenia as a sacrifice. This provides a neat contrast with the specimen of the 'knight of faith' whom Kierkegaard celebrates throughout *Furcht und Zittern*, namely Abraham, who unhesitatingly obeyed God's command to sacrifice his son Isaac. This action conflicted not only with Abraham's own inclinations but with a universal principle. By any humanly intelligible standard, it was an immoral, even an insane action. In comparison, the tragic hero had an easier task, since he only had to complete the first movement of faith, which brought him into the reassuring shelter of the universal. But the second and more difficult movement of faith brings the 'knight of faith' out of shelter and into a solitude where nothing but his faith in God can assure him that he has acted rightly. Instead of resting in the security of tragic acquiescence, he has to keep his faith alive by constant effort. And since his faith consists only in the individual's intimate and ineffable relation to God, it cannot be communicated to anyone else.

For a time Kafka was fascinated by this conception of a private, individualistic, asocial faith. Having thought through its logical consequences, he summed them up as follows in a letter to Brod in March 1918:

Denn das Verhältnis zum Göttlichen entzieht sich zunächst für Kierkegaard jeder fremden Beurteilung, vielleicht so sehr, daß selbst Jesus nicht urteilen dürfte, wie weit derjenige gekommen ist, der ihm nachfolgt. (Br 239.)

As early as 30 November 1917 we find him speculating that such individualistic faith, once it has become possible for everyone, will itself bring about the arrival of the Messiah, and on 4 December he draws the conclusion: 'Der Messias wird erst kommen, wenn er nicht mehr nötig sein wird, er wird erst einen Tag nach seiner Ankunft kommen, er wird nicht am letzten Tag kommen, sondern am allerletzten' (H 90). That is, when everyone has achieved such faith, the Messiah will be superfluous, for the Kingdom of God will already exist. On the same day, however, he treats the notion of a completely private faith with some irony in the aphorism 'A. ist ein Virtuose und der Himmel ist sein Zeuge' (H 90). While the tenor of this metaphor is the Kierkegaardian paradox of faith, its vehicle appears to be taken from Grillparzer's *Der arme Spielmann*, a story Kafka greatly admired (see T 282). Grillparzer's musician is devoted to the violin but grotesquely lacking in musical talent. To him, his playing seems to express the divine essence of music, but to others it is mere caterwauling; similarly, the faith in God of Kierkegaard's Abraham makes him violate all the principles his fellow men acknowledge. In equating such an unrecognizable faith with the violinist's inaudible music, Kafka implies mixed feelings about both. While their single-minded indifference to the opinion of others may make Abraham and the musician into heroic figures, one can scarcely help feeling them at the same time to be eccentric and pathetic.

Kafka became increasingly suspicious of Abraham, and expressed his doubts late in February 1918. First we have a jotting which says simply 'Hintergedanke Abrahams';[7] later Kafka decides that his concealed motive was the desire to transfer his whole temporal existence, including his possessions, into the world of eternity:

Die vergängliche Welt reicht für Abrahams Vorsorglichkeit nicht aus, deshalb beschließt er mit ihr in die Ewigkeit auszuwandern. Sei es aber, daß das Ausgangs-, sei es, daß das Eingangstor zu eng ist, er bringt den Möbelwagen nicht durch. Die Schuld schreibt er der Schwäche seiner kommandierenden Stimme zu. Es ist die Qual seines Lebens. (H 125.)

In thus doubting Abraham's motives, Kafka may have been provoked by a passage in Monrad's biography which, in summarizing the message of *Furcht und Zittern*, does contrive, though doubtless unintentionally, to imply that Abraham manages to have his cake and eat it:

Abraham wählt aber ohne Bedenken das Religiöse! und [. . .] weil er Glauben wählte und nicht Resignation, bekam er alles (den Sohn, das vorige Hauswesen usw.), und zwar unverändert, aber doch in der höheren Sphäre des Glaubens neu und verklärt wieder![8]

Such an Abraham rather resembles Josef K. in his calculating character and in refusing to blame himself for the failure of his schemes; instead he blames the divine voice that summoned him. There follow more notes on Abraham in which Kafka is criticizing Kierkegaard's notion of the 'knight of faith'. Kafka suggests that Abraham wants to cut himself off from the world and rely solely on God because he finds the world boringly uniform. But since one only needs to take a look at the world to see that, far from being uniform, it is extremely varied, Abraham's problem must be that he is already estranged from the world. His boredom ought therefore to propel him back into involvement with life; it should be 'ein Sprungbrett in die Welt' (H 125).[9] Thus Kafka's meditations on *Furcht und Zittern* have led him to a conclusion opposite to Kierkegaard's. Kierkegaard admires Abraham for abandoning human society and committing himself unreservedly to a precarious communion with God. In Kafka's interpretation, Abraham acts wrongly and from dubious motives in intensifying his isolation, instead of escaping from it by re-entering human society. Unlike Kierkegaard, Kafka does not think that the true way leads ever further into the wilderness. Rather, one's passage through spiritual isolation can and should be part of a circular journey which eventually brings one back to the community.

In the following notes Kafka criticizes Kierkegaard directly, complaining that, not content with the persuasive force of his arguments, Kierkegaard also exercises a literary enchantment on the reader, and that this combination leaves the reader crushed rather than convinced. He adds that Kierkegaard's brilliance enables him to ignore the sometimes intractable problems of actual living: 'Er hat zu viel Geist, er fährt mit seinem Geist wie auf einem Zauberwagen über die Erde, auch dort, wo keine Wege sind' (H 126). Not having shared other people's experiences, Kafka continues, Kierkegaard is arrogant and tyrannical in demanding that they should follow his path. Writing to Brod a few days later, Kafka confirms Kierkegaard's somewhat specious brilliance ('Kierkegaard, der das unlenkbare Luftschiff so wunderbar dirigiert'), expresses a sense of distance ('aus dem Zimmernachbar ist irgendein Stern geworden'), and repeats that Kierkegaard overlooks the problems of ordinary people: 'den gewöhnlichen Menschen [. . .] sieht er nicht und malt den ungeheueren Abraham in die Wolken' (Br 234–6). It is clear that Kafka disagreed radically with the message of *Furcht und Zittern* and that he regarded Kierkegaard, now and later, with a mixture of fascination and scepticism. More evidence for this can be found in the tantalizing first few sentences of an unfinished story, undated but almost certainly later than the Zürau period, where the speaker is a dog:

Ich bin ein Jagdhund. Karo ist mein Name. Ich hasse alle und alles. Ich hasse meinen Herrn, den Jäger, hasse ihn, trotzdem er, die zweifelhafte Person, dessen gar nicht wert ist. (H 273.)

This may have been inspired by a passage from the journals in which Kierkegaard compares himself to a hound ('Jagdhund') which obeys its master absolutely and even allows people to maltreat it so long as its master's gaze tells it to submit to such treatment, but attacks its tormentors as soon as its master gives it a signal.[10] Kafka seems to have adopted this image in order to satirize Abraham's dislike of the world and question the purity of his faith in God; the 'kommandierende Stimme' which summoned Abraham could have helped to suggest the comparison of his God to a huntsman. Altogether, there seems to be only the slenderest of evidence for Max Brod's famous and influential assertion that Kafka drew heavily on Kierkegaard and worked his doctrine of the incommensurability of divine and human law into *Das Schloß*.[11] Any influence that Kierkegaard may have exerted on Kafka was rather of the negative variety that S. S. Prawer defines as 'stimulus to rejection and counter-effect'.[12]

Kafka responded positively, however, to what he knew of the body of Jewish mystical thought called the Cabbala. Admittedly, he almost certainly knew it only at second hand; his references to it are few and casual (T 178, 553). In 1921 he asked Brod to bring to Matliary one of the Cabbalistic works which the latter was reading as preliminary study for his novel *Rĕubēni, Fürst der Juden* (Br 303); but his Hebrew was probably not yet good enough for him to make much of it, and in any case Brod states unequivocally, in an article on Kafka published in November 1921, that he had never read Cabbalistic literature.[13] Any Cabbalistic concepts known to Kafka must have reached him through Hasidism, for which the Cabbala provided the intellectual basis, and most probably derive from conversations with Langer, whose book *Die Erotik der Kabbala* demonstrates his thorough familiarity with this mystical tradition. There are two Cabbalistic concepts in particular which formed part of Hasidic thought and seem to figure prominently in Kafka's aphorisms. One is the mysterious concept of development which Kafka alludes to in describing evil as 'eine Notwendigkeit eines Augenblicks unserer ewigen Entwicklung' (H 91) and as 'eine Ausstrahlung des menschlichen Bewußtseins in bestimmten Übergangsstellungen' (H 102). The other is the element of Hasidic spirituality called *Kavvanah*, which Gershom Scholem translates as 'mystical intention'.[14]

What Kafka means by 'Entwicklung' can be partially indicated by a necessarily brief and crude account of the concept of human development to be found in the Lurianic Cabbala. This is the name given to the teachings of Isaac Luria (1534–72), which were spread among the Jewish people by his disciples and eventually provided the intellectual framework of Hasidism. Luria taught that the ten *Sefiroth*, the lights emanating from God, were originally preserved in special vessels. But the light of the seven lower *Sefiroth*, bursting forth all at once, proved too powerful for the vessels and broke them. The fragments of the vessels were the origin of what we call evil. While some of the divine light returned to its source, the rest was and still is held captive by the powers of evil, and the cosmic process (*Tikkun*) has as its goal the liberation of those sparks and the restoration of the original divine order. This process of development takes place in human history as well as in the cosmos; its consummation will be the appearance of the Messiah. Everyone can play a part in the process, for his prayer helps to speed the coming of the Messiah. This accounts for the widespread appeal of Lurianic Cabbalism, as Scholem says: 'The doctrine of *Tikkun* raised every Jew to the rank of a protagonist in the great process of restitution, in a manner never heard of before.'[15] It also provides an explanation for evil and suffering, something acutely necessary in Luria's day when the expulsion of the Jews from Spain in 1492 was still a recent calamity. Evil can be accommodated as a necessary stage in the cosmic process. This optimistic view was transmitted to Hasidism. One of the Ba'al Shem's most famous sayings runs: 'Das Böse ist nur die unterste Stufe des Guten.'[16]

The individual's share in *Tikkun* is not confined to a single lifetime. The doctrine of metempsychosis, which had figured rarely, and only as a form of punishment, in earlier Cabbalism, was reinterpreted by Luria and given a central place in his system. It was believed to affect everyone and to be a necessary part of the cosmic process. This doctrine, too, passed into Hasidism. 'Alle Menschen sind die Stätten wandernder Seelen,' says Buber in his account of the teachings of the Ba'al Shem. 'In vielen Wesen wohnen sie und streben von Gestalt zu Gestalt nach der Vollendung.'[17] Kafka too sometimes toys with this idea: in a notebook entry of 24 February 1918 he considers the evidence for pre-existence, 'Beweise für ein wirkliches Vorleben' (H 120).

The doctrine of metempsychosis seems to underlie notebook-entries like this one:

Die Freuden dieses Lebens sind nicht die seinen, sondern unsere Angst vor dem Aufsteigen in ein höheres Leben; die Qualen dieses Lebens sind nicht die seinen, sondern unsere Selbstqual wegen jener Angst. (H 108.)

Elsewhere, in a manner strongly recalling Luria's *Tikkun*, he describes the world as a transitional stage, an 'Übergang' (H 118). It is not clear, however, that Kafka is expressing a literal belief in the transmigration of souls. Often the moral connotations that he attaches to this doctrine suggest that he is using it metaphorically, like Goethe with the injunction 'Stirb und werde!' in the poem 'Selige Sehnsucht'.[18] The stages in the process of development are said to be degrees of knowledge, 'Erkenntnis' (H 110). The advance to a higher degree of knowledge is a kind of death, but it is not equivalent to physical death: 'Unsere Rettung ist der Tod, aber nicht dieser' (H 123). That Kafka is using the doctrine of metempsychosis figuratively becomes apparent when he writes succinctly: 'Die Menschheitsent-wicklung—ein Wachsen der Sterbenskraft' (H 123). By 'Sterbens-kraft' Kafka appears to mean something like the spiritual discipline described in George Herbert's poem 'Mortification'.[19]

If Kafka incorporates this doctrine into his thought as a metaphor, he borrows the concept of *Kavvanah* on a more literal plane. This is the form of prayer through which man contributes to the process of *Tikkun*. Luria sees it not as contemplative but as active. In Scholem's words:

> The task of man is seen to consist in the direction of his whole inner purpose towards the restoration of the original harmony which was disturbed by the original defect—the Breaking of the Vessels—and those powers of evil and sin which date from that time. To *unify* the name of God, as the term goes, is not merely to perform an act of confession and acknowledgement of God's Kingdom, it is more than that; it is an action rather than an act.[20]

This active concentration of one's whole being on the spiritual goal is also demanded by Kafka: 'Zwei Möglichkeiten: sich unendlich klein machen oder es sein. Das zweite ist Vollendung, also Untätigkeit, das erste Beginn, also Tat' (H 105). Scholem also makes it clear, how-ever, that *Kavvanah* is not active in the sense of demanding effort. It seems rather to require that complete renunciation of effort and abnegation of the will which, according to one of Kafka's last aphor-isms, brings the world to one's feet:

> Es ist nicht notwendig, daß du aus dem Hause gehst. Bleib bei deinem Tisch und horche. Horche nicht einmal, warte nur. Warte nicht einmal, sei völlig still und allein. Anbieten wird sich dir die Welt zur Entlarvung, sie kann nicht anders, verzückt wird sie sich vor dir winden. (H 124.)

Kavvanah is also closely allied to humility, the means by which man realizes his unity with the rest of creation. For Kafka, too, humility is the way to make contact with one's fellow men:

> Die Demut gibt jedem, auch dem einsam Verzweifelnden, das stärkste Verhältnis zum Mitmenschen, und zwar sofort, allerdings nur bei völliger und dauernder Demut. Sie kann das deshalb, weil sie die wahre Gebetsprache ist, gleichzeitig Anbetung und festeste Verbindung. (H 119.)

Unlike Kierkegaard's asocial conception of faith, then, this offers a solution to the problem of reconciling spiritual concentration with one's duties as a member of a community. It is associated with a mystical conviction of the unity of mankind. But a sentence written on 19 February 1918, 'Wir alle haben nicht einen Leib, aber ein Wachstum', indicates that human beings are not united in the Christian sense of being members of one body (cf. Rom. 12:5, 1 Cor. 12:12), but through participating in a single process of development, a conception which strikingly recalls, and is almost certainly derived from, the Lurianic idea of *Tikkun*.

We can now begin examining how these ideas fit into the system of thought which can be pieced together from Kafka's aphorisms. It will be best to start with the term 'Rechtfertigung', already alluded to, for this was the moral and spiritual purpose of Kafka's probing of his own wound, and the point where his personal problems opened out to reveal issues of concern both to him and to his fellow men, which it was the task of the Zürau aphorisms to explore. Kafka explains 'Rechtfertigung' in a paragraph which itself requires considerable explanation:

Niemand schafft hier mehr als seine geistige Lebensmöglichkeit; daß es den Anschein hat, als arbeite er für seine Ernährung, Kleidung und so weiter, ist nebensächlich, es wird ihm eben mit jedem sichtbaren Bissen auch ein unsichtbarer, mit jedem sichtbaren Kleid auch ein unsichtbares Kleid und so fort gereicht. Das ist jedes Menschen Rechtfertigung. Es hat den Anschein, als unterbaue er seine Existenz mit nachträglichen Rechtfertigungen, das ist aber nur psychologische Spiegelschrift, tatsächlich errichtet er sein Leben auf seinen Rechtfertigungen. Allerdings muß jeder Mensch sein Leben rechtfertigen können (oder seinen Tod, was dasselbe ist), dieser Aufgabe kann er nicht ausweichen. (H 121.)

Here the word 'Rechtfertigung' appears to have been borrowed from the theological context in which man's justification before God through faith or works is discussed, and to mean something like the conviction that one is leading a good life. The chance to justify oneself, in this sense, is provided by the daily need to work for one's food and clothing. But it is not as though one had to earn one's justification through work; nor can one look back over one's life and justify it after the fact. Rather, the conviction of leading a good life precedes one's life: it is the foundation on which one's life is built. It is not an intellectual conviction that can be acquired by a process of reflection.

Rather, it is the vital energy that enables one to go about one's daily tasks in the first place.

This suggests several conclusions. First, we can recognize here the vital energy that awoke in Josef K. as he was being led to his execution and made him think: 'Die Logik ist zwar unerschütterlich, aber einem Menschen, der leben will, widersteht sie nicht' (P 272). By now, however, Kafka has given this primitive energy a moral interpretation. He regards it as the soil from which religious faith can grow, as this dialogue demonstrates:

'Daß es uns an Glauben fehle, kann man nicht sagen. Allein die einfache Tatsache unseres Lebens ist in ihrem Glaubenswert gar nicht auszuschöpfen.'
'Hier wäre ein Glaubenswert? Man kann doch nicht nicht-leben.'
'Eben in diesem "kann doch nicht" steckt die wahnsinnige Kraft des Glaubens; in dieser Verneinung bekommt sie Gestalt.' (H 123–4.)

That is to say, faith is not an intellectual conviction to which theologians have privileged access; it is the bedrock vitality which sustains the lives of everyone, including the most unreflective people.

Secondly, it is evident that for Kafka faith is demonstrated in action and especially in mundane acts like earning one's food and clothing. One is reminded of Hegel's admonition: 'Trachtet am ersten nach Nahrung und Kleidung, so wird euch das Reich Gottes von selbst zufallen.'[21] The belief that one can justify one's life simply by living it helps to explain why Kafka was so fond of quoting the remark Flaubert made after visiting a family with numerous children: 'Ils sont dans le vrai.'[22] The ideal Kafka starts from is that of ordinary human beings coping with day-to-day tasks, working, and bringing up their families; and the ultimate goal he envisaged was a community in which everyone would live 'dans le vrai'. People leading such a life would not need a religion, for a religion is an attempt to retain a distant connection with the good after one has become estranged from it, as Kafka speculates when he asks: 'Ist die Tatsache der Religionen ein Beweis für die Unmöglichkeit des Einzelnen, dauernd gut zu sein?' (H 84), and adds: 'Der Gründer reißt sich vom Guten los' (H 84–5).

Thirdly, Kafka's celebration of unreflective vitality marks him as a man of his age, for if any concept dominated the early years of the twentieth century in the German-speaking world, it was *das Leben*.

Wolfdietrich Rasch has said that this concept held an even more exclusive sway over the period than the concept of reason did in the Enlightenment.[23] It would be easier, however, to find *das Leben* celebrated as amoral vitality than interpreted morally as it is by Kafka. The closest parallel would perhaps be with the young Hofmannsthal, for whom *das Leben* summons one to leave the artificial paradise of aestheticism and confront the gravity and suffering of life.

The fourth and final reflection suggested by Kafka's remarks on 'Rechtfertigung' is that they seem to contain a contradiction. If the justification of one's life is latent in the sheer fact of living, how can it be a problem? How can one be in doubt about one's justification if one already possesses it?

This is only an apparent contradiction. What makes one's justification problematic is the now familiar split between being and consciousness. One's justification may be latent in one's being, but absent from one's consciousness, so that one can be tormented by a sense of guilt—or brazenly unaware of guilt, like Josef K.—because one is repressing the vital and moral energy which is present in one's own being but which one refuses to admit to one's consciousness. This inner principle, this energy at the core of one's being, is often referred to by Kafka as 'das Unzerstörbare':

Der Mensch kann nicht leben ohne ein dauerndes Vertrauen zu etwas Unzerstörbarem in sich, wobei sowohl das Unzerstörbare als auch das Vertrauen ihm dauernd verborgen bleiben können. Eine der Ausdrucksmöglichkeiten dieses Verborgenbleibens ist der Glaube an einen persönlichen Gott. (H 90–1.)

Probably this notion can be traced back to Kafka's early reading (Br 20) of the medieval mystic Meister Eckehart, who says that the point at which God and man can meet is 'in dem Reinsten, was die Seele zu bieten vermag, in ihrem Edelsten, in dem Grunde, kurz: in dem *Wesen* der Seele'.[24] However, Eckehart's influence has since been overlaid by that of Schopenhauer, especially the chapter of *Die Welt als Wille und Vorstellung* entitled 'Über den Tod und sein Verhältnis zur Unzerstörbarkeit unseres Wesens an sich', in which Schopenhauer argues that one's true being consists in the will, a fundamental level of reality shared by all creatures and unaffected by the death of the individual.[25] The will is not an abstraction but, like 'das Unzerstörbare', a vital force supplying one's life with sustenance and impetus. Kafka may also have absorbed Buber's idea, discussed in the previous chapter, of mystical experience as an immersion in oneself which leads through absolute solitude to union with the 'Weltich' and hence with the rest of humanity;[26] though the structure of Buber's mysticism itself derives from Schopenhauer.

If, however, 'das Unzerstörbare' corresponds to one's being, then it is separate from one's consciousness. As a result of this separation, one may fancy that one's life is sustained by some other power, such as a personal god. We saw in Ch. 3 that Kafka used the word 'Gott' only metaphorically and felt that the object of his religious belief could be better described as 'einer beruhigend fernen, womöglich unendlichen Höhe oder Tiefe' (F 289). Tolstoy in his diaries, which Kafka read with interest while in Zürau, also insists on a non-anthropomorphic conception of God: 'Man sagt, man müsse Gott als eine Person verstehen. Darin liegt ein Mißverständnis: Person heißt Begrenztheit.'[27] Dora Dymant, the companion of Kafka's last year of life, was certain that he had no belief in a personal god.[28] Even if an atheist, Kafka was also a deeply religious man, and the object of his religious feelings was not some supernatural entity, but the collective being of mankind united in 'das Unzerstörbare':

Das Unzerstörbare ist eines; jeder einzelne Mensch ist es und gleichzeitig ist es allen gemeinsam, daher die beispiellos untrennbare Verbindung der Menschen. (H 96–7.)

It would be misleading, therefore, to discuss Kafka's thought in theological terms, for he had no belief in a god and hence no theology.[29] Martin Buber's claim that he had a characteristically Jewish faith in a *deus absconditus* can hardly be reconciled with Kafka's own utterances.[30] Still less is there any foundation for the strange notion, which crops up now and again in Kafka studies, that he had some sort of Manichaean belief in an evil god.[31] It would be more accurate to associate Kafka with Feuerbach's view that God, with his omnipotence, perfection, etc., is a projection of the human potential from which man is at present estranged, so that 'in religion man contemplates his own latent nature'.[32] But although, for Kafka as for Feuerbach, a belief in God is a token of estrangement, 'das Unzerstörbare' is not something that needs to be reincorporated into human life: it is there already, as the vital force upon which life is based, and the ideal relationship between it and the individual consciousness would be not union but equilibrium: 'Theoretisch gibt es eine vollkommene Glücksmöglichkeit: An das Unzerstörbare in sich

glauben und nicht zu ihm streben' (H 96). Unquestioning faith in
'das Unzerstörbare' would enable one to share its qualities: 'Glauben
heißt: das Unzerstörbare in sich befreien, oder richtiger: sich
befreien, oder richtiger: unzerstörbar sein, oder richtiger: sein'
(H 89). One would then be 'dans le vrai', able to go about one's day-
to-day life in a spirit of assurance, and it would not even matter if the
grounds for one's assurance remained unconscious: 'Nicht jeder kann
die Wahrheit sehn, aber sein' (H 94).

In the autumn of 1917, however, Kafka felt himself to be at the furthest possible remove from such a state. At times the task of discovering
the proper relation between 'das Unzerstörbare' and human life
seemed impossible, as though a problem were required to solve itself:
'Du bist die Aufgabe. Kein Schüler weit und breit' (H 83). Paradoxes
of this sort, though, are not so common in Kafka's thought as has
sometimes been supposed.[33] As in *Der Prozeß*, he tends to convert
logical problems into moral ones which are soluble in principle, even
if the exertions required are in practice too great for humanity.
Similarly, in his aphorisms, he translates the contrast between being
and consciousness into the contrast between the spiritual world and
the world of the senses, and maintains that the separation of the two is
illusory:

Es gibt nichts anderes als eine geistige Welt; was wir sinnliche Welt nennen,
ist das Böse in der geistigen, und was wir böse nennen, ist nur eine Notwendigkeit eines Augenblicks unserer ewigen Entwicklung. (H 91.)

Here Kafka is adopting the concept of *Tikkun* to explain evil as a
necessary stage in a larger process, and combining it with the Hasidic
doctrine, discussed in the previous chapter, that the divine presence
pervades the world and can be perceived at any time if one simply
rejects the delusions of the senses. But this god's-eye view of things is
of no help to somebody enmeshed in the physical world. Though
Kafka considers this problem under different aspects—moral,
spiritual and epistemological—its structure remains constant. On the
one hand we have a reality which is undivided, self-sufficient, and
therefore incapable of self-awareness, because that would require a
division between subject and object. Such a reality must also be indif-
ferent to the world outside it. Thus Kafka asserts 'daß auch die Seele
von sich selbst nichts weiß' (H 93), and maintains: 'Das Böse weiß
vom Guten, aber das Gute vom Bösen nicht' (H 84) and: 'Wahrheit
ist unteilbar, kann sich also selbst nicht erkennen; wer sie erkennen
will, muß Lüge sein' (H 99). On the other hand we have consciousness

which is by definition separate from its object, so that to be conscious of goodness and truth is to be excluded from goodness and truth and hence to be evil and false. If one were 'dans le vrai' one would not know it: 'Selbsterkenntnis hat nur das Böse' (H 84). Exclusion from the truth does not necessarily mean, however, that one's knowledge is false. Sabina Kienlechner, whose exegesis of the Zürau aphorisms is much the best that I have read, does seem to err in interpreting as a paradox Kafka's statement: 'wer sie [die Wahrheit] erkennen will, muß Lüge sein'. Her paraphrase runs: 'Nur wer *Lüge* ist, kann Wahrheit erkennen, aber wer Lüge ist, kann *Wahrheit* nicht erkennen.'[34] What Kafka means, though, is that one can be a lie *and* know the truth: one's consciousness can have accurate knowledge of the truth, and yet this may be of no good to one, since one's being can still be pervaded by falsehood.

This will become clearer through a glance at the aphorisms which have the same conceptual structure but place the emphasis on good and evil. If one has absorbed evil into one's being, it no longer matters whether one is conscious of evil: 'Wenn man einmal das Böse bei sich aufgenommen hat, verlangt es nicht mehr, daß man ihm glaube' (H 84). One can have an untroubled consciousness and yet be steeped in evil, like Josef K., or, in a sense, like Kleist's Marquise von O., who becomes pregnant while unconscious and whose call for a midwife makes her mother exclaim: 'Ein reines Bewußtsein, und eine Hebamme!'[35] The converse also applies: the Evil One persuaded Adam and Eve to sin by his promise, 'ye shall be as gods, knowing good and evil' (Gen. 3: 5), which convinced them that consciousness of good was superior to being good: 'Der trostlose Gesichtskreis des Bösen: schon im Erkennen des Guten und Bösen glaubt er die Gottgleichheit zu sehn' (H 102).

Confinement to the sensory world does not, then, preclude knowledge of the truth, but it does prevent one from incorporating the truth into one's being. The world we live in is so pervaded by untruth that untruth cannot be abolished piecemeal, by correcting one mistake after another, but only wholesale, by replacing the present world with a 'Welt der Wahrheit' (H 108). Occasionally, especially in the earlier aphorisms, Kafka says that the search for truth is a self-contradictory enterprise:

Wirklich urteilen kann nur die Partei, als Partei aber kann sie nicht urteilen. Demnach gibt es in der Welt keine Urteilsmöglichkeit, sondern nur deren Schimmer. (H 86.)

This is a banal paradox: if one is involved in a problem, one is too biased to reach the truth; if one is not involved, one is too ignorant. The only interesting thing about this conundrum is that it inspired Kafka to write several entertaining little narratives indicating how everyday life is beset by confusion and delusion ('Eine alltägliche Verwirrung') and how the prevalence of error in the world can on occasion rescue one unexpectedly from danger ('Das Schweigen der Sirenen'). Odysseus appears in the latter story, not as Homer's man of many wiles, but as a simpleton who fancies that merely putting wax in his ears and having himself chained to the mast will be adequate protection against the song of the Sirens. The Sirens apply a yet more deadly weapon than their singing, namely their silence, but since the movement of their throats makes Odysseus imagine that they are singing, his delusion saves him and he passes them unscathed.

Since the world of evil and delusion is only an enclave within the spiritual world, there might be some way of escaping from it. Kafka considers two possibilities: psychology and art.

In a letter written from Zürau to Felix Weltsch, Kafka admitted to his ambivalent fascination with 'dem verdammt psychologischen Theorienkreis, den Du nicht liebst, aber von dem Du besessen bist (und ich wohl auch)' (Br 187). He was acquainted with two main psychological theories. One was, of course, Freudian psychoanalysis, which Kafka read about in *Die neue Rundschau* and perhaps also in *Imago*; he read the psychoanalytic study by Hans Blüher, *Die Rolle der Erotik in der männlichen Gesellschaft*, met the psychoanalyst Otto Gross, and speaks with familiarity of Wilhelm Stekel, the 'Wiener, der aus Freud kleine Münze macht' (Br 169), who had mentioned *Die Verwandlung* in one of his books.[36] As a theory, psychoanalysis seemed to Kafka satisfactory only in the short run (Br 197); its pretensions to explain everything meant that in the long run it explained nothing. As a therapy, it was wholly misguided, because it failed to realize that the symptoms it proposed to treat were in fact expressions of religious need, 'Verankerungen des in Not befindlichen Menschen in irgendwelchem mütterlichen Boden' (M 292), and hence rooted in human nature itself. His opposition to Freud's ideal of psychic health was supported by a quotation from Kierkegaard: 'Überhaupt leiblich und psychisch ganz gesund ein wahres Geistesleben führen—das kann kein Mensch' (Br 240).[37] Equally helpless was the other psychological theory that Kafka knew, the empirical or descriptive psychology of the philosopher Franz Brentano. While at university Kafka attended a course of lectures on 'Grundfragen der deskriptiven Psychologie' delivered by Brentano's pupil Anton Marty, and from 1902 to 1905 he was present (how regularly, we do not know) at informal discussions of Brentano's philosophy held fortnightly by a group of students in the Café Louvre. Though the attempts that have been made to represent Brentano's psychology as the key to Kafka's thought do not carry conviction, it does receive explicit mention in this passage from the Zürau notebooks:

Es gibt keine Beobachtung der innern Welt, so wie es eine der äußern gibt. Zumindest deskriptive Psychologie ist wahrscheinlich in der Gänze ein Anthropomorphismus, ein Ausragen der Grenzen. Die innere Welt läßt sich nur leben, nicht beschreiben.—Psychologie ist die Beschreibung der Spiegelung der irdischen Welt in der himmlischen Fläche oder richtiger: die Beschreibung einer Spiegelung, wie wir, Vollgesogene der Erde, sie uns denken, denn eine Spiegelung erfolgt gar nicht, nur wir sehen Erde, wohin wir uns auch wenden. (H 72.)

Since the self belongs to the spiritual world instead of the empirical world, empirical psychology can only project on to it categories taken from earthly reality. Elsewhere Kafka says that psychology is the decipherment of mirror-writing, a task whose result is known in advance since one wrote the text oneself before reversing it (H 122). Kafka's downright dismissal of 'Beobachtung der innern Welt' does not suggest any intimate knowledge of Brentano's work, for Brentano agrees that self-observation is impossible and therefore says that the method of his philosophy is not 'innere *Beobachtung*' but '*innere Wahrnehmung*'.[38] Where Brentano thinks that we can, to a limited extent, catch ourselves in the act of thinking, Kafka denies even this and contends that, as creatures of the empirical world, we can see nothing else wherever we look. The psychologist's attempts to investigate the spiritual world are rather like James Thurber's efforts to see through a microscope: after copying a fascinating pattern of whorls and dots, Thurber discovered that he had fixed the lens so that it reflected, and had succeeded in drawing his own eye.

The imagery of light and reflection occurs in the two aphorisms where Kafka speaks of art. If truth is a light shining in darkness, then art cannot approach too close for fear of being burnt. Instead, it has to find a point from which the light can be reflected (H 104). Thus art can convey truth, without being true itself, as another aphorism indicates: 'Unsere Kunst ist ein von der Wahrheit Geblendet-Sein: Das

Licht auf dem zurückweichenden Fratzengesicht ist wahr, sonst nichts' (H 93–4). Art is a true revelation of falsehood. Given that we live in a world of deceit, art can show us accurately the false and deceptive character of our world; but art cannot embody truth and cannot recreate or provide access to the world of truth. The form of art that most interested Kafka was literature, and literature is tied to the sensory world by its medium, language:

Die Sprache kann für alles außerhalb der sinnlichen Welt nur andeutungsweise, aber niemals auch nur annähernd vergleichsweise gebraucht werden, da sie, entsprechend der sinnlichen Welt, nur vom Besitz und seinen Beziehungen handelt. (H 92.)

It is not clear whence Kafka derived this view of the inadequacy of language to express concepts, but the closest contemporary analogue would seem to be the extreme nominalism of the Prague philosopher Fritz Mauthner, whose three-volume *Beiträge zur Kritik der Sprache* was published at the beginning of the century. Believing that experience consists of sensations, Mauthner maintains that words cannot refer to concepts, because these have no existence separate from language. Instead, nouns designate sensations, and do so metaphorically.[39] This doctrine could be used either to legitimize art, by showing that art was no more fictional than ordinary language, or to downgrade art by showing that its use of language did not differ from ordinary language and therefore could not support claims to reveal truth. If Kafka had any acquaintance with Mauthner's linguistic theory, he must have drawn the latter, more pessimistic conclusion, since he thinks that art can at best transmit or reflect truth but not embody it.

Since neither psychology nor art can help to overcome the opposition of being and consciousness, Kafka resorts to the language of myth. In a series of aphorisms he appropriates the myth of the Fall as an instrument with which to explore the relation between the two opposed worlds. For appropriating the myth to his own concerns he had precedents in Kleist's *Über das Marionettentheater*[40] and in those passages from *Die Welt als Wille und Vorstellung* where Schopenhauer equates original sin with the affirmation of the will to live.[41] First of all, he inquires into the relation between the Fall and 'das Unzerstörbare'.

Wenn das, was im Paradies zerstört worden sein soll, zerstörbar war, dann war es nicht entscheidend; war es aber unzerstörbar, dann leben wir in einem falschen Glauben. (H 97.)

The Fall could only have made a decisive difference to human life if it had affected the indestructible basis of humanity. Since that is by definition impossible, we must be labouring under a false belief, the nature of which is explained in this aphorism:

Die Vertreibung aus dem Paradies ist in ihrem Hauptteil ein augenblicklicher ewiger Vorgang: Es ist also zwar die Vertreibung aus dem Paradies endgültig, das Leben in der Welt unausweichlich, die Ewigkeit des Vorganges aber (oder zeitlich ausgedrückt: die ewige Wiederholung des Vorgangs) macht es trotzdem möglich, daß wir nicht nur dauernd im Paradiese bleiben könnten, sondern tatsächlich dort dauernd sind, gleichgültig ob wir es hier wissen oder nicht. (H 94; corrected from MS.)

In this passage Kafka slips adroitly from one sense of 'ewig' to another. Starting from the datum that our expulsion from Paradise is eternal and irreversible, he suggests that it is eternal in being outside time altogether. The Fall is not an event in time but a timeless state of estrangement from Paradise, in which we can recognize the estrangement of consciousness from being. It is quite possible that our consciousness misleads us and that Paradise is all around us, enclosing us as the spiritual world does the world of the senses.

This means that time is illusory, one more of the errors into which our estranged consciousness leads us, and that time and eternity are related as consciousness to being. The illusory nature of time is a frequent theme of the aphorisms. 'Die Tatsache, daß es nichts anderes gibt als eine geistige Welt, nimmt uns die Hoffnung und gibt uns die Gewißheit' (H 93): if time is illusory, then hope, which is directed towards the future, must be illusory, since there is no future; this leaves us, not with despair, but with certainty. The certainty is that a decision is required of us in every instant:

Der entscheidende Augenblick der menschlichen Entwicklung ist immerwährend. Darum sind die revolutionären geistigen Bewegungen, welche alles Frühere für nichtig erklären, im Recht, denn es ist noch nichts geschehen. (H 73.)

Revolutionaries are right to dismiss the past, for there is no past, only the perpetual present urging a decision upon us. This idea made Kafka criticize Brod's novel *Das große Wagnis*, in which the characters have to make a single and irreversible decision whether or not to join the new state of Liberia. 'Vielleicht mißverstehe ich Dich,' he wrote to Brod, 'aber wenn es nicht zahllose Möglichkeiten der Befreiung gibt, besonders aber Möglichkeiten in jedem Augenblick unseres Lebens, dann gibt es vielleicht überhaupt keine' (Br 192).

If our conception of time needs revision, so does our conception of eternity. Kafka opposes the vulgar notion that eternity is something that will succeed the cessation of time. He found this notion expressed in a passage in Kierkegaard's *Der Augenblick* where Kierkegaard adjures his readers to refrain from worldly greed and hypocrisy because in eternity they will be punished by divine justice.[42] Kafka's note of 9 February 1918, two days after he had begun reading *Der Augenblick*, 'Ewigkeit ist aber nicht das Stillstehn der Zeitlichkeit' (H 112), looks like a response to Kierkegaard's view. For Kafka, eternity is not a track running parallel to time, but a spiritual reality which enfolds time. When eternity manifests itself, time will not be annihilated, but its 'Rechtfertigung', in the sense discussed earlier, will be revealed:

Wieviel bedrückender als die unerbittlichste Überzeugung von unserem gegenwärtigen sündhaften Stand ist selbst die schwächste Überzeugung von der einstigen, ewigen Rechtfertigung unserer Zeitlichkeit. Nur die Kraft im Ertragen dieser zweiten Überzeugung, welche in ihrer Reinheit die erste voll umfaßt, ist das Maß des Glaubens. (H 113.)

Just as each individual life is built on an unconscious justification, so is the temporal world as a whole. The entry of eternity into time will uncover this hidden justification and thus reconcile being with consciousness. The result, however, will not be a new world but rather 'the old made explicit, understood,' to quote T. S. Eliot; one may recall the Hasidic saying quoted in Ch. 3, 'Alles wird sein wie hier— nur ein ganz klein wenig anders', or this note in which Kafka seems to anticipate such a state of things: 'An diesem Ort war ich noch niemals: Anders geht der Atem, blendender als die Sonne strahlt neben ihr ein Stern' (H 82).

How is this state of union to be reached? There is no question of reversing the Fall. We cannot, so to speak, wind back the reel to return to the beginning of the film. We can only go forward, and the way forward is indicated by the fact that in the Old Testament Adam was expelled from Eden, not only because he had learnt good and evil, but also 'lest he put forth his hand, and take also of the tree of life, and eat, and live for ever' (Gen. 3:22). Hence this aphorism:

Wir sind nicht nur deshalb sündig, weil wir vom Baum der Erkenntnis gegessen haben, sondern auch deshalb, weil wir vom Baum des Lebens noch nicht gegessen haben. Sündig ist der Stand, in dem wir uns befinden, unabhängig von Schuld. (H 101.)

Our state is sinful but not guilty, because it is a timeless state, not the result of a guilty action committed in the past. To escape from our sinful state we must make the decision to eat of the tree of life and ascend to a higher stage of development. What this would involve is outlined in the following aphorism:

'Wenn——, mußt du sterben,' bedeutet: Die Erkenntnis ist beides, Stufe zum ewigen Leben und Hindernis vor ihm. Wirst du nach gewonnener Erkenntnis zum ewigen Leben gelangen wollen—und du wirst nicht anders können als es wollen, denn Erkenntnis ist dieser Wille—, so wirst du dich, das Hindernis, zerstören müssen, um die Stufe, das ist die Zerstörung, zu bauen. Die Vertreibung aus dem Paradies war daher keine Tat, sondern ein Geschehen. (H 105-6.)

In showing how the ascent to a higher stage must be performed, this aphorism introduces us to the more strictly ethical part of Kafka's thought. It appears that 'Erkenntnis', insight or knowledge, has two faces. It is part of the vital force that propels us through our lives. In this sense it is not something that has to be striven for, for we already have all the knowledge that we need, in consequence of the Fall: 'Erkenntnis haben wir. Wer sich besonders um sie bemüht, ist verdächtig, sich gegen sie zu bemühn' (H 104). That is, to strive for knowledge would probably be a disguised attempt to repress the knowledge one already has. The only sense in which 'Erkenntnis' can be acquired is that one's dormant knowledge of good and evil may be activated, as K.'s is by the intervention of the Court. Once this has happened, 'Erkenntnis' shows its other face: it reveals that to attain eternal life one must destroy the obstacle in the way, and one is oneself the obstacle, for one's ingrained habits of dishonesty and possessiveness must be discarded before one can enter eternal life. If one tries to bring along one's old self, one will end up like Abraham, whom Kafka imagined getting his furniture-van jammed in the entrance to eternity. Instead, one must cast off one's old self, or rather one must actively destroy it. 'Nicht Selbstabschüttelung, sondern Selbstaufzehrung' (H 105) is the way to be rid of the old Adam. The road to spiritual life leads through spiritual death.

Along the way there are many temptations. An error one is liable to commit at the outset is to confuse spiritual with physical death:

Ein erstes Zeichen beginnender Erkenntnis ist der Wunsch zu sterben. Dieses Leben scheint unerträglich, ein anderes unerreichbar. Man schämt sich nicht mehr, sterben zu wollen; man bittet, aus der alten Zelle, die man haßt, in eine neue gebracht zu werden, die man erst hassen lernen wird. Ein Rest von

Glauben wirkt dabei mit, während des Transportes werde zufällig der Herr durch den Gang kommen, den Gefangenen ansehen und sagen: 'Diesen sollt ihr nicht wieder einsperren. Er kommt zu mir.' (H 81.)

One would like in a way to be able to share Hans Joachim Schoeps's reaction to this aphorism: 'Ich weiß kein zweites Dokument aus neuerer Zeit, das so für die Macht der Hoffnung Zeugnis gibt und von einer solchen Urkraft messianischer Erwartung durchglüht ist wie dieser Satz.'[43] However, Schoeps's theological perspective has misled him into missing Kafka's point: in the last sentence above, Kafka is actually condemning the desire to be let off one's task of self-destruction by a divine intervention. The best gloss on the immediately preceding sentence is Baudelaire's remark that most people resemble hospital patients who think they will be cured if they are moved to a different bed. Still, these errors are productive in so far as they signal the awakening of 'Erkenntnis'. A much graver error is the frenzied activity with which one tries to repress the insight that one's subjection to the physical world depends on one's own decision; Kafka conveys this error through the parable of the king's messengers:

Es wurde ihnen die Wahl gestellt, Könige oder der Könige Kuriere zu werden. Nach Art der Kinder wollten alle Kuriere sein. Deshalb gibt es lauter Kuriere, sie jagen durch die Welt und rufen, da es keine Könige gibt, einander selbst die sinnlos gewordenen Meldungen zu. Gerne würden sie ihrem elenden Leben ein Ende machen, aber sie wagen es nicht wegen des Diensteides. (H 89-90.)

Misguided activity of this sort constitutes so strong a temptation that Kafka thinks man's chief sin is impatience (H 72). Mere effort cannot release one from the world of the senses, though it can provide a pleasing illusion of release:

Je mehr Pferde du anspannst, desto rascher gehts—nämlich nicht das Ausreißen des Blocks aus dem Fundament, was unmöglich ist, aber das Zerreißen der Riemen und damit die leere fröhliche Fahrt. (H 89.)

Another dangerous temptation is to engage in open conflict with evil. Such conflict has a way of ending in collaboration (H 74). Yet another is the attempt to exercise rigid control over one's thoughts and impulses, for one can in fact control only a tiny and randomly chosen part of one's spiritual existence (H 85-6).

Nevertheless, spiritual progress means a confrontation, as Kafka indicates through the image of the burning bush (H 84), but the encounter with one's real antagonist gives one endless courage: 'Vom wahren Gegner fährt grenzenloser Mut in dich' (H 83). One's true antagonist is not the Evil One but one's own self, and so one must take the side of the world against oneself (H 91). One's faith must become one's guillotine: 'Ein Glaube wie ein Fallbeil, so schwer, so leicht' (H 104). One must mortify oneself, and let oneself be hollowed out, as a humble wooden stair is by the passage of feet: 'Eine durch Schritte nicht tief ausgehöhlte Treppenstufe ist, von sich selbst aus gesehn, nur etwas besonders zusammengefügtes Hölzernes' (H 93; amended from MS). As this aphorism suggests, one may not be conscious, any more than the stair, of making spiritual progress, yet be on the right path just the same. Another aphorism also refers to the difference between appearance and reality, pointing out that opposite states can look identical to the observer:

Der Verzückte und der Ertrinkende, beide heben die Arme. Der erste bedeutet Eintracht, der zweite Widerstreit mit den Elementen. (H 87.)

Here Kafka has adapted and compressed a Hasidic saying, in which the Ba'al Shem defended the extravagant gesticulations made by his followers during ecstatic prayer:

When a man is drowning in a river and gesticulates while in the water that people should save him from the waters which threaten to sweep him away, the observers will certainly not laugh at him and his gestures. So, too, one should not pour scorn on a man who makes gestures while he prays for he is trying to save himself from the waters of presumption.[44]

Self-destruction is not self-knowledge, unless the injunction 'Erkenne dich selbst' is interpreted to mean 'Verkenne dich! Zerstöre dich!' (H 80). It means going before the Holy of Holies and stripping oneself not only of one's shoes and clothes but of one's very nakedness, and then even of what is left (H 104–5). Only if one submits to this process will one become aware of the good purpose it serves: 'Um Dich zu dem zu machen was Du bist' (H 80).[45] What remains will be the indestructible core of one's own being, which is part of 'das Unzerstörbare'.

It may not be clear how this static self-mortification is compatible with the active spiritual progress implied by the image of the way, on which Kafka offers several variations. Sometimes the true way is a tightrope stretched just above the ground, so as to make one stumble constantly (H 70–1); sometimes it is an uphill path with a steep gradient

on which one keeps slipping back (H 81), but this latter image provides some unexpected consolation, for it means that one's slow progress may be due to the difficulty of one's task rather than to one's
own shortcomings. Finally, however, Kafka supplies an image which
reconciles dialectically the opposed notions of spiritual effort and the
renunciation of effort:

So fest wie die Hand den Stein hält. Sie hält ihn aber fest, nur um ihn desto
weiter zu verwerfen. Aber auch in jene Weite führt der Weg. (H 83.)

One must be as passive as the stone, submitting oneself to a higher
authority and gaining a certain security from one's absolute submission. Since *verworfen* means both 'thrown away' and 'dismissed with
contempt', this leads to humiliation; but the image of the stone being
thrown shows that this humiliation brings one further along the way,
and hence that self-abnegation is the means of spiritual advance. It is
just this combination of activity and passivity, intense yet static concentration, which is expressed in the Hasidic concept of *Kavvanah*.

We saw earlier that Kafka was able to overcome the opposition
between being and consciousness by adapting the concept of *Tikkun*.
Instead of being fixed and unalterable, the opposition turned out to
belong to one stage in a process of spiritual development, the ultimate
end of which would be the reconciliation of the two. The concept of
Kavvanah now comes to Kafka's aid and enables him to reconcile the
second of his two oppositions, that between the spiritual integrity of
the individual and responsibility towards the community. Since 'das
Unzerstörbare' is common to all humanity, withdrawal into solitary
and rigorous self-mortification in order to uncover the indestructible
core within one's own being is the way to the only true integration
with humanity. This integration must be based on humility and
prayer:

Das Verhältnis zum Mitmenschen ist das Verhältnis des Gebetes, das
Verhältnis zu sich das Verhältnis des Strebens; aus dem Gebet wird die Kraft
für das Streben geholt. (H 119.)

To cut oneself off from humanity is suicidal: one would be like the
man who lives on the crumbs from his own table and starves when the
supply runs out (H 97). What links one to one's fellow-men is not
only prayer, but shared suffering. Another aphorism runs:

Du kannst dich zurückhalten von den Leiden der Welt, das ist dir freigestellt
und entspricht deiner Natur, aber vielleicht ist gerade dieses Zurückhalten
das einzige Leid, das du vermeiden könntest. (H 117.)

This emphasizes the importance which Kafka assigns to suffering. He goes even further in saying: 'Das Leiden ist das positive Element dieser Welt, ja es ist die einzige Verbindung zwischen dieser Welt und dem Positiven' (H 108). One is reminded of the words Büchner is reported to have uttered three days before his death: 'Wir haben der Schmerzen nicht zu viel, wir haben ihrer zu wenig, denn durch den Schmerz gehen wir zu Gott ein!'[46] For Kafka, however, pain is not the means of access to God but the medium in which one is linked to one's suffering fellow men:

Alle Leiden um uns müssen auch wir leiden. Christus hat für die Menschheit gelitten, aber die Menschheit muß für Christus leiden. Wir alle haben nicht einen Leib aber ein Wachstum, und das führt uns durch alle Schmerzen, ob in dieser oder in jener Form. So wie das Kind durch alle Lebensstadien bis zum Greis und zum Tod sich entwickelt—und jedes Stadium in Verlangen oder in Furcht im Grunde dem früheren unerreichbar scheint—, ebenso entwickeln wir uns (nicht weniger tief mit der Menschheit verbunden als mit uns selbst) durch alle Leiden dieser Welt gemeinsam mit allen Mitmenschen. (H 117; corrected from MS.)

Christ is mentioned here, not because Kafka feels any affinity with Christianity, but because he wants to reject the notion of a god intervening in the world to take its suffering upon himself. In reality, suffering is borne by mankind, not by Christ. The image of metempsychosis returns, to convey that one must experience every variety of suffering for oneself in the course of the cosmic process. Even taking metempsychosis as an image for the individual's spiritual development during a single lifetime, this would seem a terrifyingly pessimistic view, were it not that sharing the suffering of others links one with them in a relationship as intimate as one's relation to oneself. Moreover, suffering derives its painful character from the state of estrangement from being in which we live, and in another world, at the end-point of the cosmic process, its character will change:

Nur hier ist Leiden Leiden. Nicht so, als ob die, welche hier leiden, anderswo wegen dieses Leidens erhöht werden sollen, sondern so, daß das, was in dieser Welt leiden heißt, in einer andern Welt, unverändert und nur befreit von seinem Gegensatz, Seligkeit ist. (H 108.)

This peculiarly Delphic utterance implies that suffering is a composite state, whose two elements are related as consciousness to being. The sufferer is conscious only of pain and isolation, yet his sufferings serve to destroy his old self and bring him closer to the solidarity with his fellow-men in which true being consists. In a world where being is no longer at odds with consciousness, the solidarity will survive, freed from the pain which is its opposite but also the only means by which it can be achieved. This is the ultimate goal of the dialectical process worked out in the Zürau aphorisms.

Not only do the aphorisms state the principles on which a future community should be founded; by writing them, Kafka has fulfilled his responsibility and thus, in a sense, overcome his own estrangement from society. One of the last aphorisms runs: 'Der Weg zum Nebenmenschen ist für mich sehr lang' (H 131); the aphorisms themselves are the circuitous path that leads Kafka to his neighbour. On the other hand, his estrangement from society was in large part due to his commitment to literature, and the aphorisms, whatever their function, are themselves literature, so that one could turn a sentence from a well-known Kafka parable against Kafka himself and say that, if he has overcome his isolation, he has done so 'leider nur im Gleichnis' (B 96). Near the end of the second notebook containing the aphorisms is 'Die besitzlose Arbeiterschaft', Kafka's scheme for an ascetic, all-male community, which is evidently intended for Palestine, since the members are to live on bread, water, and dates. This plan may owe something to Kafka's reading about the celibate communities of Essenes who lived in Palestine at the time of the Roman occupation and whose aim was 'Abtötung der Sinnlichkeit durch Übung größtmöglichster Enthaltsamkeit zum Zwecke seelischer Erhebung'.[47] If so, the plan was not quite so impractical as it looks on paper.

The foregoing exposition has concentrated on the content rather than the form of Kafka's aphorisms. It is, however, worth drawing attention to a figure of thought for which he has a particular fondness. This is a technique of drawing comfort from an apparently hopeless situation by a sudden mental leap which enables one to view the situation from a different perspective. An instance would be the conclusion Kafka draws after establishing that the soul is inaccessible to consciousness: 'Sie muß also unbekannt bleiben. Das wäre nur dann traurig, wenn es etwas anderes außer der Seele gäbe, aber es gibt nichts anderes' (H 93). In other words, it does not matter if spiritual reality is unknowable, for all reality is spiritual, so there is a still unspecified sense in which we already know it. This is the kind of mental leap, leading to a transformation of consciousness, which might have saved Josef K. It is remarkably common in the Talmud and in Jewish folk-tales. One very striking example occurs in a story about the Ba'al Shem which Kafka heard from Langer:

Einem Zaddik soll man mehr gehorchen als Gott. Baalschem sagte einmal einem seiner liebsten Schüler, er solle sich taufen lassen. Er ließ sich taufen, kam zu Ansehn, wurde Bischof. Da ließ ihn Baalschem zu sich kommen und erlaubte ihm, zum Judentum zurückzukehren. Er folgte wieder und tat wegen seiner Sünde große Buße. Baalschem erklärte seinen Befehl damit, daß der Schüler wegen seiner ausgezeichneten Eigenschaften vom Bösen sehr verfolgt gewesen sei und daß die Taufe den Zweck gehabt habe, den Bösen abzulenken. Baalschem warf den Schüler selbst mitten ins Böse, der Schüler tat den Schritt nicht aus Schuld, sondern auf Befehl und für den Bösen schien es hier keine Arbeit mehr zu geben. (T 482.)

Apostasy, otherwise the most heinous of sins, is transformed into the virtue of obedience to the command of the Ba'al Shem. Other examples of this figure of thought can be found in the Ba'al Shem's comment on Elisha ben Abuyah, who had been told by a voice from heaven that he would not be saved: 'In wie glücklicher Lage war doch Elischa ben Abuja. Gerade er hätte wie kein anderer jemals mit voller Uneigennützigkeit Gott dienen können';[48] or Rabbi Elimelech's prediction that he would be saved because his confession to the divine judge that he had neither studied, prayed, nor done good works would ensure his salvation as a reward for his truthfulness;[49] or the saying in which Rabbi Akiba drew comfort from the good fortune of the wicked: 'If God allows those who transgress His will to live happily on earth, how infinitely great must be the happiness which He has stored up in the world to come for those who observe His commands!'[50] Much the neatest example, however, is a Hasidic saying attributed to the *tsaddik* Schneur Salman of Ladi and retold by Buber (for which one has to know that a 'Mitnaged' is an orthodox opponent of Hasidism):

Einer fragte den Raw scherzend: "Wird der Messias ein Chassid oder ein Mitnaged sein?" "Ich denke, ein Mitnaged," sagte er. "Denn würde er ein Chassid sein, die Mitnagdim würden ihm nicht glauben. Die Chassidim aber werden ihm glauben, was immer er sei."[51]

It is through this ingenious technique of drawing unexpected conclusions, more than through their content, that Kafka's aphorisms are related to traditions of Jewish thought.

In so far as the problems dealt with in the aphorisms were pressingly personal and not merely intellectual, they could not be solved once and for all by writing. Since, as Kafka says, there is a certain pleasure in understanding one's situation, even if that situation is painful, writing can raise one above one's sufferings, in the manner of Münchhausen pulling himself out of the swamp by his own pigtail (H 71). But this feat has to be performed repeatedly, and so images of imprisonment with no visible escape, sometimes no conceivable escape, recur in Kafka's work, most starkly in this aphorism from the later series, 'Er', written in 1920: 'Sein eigener Stirnknochen verlegt ihm den Weg, an seiner eigenen Stirn schlägt er sich die Stirn blutig' (B 292). This is a condensed and developed version of an earlier narrative in which a gentleman out riding in his coach comes to a long, white wall which terminates in an arch and which his coachman identifies as a forehead (H 153). As Hiebel says, this must represent the concave inner side of the forehead and hence the limit of the subjective world, from which there is no escape.[52] But against these images of confinement Kafka sets images of responsibility, as in the aphorism about the man who feels a duty to an unknown family and an unknown law (B 295), or in the short sketch 'Nachts', also dating from 1920:

Versunken in die Nacht. So wie man manchmal den Kopf senkt, um nachzudenken, so ganz versunken sein in die Nacht. Ringsum schlafen die Menschen. Eine kleine Schauspielerei, eine unschuldige Selbsttäuschung, daß sie in Häusern schlafen, in festen Betten, unter festem Dach, ausgestreckt oder geduckt auf Matratzen, in Tüchern, unter Decken, in Wirklichkeit haben sie sich zusammengefunden wie damals einmal und wie später in wüster Gegend, ein Lager im Freien, eine unübersehbare Zahl Menschen, ein Heer, ein Volk, unter kaltem Himmel auf kalter Erde, hingeworfen wo man früher stand, die Stirn auf den Arm gedrückt, das Gesicht gegen den Boden hin, ruhig atmend. Und du wachst, bist einer der Wächter, findest den nächsten durch Schwenken des brennenden Holzes aus dem Reisighaufen neben dir. Warum wachst du? Einer muß wachen, heißt es. Einer muß da sein. (B 116.)

As in *Der neue Advokat* and *Beim Bau der chinesischen Mauer*, Kafka uses a technique of superimposition. The phrase 'wie damals einmal' refers to the Israelites camping in the wilderness on their way to the Promised Land, though this turns out to be not merely a historical event but rather an image for the permanent condition of humanity. If the guardian, appointed by an unknown authority ('Einer muß wachen, heißt es'), suggests Moses, a figure who fascinated Kafka increasingly in his later years, there seems also to be a reminiscence of the picture of Napoleon on the battlefield of Wagram which Kafka saw in Versailles in 1911 and described as follows: 'Napoleon sitzt allein, das eine Bein auf einen niedrigen Tisch gelegt. Hinter ihm ein rauchendes Lagerfeuer' (T 619). The problem of one's responsibility towards mankind continued to preoccupy Kafka, and several different ways of exercising one's responsibility are examined in *Das Schloß*, which was written in the first half of 1922 and is the subject of the next chapter.

6

The Last Earthly Frontier
Das Schloß (1922)

Das Schloß is Kafka's most ambitious attempt to achieve the new artistic purpose that he had formulated in September 1917: 'die Welt ins Reine, Wahre, Unveränderliche heben' (T 534). His manifesto probably owes something to Schopenhauer's definition of the artist's task as 'reine, wahre und tiefe Erkenntnis des Wesens der Welt',[1] but goes beyond Schopenhauer, since, as we saw in the last chapter, Kafka regarded cognition ('Erkenntnis') not as a goal but as a starting-point. Philosophers like Schopenhauer had interpreted the world; Kafka wants to change it. Since his literary vocation compels him to do so 'im Gleichnis', his aim is to confront the world of falsehood, denounced in the Zürau aphorisms, by opposing to it a fictional world which, just because it is fictional, rises above the deceits of the physical world and approaches the truth.

A novel based on such principles can no longer be a reflection, however oblique, of the empirical world. It cannot be a mirror travelling down the highway, not even a distorting mirror like *Die Verwandlung* and *Der Prozeß*. Instead, it must be a self-contained fictional world whose relation to the empirical world is, in the terms proposed by the late Roman Jakobson, not metonymic but metaphoric.[2] The realistic novel, Jakobson suggested, tends towards the metonymic pole of language, because it presents itself as the copy of the world which is outside it and contiguous to it, while the modernist novel tends increasingly to sacrifice referential content to metaphoric, poetic imagery. (Contrast *Middlemarch* with *The Waves*.) Likewise, film is metonymic, theatre is metaphoric: we accept the stage as a self-contained image of the world, as in the phrase *theatrum mundi*. Within this polarity, *Das Schloß* is clearly metaphoric; while working on it, Kafka compares himself to a theatre director who has to create the entire theatre himself and even father the actors (T 574). Accordingly, the world of the novel is self-contained to a degree unusual in fantasy literature. The 'Traumstadt' of Kubin's *Die andere Seite* is situated somewhere in Central Asia, but one cannot even ask where Kafka's Castle is located, or what route leads to it; Frieda's proposal that she and K. should emigrate to Spain or the south of France (S 215) gives the reader a brief jolt but does not invite speculation about the length of their journey to the Mediterranean. The astonishing thing is that on this imaginary stage Kafka has placed a solid and elaborately structured society which Walter Sokel, a shade extravagantly, has compared to Dickens's London and Flaubert's Yonville.[3] An apter comparison might be with the intricate world of Peake's Gormenghast trilogy. The characters inhabiting this society are no longer, as in *Der Prozeß*, mere wraiths, important only in their functional relation to the hero or as projections of his psyche. Instead, *Das Schloß* contains three-dimensional characters with complex relationships and deep emotions. If the hero of *Der Prozeß* was isolated, as the subject of a moral experiment, in a sealed chamber where he could hurt nobody but himself, his counterpart in *Das Schloß* is exposed to risks and ambiguities which much more resemble those of actual experience. Not only can he harm himself, he can also hurt other people irretrievably. We have emerged from the confinement of *Der Prozeß* and entered a more spacious, less predictable world.

Creating this world was for Kafka a way of regaining contact with society after his relations with other people had reached an apparent crisis. In the second week of January 1922 he suffered a nervous breakdown which probably resulted in part from the strain of his relationship with Milena Jesenská. Though they were still close, their sexual relationship had ceased a year earlier, leaving Kafka with a renewed feeling that he was doomed to fail shamefully in his attempts to marry and found a family. No doubt the persistent ill-health which obliged him to spend much of his time in sanatoria also contributed to his nervous collapse. Looking back on the experience, he described it as one of living simultaneously in two time-scales: 'Die Uhren stimmen nicht überein, die innere jagt in einer teuflischen oder dämonischen oder jedenfalls unmenschlichen Art, die äußere geht stockend ihren gewöhnlichen Gang' (T 552). On further reflection, however, he felt that this frenzied mental activity was only an intensification of the relentless self-observation in which he normally indulged. He attributed this compulsion to his habitual solitude, and feared that it was leading him into yet greater solitude: 'Dieses Jagen nimmt die Richtung aus der Menschheit' (T 552). Writing was a possible means of re-establishing contact with mankind, but a dangerous one, for the writer was always under suspicion of merely feeding his own vanity. The only way to elude this danger was to use writing as a way of exercising one's responsibility towards the rest of mankind, as Kafka had done in the Zürau aphorisms.

The spirit of responsibility in which Kafka began work on *Das Schloß* is attested by several diary entries from this period in which he speaks of the task facing him. One dates from 21 January 1922, about a week before he started on the novel:

So schwer war die Aufgabe niemandes, soviel ich weiß. Man könnte sagen: es ist keine Aufgabe, nicht einmal eine unmögliche, es ist nicht einmal die Unmöglichkeit selbst, es ist nichts, es ist nicht einmal so viel Kind wie die Hoffnung einer Unfruchtbaren. Es ist aber doch die Luft, in der ich atme, solange ich atmen soll. (T 557.)

Here Kafka seems to be undertaking the task for his own sake, as the only medium in which he can survive. On 27 January he arrived in the health-resort of Spindlermühle in the Riesengebirge and in all likelihood set to work on *Das Schloß* on the same day.[4] Another diary-entry, of 10 February, repeats the image of air but suggests that the writer is seeking it on behalf of a larger body of people:

Es ist klarer als irgend etwas sonst, daß ich, von rechts und links von übermächtigen Feinden angegriffen, weder nach rechts noch links ausweichen kann, nur vorwärts, hungriges Tier, führt der Weg zur eßbaren Nahrung, atembaren Luft, freiem Leben, sei es auch hinter dem Leben. Du führst die Massen, großer langer Feldherr, führe die Verzweifelten durch die unter dem Schnee für niemanden sonst auffindbaren Paßstraßen des Gebirges. Und wer gibt dir die Kraft? Wer dir die Klarheit des Blickes gibt. (T 572.)

This passage recalls the notebook-entry of 1918, discussed in the previous chapter, in which Kafka describes his task of creating soil, air, and a commandment not just for himself but for the age in which he lives (H 120). Now, in 1922, the task has become more urgent, and Kafka imagines himself as a military commander leading a crowd of desperate people through a snowy wasteland.

This is one of several images that Kafka uses to define the mission that he feels has been entrusted to him. All imply spiritual leadership; some emphasize that the task of leadership must be performed by verbal communication; and all include the possibility that the mission has been assigned to a grotesquely incongruous figure, or, worse still, that the would-be leader has responded to a summons that was really intended for someone else.[5]

The first of these images, the military commander, springs of course from Kafka's long-standing fascination with figures like Napoleon and Alexander. His being described as a 'großer langer Feldherr' makes him into a self-ironizing projection of Kafka, who was a thin, gangling man just under six feet tall and self-conscious about his height. By leading 'Massen', civilians rather than soldiers, the commander resembles a national leader, like Moses, in whom Kafka was increasingly interested. In his diary for October 1921 Kafka meditates on why Moses was not allowed to enter the Promised Land, and decides that the Promised Land represents a goal too great to be realized within the limitations of human life (T 545). The same problem had been discussed by Brod in his book *Heidentum, Christentum, Judentum* (1921), which Kafka read before its publication (Br 279). Here Brod discusses the episode in Num. 20 in which Moses, commanded by the Lord to make a rock give forth water by speaking to it, is so anxious to assuage his people's thirst that he strikes the rock and thus earns the Lord's displeasure. In Brod's interpretation, Moses finds himself in a tragic dilemma, puts his duty to his people before obedience to the Lord, and is therefore permitted only to glimpse Canaan from the distance.[6] This interpretation may have encouraged Kafka to use Moses as an example of the conflicts inherent in carrying out a mission. In Brod's analysis, it is the intensity of Moses' devotion to his people that prevents him from sharing their final triumph; so, in Kafka's case, his vocation of serving humanity through his writing cut him off from immediate contact with other people, even if, by way of symbolic recompense, it united him with them on a different level.

Another image which seems to have contributed to the 'Feldherr' passage is that of the explorer. In associating the strength which enables the commander to perform his task with his 'Klarheit des Blickes', Kafka implies that the journey into the snow-covered mountains is among other things a quest for truth. He almost certainly knew the passage in *Zur Genealogie der Moral* where Nietzsche uses the image of an Arctic explorer to represent the disinterested search for truth:

Man sieht einen traurigen, harten, aber entschlossenen Blick—ein Auge, das *hinausschaut*, wie ein vereinsamter Nordpolfahrer hinausschaut (vielleicht um nicht hineinzuschauen? um nicht zurückzuschauen? . . .). Hier ist Schnee, hier ist das Leben verstummt; die letzten Krähen, die hier laut werden, heißen 'Wozu?', 'Umsonst!', '*Nada!*'[7]

Nietzsche's explorer leaves behind all questions of meaning and value and devotes himself to the increasingly sterile task of pure inquiry. Like Nietzsche, Kafka distrusts the pursuit of knowledge as an end in itself. He sees knowledge rather as the precondition of effective action. Hence his 'Feldherr' must use the gift of clear vision to lead people not into but out of the snowy waste, with its suggestions of spiritual desolation, to a more habitable country. Nietzsche's Arctic wasteland may have helped to suggest the landscape surrounding the Castle, which also has crows flying round it, though the snow-covered landscape had appeared in Kafka's fiction since 1914 ('Erinnerung an die Kaldabahn', T 422–35) and its presence in *Das Schloß* doubtless owes something to the actual landscape around Spindler-mühle, where Kafka furthered his convalescence by tobogganing and skiing.

An image of leadership which Kafka rejected was the one offered by Werfel in his play *Schweiger* (1922), which provoked Kafka into composing a letter of remonstrance. Though this letter, and a more strongly worded draft (H 275–8), were written in December 1922, after Kafka had abandoned work on *Das Schloß*, it is so closely related to Kafka's conception of the writer as spiritual leader that one is probably justified in deducing from it how Kafka understood his own task in *Das Schloß*. Werfel's play is set in a provincial town in post-war Austria. Schweiger, its hero, is a man with an inexplicable spiritual presence. Representatives of various contemporary ideologies— socialism, *völkisch* politics, Christianity—see a potential leader in him and try to win him over, but he refuses their blandishments and perishes as a result of his private traumas. Kafka was disappointed and disgusted by this play. Instead of using Schweiger to point out new spiritual possibilities for a perplexed age, Werfel had degraded his character into a psychiatric case and had thus betrayed the generation which regarded him as a leader:

Sie sind gewiß ein Führer der Generation, was keine Schmeichelei ist und niemandem gegenüber als Schmeichelei verwendet werden könnte, denn diese Gesellschaft in den Sümpfen kann mancher führen. [. . .] Und nun dieses Stück. Es mag alle Vorzüge haben, von den theatralischen bis zu den höchsten, es ist aber ein Zurückweichen von der Führerschaft, nicht einmal Führerschaft ist darin, eher ein Verrat an der Generation, eine Verschleierung, eine Anekdotisierung, also eine Entwürdigung ihrer Leiden. (Br 424–5.)

To understand why Kafka felt the shortcomings of Werfel's play to be so serious, one must realize that it confirmed the doubts Kafka had been developing about a writer whom he admired far more than he did Brod or any other literary contemporary in Prague. He was intermittently aware (F 300) that friendship for Brod made him overestimate the latter's writings, but towards Werfel he felt an awestruck humility. Werfel, who was seven years younger than Kafka and had had his first collection of ecstatic, hymnic poems, *Der Weltfreund*, published when he was twenty-one, was considered the boy genius of the Prague circle.[8] To Kafka he seemed 'ein Wunder' (F 178), 'ein Ungeheuer' (T 286) in his overpowering creative energy, and his early poems and plays were 'fortreißend' (T 444), whether Kafka read them in private or heard them recited by Werfel, who knew all his own poems by heart (F 281). His later plays, however, did not live up to these expectations. Kafka's comment on *Bocksgesang* (1921)—'Äußerst interessant ist es. Dieser Kampf mit den Wellen und immer wieder kommt er hervor, der große Schwimmer' (Br 363)—is already qualified, and stronger reservations are implied in a prose piece beginning ' "Der große Schwimmer! Der große Schwimmer!" riefen die Leute' (H 319). The great swimmer, returning from the Antwerp Olympics (1920), announces that although he has established a world record for swimming, he has actually never learnt to swim. If this is a covert reference to Werfel, it confirms that Kafka was beginning to sense something spurious about Werfel's achievements.

Another cautiously disparaging allusion to Werfel and his evasion of his responsibilities occurs in 1921 in the famous letter to Robert Klopstock where Kafka discusses the figure of Abraham. Despite his disapproval of Kierkegaard's version of the story, the Biblical Abraham continued to typify for Kafka the man who receives a divine summons. In his letter Kafka considers various versions of Abraham. There are 'die oberen Abrahame' (Br 333) who ignore the summons and awaken the suspicion that they '—um ein sehr großes Beispiel zu nennen—das Gesicht in magischen Trilogien verstecken, um es nicht heben zu müssen und den Berg zu sehn, der in der Ferne steht'. The great example is Werfel, whose play *Spiegelmensch: Magische Trilogie* had been published the year before; Kafka had read it avidly in a single afternoon (M 283), but on reflection it evidently seemed to him a diversion from the responsibilities of a major writer. If people like Werfel were going to ignore the summons, humble people like Kafka would have to answer it, even though it hardly seemed possible that it could be meant for them and they were likely to make fools of themselves by responding to it, like the other and humbler Abraham whom Kafka now proceeds to imagine:

Aber ein anderer Abraham. Einer, der durchaus richtig opfern will und überhaupt die richtige Witterung für die ganze Sache hat, aber nicht glauben kann, daß er gemeint ist, er, der widerliche alte Mann und sein Kind, der schmutzige Junge. [. . .] Er fürchtet, er werde zwar als Abraham mit dem Sohne ausreiten, aber auf dem Weg sich in Don Quixote verwandeln. (Br 333.)

Like the small tradesmen in *Ein altes Blatt*, Kafka saw himself obliged to assume a responsibility which greater people had refused.

Another image for this combination of humility with supreme responsibility is implied in the phrase 'Führer der Generation' which Kafka uses in his letter to Werfel. This is the literal equivalent to the Hebrew phrase *rosh ha-dor*, much used by the Ba'al Shem, and defined as follows by Gershom Scholem: 'Er ist der Mann, der in Gemeinschaft mit Gott lebt, aber seine Macht benutzt, um seine Mitmenschen mit sich nach oben zu ziehen.'[9] Kafka knew of this tradition from Jiří Langer, who told him about the 'Zaddik Hador' (T 482), a supreme *tsaddik* who appears in every century. Such a person exercises his spiritual powers in obscurity and does not emerge as a religious leader. In the early eighteenth century the *tsaddik ha-dor* contemporary with the Ba'al Shem was an ordinary merchant living in the Galician town of Drohobycz. Kafka also knew about the Lamed Vov, the thirty-six just men in every generation on whom the world reposes, even though no-one is permitted to know who they are.[10] In these figures, who carried out their spiritual tasks in complete obscurity, Kafka found models for his own role as a responsible writer.

As this allusion shows, Kafka had by now acquired a considerable knowledge of Jewish and especially Hasidic traditions. Since early in 1917 he had also been learning Hebrew. He began by using Moses Rath's grammar of classical Hebrew, but since his long-term plan was to emigrate to Palestine, he also learnt modern conversational Hebrew from several teachers: Langer, the writer and philosopher Friedrich Thieberger, and Puah Bentovim, a girl who had been brought up in Palestine, had spoken Hebrew constantly since childhood, and had come to Prague to study.[11] Dora Dymant, whom he met in July 1923, was impressed by his thorough and accurate command of Hebrew; she was a good judge, since she had been familiar with

Hebrew since her childhood, and during one of their earliest conversations she read Kafka a passage from Isaiah in the original.[12] While living together in Berlin they read the Hebrew Bible and Rashi's medieval commentary on the Pentateuch (an elementary text much used in Jewish schools),[13] and Kafka also struggled through some thirty pages of a modern Hebrew novel by Yosef Haim Brenner (Br 453, 456).[14] We can be sure that even at the beginning of 1922, when he started work on *Das Schloß*, his knowledge of Hebrew was extensive. Combined with his acquaintance with Jewish traditions, it formed part of the equipment he needed for the novel, as the following diary entry of 16 January 1922 indicates:

Diese ganze Literatur ist Ansturm gegen die Grenze, und sie hätte sich, wenn nicht der Zionismus dazwischengekommen wäre, leicht zu einer neuen Geheimlehre, einer Kabbala entwickeln können. Ansätze dazu bestehen. Allerdings ein wie unbegreifliches Genie wird hier verlangt, das neu seine Wurzeln in die alten Jahrhunderte treibt oder die alten Jahrhunderte neu erschafft und mit all dem sich nicht ausgibt, sondern jetzt erst sich auszugeben beginnt. (T 553.)

This passage needs some exegesis. Kafka has just been reflecting that his customary solitude makes him exaggeratedly introspective and thus isolates him still more from other people; his recent nervous breakdown was only an intensification of this state. On the other hand, his introspection can be seen, not as neurotic self-torment, but, more positively, as an 'Ansturm gegen die letzte irdische Grenze' (T 553), an assault on the last earthly frontier in the attempt to force his way beyond it into unexplored regions of consciousness. That description, he now continues, would apply to all his writing. As a series of attempts to annex new territory for literature, it runs the risk of coming to resemble the Cabbala, not in its content (we saw in the last chapter that Kafka had no first-hand knowledge of the Cabbala), but in being wholly esoteric, accessible only to Kafka and selected initiates. 'Ansätze dazu bestehen', he admits: we may think of *Elf Söhne*, a work that would have been altogether cryptic if Kafka had not mentioned to Brod that the 'sons' were eleven stories on which he was engaged.[15]

What has saved Kafka's writings from becoming totally hermetic is Zionism. Again, this needs explanation. As we saw in Chapter 4, Zionism interested Kafka not in its day-to-day aspect but as 'der Eingang zu dem Wichtigern' (F 675), as the possibility of building up a new religious community. For this purpose it would be necessary not only to think through the problems of religion afresh, as Kafka had done in the Zürau aphorisms, but also to draw in some way on the traditions of the past; hence Kafka's interest in figures like the Belzer Rabbi, and his incorporation of motifs from the Hasidic tale into his short stories, notably *Ein Landarzt*. In the passage just quoted, however, he expresses a desire to do more than that and to sink roots into past centuries or to create past centuries anew. That is, he means to draw on his knowledge of Jewish tradition much more deeply than he has yet done. Thus, although *Das Schloß* will be to some degree on obscure work, since it will attempt a further 'Ansturm gegen die letzte irdische Grenze' and engage in spiritual exploration, it will be saved from complete hermeticism by drawing on traditions known to other people besides Kafka.

What this means in practice is that Kafka's knowledge of Hebrew and of Jewish, especially Hasidic, traditions supplied him with a set of cultural allusions which he worked into *Das Schloß*. Once recognized, these allusions bring some episodes of the novel into sharper focus and open up new levels of meaning in others. The chief aim of the pages that follow is to point these allusions out and explore their implications for the interpretation of the novel. At this point, however, certain reservations are in order. First, it must not be imagined that these allusions form a code that can be cracked, revealing that the meaning of *Das Schloß* was all along something perfectly simple. Far from it: their function is not to reduce but to increase the complexity and richness of Kafka's text. Second, these allusions throw light on certain episodes, but, unless the limited knowledge of the present writer is to blame, they do not provide any master-key to the novel as a whole. Consequently, even if Kafka has preserved it from hermeticism, *Das Schloß* remains one of his obscurest works. The broad outline of its meaning is clear, thanks above all to the work of Richard Sheppard, but many passages and many details refuse to come into focus. It is worth considering briefly why this is so.

The main reason is, I think, that *Das Schloß* is an only partially successful work of art. One cannot fairly blame it for lacking the dramatic intensity of *Der Prozeß*, since it is planned as a more expansive work in which the hero has leisure to explore various milieux. Still, as we saw in Ch. 1, it was contact with drama that enabled Kafka's writing to take off, and in adopting a less concentrated narrative mode he was running the risks of meandering and of losing thematic control. As a result, *Das Schloß* contains some deplorable *longueurs*, notably the long excursus into the history of the Barnabas family and the later conversation between K. and Pepi, which, to make matters worse, is given in reported speech, like over-faithful minutes of a committee meeting. The imagined world of the novel is less vivid than in *Der Prozeß* and less charged with thematic significance. The novel suffers not only from incomplete realization but also from an inattention to detail which means that some of its narrative pledges are never redeemed. In the opening chapter, for example, K. makes a promise to call on the schoolmaster, which he subsequently never fulfils; and Count Westwest is mentioned with great portentousness, only to be forgotten about for the rest of the novel.[16] By contrast, *Der Prozeß* was composed with meticulous care: Staatsanwalt Hasterer, for instance, is mentioned near the outset as a good friend of K.'s, and duly makes his appearance in one of the unfinished chapters.

These criticisms do not affect the strengths of *Das Schloß*. Besides its moving portrayal of the relationship between Frieda and K., it contains, on the one hand, pregnant episodes like K.'s first attempt to reach the Castle or the ironic interview with Bürgel and, on the other, some of Kafka's finest comic writing. But they do set limits to the possibilities of interpretation. Trying to make sense of the scanty references to Count Westwest, for example, does not involve using external evidence to help interpret the text, but rather using the text along with external evidence in order to reconstruct Kafka's half-realized intentions—a speculative and unsatisfactory procedure which needs the greatest caution. Elsewhere Kafka supplies scraps of information which look like clues to his meaning but turn out to be red herrings. The characters' names, in particular, have provoked many ingenious conjectures,[17] but Brod tells us that Kafka took names at random from whatever books he happened to be reading: 'Bertuch' comes from a book about Goethe and is the name of a publisher in Weimar; 'Galater' and 'Barnabas' come from the New Testament; while 'Gerstäcker' was suggested by the adventure-stories of Friedrich Gerstäcker which Kafka's parents had on their shelves.[18] Of course Kafka's choice of names may have been influenced by subliminal associations, so that Richard Sheppard need not be wide of the mark in connecting 'Bertuch' with *Bahrtuch* 'shroud' and 'Gerstäcker' with *Gottesacker* 'churchyard', but that would be a flimsy basis for interpretation.[19] I should be inclined to doubt whether *Das Schloß* contains more than a handful of *sprechende Namen*.

It is now time to turn to the four main components of the novel and try to bring each one into a sharper focus by means of the appropriate internal and external evidence.

The Land-Surveyor

K.'s profession of land-surveyor seems to invite interpretation, and has received plenty. Many critics have seen the word 'Landvermesser' as alluding to the 'Vermessenheit' (boldness) with which K. challenges the Castle.[20] Wilhelm Emrich argues that land-surveying would be a revolutionary act, because it would query the present distribution of land.[21] Hulda Göhler has recently drawn attention to Ezek. 40, where a man with a measuring-rod measures the dimensions of the Temple, and surmised that K.'s mission is to help in rebuilding Zion.[22] While none of these associations can be ruled out altogether, they must be subordinate to the main significance of 'Landvermesser'. K.'s profession represents a pun on two almost identical Hebrew words, *mashoah* 'land-surveyor' and *mashiah* 'Messiah'.[23] In making such a pun, Kafka was not only exploiting his knowledge of Hebrew but borrowing a technique of word-play from the Hebrew Bible. Several biblical passages are unintelligible in translation because their meaning depends on puns in the original, as in the first chapter of Jeremiah:

Moreover the word of the Lord came unto me, saying, Jeremiah, what seest thou? And I said, I see a rod of an almond tree.

Then said the Lord unto me, Thou hast well seen: for I will hasten my word to perform it. (Jer. 1: 11–12.)

The Lord, by punning on the words *shaqed* 'almond tree' and *shoqed* 'watch', is here promising to watch over his people.[24] Kafka's similar pun serves to associate his text with Jewish tradition and to provide a further level of meaning which, however, is not private, but accessible to anyone who shares his knowledge of Hebrew. By its salience, the pun offers a crucial clue to the meaning of *Das Schloß*. To understand it, we must first try to reconstruct the associations that the term 'Messiah' had for Kafka, by recalling the numerous Messianic episodes in Jewish history that were known to him.

Kafka was familiar with the Bible, as his diaries attest, and would have known the prophecies concerning the Messiah in the books of Isaiah, Jeremiah, and Micah. He was aware also, from his reading in religious history, that Messianic expectations had been widespread among the less educated Jewish population in Palestine from the period of the Maccabean uprising (167 BC) till after the destruction of the Temple (AD 70). In *Heidentum, Christentum, Judentum* Brod fitted

Jesus into the pattern of Jewish Messianism.[25] These chiliastic hopes culminated in the rebellion against the Romans led by Bar Kokhba, whom the teacher Rabbi Akiba actually hailed as Messiah. After the suppression of the rebellion in AD 135, the rabbinate strictly condemned all Messianic movements, insisting on the supreme importance of the study of the Torah and the Talmud.[26] People who were not content to await the coming of the Messiah but tried to hasten it by their own efforts were denounced as 'forcers of the end'.

The opposition between the learned rabbinate and the common people, with their susceptibility to Messianic expectations, persisted, and came to a head after every major catastrophe in Jewish history. The expulsion of the Jews from Spain in 1492 was followed by a Messianic ferment. Two of its principal figures, the self-proclaimed Messiah David Re'uveni and his acolyte Salomon Molcho, appear in Brod's novel *Rëubēni, Fürst der Juden* (1925). Re'uveni turned up in Venice in 1524, claiming to come from a Jewish kingdom in Central Asia, and sought help from various European potentates for the reconquest of Palestine from the Turks. While conferring with the King of Portugal, he found an associate in Diego Pires, a young man of Jewish descent, who submitted to circumcision and assumed the name Salomon Molcho. Re'uveni and Molcho continued their Messianic propaganda for several years, but were finally put to death by the Inquisition. Although Brod's novel about them was not published till after Kafka's death, he did the necessary historical research and wrote the first four chapters during Kafka's lifetime, so that Kafka, though unacquainted with the original sources, would have known something about this period at second hand.

A Messianic movement much more influential than Re'uveni's arose in reaction to the massacres of Ukrainian Jews in Khmelnitsky's Cossack uprising in 1648. The shock felt by the entire Jewish world helps to explain the fervent response to the emergence of Shabbetai Tsevi as Messiah. Shabbetai (1626–76) was an educated Jew from Smyrna who suffered from severe manic-depressive instability. He was considered a local eccentric until 1665, when a young rabbi, Nathan of Gaza, had a vision of him as the Messiah and persuaded him that the bizarre antics he indulged in during his manic spells proceeded from divine illumination. With a prophet to vouch for them, Shabbetai's Messianic claims were widely accepted, and for a year the Jewish communities of Europe and Asia were swept by apocalyptic hysteria, vividly described in Isaac Bashevis Singer's novel *Satan in*

Goray. Many Jews abandoned their homes and professions and prepared to set out for Palestine. In September 1666, however, Shabbetai was brought before the Sultan in Adrianople and given the
choice between being martyred as the Messiah, or renouncing his
claims and converting to Islam. He chose the latter option and was
rewarded with a sinecure as Keeper of the Palace Gates.[27] Despite his
apostasy, Messianic movements persisted among the Jews of Eastern
Europe in the seventeenth and eighteenth centuries, the largest being
the Frankist movement. Its leader, Jacob Frank (1726–91), believed
in redemption through sin, and therefore he and his adherents committed the two most heinous offences possible for Jews: they abandoned their religion for Catholicism, and then incriminated the Jews
by accusing them of employing the blood of Christians for ritual purposes. Instead of meeting the end he deserved, Frank died as the
owner of a castle near Frankfurt am Main, bearing the title Baron
von Offenbach, and supported in luxury by gifts from his Polish and
Bohemian followers; he may have met with poetic justice, however,
by helping indirectly to suggest the character of Moritz Spiegelberg,
the villainous Jew in Schiller's *Die Räuber*.[28]

Kafka knew about the Sabbatian and Frankist movements from
various sources. The response of German Jews to Shabbetai's procla-
mation is described in the 'Vorspiel' to Wassermann's novel *Die Juden
von Zirndorf*, which he owned;[29] Jacob Frank figures in the story 'Der
Hirt' in Buber's *Die Legende des Baalschem*; and he also heard about
these movements in conversation with Langer (T 482), who gives a
long account of them in *Die Erotik der Kabbala*. He also knew about the
attitude to Messianism held by the Ba'al Shem. The Ba'al Shem was
opposed to Messianism, but did not attack it outright, recognizing,
perhaps, that it was too tenacious a feature of Jewish religious life
ever to be eradicated; instead, his achievement consisted in what Gershom Scholem calls the neutralization of the Messianic impulse.[30] He
adjured his followers to redirect their energy away from yearning for
the advent of the Messiah and towards the attainment of individual
sanctity. Once everyone had achieved such sanctity, there would no
longer be any need to await the Messiah, since he would already
be present in their hearts and minds. The Ba'al Shem expressed
this idea in a story which came to be regarded as the manifesto of
Hasidism, and which describes a spiritual ascent to Heaven. In the
course of this experience the Ba'al Shem came to the palace of the
Messiah:

Und ich fragte den Messias: wann wird der Herr kommen? Und er erwiderte mir: 'Daran sollst du es erkennen: wenn deine Lehre weitbekannt und du der Welt offenbart sein wirst, und deine Quellen nach außen verströmen, was ich dich gelehrt und du erfaßt hast, und auch sie Einungen und Aufstiege werden vollbringen können wie du; dann wird die böse Macht vernichtet und eine Zeit der Gnade und Hilfe sein.'[31]

This interpretation of the Messianic impulse was evidently known to Kafka, for it appears in the Zürau notebooks where he speculates that once everyone has attained individual faith, the Messiah will in effect have arrived, so that 'Der Messias wird erst kommen, wenn er nicht mehr nötig sein wird' (H 90).

The Ba'al Shem was one of the two most influential figures among the eighteenth-century European Jews; the other, incongruously enough, was Moses Mendelssohn, under whose influence the Messianic tradition underwent a different transformation. The advent of the Messiah was reinterpreted in secular terms as the ultimate stage in an optimistic, Enlightened conception of the historical process. In the nineteenth century the leaders of Reform Judaism propagated this view, claiming that Jewish emancipation was the prelude to a secular millennium. Similarly, the Communist Moses Hess wrote in 1862:

Denn das Ende der Tage, von welchem das Judenthum seit dem Anfange der heiligen Geschichte, in seinen guten und bösen Tagen, stets geweissagt hat, ist nicht, wie andere Völker es mißverstanden haben, das Ende der Welt, sondern die Vollendung der Entwicklungsgeschichte und Erziehung des Menschengeschlechts.[32]

Despite the echo of Lessing in the final phrase, Hess by this time had already turned away from the Enlightenment ideal of Jewish assimilation, and had concluded that the Jews could not hope to be absorbed into Western society and should instead aim at national autonomy, as other European peoples were doing. His treatise is among the earliest documents of Zionism, a movement in which Messianic notions have never been far below the surface. Theodor Herzl claimed that as a child he had dreamt about meeting the Messiah, who said to him: 'Go and declare to the Jews that I shall come soon and perform great wonders and great deeds for my people and for the whole world!'[33] Herzl also compared himself to Shabbetai Tsevi, a figure who fascinated him and who is discussed in his novel *Altneuland*, set in the Jewish state of the future. After seeing an opera about Shabbetai, a group of characters judge his case leniently and conclude that the Jews were misguided only in expecting their deliverance to come from an individual rather than from the reawakening of their national spirit.[34]

Das Schloß is deeply indebted to Kafka's knowledge of the Messianic tradition. Through the figure of K. Kafka expresses the Messianic impulse, examines it critically, and finally condemns it. K. resembles the would-be Messiahs of history, not only in the pun implicit in his profession, but in four of his salient characteristics.

The first of these is the suspect nature of his calling. Since all previous Messiahs have been impostors, it is appropriate that K.'s credentials as a land-surveyor should be questionable. When roused by Schwarzer in the Brückenhof, he claims to have strayed into the village and to know nothing of any Castle, yet immediately afterwards he announces himself as the land-surveyor summoned by Count Westwest. After first disclaiming all knowledge of him, the Castle authorities then confirm his status, to his own surprise. Later the 'Gemeindevorsteher' turns out to have been expecting K. for a long time, and informs him that he was indeed summoned, but in consequence of an administrative error. Though there is no way of resolving these ambiguities, they are not mere wilful mystifications, nor are they simply a renewed expression of Kafka's fear that in answering a summons one may be thrusting oneself forward impudently or responding to the 'Fehlläuten der Nachtglocke' (E 153). Such ambiguity is, above all, an essential feature of K.'s role as land-surveyor/Messiah.

Similarly, two of K.'s most prominent attributes, his aggressiveness and his ruthless ambition, are not accidental features of his personality but integral to his concealed Messianic role. The Messianic movements described above had necessarily to challenge the existing order, and usually found their first antagonist in the orthodox rabbinate, the upholders of law and tradition. No wonder, therefore, that K. is constantly spoiling for a fight with the Castle authorities. 'Kampf' and 'Sieg' are among his favourite words; it is appropriate that he remembers his military service as 'diese glücklichen Zeiten' (S 31). The moment he learns of his appointment as land-surveyor, he assumes that the Castle is embattled against him (S 12), and on first meeting Frieda he quite gratuitously supposes that she is engaged in a 'Kampf' with the Castle (S 63). He regards himself as the 'Angreifer' (S 93) and fancies that many other people, unknown to him, are also attacking the Castle. He recollects climbing the churchyard wall in his home town as a child, a flag between his teeth, and the 'Gefühl dieses Sieges' (S 50) sustains him later; he wins a victory over Momus, Klamm's secretary, by insisting on waiting for Klamm in the courtyard; and while asleep in Bürgel's room he dreams about defeating a naked official. But all these victories are questionable. The first was 'überraschend leicht' (S 49) and took place in an unusual blaze of light, suggesting quasi-divine intervention and recalling the cancelled passage from *Der Prozeß* in which Josef K. and Titorelli fly effortlessly towards a dazzling light (P 294–5). The second is 'ein Sieg, der keine Freude machte' (S 168), a mere assertion of K.'s will with no further purpose, and the third appears to be a laughable surrogate for the victory that is impossible in reality. These illusory and futile victories show aggression to be pointless as a means of achieving a goal and illustrate Kafka's aphorism: 'Eines der wirksamsten Verführungsmittel des Bösen ist die Aufforderung zum Kampf' (H 74).

Kafka continues the critique of Messianism by showing how mercilessly K. is prepared to exploit other people in pursuit of his ambitions. This theme is explicit in the first part of *Das Schloß* to be written, the subsequently discarded passage beginning 'Der Wirt begrüsste den Gast', in which the unnamed stranger says to the parlourmaid Elisabeth (later replaced by Frieda):

Ich habe eine schwere Aufgabe vor mir und habe ihr mein ganzes Leben gewidmet. Ich tue es fröhlich und verlange niemandes Mitleid. Aber weil es alles ist was ich habe, diese Aufgabe nämlich unterdrücke ich alles was mich bei ihrer Ausführung stören könnte, rücksichtslos. Du, ich kann in dieser Rücksichtslosigkeit wahnsinnig werden. (SA 116.)

This draft anticipates the ruthlessness K. shows towards others. When his relationship with Frieda is crumbling, she accuses him of having made advances to her solely as a means of reaching Klamm (S 244), and while this may not be the whole truth, it is supported by the dejection K. feels when Frieda detaches herself from Klamm by crying: 'Ich bin beim Landvermesser!' (S 69), by the lust K. feels the instant he meets Pepi, her successor as barmaid (S 160), and by numerous paralipomena which charge K. with base and self-interested motives (SA 185, 240, 272–4). Messianic pretenders have always been open to the suspicion of mere self-seeking, in gross contrast to the supposedly redemptive character of their mission. K. shows little concern to benefit other people, but several characters, especially the Barnabas and Brunswick families, expect some undefined help from him. Even the peasants who pester K. and gape at him seem to want something from him which they cannot put into words: 'vielleicht wollten sie wirklich etwas von ihm und konnten es nur nicht sagen' (S 44). If K.'s mission is capable of benefiting others, then his readiness to exploit people must throw further doubt on the authenticity of his calling.

The fourth characteristic common to K. and other would-be Messiahs is having a prophet to announce and validate their mission. Bar Kokhba was proclaimed the Messiah by Rabbi Akiba, Re'uveni by Salomon Molcho, Shabbetai by Nathan of Gaza. K.'s status is acknowledged only by the child Hans Brunswick, who believes: 'jetzt sei zwar K. noch niedrig und abschreckend, aber in einer allerdings fast unvorstellbar fernen Zukunft werde er doch alle übertreffen' (S 237). Hans's vision of the future suggests that Kafka is alluding to the tradition of Messianic prophecy; there seem also to be puns on his prophetic foresight implied when K. judges him to be 'fast ein energischer kluger weitblickender Mann' (S 225) and calls him a 'vorsichtigen kleinen Mann' (S 251).

The word-play concealed in 'Landvermesser', then, is more than a passing allusion. It would appear that Kafka's portrayal of K. throughout the novel was guided by his conception of K. as a Messiah-figure. By his critical depiction of K., Kafka was contributing to a central and controversial Jewish tradition. Besides being a propelling force in Jewish history, Messianism has always aroused hostility and criticism within the Jewish world: orthodox Judaism has generally opposed it—even today there are groups of orthodox Jews who condemn the state of Israel as a sacrilegious attempt to realize the Messianic kingdom—and, from a different standpoint, so has Hasidism. The Messianic idea has been searchingly questioned in a famous article by Gershom Scholem. Scholem argues that by urging people to live in hope of redemption in the future, the Messianic idea has discouraged them from finding any value in the present. It reduces the present to an empty period of waiting, during which no achievement can be more than provisional and even the individual cannot be recognized at his full worth. 'The Messianic idea', Scholem concludes, 'is the real anti-existentialist idea.'[35] In *Das Schloß* Kafka undertakes a similar critique of Messianism. K. discards Frieda because his energies are for the most part directed towards a future goal which even he cannot define: asked why he wants to see Klamm, he admits: 'was ich von ihm will, ist schwer zu sagen' (S 137); and later he acknowledges to himself that Klamm is not his ultimate goal:

denn nicht Klamms Nähe an sich war ihm das erstrebenswerte, sondern daß er, K., nur er, kein anderer mit seinen, mit keines andern Wünschen an Klamm herankam und an ihn herankam, nicht um bei ihm zu ruhen sondern um an ihm vorbeizukommen, weiter, ins Schloß. (S 176.)

As one would expect, there are also non-Jewish prototypes for K.'s. insatiable striving. The most obvious is indicated by another pun, in the phrase 'auf eigene Faust' (S 138, 144), which draws attention to the similarities between K. and Goethe's Faust. Both strive towards an indefinable goal, and both callously abandon the women (Frieda, Gretchen) whom they encounter on the way.[36] Another prototype is Michael Kohlhaas, the hero of Kafka's favourite story (he informed Felice in February 1913 that he had just read it for the tenth time, F 291).[37] Having had two horses illegally confiscated by Junker Wenzel von Tronka, Kohlhaas eventually resorts to force in order to regain them and storms the Junker's castle. This anticipates the aggressive side of K. But Kohlhaas's aims grow increasingly nebulous. Not satisfied with the restitution of the horses, he ends up demanding an abstract justice which the imperfect world around him cannot provide. As the reader (though not K.) learns from Bürgel, K.'s ambition to penetrate the Castle is equally unrealizable.

K.'s obsession makes him forfeit the alternative which is offered to him, namely, domestic life with Frieda. To understand what his choice involves, we must examine Kafka's presentation of the Castle and then look more closely at the positive alternative which is held out to K.

The Castle

If K. cannot define his goal, the reason may lie in the sheer difficulty of understanding the significance of the Castle. The interpretations offered by commentators have been extraordinarily diverse. Those at one end of the spectrum see it as a religious emblem with a fixed meaning, as Brod did when he explained it as 'genau das, was die Theologen "Gnade" nennen'.[38] At the other extreme, Klaus-Peter Philippi considers it only an empty sign, 'etwas, eine Chiffre, das durch seine Existenz nur mehr auf den Verlust der echten Identität von Sache und Bedeutung verweist'.[39] The truth, I think, lies somewhere between these extremes. The Castle is neither an emblem nor a cipher. However, Kafka certainly draws on an allegorical tradition employing univocal images, and a rapid survey of this tradition will show how far Kafka is indebted to it for some of the Castle's associations and how far he distances himself from it by not assigning a fixed religious significance to the Castle.

The earliest prototype of the Castle is the Old Testament Zion, which is spoken of as both a castle and a city: 'Aber David gewann die Burg Zion, das ist Davids Stadt' (2 Sam. 5 : 7). This passage seems to have suggested the ambiguous physical appearance of Kafka's Castle. Only from a distance does it resemble a castle; seen close up, it proves to be 'nur ein recht elendes Städtchen, aus Dorfhäusern zusammengetragen' (S 17). The indebtedness is still clearer in a fragmentary dialogue about a distant city, which ends:

O ja, ich sehe es, es ist ein Berg mit einer Burg oben und dorfartiger Besiedelung auf den Abhängen.
Dann ist es jene Stadt, du hast recht, sie ist eigentlich ein großes Dorf. (H 333.).

The Old Testament uses the castle or city of Zion as an image of God's dwelling-place, thus founding a tradition of imagery which Kafka also encountered in Maimonides. He knew Maimonides at second hand from the autobiography of Salomon Maimon, which, as Kafka mentions with evident interest (Br 203), contains a summary of Maimonides' theological and philosophical work, the *Guide for the Perplexed*. The summary includes a lengthy allegory in which Maimonides compares God to a king sitting in his palace and surrounded by his subjects:

Der König, sagt er, wohnt in seinem Palast. Von seinen Untertanen sind einige in seiner Residenz; andere wiederum außer derselben. Von den ersteren gibt es einige, die dem königlichen Palast den Rücken zukehren und sich von demselben entfernen. Andre gehn zwar nach dem Palast mit dem Vorsatz, dem König aufzuwarten, gelangen aber nie dahin. Andere gelangen zwar dahin, können aber den Eingang nicht finden. Einige kommen in den Vorhof, einige sind sogar schon in dem Palast, können aber dennoch den König nicht so leicht zu sehen oder zu sprechen bekommen, bis sie durch viele Mühe endlich dazu gelangen.[40]

Since this is the kind of allegory based on one-to-one correspondences, each of these groups has an equivalent. Those outside the royal capital are people with neither natural nor revealed religion, like the

Tartars and the Moors; those with their backs to the palace have a religion, but a false one; those who set out for, but do not find, the palace have the true religion, but practise it mechanically, without understanding; those who cannot find the entrance to the palace are Talmudists, who understand religious truth but have never thought about the fundamental principles of religion; while people who do ponder these principles have reached the forecourt, and those inside the palace are on the way to attaining knowledge of God. Though *Das Schloß* is very differently composed, Maimonides' allegory may have helped to suggest K.'s efforts to approach the Castle and the elaborate hierarchy of villagers, innkeepers, secretaries, and officials surrounding it.

Another allegory which appears to have been known to Kafka is *The Labyrinth of the World and the Paradise of the Heart* (1631) by the Czech humanist Jan Amos Komenský. It contains two allegorical castles. One is the Castle of Fortuna, which has crowds of men walking round it looking for an entrance. The other, the Palace of Worldly Wisdom, is accessible only to the privileged members of a hierarchy:

Behold, the outer walls of this palace gleamed everywhere with divers beautiful paintings; and it had a gate at which guards stood; thus no one except those who had some power or office in the world could enter. To these only, as being servants of the queen and executors of her orders, liberty to go in and out was granted. Others, if they wished to behold the palace, had to gape at it from the outside only. (For it was said that it was not seemly that all should spy on the secrets by which the world is ruled.)[41]

This is an ironic allegory in which the castle, a secular building, is shown to attract only worldlings, and is contrasted with the church in which Komenský's pilgrim later gains access to the divine. It should help to dissuade interpreters of *Das Schloß* from trying to find a univocal religious meaning in the Castle.

Kafka was also familiar with philosophical writings employing the image of a castle. Schopenhauer uses it to indicate that empirical inquiry can never provide access to the 'Wesen der Dinge': 'Man gleicht Einem, der um ein Schloß herumgeht, vergeblich einen Eingang suchend und einstweilen die Fassaden skizzirend.'[42] Kierkegaard employs the image to enforce his contention that a man should regard his social superiors simply as fellow men and face them with proper self-respect:

Auch von der Herrlichkeit des königlichen Schlosses soll er sich keine abenteuerliche, märchenhafte Vorstellung machen; er soll sich getrauen, auch in des Königs Saal mit zuversichtlicher Würde einzutreten. Nicht daß er mir nichts dir nichts, unter Mißachtung jeglichen Abstands und Anstands, von der Gasse weg in des Königs Saal stürmen dürfte.[43]

The conduct Kierkegaard condemns resembles that of K., who willingly discards his dignity in the hope of gaining entry to the Castle, and intrudes into the corridors of the Herrenhof before being turned out by the landlord and landlady. Besides these philosophical images, Kafka knew several literal castles from his reading: the Tronkenburg in *Michael Kohlhaas*, and the castle of the Princess in Božena Němcová's *Babička* ('Grandmother'), with its staff of lazy and dishonest servants.[44] There has also been much debate about which of the real castles that he saw in Bohemia is most likely to have influenced *Das Schloß*.[45] Here, however, the search for sources risks tipping over into the trivia of merely biographical criticism, and we had better call a halt.

The diversity of Kafka's sources matches the multivalence of the Castle. Its religious associations, which will shortly be discussed in detail, sometimes recall the divine castles of the Old Testament and the *Guide for the Perplexed*; yet at other times the behaviour of its officials and their servants makes it appear as suspect as Komenský's Palace of Worldly Wisdom, or as oppressive as Kleist's Tronkenburg. Not only its metaphorical significance, but even its physical appearance is uncertain. Kafka takes care to remind us that we are seeing it through K.'s eyes:

Im Ganzen entsprach das Schloß, wie es sich hier von der Ferne zeigte, K.s Erwartungen. Es war weder eine alte Ritterburg, noch ein neuer Prunkbau, sondern eine ausgedehnte Anlage, die aus wenigen zweistöckigen, aber aus vielen eng aneinanderstehenden niedrigen Bauten bestand; hätte man nicht gewußt daß es ein Schloß ist, hätte man es für ein Städtchen halten können. (S 17.)

This incoherent description seems to tell us more about the state of K.'s mind than about the appearance of the Castle. The Castle fulfils K.'s expectations, yet we are promptly told that it looks so unlike a castle that unless one knew what it was in advance, one would take it for a village. One might be tempted to agree with Philippi that it only looks like a castle because K. is determined to see it as one: 'Ein Schloß ist es nur, weil K. es aufgrund seiner Erwartungen dafür hält; weil er es dafür halten *will*, denn auf den zweiten Blick muß er seinen

Eindruck wieder zurücknehmen.'[45] This would be a defensible view if Kafka had written 'daß es ein Schloß sei', which is printed in the edition Philippi was obliged to rely on. Now that Kafka's authentic text is available in the Critical Edition, we can see that he used not the subjunctive, which would imply doubt, but the indicative—'daß es ein Schloß ist'—which shows that the narrator is intervening to supply privileged information and to confirm that it is indeed a castle, despite appearances.

The Critical Edition also disproves the still more radical view, upheld by Ingeborg Henel, that the Castle, and indeed the whole world of the novel, only exists as a projection of K.'s beliefs.[47] She argues that the opening paragraph of the novel, narrated from K.'s standpoint, reveals his conviction that the Castle must exist even though nothing is visible through the fog and darkness. What Kafka wrote, however, was as follows:

Es war spät abend als K. ankam. Das Dorf lag in tiefem Schnee. Vom Schloßberg war nichts zu sehn, Nebel und Finsternis umgaben ihn, auch nicht der schwächste Lichtschein deutete das große Schloß an. Lange stand K. auf der Holzbrücke die von der Landstraße zum Dorf führt und blickte in die scheinbare Leere empor. (S 7.)

The crucial word here is 'führt'. Previous editions had 'führte', which would be appropriate if this paragraph really were being narrated entirely from K.'s viewpoint. But the present tense of 'führt' is the appropriate one for a narrator whose viewpoint differs from K.'s, and who can vouch for the reality of K.'s surroundings. The fact that the paragraph comes from a narrative voice independent of K. particularly affects the interpretation of the word 'scheinbar'. On Henel's reading, the word would come from K. and indicate his *a priori* conviction that there must be a castle and that the apparent void is only 'scheinbar'. On the reading required by Kafka's authentic text, the word comes from the narrator and guarantees the independent reality of the Castle, despite its 'scheinbar' absence. The nature and meaning of the Castle are still perplexing, but Kafka has at least given us the assurance that there is something up there. As with the *Ding an sich*, we can be certain of the Castle's existence, though perhaps of nothing else about it.

This applies also to the spiritual reality of which Kafka speaks in the Zürau aphorisms. It cannot be known intellectually; one can apprehend it only from inside, by living in a certain way and thus being part of it. 'Nicht jeder kann die Wahrheit sehn, aber sein'

(H 94). Indeed, there is a sense in which everyone already inhabits the spiritual world, for its basis, 'das Unzerstörbare', is also the basis of each individual's existence and the link between him and the rest of humanity. Most people, however, are estranged from the indestructible core of their being by self-deception, and one form of self-deception is the attempt to perceive the spiritual world intellectually. That, I suggest, is what K. is doing when he scrutinizes the Castle from below, and that is why it does not present any stable appearance to his gaze. It cannot be apprehended from outside, still less approached: when K. sets out for the Castle, the road that seems to lead to it simply winds round the Castle interminably. By being in the village, however, K. in an important sense is already in the Castle. Schwarzer tells him: 'Dieses Dorf ist Besitz des Schlosses, wer hier wohnt oder übernachtet, wohnt oder übernachtet gewissermaßen im Schloß' (S 8, cf. 20, 309). In the village it is possible to live in accordance with the demands of the Castle, with no need to strive towards it. Similarly, one cannot make contact with 'das Unzerstörbare', because it is already within one, so that the attempt to reach it is like trying to jump over one's own shadow; but one has no need to make the attempt: 'Theoretisch gibt es eine vollkommene Glücksmöglichkeit: An das Unzerstörbare in sich glauben und nicht zu ihm streben' (H 96). That, however, is a lesson which K. learns, if at all, only when it is too late for him to profit from it.

What I am arguing, therefore, is that the assumptions underlying *Das Schloß* are the same as those of the Zürau aphorisms, and that the Castle is to be identified with 'das Unzerstörbare', which was discussed in the last chapter as a concept central to Kafka's thought. However, the Castle cannot represent 'das Unzerstörbare' in the way that the palace in Maimonides' allegory represented the dwelling-place of God. Since Kafka assumes that being cannot be present to consciousness, and 'das Unzerstörbare' is part of being, Kafka cannot use any fixed, stable image to represent 'das Unzerstörbare'; instead, the Castle can only be an unstable image, one which changes its appearance every time the observer tries to focus his gaze on it. Moreover, as we also saw in the last chapter, 'das Unzerstörbare' cannot be identified with the object consciously worshipped by any religion, although it is itself both the origin and the real object of the religious impulse. But since religion is, by definition, a form of estrangement from 'das Unzerstörbare', the latter, as the real object of religion, must remain occluded from it by fictions like that of a personal god. Religion is not an illusion, as Freud thought, since for Kafka the religious impulse is essential to humanity; but it must always be under an illusion. Hence the imagery of religion is valid as the expression of the religious impulse, but misleading as an interpretation of this impulse. Kafka is therefore debarred from making any such straightforward use of religious imagery as he found in Maimonides and his other sources: he can only use religious imagery with qualifications. One method of qualifying it is the eclecticism that we noted in *Der Prozeß*. If Kafka uses a religious image, he must promptly deny its claim to privileged authority by following it with an image drawn from a different tradition. Although, as we shall see, Kafka's eclecticism is not wholly even-handed, this does explain why certain images used in *Das Schloß* are charged with a significance which is intense yet desperately hard to formulate.

In the very first chapter, Kafka distances himself from the imagery of traditional religion by contrasting the Castle with the church spire in K.'s home town:

Und er verglich in Gedanken den Kirchturm der Heimat mit dem Turm dort oben. Jener Turm, bestimmt, ohne Zögern, geradenwegs nach oben sich verjüngend, breitdachig abschließend mit roten Ziegeln, ein irdisches Gebäude—was können wir anderes bauen?—aber mit höherem Ziel als das niedrige Häusergemenge und mit klarerem Ausdruck als ihn der trübe Werktag hat. (S 18.)

Unlike the church spire, the Castle only looks distinct from a distance. When K. gets closer, he sees that the battlements are 'unsicher, unregelmäßig, brüchig wie von ängstlicher oder nachlässiger Kinderhand gezeichnet' (S 18), and the stone appears to be crumbling. Recalling how Kafka, in *In der Strafkolonie*, represented the decline of religion by a disintegrating machine, we might want to attach a similar association to the shapeless and decrepit-looking Castle. But we should also recall the notebook-entry in which Kafka says that he has been born too late to share in Jewish or Christian traditions and is 'Ende oder Anfang' (H 121). If he is continuing the project, begun in the Zürau aphorisms, of exploring how a new religious life could be based on 'das Unzerstörbare', it is appropriate that the novel's dominant image should be associated both with decay and, through the word 'Kinderhand', with renewal.

The church spire in K.'s home also symbolized a clear division between Sunday and weekdays, between the religious and the secular aspects of life. Even if workaday existence was as squalid and aimless as the phrase 'das niedrige Häusergemenge' implies, the spire pointed unmistakably towards a transcendent goal. The Castle's resemblance to a town suggests, however, that such distinctions are blurred, and that Kafka's project includes questioning the accepted division of the sacred from the secular.

The other associations surrounding the Castle are diverse and incongruous, but we can now understand their incongruity as part of Kafka's meaning: the implications of each image must be ironically qualified by its juxtaposition with an unexpected successor. K.'s attempts to communicate with the Castle by telephone provide an example. In the receiver he hears a buzzing like the 'Gesang fernster, allerfernster Stimmen' (S 36), later described as 'Rauschen und Gesang' (S 116), which seem to combine and form a single, powerful voice. Though unintelligible, this sound contains more truth than any verbal reply, for an answer could only be an inconsequential joke on the part of a tired official, while the buzzing comes from the incessant telephoning that goes on inside the Castle. The telephone permits one to overhear the deliberations of remote officials, though one cannot make sense of what one hears. Malcolm Pasley has discerned an echo of Ezek. 10: 5: 'Und man hörete die Flügel der Cherubim rauschen bis heraus vor den Vorhof, wie eine Stimme des allmächtigen Gottes, wenn er redet.' He has also pointed out that Nietzsche, in *Zur Genealogie der Moral*, pauses in his analysis of the priestly function to accuse Wagner of giving music the status of a religious oracle, a 'Telephon des Jenseits'.[48] It is possible that Kafka is not only juxtaposing the numinous atmosphere of the passage in Ezekiel with Nietzsche's reductive scepticism, but also subsuming both under the idea, found in some Jewish biblical commentators, that inarticulate sound is more reliable than language as a channel of communication between God and man: our estrangement from God may mean that we have forgotten his language, and the wordless sound of the *shofar*, the ram's horn blown on New Year's Day, may be the most effective way of communicating with him.[49]

There is somewhat less ambivalence in the presentation of Barnabas, the messenger sent from the Castle to K. Many commentators have picked up the religious undertones present when he is introduced:

Er war fast weiß gekleidet, das Kleid war wohl nicht aus Seide, es war ein Winterkleid wie alle andern, aber die Zartheit und Feierlichkeit eines Seidenkleides hatte es. Sein Gesicht war hell und offen, die Augen übergroß.

Sein Lächeln war ungemein aufmunternd; er fuhr mit der Hand über sein Gesicht, so als wolle er dieses Lächeln verscheuchen, doch gelang ihm das nicht. 'Wer bist Du?' fragte K. 'Barnabas heiße ich', sagte er, 'ein Bote bin ich.' (S 38–9.)

Kafka no doubt knew the etymology of 'Barnabas' as 'Sohn des Trostes' given in the New Testament (Acts 4: 36), but he certainly knew that *mal'akh*, the Hebrew equivalent of the word 'Bote', to which he draws attention by a curious syntactic inversion, means 'angel' as well as 'messenger'. Even if he had overlooked this fact in his Hebrew studies, it would have been brought to his notice by a passage from Maimon's autobiography which denounces the perverse ingenuity brought by Talmudists to the interpretation of the Old Testament and singles out their treatment of this word as an example:

Wenn es z. B. im ersten Buch Mosis heißt: Jakob schickte Boten an seinen Bruder Esau usw., so gefiel es den Talmudisten vorzugeben, daß diese Boten Engel gewesen. Denn obgleich das Wort Malachim im Hebräischen sowohl Boten als Engel bedeutet, wählten diese Wunderhäscher doch lieber die zweite Bedeutung, da die erste nichts Wunderbares in sich enthält.[50]

Besides exploiting this ambiguity, Kafka emphasizes it further by making K. say, after catching up with Barnabas, 'wie Du fliegst' (S 47). K., however, is so spellbound by Barnabas' status as messenger that he fails to grasp his real message. Thinking that by accompanying Barnabas he will gain entry to the Castle, K. instead finds himself led to Barnabas' household—the first of many signs that the proper object for his efforts is not the Castle but integration in domestic life.

Not only, therefore, is communication with the Castle misleading, but the images of communication that Kafka employs, the telephone and the messenger, are themselves designed to mislead the unwary reader. We should therefore expect ambivalent associations to be thickly clustered around Count Westwest, the owner of the Castle, whose flag flies above the Herrenhof. Even if the references to him were less sparse, interpreting this figure would still be a baffling problem. He has some prototypes in Kafka's earlier writings, including the Emperor in *Ein altes Blatt* who is unable to protect his people from the nomads and has withdrawn into the recesses of his palace. Another prototype is the Count who figures in a Gothic-sounding fragment from the year 1917:

Es war schon spät nachts, als ich am Tor läutete. Lange dauerte es, ehe, offenbar aus der Tiefe des Hofs, der Kastellan hervorkam und öffnete.

'Der Herr läßt bitten', sagte der Diener, sich verbeugend und öffnete mit geräuschlosem Ruck die hohe Glastür. Der Graf in halb fliegendem Schritt eilte mir von seinem Schreibtisch, der beim offenen Fenster stand, entgegen. Wir sahen einander in die Augen, der starre Blick des Grafen befremdete mich. (H 159–60.)

Here, as in *Das Schloß*, the stranger arrives at night. The Count, found at his desk in the middle of the night, resembles an overworked bureaucrat; with his 'halb fliegendem Schritt' he recalls a quasi-angelic messenger like Barnabas; and his 'starre Blick' has a suggestion of death. In *Das Schloß* the first two features have been transferred to the Count's subordinates, while the implication of death has been found by many commentators in the name 'Westwest'. Some proceed from this to argue, as Politzer does, that 'The West of the West may indicate the decline of the decline, that is, an ascent', so that the name alludes to resurrection and eternal life.[51] This seems strained, though less so than Marthe Robert's conjecture that the name refers to Kafka's imperfect integration as a Jew in Western society, 'l'horizon extrême-occidental dont le comte West-West incarne la civilisation'.[52] All these interpretations should be received with caution, since Kafka seems to have been sparing in his use of *sprechende Namen*, and it might be wiser to regard the name not as a conundrum but as a potential clue to Kafka's reading and hence to his preoccupations while writing the early chapters of *Das Schloß*.

A book that had made a strong impression on Kafka some years earlier was *Das Werden des Gottesglaubens* by Nathan Söderblom. Kafka copied extracts from it into his diary for 1916 (T 500–1). It has much in common with the better-known work of Rudolf Otto, *Das Heilige* (1917), which develops the concept of the numinous, and also with the research into the Cabbala that Gershom Scholem was to begin in the 1920s. In different ways, Söderblom, Otto, and Scholem were all reacting against the rationalistic interpretation of religion that had been gaining ground since the Enlightenment, but unlike Kierkegaard and Barth, who were also engaged in this reaction, they sought the foundation of religion not in the existential situation of the modern individual but rather in the religious experience of mystics and primitive peoples. The essential element in religion, Söderblom insists, is a matter not of intellectual reflection but of immediate experience:

Das, was entscheidend dafür ist, wie weit wirkliche Religiosität zu finden ist oder nicht, ist nicht die Ausgestaltung eines Gottesglaubens, sondern die wirkliche Empfindung des Göttlichen; mit andern Worten: die Befruchtung des Sinnes durch das Heilige.[53]

He finds this essential element to be present, even if rudimentarily, in primitive religious beliefs. Animism, which ascribed souls to trees and stones, also gave rise to the conception of the human soul; while the primitive belief in supernatural power or *Mana* attaching to certain individuals has been transformed into the concept of sanctity. Primitive modes of thought are still alive at the present day and are particularly apparent in popular customs. These are not to be regarded as survivals from a barbarous past, but as evidence of the abiding mental qualities shared by 'primitive' and 'modern' man: 'Volkssitte und Volksbräuche geben nicht ohne weiteres Kunde von grauer heidnischer Vorzeit, wohl aber legen sie Zeugnis ab für die Unausrottbarkeit primitiver Mentalität.'[54] Reading this would strengthen Kafka's conviction that the religious impulse was innate in human nature and increase his interest in primitive manifestations of it. One of the Zürau aphorisms says, rather wistfully: 'Was ist fröhlicher als der Glaube an einen Hausgott!' (H 96).

One mode of thinking that particularly interests Söderblom is the taboo. He describes, for example, the taboos surrounding certain African rulers, who are obliged to live in strict seclusion from their subjects, because the king is regarded as 'die zentrale Kraftquelle des Stammes oder Reiches'.[55] In *Das Schloß* there are two indications that Kafka may have conceived Count Westwest as a ruler concealed and protected by taboos. When K. asks the schoolmaster about him, the reply comes, with evident embarrassment, in French: 'Nehmen Sie Rücksicht auf die Anwesenheit unschuldiger Kinder' (S 20). As Karin Keller has noted, this suggests that the Count is surrounded by the 'Tabu des Heilig-Verruchten'.[56] Just before this incident, K. has had his first sight of the Castle and observed the jagged, irregular shape of the battlements at the top of the tower:

Es war wie wenn irgendein trübseliger Hausbewohner, der gerechter Weise im entlegensten Zimmer des Hauses sich hätte eingesperrt halten sollen, das Dach durchbrochen und sich erhoben hätte, um sich der Welt zu zeigen. (S 18.)

This curious passage, which I have never seen satisfactorily explicated, does not help one to visualize the Castle, but, combined with the remark that the tower is 'zum Teil gnädig von Epheu verdeckt' (S 18), it suggests that the Castle should have remained concealed but has been exposed, as though through the breaking of a taboo.

A source for the 'Hausbewohner' image, and further evidence for Kafka's interest in primitive religion, can be found in Werfel's play *Bocksgesang*, which, as we have seen, Kafka read in 1921 with qualified admiration. The play concerns a misshapen monster that has been born to Serbian peasants and confined all its life in an outhouse. Accidentally released, it takes refuge behind the altar of a church and becomes the object of a religious cult among the peasants. They assemble in the church and celebrate a festival, at whose culmination a girl goes behind the altar and copulates with the monster. Werfel's title, a calque on the literal meaning of 'tragedy', indicates his wish to recreate the orgiastic religious festivities from which tragedy is said to have developed; a sense of awe comes from the fact that we never see the monster and know only that it is larger than a human being, semi-animal, and sexually potent. Though we need not ascribe any of these qualities to Count Westwest, we may conclude that Kafka intended the Castle and its occupant to be the object of primitive rather than sophisticated religious feeling, and that he was well aware of the link between primitive religion and sex. This connection is repeatedly hinted at in *Das Schloß*, notably in the festival of the fire-brigade, where Sortini is aroused by the sight of Amalia.

Another clue to the nature of Count Westwest occurs in a passage which Kafka copied into his diary from the chapter in which Söderblom describes how many primitive peoples attribute their religions to a divine or semi-divine founder. Certain Australian tribes believe in a group of primeval beings of whom the greatest is called Bäjämi:

Er wird als ein mächtiger Medizinmann geschildert, der einst von Westen kam, Menschen, Tiere, Bäume, Flußläufe, Gebirge machte, die heiligen Zeremonien einsetzte und bestimmte, aus welchem Klan ein Mitglied eines bestimmten andern Klans sein Weib nehmen sollte, d.h. die festen Eheregeln einführte. Als er das alles fertig gebracht hatte, ging er davon. Die Medizinmänner können an einem Baum oder Seil zu ihm hinaufsteigen und Kraft holen.[57]

It may be justified to detect a reminiscence of this passage in the name of Count Westwest, in which case the reduplication of the syllable 'West' could be explained as Kafka himself did the syllable 'mann' in the name 'Bendemann' in *Das Urteil*, as 'eine für alle noch unbekannten Möglichkeiten der Geschichte vorgenommene Verstärkung' (T 297). To venture any further would be to risk over-interpreting a cluster of associations which seems to have left traces in *Das Schloß* without crystallizing into a fully significant pattern. One association seems to be between Söderblom's medicine-man and the passage in which K., on hearing that Hans Brunswick's mother is ill, announces that he himself has some knowledge of medicine:

Nun habe er, K., einige medicinische Kenntnisse und was noch mehr wert sei, Erfahrung in der Krankenbehandlung. Manches was Ärzten nicht gelungen sei, sei ihm geglückt. Zuhause habe man ihn wegen seiner Heilwirkung immer das bittere Kraut genannt. (S 229.)

From this passage associations run off in many directions: to the doctor's ill-fated mission in *Ein Landarzt*; to the play on the medical and spiritual meanings of 'heilen' indulged in both by Kafka (e.g. M 293) and by Nietzsche in *Zur Genealogie der Moral*; and to the bitter herbs which form part of the Passover meal (Exod. 12: 8) and hence back to Kafka's interest in Moses.[58] But even taken together, these associations do not form a basis for interpreting these parts of *Das Schloß*. Either they contain allusions whose point is still obscure, or they are gratuitous additions that indicate only the comparative weakness of the author's thematic control.

So far as these allusions can be interpreted, however, they illustrate the eclecticism with which Kafka employed religious images as more or less misleading metaphors whose ultimate tenor, 'das Unzerstörbare', was nevertheless an unquestionable reality, just as the reality of the Castle, behind its misleading appearances, is established by the narrator at the very outset of the story. The allusions discussed in this section also indicate Kafka's readiness to sympathize with more primitive versions of religion. The next section will provide some evidence for his scepticism about more sophisticated versions of religion which interposed an elaborate theological or hieratic superstructure between the believer and the basis of religion.

The Officials

If Count Westwest evokes primitive associations, the officials arouse a much wider range of associations whose extremes are juxtaposed in the description of Bürgel:

Es war ein kleiner, wohl aussehender Herr, dessen Gesicht dadurch einen gewissen Widerspruch in sich trug, daß die Wangen kindlich rund, die Augen kindlich fröhlich waren, aber die hohe Stirn, die spitze Nase, der schmale Mund, dessen Lippen kaum zusammenhalten wollten, das sich fast verflüchtigende Kinn gar nicht kindlich waren, sondern überlegenes Denken verrieten. (S 404–5.)

The officials' childlike aspect is most in evidence near the end of the novel, especially in the comic scene where documents are distributed in an atmosphere of hilarity that is said variously to suggest children preparing for an outing or poultry waking up at sunrise. Their intellectuality is intimated in the first chapter, when K. sees the portrait of a 'Kastellan' that chiefly reveals his 'hohe lastende Stirn' (S 15). It will be convenient to discuss their intellectual aspect first, then their more playful side, and turn finally to their most perplexing feature, the lechery evinced by Klamm, Sortini, and others who remain unnamed.

The intellectuality of the Castle bureaucrats is anticipated in the little sketch 'Poseidon', written in September 1920. Here we learn that the god of the oceans bears no resemblance to the image of him in traditional iconography, which shows 'wie er etwa immerfort mit dem Dreizack durch die Fluten kutschiere' (B 98). Not only does he never travel through the seas, he has never even seen them, except for fleeting glimpses while on his way to visit Jupiter. His relation to the oceans is abstract: instead of ruling them like a feudal monarch, he administers them like a bureaucrat. He is constantly at his desk, and though a huge staff of 'Hilfskräfte' assists him, he cannot refrain from checking all their calculations, so that they do nothing to reduce his work-load. Though his labours are irritating as well as arduous, the very thought of retirement makes his bronze chest shudder, and in any case nobody thinks seriously of transferring him to another department: 'seit Urbeginn war er zum Gott der Meere bestimmt worden und dabei mußte es bleiben' (B 97).

There are several similarities between Poseidon and the officials who administer the domain of Count Westwest. These are harassed bureaucrats who not only produce masses of documents but check one another's work meticulously, even though mistakes are considered impossible. They travel between the Castle and the village at maximum speed, studying documents during the journey. Yet this frenzied activity seems pointless. The near-impossibility of telephone communication with the Castle and the absence of a central switchboard suggest that their work is self-enclosed, self-perpetuating, and without a governing purpose. One recalls the couriers who dash about in the service of a non-existent king (H 89–90).

Like the couriers and Poseidon, the officials seem to take the necessity of their activities for granted, and their authority is accepted just as unquestioningly by the villagers. When K. declares that he wishes to consult Klamm about his marriage, Gardena, whom Keller aptly calls the 'Hüterin des Bestehenden',[59] expresses her outrage in revealing terms: 'Der Herr Landvermesser hat mich gefragt und ich muß ihm antworten. Wie soll er es denn sonst verstehen, was uns selbstverständlich ist, daß Herr Klamm niemals mit ihm sprechen wird, was sage ich "wird", niemals mit ihm sprechen kann' (S 79). By using the word 'wird', hastily changed to 'kann', she betrays how ill-founded her beliefs are. It may well be that Klamm will in fact refuse to speak to K., but that does not mean that an interview is *a priori* impossible. Though Gardena takes the present state of affairs so much for granted that she believes it to be unalterable, in her heart of hearts she knows otherwise, and she comes round to conceding that the interview K. wants is actually possible, though contrary to all rules and traditions: 'ganz gegen die Vorschriften und gegen das Althergebrachte' (S 84). By pleading with K. not to speak to Klamm, she implicitly acknowledges that such an encounter would be feasible but dangerous, and justifies K.'s audacious suggestion that there might be more danger for Klamm than for himself: 'Sie fürchten doch nicht etwa für Klamm?' (S 91). Later the 'Gemeindevorsteher' offers K. the job of school caretaker precisely because he fears K. may attempt something 'auf eigene Faust' (S 144). Authority in this society rests on weak foundations and might be unable to resist a challenge from an outsider.

If the Castle bureaucracy has any religious connotations, it suggests a religion that has become abstractly intellectual and lost contact with immediate experience, and has called into being a hierarchy of functionaries whose sole purpose is to administer the institution that employs them. We saw in Ch. 3 that the hierarchy of advocates in *Der Prozeß* was subjected to similar criticism and associated satirically with the Catholic priesthood and ritual. There is a touch of anti-Catholic satire in *Das Schloß* when the wife of the 'Gemeindevorsteher', having emptied a cupboard of documents, kneels before it with a candle nearby, and when she folds her hands, as though in prayer, on seeing Klamm's letter (S 99, 113). It may also be relevant that the 'Gemeindevorsteher', like the Advocate, is bedridden, and that Nietzsche in *Zur Genealogie der Moral* ironically describes the ascetic priest as using medical techniques to dominate a flock whose sickness he himself shares.[60]

This type of satire, however, occurs only in one short episode of *Das Schloß*. Elsewhere, when Kafka brings his presentation of the Castle bureaucracy into a satiric focus, he makes it resemble more the orthodox Jewish rabbinate as seen from the standpoint of Hasidism. The Hasidim regarded the orthodox rabbis as misguided teachers who, instead of leading people to intimacy with God, wasted their time with ritual observances and supersubtle disputations. Kafka had gathered from his reading that even in the period before the destruction of the Temple there had been a gulf between the rabbis and the *'am ha-'arets* ('countrymen'). He had learnt that the two groups were so hostile that a rabbi was forbidden to marry the daughter of an *'am ha-'arets*, to ask him to give testimony, to travel in his company, or even to study the Torah in his presence.[61] We may compare the arrogance which the officials display towards the villagers, and the care with which they avoid them. Officials are said to be 'empfindlich' (S 56) and unable to endure the unexpected sight of a stranger. Kafka also knew that the gulf between the learned and the unlearned still existed in the eighteenth-century Jewish communities of Eastern Europe, and that the Ba'al Shem had directed his teaching towards the unlearned. The chief orthodox opponent of Hasidism, the Gaon of Vilna, was a scholar renowned for spending his days and nights in intense study of the Torah. Once he came across a difficult passage in the Jerusalem Talmud and spent three.days pondering it, during which time he took no food.[62] Such marathon feats of scholarship seem to have provided Kafka with prototypes for a figure like Sordini, though Kafka adds a characteristic touch of grotesque exaggeration in saying that Sordini's room emits a continual crashing noise, because the documents on which Sordini is working are always stacked in pillars which keep toppling to the floor. The authority which the officials exercise in the village may have been suggested by Maimon's hostile description of the orthodox rabbinate in eighteenth-century Poland:

Die jüdische Nation ist [. . .] eine *unter dem Schein der Theokratie immerwährende Aristokratie*. Die Gelehrten, welche den *Adel* dieser Nation ausmachen, wußten sich seit vielen Jahrhunderten als das gesetzgebende Korpus bei den Gemeinen in ein solches Ansehen zu setzen, daß sie mit ihnen machen konnten, was sie wollten.[63]

The officials are therefore vulnerable to K., since their authority cannot withstand hostile scrutiny, and since they share the repugnance of Jewish orthodoxy in all periods to Messianic pretenders. The word 'Sekretär', used for the lower rank of officials like Momus or Bürgel, conceals another clue to their status, for it is the accepted German equivalent for the Hebrew *gabbai*, meaning the assistant to a rabbi. Kafka himself uses this word to describe the attendants of the Belzer Rabbi, and explains it as 'die "Nächsten", Angestellte, Sekretäre' (Br 144).

The Castle officials, then, are far from being a 'company of Gnostic demons', to quote Erich Heller's extravagant description.[64] They may govern the village with a high hand, but their rule depends on people's readiness to mistake it for the natural order. They are made even less demonic by their playfulness, though they do not manifest this in the village, but only among themselves. When they answer the telephone their tone is imperious, but the noise of their telephoning each other is like 'dem Summen zahlloser kindlicher Stimmen' (S 36). At the distribution of documents in the Herrenhof corridor, a ceremony which no outsider is supposed to witness, the officials sound and behave like children. One of them imitates the crowing of a cock, another empties a basin of water over a servant's head, and even when they are annoyed the sound they make is like 'Kinderweinen' (S 437). Richard Sheppard seems to be right in arguing that the malevolence of the Castle authorities is an illusion produced by K.'s projection of his Faustian will on to them, and that after his interview with Bürgel he is freed from his aggressiveness and able to perceive the playfulness which is the officials' real nature.

Two of the officials are of particular importance for K. and deserve separate discussion. One is his superior, Klamm, who is apparently endowed with supernatural attributes. Olga tells K. that Klamm's physical appearance is constantly changing, though she adds that his protean quality is not due to magic but to the intense emotions of hope or despair with which the villagers regard him. Her explanation seems to remove Klamm's supernatural aura, but in fact reinforces it, for one wonders what it is about Klamm that inspires such emotions. The villagers say mysteriously that he is indispensable in both the Castle and the village (S 380): are we to infer that he is always in some sense present in both, in a manner recalling the Ba'al Shem's teaching that 'all things are in God and "there is no place empty of him"'?[65] Frieda brings the Castle servants to heel by addressing them 'im Namen Klamms' (S 66), as though his name induced religious awe; it may be a sign of K.'s outsider status or of his strength of will that he is unimpressed by Momus's invocation of Klamm with the words 'Im Namen Klamms fordere ich Sie auf, meine Fragen zu beantworten' (S 176). Klamm is mostly silent: he has never spoken to Frieda except to call her to his bed; Gardena's comparison of Klamm to an eagle sets K. thinking of 'seine, nur vielleicht von Schreien, wie sie K. noch nie gehört hatte, unterbrochene Stummheit' (S 183). A notebook entry by Kafka, 'Stummheit gehört zu den Attributen der Vollkommenheit',[66] may be a clue to Klamm's character. Admittedly, his secretary Erlanger, who summons K., has a limp which recalls the cloven hoof of the Devil; but so has the church servant who in *Der Prozeß* leads Josef K. to the pulpit and ensures that he hears the ineffectual warning represented by the Chaplain's legend. Erlanger's summons, likewise, is the indirect reason why K. strays into the wrong room and has his crucial encounter with Bürgel. In both these instances, evil, symbolized by lameness, leads to potential good. Kafka knew from Roskoff's *Geschichte des Teufels* that many primitive peoples had a dualistic conception of their god as composed of a good and an evil aspect, and in his diary for 1913 he quoted the last sentence of a passage in which Roskoff discusses this dualism:

Bei den *Karaiben* finden sich zwei Arten von Wesen, wohlthätige, die ihren Sitz im Himmel haben, wovon jeder Mensch das seinige als Führer auf Erden hat; boshafte, die durch die Luft ziehen und ihre Lust daran finden, den Menschen Schaden zuzufügen. [. . .] Bei den jetzigen Karaiben gilt [. . .] 'der, welcher in der Nacht arbeitet', als der Schöpfer der Welt, auf den sie alles Gute zurückführen.[67]

Though the last sentence was probably quoted by Kafka (T 314) with an ironic reference to his own nocturnal writing, it fitted in with his imaginative habit of degrading gods to bureaucrats, as in the case of Poseidon, and could have lodged in his mind firmly enough to guide his portrayal of Klamm as an inaccessible, quasi-divine being with an apparently evil earthly subordinate.

Some evidence suggests that Klamm is a benevolent guardian. K. finds it plausible that Klamm has watched over his ex-lover Gardena and supplied her with a husband and a livelihood, even if she does not appreciate them. He dismisses Klamm's alleged forgetfulness of his former lovers as a 'Legende' (S 136) and maintains: 'Der Segen war über Ihnen, aber man verstand nicht ihn herunterzuholen' (S 135). Ironically, K.'s rebuke to Gardena may also apply to himself. Frieda thinks that it was Klamm's doing that she and K. found each other, and exclaims: 'gesegnet, nicht verflucht, sei die Stunde' (S 83–4). The first letter that Barnabas brings assures K. that Klamm is watching over him, and K.'s desperate efforts to read a deeper significance into the slightest details of the letter need not deter the reader from accepting the statement at face value. The second letter, urging K. to keep up the good work that he and his assistants have begun, hardly lends itself to a literal reading, since K. has not done any land-surveying, yet this time K. is inconsistent enough to interpret the letter literally. If we again reject K.'s reading, we can make sense of the letter along the lines suggested by Sheppard. Klamm is trying to induce K. to settle down in domestic life with Frieda and the assistants, as a positive alternative to his misguided attempts to reach the Castle; the good work is the effort K. has already made to establish his relationship with Frieda, and Klamm is pleased that K. is beginning to accept his own lowly status. Frieda suspects, and Jeremias later confirms, that the assistants are emissaries from Klamm, as though intended to provide K. and Frieda with a kind of surrogate family. The importance of domestic life as the central value in *Das Schloß* will be argued for in the next section, but it will be recalled from Ch. 5 that Kafka regarded marrying and bringing up a family as an almost sacred responsibility.

If Klamm is pressing K. to fulfil this responsibility, then we can explain why K. never meets him and why he keeps changing his appearance. The religious impulse that, in Kafka's opinion, finds its best fulfilment in domestic duties springs from the indestructible basis of humanity. Given that Klamm embodies this impulse, then he is part of 'das Unzerstörbare' and, like it, cannot be perceived in any permanent form by observers. His appearance depends on the observer's feelings because he is himself a projection of human feeling. This is supported by Elizabeth Rajec's suggestion that his name comes from the Czech word *klam* 'illusion, deception' (as in *klam optický* 'optical illusion').[68] Klamm's separate existence is illusory. K. already, in effect, has Klamm within himself, and the way to obey Klamm's wishes is indicated in the already quoted aphorism: 'An das Unzerstörbare in sich glauben und nicht zu ihm streben' (H 96).

An official whom K. actually meets is Bürgel, the 'Verbindungs-sekretär' to Friedrich: 'ich bilde die stärkste Verbindung [. . .] zwischen Friedrich und dem Dorf' (S 407). Having been summoned by Erlanger for what turns out to be a trivial reason, K. stumbles into

Bürgel's room instead. By an improbable accident he has slipped through the elaborate defences which the bureaucracy has erected against its clients, and has come upon a secretary who is not only competent to deal with his case but is in the condition of lowered resistance which afflicts the officials at night and makes them positively anxious to grant their clients' requests. Bürgel is exceptional both in his potential helpfulness and in his function as a kind of mediator between the Castle and the village. In giving him powers which the other officials lack, Kafka seems to have dropped his satire on the orthodox rabbinate and to be alluding to its opposite, namely to the Hasidic *tsaddik*, who, unlike a rabbi, is credited with a spiritual authority that enables him to mediate between God and man. Alexander Eliasberg explains this in an account of the *tsaddikim* which was known to Kafka, and adds: 'Der Zaddik ist aber noch mehr als Priester: er ist beinahe Halbgott.'[69] This allusion underlines Bürgel's powers. The scene with Bürgel recalls Josef K.'s meeting with the Information Officer in *Der Prozeß*. The hero is in one case offered, in the other case actually given information which he is too exhausted to take in. Bürgel explains K.'s failure as follows:

Die Leibeskräfte reichen nur bis zu einer gewissen Grenze, wer kann dafür, daß gerade diese Grenze auch sonst bedeutungsvoll ist. Nein, dafür kann niemand. So korrigiert sich selbst die Welt in ihrem Lauf und behält das Gleichgewicht. Das ist ja eine vorzügliche, immer wieder unvorstellbar vorzügliche Einrichtung, wenn auch in anderer Hinsicht trostlos. (S 425.)

In other words, K.'s Messianic ambitions to penetrate the Castle were a futile attempt to cross a frontier which is impassable to human beings. The effort required to reach this frontier ensures that if one gets there one will not have the strength to cross it. Accordingly, K. cannot use the opportunity Bürgel offers him, but falls asleep on Bürgel's bed. It is as though the world contained a self-regulating mechanism which ensures, as it were, that people are always turned back at the frontier between being and consciousness.

Bürgel seems to have spiritual influence as well as access to truth. Hence K.'s dream in which he fights and overcomes a Castle secretary, who is naked, like the statue of a Greek god, and who squeals like a girl. This ludicrous combat reveals how futile K.'s aggressiveness was all along, especially as it leaves K. alone in a large room, looking around for another opponent but only injuring himself. In his dream he confronts the side of the officials that has hitherto been concealed from him and finds it to be nothing other than the childishly playful character that comes to the fore in the Herrenhof corridor. This surrogate victory cures K. of his aggressiveness, so that his behaviour to the people he encounters in the remaining chapters is much more accommodating than before. When he sees a tiny scrap of paper left over after all the other documents have been distributed, and being torn up by the servant, the thought occurs to him: 'Das könnte recht gut mein Akt sein' (S 438), a recognition of his own unimportance which would previously have been impossible for him. The destruction of the document no doubt signifies that the Castle's business with K. is over. The administrative error that caused him to be summoned in the first place has been cancelled out by the servant's irregular conduct in tearing up the scrap of paper. The intervening events have taught K. humility, but, tragically, he has acquired it too late: by sacrificing his relationship with Frieda to his misguided ambition, he has forfeited his chance of settling down in domestic life, and has nothing ahead of him but the prospect of joining Pepi and the other two maids in the tiny subterranean room that sounds disturbingly like the grave.

The Women

One of the most puzzling features of *Das Schloß* is the apparent lechery of the officials. Klamm, we gather, is 'wie ein Kommandant über die Frauen' (S 309). When Frieda became his mistress, it was in response to a summons as crude as the one Sortini sent to Amalia. Nonetheless she is proud of her position, while Gardena, though Klamm only summoned her three times and twenty years have since passed, still cherishes her mementos of the affair. Sexual allusions are most heavily concentrated in ch. 17, in which Olga describes to K. the fire-brigade festival to which the Castle contributed a new hosepipe. This festival takes place beside a stream and in summer, contrasting with the winter in which the action of the novel occurs, and the many references to the elements of fire and water tempt one to agree with Sheppard in calling it 'a festival of procreation and renewal'.[70] The German word for the fire-hose, 'Feuerspritze', combines the motifs of fire, water, and sex, since *spritzen* can mean 'to ejaculate'. Noise and intoxication help to suggest an orgy: the Castle has also presented the fire brigade with trumpets which make a deafening noise, and by the end all the villagers, except for the sedate Amalia, are 'von dem süßen Schloßwein wie betäubt' (S 301).

This episode contains several reminiscences of Němcová's *Babička*. Among the country festivals she describes is one in which homecoming pilgrims are greeted by little boys with toy trumpets, and a wedding at which the bride wears a garnet necklace, like the 'Halsband aus böhmischen Granaten' (S 296) which Olga gives Amalia and which attracts the attention of Sortini. A repeated motif in *Babička* is the harassment of girls by unwanted lovers. One girl, Viktorka, acquires a reputation for pride by refusing all suitors, until she is seduced by a soldier whose sinister power she cannot resist, after which she goes mad and lives in the woods, shunning all human beings. The eventual bride has first to fight off the attentions of an Italian servant from the local castle and then those of the steward from the castle.[71] These two figures have been fused into the Italian-sounding Sortini, while Viktorka seems to be a prototype for Amalia.

The significance of these motifs in the context of *Das Schloß* is harder to explain, but one can begin by pointing out that the attraction of village women to Castle officials provides a series of parallels to K.'s attitude to the Castle. Just as his credentials as land-surveyor are open to doubt, so is their position as the lovers of officials. Gardena questions whether Frieda really was Klamm's lover, and considers the term 'eine sehr übertriebene Bezeichnung' (S 81); it is surely just as exaggerated for someone who was with Klamm only three times. Besides the reality of these relationships, their value is called into question, so that they seem as self-willed and misguided as K.'s striving towards the Castle. When Frieda expresses pride at being barmaid in the Herrenhof, K. reflects: 'Ihr Ehrgeiz war offenbar toll' (S 62), a clear case of *de te fabula*. We have already seen how the rebuke he delivers to Gardena for her obsession with Klamm likewise applies ironically to himself. The people most destructively obsessed with the Castle are the Barnabas family. Since Amalia refused Sortini's summons, the others have devoted all their energies to obviously futile expedients for regaining the Castle's favour. Her sister Olga spends every night in the Herrenhof stables with the Castle servants, in the hope of meeting or at least hearing of the servant who carried Sortini's message. Yet all these efforts have achieved next to nothing: the Castle insists that there is nothing for it to forgive, and Olga admits that if they had been able to present the occurrence as a misunderstanding, they would have been welcomed once again by the villagers who at present ostracize them. Despite K.'s initial scepticism, he is eventually won round to praising her courage, wisdom, and self-sacrifice (S 366) and does not see that her ambitions are as irrational as his own. The parallel is made clearer still by the fact that the Barnabas family regard K. as their lifeline to the Castle, which is just how he sees their value for him. The resulting vicious circle has been well described by Philippi: 'Jeder will mit Hilfe des anderen das erreichen, was auch dieser umgekehrt vom anderen erwartet. [. . .] Indem sie aber den anderen zum Mittel machen, um durch ihn zu erreichen, was dieser selbst nicht erreichen kann, verkehrt sich ihnen ihre Absicht unter den Händen in etwas Sinnloses.'[72]

Having acknowledged the function of these parallels, however, one may still wonder why Kafka insists on female sexuality as an analogy for K.'s Faustian ambition. His revulsion from female sexuality is certainly apparent from passages in his diary which present women with disgust as primarily sexual and physical beings, like this account of an outing with Felix Weltsch to Rostock (now Roztok), near Prague:

Mit Felix in Rostock. Die geplatzte Sexualität der Frauen. Ihre natürliche Unreinheit. Das für mich sinnlose Spiel mit dem kleinen Lenchen. Der Anblick der einen dicken Frau, die zusammengekrümmt in einem Korbstuhl, den einen Fuß auffällig zurückgeschoben, irgend etwas nähte und mit einer alten Frau, wahrscheinlich einer alten Jungfer, deren Gebiß auf einer Seite des Mundes immer in besonderer Größe erschien, sich unterhielt. Die Vollblütigkeit und Klugheit der schwangeren Frau. Ihr Hinterer mit geraden abgeteilten Flächen, förmlich facettiert. (T 314.)

The precise and observant revulsion in this passage connects it with characters like Leni in *Der Prozeß* and Klara in *Der Verschollene*, and also with Kafka's association of sex with dirt (e.g. M 196–9). But, while his portrayal of the women in *Das Schloß* is obviously related to his own experience, personal experience happens within a framework of cultural assumptions, and Kafka owes much to the widespread anti-feminist assumptions of his time. One version of anti-feminism had Otto Weininger as its most influential spokesman. In *Geschlecht und Charakter* Weininger says that women, in so far as the feminine principle (W) is dominant in them, are primarily sexual beings:

Der Zustand der sexuellen Erregtheit bedeutet für die Frau nur die höchste Steigerung ihres Gesamtdaseins. *Dieses ist immer und durchaus sexuell. W geht im Geschlechtsleben, in der Sphäre der Begattung und Fortpflanzung, d. i. im Verhältnisse zum Manne und zum Kinde, vollständig auf*, sie wird von diesen Dingen in ihrer Existenz vollkommen ausgefüllt, während M *nicht nur* sexuell ist.[73]

Whatever appeal this view of women had for Kafka, he probably knew Weininger's work only at second hand, while he had first-hand acquaintance with another version of anti-feminism in Strindberg, whose writings he greatly admired. In his diary for 1915 Kafka records the 'Wohlbehagen' with which he read Strindberg's *Am offnen Meer* (T 467), a novel about a scientist who falls in love with a young woman and tries for some time to avoid admitting to himself that she is a shallow, brainless creature whose attraction towards him is only physical. Eventually he brings about the dissolution of their engagement by fostering a romance between her and his assistant. Left on his own, however, he realizes that although woman cannot be man's moral or intellectual equal, man cannot live without her, for she is the essential link between the masculine intellect and unconscious, vital forces of nature. Cut off from these forces, Strindberg's hero loses his interest in life, pines away, and dies. One of his last utterances is: 'das Weib ist des Mannes Wurzel in der Erde'.[74] Weininger, no doubt because of his own homosexuality, takes a dimmer view of woman, seeing her as an evil made necessary by man's failure to liberate himself from sexuality. Strindberg's view was accepted enthusiastically, however, by Wedekind, who portrays his heroine Lulu as a mindless, amoral incarnation of the life-force, while Karl Kraus declared in a famous aphorism: 'Des Weibes Sinnlichkeit ist der Urquell, an dem sich des Mannes Geistigkeit Erneuerung holt.'[75]

The extreme anti-feminism of Weininger seems to underlie Kafka's depiction of Olga, who has no scruples about making herself into a sexual object. If she embodies promiscuity, Amalia represents the opposite pole of asceticism. Her dominant trait is 'ein fortwährendes, jedem andern Gefühl überlegenes Verlangen nach Einsamkeit' (S 264), expressed in her cold, reserved gaze which seems to bypass whatever object she is looking at. Her will and intellect are powerful: she strikes K. as 'herrisch' (S 270) and takes all the decisions in her family, though she is its youngest member; and Olga describes her rejection of Sortini as a confrontation with the truth: 'Aug in Aug mit der Wahrheit stand sie' (S 331). It may be pertinent to recall Nietzsche's Arctic explorer whose ascetic search for truth leads him into a snowy wasteland of meaninglessness. However, Amalia is an opaque character. Since she hardly speaks, we have to learn her story from Olga, who admits: 'wir sind ihr fremd' (S 271) and stresses her inscrutability: 'ihre Beweggründe hält Amalia in ihrer Brust verschlossen, niemand wird sie ihr entreißen' (S 312).

There seems no way of deciding whether, as Camus thought, Amalia is an existential sinner who has forfeited the grace of God by her attachment to her honour, or whether, as in Politzer's view, she is a heroic exemplar of existential solitude.[76] The latter is rendered somewhat doubtful by the obvious parallel between Amalia's rejection of human contact and the isolation K. experiences in the snow-covered courtyard after he has successfully but pointlessly opposed his will to that of the Castle as represented by the secretary Momus and is left with the feeling that there is 'nichts Sinnloseres, nichts Verzweifelteres als diese Freiheit, dieses Warten, diese Unverletzlichkeit' (S 169).

The contrast between Olga and Amalia can perhaps be clarified further by referring to the passage of *Heidentum, Christentum, Judentum* in which Brod distinguishes the different attitudes to love held by these three religions. Leaving aside the Jewish attitude to love for the moment, it appears that pagan and Christian love form an extreme contrast, since the former is mindlessly sensual, while the latter tries to transfer love from the body to the mind and attributes the highest value to the yearning for an inaccessible beloved. Brod illustrates this from Dante's love for Beatrice and Kierkegaard's renunciation of Regina Olsen. The opposition beween pagan and Christian love corresponds quite neatly to that between Olga and Amalia. By insisting on the obscurity of Amalia's motives, Kafka leaves open the possibility that she may have rejected Sortini in order to keep her emotions spiritual, and the phrase in which Brod sums up this kind of Christian love, 'geradezu spiritualer Egoismus',[77] might well apply to her. This does not mean that Kafka is writing in code about the same themes as Brod, but that the contrast drawn by Brod has served him as a means of structuring and focusing his opposition between Olga's promiscuity and Amalia's asceticism.

One might well think, however, that Amalia could hardly do anything but reject such a coarse invitation as Sortini's is said to have been. But Kafka knew that the vehicle of an image can clash violently with its tenor. A striking example is the Talmud passage referred to by Maimonides which was mentioned in Ch. 3 in connection with the pornographic pictures K. finds on the Court premises, and which also provides the epigraph for Langer's *Die Erotik der Kabbala*:

Es sagte Rabbi Katina: Wenn die *Israeliten* an den drei Festen in den Tempel zu Jerusalem kamen, da öffnete man vor ihnen den Tempelvorhang und man zeigte ihnen die Cherubim, wie sie sich innig umschlungen hielten, und man sagte ihnen: Sehet, euere und Gottes gegenseitige Liebe ist wie die Liebe des Mannes und der Frau!

Resch Lakisch sagte: Als die *Barbaren* den Tempel betraten, sahen sie die Cherubim, die sich innig umschlungen hielten. Sie schleppten sie auf den Markt hinaus und sagten: Sehet! Israel, dessen Segen ein Segen und dessen Fluch ein Fluch ist, beschäftigt sich mit derartigen Dingen?! Dann schmähten sie sie.[78]

Jewish thought includes several other instances of sexual imagery with a spiritual meaning. Brod quotes Rabbi Akiba as saying that the Song of Songs is the holiest book in the Bible, and a pupil of the Ba'al Shem as saying that, alone of all the Scriptures, it provided a direct link between man and God.[79] Maimonides interpreted it as a dialogue between God and the soul. Many passages in the Zohar describe man's relation to God in terms of erotic symbolism; Langer summarizes one of them as follows: 'Gott ruht in dem, der sich reinen Gefühls mit seiner Frau geschlechtlich vereinigt: dies ist—nach "Sohar"—der wahre Sinn der ganzen Thora.'[80] In the Zohar the Shekhinah (the 'divine presence' emanating from the Godhead) is imagined as the female element in the Godhead, and it is stated that when a man cannot be with his wife he has the Shekhinah as a substitute partner.[81] Even bolder comparisons are to be found in the sayings of the Ba'al Shem, who speaks of mystical prayer as sexual union:

Prayer is copulation with the Shekhinah. Just as there is swaying when copulation begins so, too, a man must sway at first and then he can remain immobile and attached to the Shekhinah with great attachment.[82]

The erotic and the religious associations of the Castle may therefore be more compatible than they seem, and Amalia's *gran rifiuto* may be less defensible. In suggesting this, I am not proposing to revive Brod's Kierkegaardian interpretation of Sortini's summons as an absolute command whose outrageousness simply illustrates 'die Inkommensurabilität irdischen und religiösen Tuns',[83] for outrageous commands with absolute authority could also be issued by Hasidic *tsaddikim*, as Kafka well knew. In the last chapter I quoted the anecdote told to Kafka by Langer in which the Ba'al Shem commands one of his followers to apostatize, and in which the merit of obedience was paradoxically enhanced by the gravity of what would otherwise have been a heinous offence. It would seem likely that in asserting her own will against that of the Castle, Amalia is arrogantly rejecting something of potential religious as well as human value.

Kafka's portrayal of Amalia is a curious instance of the triumph of ideology over experience. Of the women in his own life, at least four—Felice, Milena, Dora Dymant, and his sister Ottla—were intelligent, spirited, and independent, and attracted him by these qualities. Yet Amalia, the most intellectual and independent woman in *Das Schloß*, is treated with a distinct lack of sympathy, while Frieda, her positive counterpart, has some affinity with the anti-feminist ideal of the supportive woman who keeps the man in contact with vital energies. Still, this affinity must not be exaggerated. Frieda resembles Amalia in the quality of her gaze, a 'Blick von besonderer Überlegenheit' (S 60), later described as 'sieghaft' (S 62). Her air of superiority, however, does not prevent her from being friendly to K., showing him Klamm through the peep-hole, conspiring with him to let him stay the night in the Herrenhof, and indeed falling in love with him with a rapidity possible only in a male fantasy. Her behaviour contrasts with Amalia's frosty reserve and also with Olga's promiscuity, since she remains faithful to K. until the breakdown of their relationship. The difference between her and Olga is pointedly conveyed when she drives the servants into the stable with a whip and Olga accompanies them. The servants, whom Frieda describes as 'Vieh' and dismisses, using the dehumanizing neuter gender, as 'das Verächtlichste und Widerlichste was ich kenne' (S 65), seem to symbolize animal lust. Her whip is not a sign of sadism, as Peter Cersowsky has recently claimed;[84] it symbolizes the very opposite of perversion, namely the power to exercise control over the lust of which Olga is the helpless and not unwilling victim. Frieda is one of the few characters to have an obviously significant name, for Kafka encourages us to associate it with 'Frieden' ('peace') by using the word in close proximity to Frieda's name on three occasions (S 79, 128, 216), while elsewhere 'Frieda' is juxtaposed with 'befriedigen' ('to satisfy', S 241). Although her love-making with K. first takes place among the dirt and beer-puddles on the floor of the Herrenhof bar, its description is the first of those memorable and poignant passages that Sheppard has identified as 'moments of lyricism':[85]

Dort vergiengen Stunden, Stunden gemeinsamen Atems, gemeinsamen Herzschlags, Stunden, in denen K. immerfort das Gefühl hatte, er verirre sich oder er sei soweit in der Fremde, wie vor ihm noch kein Mensch, eine Fremde, in der selbst die Luft keinen Bestandteil der Heimatluft habe, in der man vor Fremdheit ersticken müsse und in deren unsinnigen Verlockungen man doch nichts tun könne als weiter gehn, weiter sich verirren. (S 68–9.)

K.'s entry into this strange country, whose unfamiliar air recalls the image of 'atembaren Luft' from Kafka's diary (T 572), is an exploration of new emotional territory. The repeated word 'gemeinsam' indicates a change from K.'s usual self-absorption, while the reference in the previous sentence to the 'Besinnungslosigkeit, aus der sich K. fortwährend aber vergeblich zu retten suchte' (S 68) reminds us that for much of the novel K. is struggling to remain conscious and in control of himself; he finally gives up this struggle when he falls asleep in Bürgel's bedroom, wins the dream-victory over a Castle secretary, and awakes in the transformed state described earlier. The unappetizing surroundings in which he and Frieda make love do not negate the value of the experience. While living with Felice in the 'Schloß Balmoral und Osborne' hotel in Marienbad in July 1916, Kafka made a poignant remark in his diary: 'Mühsal des Zusammenlebens. Erzwungen von Fremdheit, Mitleid, Wollust, Feigheit, Eitelkeit und nur im tiefen Grunde vielleicht ein dünnes Bächlein, würdig, Liebe genannt zu werden, unzugänglich dem Suchen, aufblitzend einmal im Augenblick eines Augenblicks' (T 503). Just as love is mostly submerged under the odious emotions that make up the bulk of mental life, so the love-affair between K. and Frieda is played out in unpleasant, cramped, or ludicrously inconvenient surroundings which externalize those mundane obstacles to love. If the affair seems to K. like a 'Verirrung', that is because his viewpoint is distorted by his Faustian ambitions, as Sheppard points out: 'Far from estranging K. from his true being, this sexual act helps him to realise unconsciously that he can only truly discover himself in the peace and timelessness of a relationship with someone like Frieda.'[86]

The relationship between K. and Frieda represents the central value of *Das Schloß*, the positive alternative to K.'s efforts to reach the Castle. In depicting it, Kafka was again drawing on his knowledge of Jewish and especially Hasidic traditions. As we have seen, his friends Brod and Langer wrote at length about the sanctity attributed by Judaism to sexual love. In *Heidentum, Christentum, Judentum* Brod analyses the Song of Songs in order to illustrate the Jewish attitude to erotic love, which he regards as superior to the pagan and Christian attitudes and defines as a 'Diesseitswunder', a miraculous spiritual experience in physical form.[87] Hasidism not only used erotic love as an image of the union between man and God, but found spiritual value in the humblest details of everyday life. Since God was omnipresent in the world, there was no need for feats of asceticism or scholarship in order to make contact with him. Instead, one should continue with one's ordinary life in a spirit of *devekut* ('attachment to God'), conscious of the divine reality underlying appearances. In a book that Kafka read during work on *Das Schloß*, Buber summed up this doctrine as 'die Heiligung des Alltags' and illustrated it by this anecdote: 'Henoch war ein Schuhflicker. Mit jedem Stich seiner Ahle, der Oberleder und Sohle zusammennähte, verband er Gott und seine Schechina.'[88] Barnabas and his father are also cobblers, but neglect their trade because of their misguided anxiety to make contact with the Castle.

K. is given the chance to realize the ideal of 'Heiligung des Alltags' by founding a household with Frieda. Though he takes up with her originally in order to gain access to Klamm, his purposes are defeated, as though by a kind of providential guidance, and he finds himself admitted to the unfamiliar experience of love and self-loss. The clash between new and habitual emotions in him on the morning after his first encounter with Frieda is finely described: he is 'ängstlich-glücklich', 'denn es schien ihm, wenn Frieda ihn verlasse, verlasse ihn alles, was er habe' (S 69), yet when Frieda defies Klamm K. feels despair over the collapse of his ambitions. However, he is now committed to Frieda, and is even provided with the post of 'Schuldiener' so that he can support her. Their housekeeping is of course attended by farcical difficulties: they are expected to live in the school, constantly moving to whichever classroom happens not to be in use, and they have a kind of family in the two assistants, who behave like overgrown and irrepressible children. Kafka's choice of an occupation for K. may have been determined by his knowledge, from at least two sources, that as a young man the Ba'al Shem had worked as a *Belfer* or teacher's assistant, a job which was considered particularly lowly;[89] similarly, K. is treated by Schwarzer 'mit unmäßiger Verachtung, wie sie einem Schuldiener gebürte' (S 257).

Given the deeper implications of K.'s relationship with Frieda, his neglect of her cannot be so easily excused as it is by Walter Sokel, who says: 'Er kann, sosehr er auch möchte, den animalischen Komfort, das Simpel-Vitale und Geistlos-Hausbackene der Familiengründung mit Frieda nicht wirklich ernst nehmen.'[90] What prevents him from taking the relationship with Frieda seriously is the fatal obsession which transfers itself from the Castle to the Barnabas family. They have the effect on K. of an irresistible drug: when he hears a knock at

the classroom door, he shrieks 'Barnabas!' and leaps to open it, only
to find Hans Brunswick (S 223); and later that evening he resolves to
visit the family only for a moment, without even entering their house
(S 263), but ends up listening to Olga's 'Schloßgeschichten' (S 323)
till late at night. It is hardly surprising that Frieda leaves him, but
when he next meets her she is 'starr' (S 385), almost corpse-like, and
feels that without him she has nothing else to live for: 'wie bin ich,
seitdem ich Dich kenne, ohne Deine Nähe verlassen', she says
(S 399). After losing her, and after his interview with Bürgel, K. is
likewise without any prospects except the approach of death: an illustration of Strindberg's thesis, mentioned earlier, that sexual union,
though it may harm one's intellectual ambitions, is indispensable as a
source of vital energy.

One may wonder whether the relationship between Frieda and K.
is helped or hindered by the assistants, those ungainly characters with
black beards and a taste for childish antics, who seem unable to leave
the couple alone. It turns out that they have been present in the bar
throughout K.'s and Frieda's night of love; expelled from the
couple's bedroom, they climb back in through the window; and they
keep peering at K., using their cupped hands as telescopes. As Binder
has pointed out, they were partly inspired by Spiegelmensch in
Werfel's play of that name.[91] On his first appearance Spiegelmensch
leaps about as restlessly as the assistants, and his function is to externalize and mock some aspects of the hero's character, as the assistants
do K.'s. Their self-importance mimics his, while their extravagant
rejoicing over small achievements, like closing a cupboard crammed
with documents, helps to indicate the absurdity of K.'s ambitions.
But they also embody something K. signally lacks, the capacity for
sheer fun. While K. is talking to Barnabas, they mock his seriousness
by pretending to hide behind Barnabas's back and imitating the
whistling of the wind; and their noisy pleasure over Klamm's second
letter contrasts with most of K.'s actions in having no ulterior motive:
'K. sah vom Brief erst auf, als die viel langsamer als er lesenden
Gehilfen zur Feier der guten Nachrichten dreimal laut Hurra riefen
und die Laternen schwenkten. "Seid ruhig", sagte er' (S 187).

A more important and significant source for the assistants, however, is to be found in the Yiddish theatre.[92] In his diary for 4 October
1911 Kafka describes a performance of Latayner's *Der meshumed*,
which included two comic figures who, like Artur and Jeremias, kept
bouncing about and expressing their emotions by grimaces. Such

pairs of clowns were a staple feature of the Yiddish theatre, but they could also have a religious significance. Kafka describes them as 'irgendwie aus religiösen Gründen bevorzugten Schnorrer' and 'Leute, die in einer besonders reinen Form Juden sind, weil sie nur in der Religion, aber ohne Mühe, Verständnis und Jammer in ihr leben' (T 80). Either then or later, he must have learnt about the value attached to such characters in Hasidism. As we have seen, Hasidism was originally, at least, a religion of joy. Weeping is harmful, said the Ba'al Shem, for man should serve the Lord joyfully; the only permissible tears are tears of happiness.[93] One of the Ba'al Shem's favourite stories is recounted as follows by Scholem:

Diese talmudische Anekdote, für die der Baalschem offenbar besonders viel übrig hatte und die in der Tat einen echt chassidischen Klang hat, erzählte davon, daß Rabbi Beroka den Marktplatz seiner Stadt in Babylonien aufzusuchen pflegte und der Prophet Elias ihn dort besuchte. Einmal fragte er ihn: Sind jetzt auf diesem Marktplatz irgendwelche Kinder der künftigen Welt [das heißt Anwärter auf die ewige Seligkeit]? Während er fragte, gingen zwei Brüder vorüber, und der Prophet Elias sagte: Diese beiden. Er ging und fragte sie: Was macht ihr? Sie sagten: Wir sind Possenreißer. Ist jemand traurig, so suchen wir ihn aufzuheitern, und sehen wir Leute streiten, so suchen wir Frieden zwischen ihnen zu stiften.[94]

That Kafka knew this story is suggested by Jeremias's explanation that he and Artur are indeed, as Frieda has surmised, 'Abgesandte Klamms' (S 219), and that they were sent by Galater, who happened to be standing in for Klamm, with the following instructions:

Als er uns zu Dir schickte, sagte er—ich habe es mir genau gemerkt, denn darauf berufen wir uns ja—: Ihr geht hin als die Gehilfen des Landvermessers. Wir sagten: Wir verstehn aber nichts von dieser Arbeit. Er darauf: Das ist nicht das Wichtigste; wenn es nötig sein wird, wird er es Euch beibringen. Das Wichtigste aber ist, daß Ihr ihn ein wenig erheitert. Wie man mir berichtet, nimmt er alles sehr schwer. (S 367–8.)

Besides trying to cheer up the humourless, single-minded K., the assistants also seem to exert a good influence on his sexual relationship with Frieda. It is when they are present, unknown to him, that K. is able to achieve momentary self-forgetfulness in sex; but in their absence, sex is described as a disappointing, merely animal activity (S 75). They are also associated with childhood: Frieda refers to them as 'läppische Jungen' but adds that she cannot really be angry at their 'kindisch-närrischen Benehmen' (S 218). By driving the assistants away, therefore, K. is taking the first step to destroying his relationship with Frieda, and she is no doubt right in fearing that his severity towards them will cut him off from Klamm: 'Wenn ich dann aber wieder bedenke, daß Du, wenn Du gegen sie hart bleibst, damit vielleicht Klamm selbst den Zutritt zu Dir verweigerst, will ich Dich mit allen Mitteln vor den Folgen dessen bewahren' (S 220).

Thus the assistants are a Hasidic image for some of the qualities that K. needs to incorporate into his daily life. Another Hasidic image appears in the opening chapter on the novel and constitutes an admonition which K. ignores. K. is trying to reach the Castle on foot and discovering that the apparently endless village street is bringing him no nearer to his objective. Exhausted by tramping through the snow, he enters the house of the peasant Lasemann and comes upon a curious scene:

Es schien ein allgemeiner Waschtag zu sein. In der Nähe der Tür wurde Wäsche gewaschen. Der Rauch war aber aus der linken Ecke gekommen, wo in einem Holzschaff, so groß wie K. noch nie eines gesehen hatte, es hatte etwa den Umfang von zwei Betten, in dampfendem Wasser zwei Männer badeten. (S 22–3.)

The importance of the bath is emphasized by the allusion in Lasemann's name to the Czech *lázeň* 'bath'.[95] As a means of ritual purification, the bath is an important feature of Judaism, and was given special prominence in the teaching of the Ba'al Shem, who considered immersion in the ritual bath a far more valuable exercise than ascetic practices like fasting. In his introduction to *Der große Maggid* Buber dwells on the bath as a symbol of spiritual renewal:

Urzeitliches Symbol der Wiedergeburt (die wahrhaft nur ist, wenn sie Tod und Auferstehung umschließt), aus alten Überlieferungen, insbesondere der Essäer und 'Morgentäufer', in die kabbalistische Praxis aufgenommen, wird es von den Zaddikim mit einer hohen und freudigen Leidenschaft geübt, die nicht asketischer Art ist.[96]

It is pleasing to find this confirmation for Sheppard's intuitively convincing interpretation of this scene as representing a 'purgatorial experience' in which one can be 'renewed'.[97]

The meaning of the bath is enriched by its setting. It is the centre of the Lasemanns' and Brunswicks' family life. The children round the tub symbolize the childlike playfulness shared by the assistants and the officials but alien to K.'s character. The natural vitality and enjoyment suggested in the description of the scene anticipate Olga's account of the fire-brigade festival, which also takes place beside water. Even the word 'Spritzer' occurs, anticipating the later 'Spritze'. The only person who does not fit into this setting is the woman in the armchair, who looks tired and ill, in contrast to the health and vigour of her counterpart at the wash-tub:

Die Frau beim Waschtrog, blond, in jugendlicher Fülle, sang leise bei der Arbeit, die Männer im Bad stampfen und drehten sich, die Kinder wollten sich ihnen nähern, wurden aber durch mächtige Wasserspritzer die auch K. nicht verschonten immer wieder zurückgetrieben, die Frau im Lehnstuhl lag wie leblos, nicht einmal auf das Kind an ihrer Brust blickte sie hinab, sondern unbestimmt in die Höhe. (S 23–4.)

If the scene around the bath symbolizes the positive values of the novel, their opposite is represented by the woman in the armchair, who provides the first of several parallels to K.'s obsession with the Castle. Eventually K. will learn that she is Frau Brunswick, the mother of Hans, but for the moment she simply calls herself 'Ein Mädchen aus dem Schloß' (S 25). The pale light gives her clothes the appearance of silk, like the garments worn by Barnabas as a token of his status as a Castle messenger; later she is said to be wearing 'ein seidenes durchsichtiges Kopftuch' (S 25). Instead of joining in the healthy and cheerful life around her, she gazes upwards, as if towards the Castle. Her gaze is 'unbestimmt', like K.'s indefinable goal, and her inattention to the child at her breast corresponds to K.'s later neglect of Frieda. The scene as a whole forms a microcosm of *Das Schloß* by juxtaposing the alternatives between which K. has to choose: domestic life pursued in accordance with Klamm's wishes, or a self-destructive neglect of domestic responsibilities for the sake of direct contact with Klamm and the Castle.

It appears, then, that Kafka has indeed sunk roots deep into past centuries in order to recount K.'s tragedy. Jewish traditions supplied him with a repertory of allusions and images with which to express these alternatives, notably the Hasidic images for the former and the Messianic allusion implicit in the word 'Landvermesser' for the latter. To understand how these images and allusions function, however, we need to understand in what framework Kafka has placed them—that is, to define the literary genre in which it is writing; and this means grappling with the vexed question of allegory.

Allegory

The word 'allegory' has led a ghostly existence in Kafka-criticism since 1930, when Edwin Muir used it in presenting his and his wife's translation of *Das Schloß* to the British reading public. Instead of making the novel more accessible, Muir caused confusion, partly by employing the word 'allegory' in a loose and semi-private sense and partly by taking Bunyan's *Pilgrim's Progress* as his example of allegory. He would have done much better to remind his readers not of Bunyan's simple one-to-one correspondences but of a complex allegorical work like Spenser's *Faerie Queene*. As it was, the damage done by Muir's inappropriate comparison could not be undone by his qualification that Kafka's 'allegory is not a mere recapitulation or recreation; it does not run on lines already laid down; it is a pushing forward of the mind into unknown places'.[98] The term 'allegory', understood in a more simplistic sense than Muir intended, was rejected by Brod, Anders, and Emrich, the last of whom argued that Kafka's images were beyond allegory and symbol in having neither the univocality of allegory nor the universality of symbols.[99] Since then, however, the term has reappeared in Kafka-studies. As early as 1964 Sokel argued that Kafka's works show a development from symbol to allegory, with *In der Strafkolonie* as the turning-point; in 1973 Ingeborg Henel described *In der Strafkolonie* as a full-fledged allegory, though she thought it unique in Kafka's work; in recent years Gerhard Kurz and Hans Hiebel have applied the term liberally to the whole of Kafka's fiction.[100] Meanwhile, writers on allegory have long taken it for granted that some at least of Kafka's works are allegorical.[101] I believe that they are right, and that the confusion among critics arises from a misunderstanding of allegory rather than of Kafka. To be useful, however, the word 'allegory' needs to be employed in a precise and not over-inclusive sense, and to be freed from the misconceptions that still surround it.[102]

One of these misconceptions, the inferiority of allegory to symbol, bears the authority of Goethe and Coleridge. Both suggest that an allegorical image is reductive in having a univocal conceptual meaning, in contrast to the inexhaustibility of the symbol, and in being separate from the reality it represents, whereas the symbol is a synecdoche which partakes of the nature of its object.[103] Now it must be pointed out, firstly, that the latter claim is demonstrably spurious. As Schopenhauer argues in a typically trenchant passage, there is no form of language, poetic or otherwise, which can provide direct access to its object without the mediation of concepts. Tropes and metaphors, which rely in different ways on the distance between image and concept, are the very stuff of poetry, and are distinguished from allegory only by their brevity.[104] Secondly, the definitions put forward by Goethe and Coleridge are prescriptive, and do not reflect the normal usage of their time, in which the terms 'symbol' and 'allegory' are frequently interchangeable. In his *Gespräch über die Poesie* (1800) Friedrich Schlegel originally wrote: 'Das Höchste kann man, eben weil es unaussprechlich ist, nur allegorisch sagen', but substituted 'symbolisch' in a later edition.[105] If the two terms can in fact be usefully distinguished, the best way would be to adopt the distinction between metaphor and metonymy outlined at the beginning of this chapter. Allegory, which is already associated with metaphor by the classical rhetoricians, is then a kind of imagery in which there is no necessary or intrinsic connection between the vehicle of an image and its tenor; a symbol, on the other hand, is a metonymic image whose tenor, though not consubstantial with the vehicle, can be accepted as a natural or obvious extension of it. Verisimilar fiction tends to use symbolism, since it purports to describe the empirical world in a manner that readily evokes symbolic implications; while the literature of fantasy, though not debarred from using symbolism, tends more towards the allegorical mode.[106]

Other misconceptions can be dealt with more briefly. Many hostile critics of allegory think first and foremost of allegorical paintings, and imagine that an allegory is typically a single image, such as the anchor which conventionally represents hope.[107] Here allegory is being confused with the tradition of the emblem. But since an emblem, that is, a picture with an explanatory caption, combines visual with verbal art, we cannot properly speak of literary emblems. Allegory is also often confused with personification, as in Christian, Ignorance, Giant Despair, and the rest of Bunyan's characters. Personification, however, is not necessarily allegorical: since Ignorance is an ignorant man, the relation between his character and his significance is intrinsic and hence metonymic, so that he is best described as a symbolic figure. Allegory seems to have originated from personification, and personification is a frequent device in allegorical works, but the two cannot be identified.

These confusions have probably been encouraged by Quintilian's definition of allegory as an extended metaphor. This is accurate in associating allegory with metaphor and in insisting on its extension, since in both literature and painting an allegory is not an isolated image but a complex narrative or description.[108] But its extension distinguishes allegory from metaphor in that the two levels of meaning, which are inseparable in metaphor, are capable in allegory of being developed in considerable independence of each other.[109] Not all allegories are elaborate set-pieces like Maimonides' palace or Spenser's House of Alma, in which there is a neat one-to-one correspondence between each image and its meaning. In many allegorical works the relation between image and meaning is intermittent, fluctuating, and diverse. Thus C. S. Lewis says of *The Faerie Queene*: 'Not everything in the poem is equally allegorical, or even allegorical at all. We shall find that it is Spenser's method to have in each book an allegorical core, surrounded by a margin of what is called "romance of types", and relieved by episodes of pure fantasy.'[10] If allegory is understood as a complex and subtle mode of literary expression, it can be seen that *Das Schloß* belongs to this mode, and to substantiate this assertion I wish, finally, to list some major features of the allegorical mode which *Das Schloß* shares.

(1) Allegory presupposes a distinction between two levels of reality. In Spenser the higher level is variously Christian and Platonic. In Melville's allegorical narrative *Moby-Dick* the higher level is the inscrutable spiritual reality concealed behind the 'pasteboard masks' of the visible world but linked to it by innumerable analogies.[111] Kafka distinguishes sharply between the spiritual world of 'das Unzerstörbare' and the physical world, and uses the Castle as an allegorical image and Klamm and the assistants as allegorical figures connecting the physical and the spiritual worlds.

(2) In literary terms, the disjunction between the two levels appears as the relation between the text and what Maureen Quilligan calls its 'pre-text', a master-text to which the allegorical work alludes and on which it relies for its own authority. For medieval and Renaissance allegorists the master-text was the Bible. For a contemporary allegorist, Thomas Pynchon, it is the language of myth and ritual now made accessible by Eliade and other mythographers.[112] For Kafka, the pre-text that endows his own text with authority is the stock of Jewish and especially Hasidic tradition with which he wishes to regain contact.

(3) The disjunction between the two levels is conveyed linguistically through word-play. Spenser's polysemy includes etymological puns

on 'error' and 'wandering' in Book 1 of *The Faerie Queene*. 'Etymology' is the first word of *Moby-Dick*, heading a pseudo-learned list of words for 'whale' in languages from Hebrew to Erromangoan. Kafka's concealed puns on 'Landvermesser' and 'Bote' are characteristic of allegory, as is his scepticism about the possibility of using language to refer to spiritual realities.

(4) Besides the master-text, a body of other pre-texts of varying degrees of authority serves as a fund of allusions. The allegorist is, or affects to be, a *poeta doctus* writing for a small group of well-informed readers. Hence Spenser's wide use of classical mythology, Melville's biblical and literary references, and the already noted eclecticism with which Kafka draws on diverse religious images.

(5) The two levels can be related in very various ways. An allegorical work can accommodate a considerable quantity of realism without ulterior significance. Spenser's Britomart represents married love, but this concept does not determine every trait of her character or every episode of her adventures. Melville's allegorical method is unmistakable, for example, in the *Pequod*'s encounters with significantly named ships (the *Virgin*, the *Rachel*, the *Bachelor*), but absent from the realistic account of the pursuit, slaughter, and dismemberment of the sperm-whale. In Kafka's treatment of K.'s relationship with Frieda, allegorical significance frequently recedes behind psychological realism. When present, allegorical meaning can be highly oblique. Spenser's allegorical passages require learned exegesis; the significance of Moby-Dick, as of the Castle, is intentionally obscure; and Kafka's usual technique of allegory is one which, instead of presenting emblematic images, uses puns and allusions to give the reader a fleeting glimpse of unfamiliar vistas of meaning. It has been admirably described by Gerhard Kurz as 'Eine Allegorie, die nicht die semantische Geste "dies bedeutet nur" erfüllt, sondern eine Tiefenperspektive an Bedeutungen evoziert'.[113]

In conclusion, I shall leave it to the reader to decide how much of Kafka's fiction can be called allegorical in the proper sense, and simply say that I should be inclined to agree with Sokel in seeing in Kafka's work a gradual transition from symbol to allegory, with many intermediate stages. Near the one pole, we find images like that of the insect in *Die Verwandlung*, whose various implications, as Kafka gradually explores them, turn out to be largely metonymic. Gregor's increasing isolation from his family, his loss of power, his regression to an infantile state, the dominance of his physical being over his mind, the sensations of horror and self-disgust, and so on, are suggested readily and naturally by the central image, without the mediation of a distinct conceptual system. Much of *Das Schloß*, on the other hand, does presuppose the conceptual system outlined in the Zürau aphorisms, as well as drawing on a body of Jewish traditions, so that *Das Schloß* is less immediately accessible to the reader than *Die Verwandlung*. Some of Kafka's late animal stories are also allegorical, since they are not explorations of animality, like *Die Verwandlung*, but use animals metaphorically with oblique reference to human life. A brief consideration of two of these, *Forschungen eines Hundes* and *Josefine, die Sängerin oder das Volk der Mäuse*, will serve to round off this study.

7

Epilogue
Forschungen eines Hundes (*1922*)
and Josefine, die Sängerin oder das Volk
der Mäuse (*1924*)

KAFKA'S late fiction is for the most part quiet and restrained. It lacks the disturbing or disgusting images of such early stories as *Das Urteil* and *Die Verwandlung*, and also their dramatic intensity. As in *Beim Bau der chinesischen Mauer*, narrative has largely given way to reflection: these stories tend to begin after the events mentioned in their titles are over—after the completion of the Great Wall, of the burrow in *Der Bau* (1923), and of the dog's researches—and their narrators meditate, in a tone of perplexity mingled with grave humour, on the enigmas that remain unsolved after the work has been done. The atmosphere of these stories made Edwin Muir compare them with the plays of Shakespeare's last period. 'The charged air which fills *The Castle* and *The Trial* has cleared,' he wrote; 'the conflict and the passion have died away. There still remains a sense of vast and incomprehensible powers presiding over human destiny, but they no longer press upon the hero so stiflingly.'[1]

When he wrote these stories, Kafka was already very ill. His tuberculosis obliged him to spend much of his time in sanatoria and to retire from the Anstalt on full pension in the summer of 1922. It increased his desire to emigrate to Palestine, especially after the winter of 1922–3, when he suffered from fever and abdominal and intestinal pains which abated only to be followed by prolonged insomnia (O 145–6). In April and May 1923 a visit from Hugo Bergmann, who had been in Palestine since 1920, made him still more anxious to go there. However, an unexpected and fortunate event intervened. In July 1923 Kafka accompanied his sister Elli and her children to Müritz, a resort on the Baltic coast, where a party of children from the Jüdisches Volksheim in Berlin was also staying. Kafka's fondness for children is well attested,[2] and the pleasure he took in the company of these children emerges from a letter to Bergmann:

50 Schritte von meinem Balkon ist ein Ferienheim des Jüdischen Volksheims
in Berlin. Durch die Bäume kann ich die Kinder spielen sehn. Fröhliche,
gesunde, leidenschaftliche Kinder. Ostjuden, durch Westjuden vor der
Berliner Gefahr gerettet. Die halben Tage und Nächte ist das Haus, der
Wald und der Strand voll Gesang. Wenn ich unter ihnen bin, bin ich nicht
glücklich, aber vor der Schwelle des Glücks. (Br 436.)

Among the helpers taking care of these children was Dora Dymant, a
girl of about twenty-five who had broken away from her Hasidic
family in Poland, and worked first in Breslau and later in Berlin.
When Kafka got to know her, he must have been impressed, among
other things, by her determination to lead her own life. Ten years
earlier his friendship with a similarly independent person, Jizchok
Löwy, had encouraged him to offend his family's assimilationist
ideals by immersing himself in Yiddish culture. Dora's moral support
now enabled him to take the still more radical step of leaving Prague
altogether and settling down with her in September 1923, two months
after they had first met, in the Berlin district of Steglitz. They stayed
there till March 1924, when Kafka returned to Prague so that he
could be admitted to a sanatorium near Vienna. He died in a
sanatorium at Klosterneuburg, north-west of Vienna, on 3 June
1924.

The months with Dora in Berlin were probably the happiest of
Kafka's life, even though his illness was worsening and the German
post-war inflation was at its notorious height. He was reluctantly
obliged to accept food-parcels from his family and friends, and it was
probably the fuel-shortage that made him order Dora to burn a large
number of his manuscripts, which are said to have included a play
and a story about the Beilis affair. After learning of this destruction
from Dora, two years later, Brod wrote with horror to Buber:
'Wissen Sie, daß er im letzten Lebensjahr an 20 dicke Hefte durch
seine Freundin hat in den Ofen werfen lassen? Er lag zu Bett und sah
zu, wie die Manuskripte verbrannten.'[3] At the same time, Kafka was
steeped in Jewish atmosphere. Dora, who had an excellent knowledge
of Hebrew as well as Yiddish, encouraged him to keep up his Hebrew
studies, as did Puah Bentovim on her occasional visits. They read
Hebrew texts together, and Kafka attended lectures on the Talmud at
the Hochschule für Wissenschaft des Judentums.[4] They also planned
to emigrate to Palestine, and had thoughts of working in a restaurant,

where Dora would be a cook and Kafka a waiter, though, looking back, Dora was not sure whether this scheme had been more than fanciful.[5]

Although we cannot say how far Kafka's life with Dora corresponded to the ideal of domesticity outlined in *Das Schloß*, we can be sure that it enhanced his sense of belonging to the Jewish people. The relationship between the speculatively or artistically inclined individual and the society he or she belongs to is a theme in both the late stories that I have chosen to discuss. In *Forschungen eines Hundes*, written in the summer of 1922, this theme is subordinate to the solitary researches pursued by the dog, but the dual title of *Josefine*, Kafka's last story, indicates that he wanted to give equal weight to both the heroine and her society. This story was written in March 1924 and published in the *Prager Presse* on 20 April under the title *Josefine, die Sängerin*; Kafka, at a time when he could no longer speak, gave written instructions that the title should be lengthened, adding: 'Solche Oder-Titel sind zwar nicht sehr hübsch, aber hier hat es vielleicht besonderen Sinn. Es hat etwas von einer Wadge.'[6]

In *Forschungen eines Hundes* the canine narrator does his research, not in isolation, but on the fringes of the 'Hundeschaft', as the dogs' community is repeatedly called. His unavailing search for truth has often been solemnly interpreted as representing man's futile search for absolute truth, or certainty, or God.[7] More recently Horst Steinmetz has called this story 'eine Art Schlüsselerzählung für das Gesamtwerk'[8] on the grounds that it thematizes the process of trying unsuccessfully to interpret an alien reality in terms of one's familiar categories, a process which, in Steinmetz's view, the rest of Kafka's fiction requires the reader to engage in. Against all these approaches I should like to put forward two arguments. First, we have already seen that in *Der Prozeß* and *Das Schloß* the narrator's perspective differs from that of the hero and thus enables the reader to understand the hero's situation as the hero himself cannot; likewise, although *Forschungen eines Hundes* differs from the novels in being told in the first person, it has an unreliable narrator whose perspective is as limited as those of the K.s and needs constantly to be corrected by the reader. Second, *Forschungen eines Hundes* was written just after *Das Schloß* and shares with it the idea of a frontier that consciousness cannot cross. If the Castle corresponds to the indestructible basis of human life, then K.'s efforts to penetrate the Castle and apprehend 'das Unzerstörbare' intellectually are as futile as the attempt to jump over one's own shadow would be. Similarly, the dog's researches keep coming up against a barrier which reduces them to futility. The difference is that while the nature of the impassable frontier in *Das Schloß* remains mysterious, and is disclosed to the reader by Bürgel only in an oblique manner, the barrier in *Forschungen eines Hundes* is obvious to the point of caricature. If *Das Schloß* is a tragedy, then *Forschungen eines Hundes* corresponds to the satyr-play that rounded off the Greek tragic cycles.

The barrier to the dog's researches, and the reason why he is an unreliable narrator, are the same. He is unaware of the existence of human beings.[9] 'Denn was gibt es außer den Hunden?' he asks rhetorically. 'Wen kann man sonst anrufen in der weiten, leeren Welt?' (B 255). This establishes an ironic distance between the narrator and the reader, who can see that all the dog's researches must founder on the limitations built into his own mind, and that all the enigmas which perplex the dog result from the power of human beings over the canine world. For example, he is puzzled by the contradiction between the dogs' desire to live in a warm huddle ('die Sehnsucht nach dem größten Glück, dessen wir fähig sind, dem warmen Beisammensein', B 242) and the fact that they live far apart from each other and obey 'Vorschriften, die nicht die der Hundeschaft sind' (B 242). Although Fingerhut interprets this as a trenchant exposure of bourgeois hypocrisy, in which 'die Phrase der menschlichen Solidarität entlarvt [wird] als eine sentimentale Verdeckung der totalen Zersplitterung der Gesellschaft und der vollkommenen Isolierung des einzelnen',[10] it can be explained less ponderously as a sign of the narrator's ignorance that dogs have human owners whom they have to obey. There is an equally simple explanation for the contradiction between the dogs' belief that they get their food from the earth either by cultivating it (i.e. scraping it) or by ritual dances, formulae, and songs, and the empirical fact that the food appears from above and indeed is often snapped up by the dogs before it reaches the ground.

The two most memorable incidents in the dog's biography can also be explained as due to human beings. The first was when, after roaming about in darkness, he suddenly found himself in a brightly illuminated place ('überheller Tag', B 243), filled with exciting smells, where he saw seven dogs walking on their hind legs to the accompaniment of music. The reader can see that the dog has found his way into a lighted room where a troupe of dancing dogs is performing before an audience which is 'voll durcheinander wogender, berauschender Gerüche' (B 243); if the smells coming from the audience include tobacco smoke, that would explain why the room is 'ein wenig dunstig' (B 243), while the 'Gewirr von Hölzern' (B 246) among which the dog hides must be the chairs on which the audience is sitting. Unable to perceive the audience itself, the narrator cannot understand why the seven dogs are breaking the canine law against walking on their hind legs, and why they do not reply to his bark. The conclusion he reaches is that the dogs are in the seclusion of their own home ('gewissermaßen in den eigenen vier Wänden', B 249) and hence entitled to behave as they please , which is, of course, the exact opposite of the truth. The second remarkable incident occurs when the narrator has gone to a remote spot in order to starve by way of scientific experiment. He is disturbed by a 'Jäger' (B 286), evidently a retriever or pointer, who claims to be under a compulsion to hunt and yet reluctant to drive his fellow-dog away from the hunting-ground. Although the narrator detects a contradiction here, there is none, for the retriever is compelled to hunt by his master, irrespective of his own feeling of canine solidarity. Both these incidents are accompanied by unfamiliar and deafening music which presumably comes, in the first instance, from a band accompanying the dogs' performance, and, in the second, from a huntsman's horn.[11] In both of them, the dogs' abnormal behaviour results from obedience to their human masters, although the narrator, unable to comprehend this cause, resorts to ludicrous conjectures to explain it.

Kafka, then, is satirizing the narrator by showing that the problems he investigates arise from the limitations of his consciousness. The dogs' ignorance of human beings seems to be as irremovable as the barrier between being and consciousness. Other themes from the Zürau aphorisms occur explicitly. The narrator, aware that he inhabits a 'Welt der Lüge' (B 284), suspects that the truth he seeks is somehow embodied in the dogs themselves. If it could be uttered, their lives might be transformed: 'Das Dach dieses niedrigen Lebens [. . .] wird sich öffnen und wir werden alle, Hund bei Hund, aufsteigen in die hohe Freiheit' (B 256). But if the truth could be extracted, it might be poison, and the dogs' obstinate taciturnity seems like an unconscious determination to guard the truth which sustains their lives as long as it remains inarticulate. The narrator does dimly feel that something is missing from their 'Hundeleben' (B 269; the word has the same connotations as 'a dog's life', and is used ironically), as though their ancestors had taken the wrong turning some time in the distant past; but now that the Fall from being into consciousness has happened, there is no going back, and the story shows elaborately that the attempt to reunite being with consciousness by an intellectual search for truth is eventually bound to fail.

Kafka sharpens his satire by emphasizing the dog's commitment to scientific investigation. The dogs have an extensive 'Wissenschaft' which sometimes sounds like Talmud study, as when we hear of a conversation between two sages and of the activities of commentators (B 281), but at other times seems to be experimental science; the narrator tries to make his researches sound more rigorous by talking about them in *Fremdwörter* (which Kafka normally uses very sparingly), as when he speaks of conducting 'ein ganz präzises Experiment' (B 275). His contempt for the arts is shown by his disapproval of the 'Lufthunde'. These are said to be small, fragile dogs which float in mid-air; the narrator has never seen one, not because they are invisible, as Emrich thinks,[12] but because they are lapdogs, and he has presumably never been inside a house where a lapdog is kept. Lapdogs are apparently the artists and intellectuals of the canine world: they are associated with 'Kunst und Künstlern' (B 261), have 'ein schönes Fell' (B 263), and utter philosophical observations which the narrator dismisses as being devoid of scientific value. He is scandalized by the 'Lotterleben' (B 262) they lead, and a similar criticism is implicit in the term 'Lufthund', which seems to be a play on *Luftmensch*, 'an idle, impractical person'. This word-play may imply a criticism of the 'Lufthunde' which comes not simply from the narrow-minded and Philistine perspective of the narrator, but also from the viewpoint of the author. If so, Binder may be right in relating them to the stereotype of the Western Jewish intellectual discussed in Ch. 4, and in citing self-critical remarks by Kafka such as: 'Der Schriftsteller in mir wird natürlich sofort sterben, denn eine solche Figur hat keinen Boden' (Br 385), especially since the closeness of the other dogs to the soil is repeatedly mentioned.[13] Kafka may also have had in mind the impractical scholars who inhabit the floating island of Laputa in Swift's *Gulliver's Travels*, a book he alludes to frequently in 1921 and 1922 (Br 342-7, 405, 415), though in that case the narrator would correspond to the equally impractical projectors down below who are busy wrecking the kingdom of Balnibarbi with their ludicrous schemes.

The lapdogs, like the performing dogs and the retriever, perplex the narrator because their strange behaviour results from the intervention in their lives of human beings, whom he is incapable of perceiving. *Forschungen eines Hundes* resembles *Das Schloß* in technique, since in each the reader is offered a perspective superior to that of the unreliable protagonist, and in theme, since both imply that one can live in accordance with the basic truth of life but not perceive it intellectually. Since the dominant tone of *Forschungen* is satirical, however, attempts to extract recondite metaphysical messages from it risk being heavy-handed.

The humour of *Josefine*, where the central character is not a scientist but an artist, is more subtle and poignant. Meditating on the relationship between Josefine and her people, the narrator unfolds a series of paradoxes. The very nature of her art is problematic, for she does nothing but squeak, and this is the sound made by all the mice as a matter of course: 'Pfeifen ist die Sprache unseres Volkes' (E 282).[14] Yet how is it that Josefine's performances hold the audience spellbound (E 268, 272), even at times of crisis, when they are in constant danger of being attacked by their enemies (E 283)? The explanation cannot be the one asserted by Josefine, who is convinced that her singing has often saved the community from political or economic perils (E 276), for her performances are more likely to betray the mice to their enemies. This belief in the importance of her art to the nation is a product of Josefine's vanity, which also makes her throw tantrums when she considers her audience too small, and demand to be kept at the public expense. She does not realize what pains the mice go to in order to protect her self-esteem by drumming up an audience for her. Still less does she realize that the mice would never take this trouble if she were a real artist, for, living as they do in constant danger, they could not afford the time to attend artistic performances. 'Möge Josefine beschützt werden vor der Erkenntnis, daß die Tatsache, daß wir ihr zuhören, ein Beweis gegen ihren Gesang ist,' says the narrator (E 279).

These reflections, which leave unsolved the question of the nature and value of Josefine's performances, belong to a series of meditations on art which had occupied Kafka intermittently since 1917, when, as we saw in Ch. 5, he abandoned an expressive view of art for a mimetic one. His writing was no longer to express his own feelings and his own situation, for self-exposure in art was simply a form of vanity; instead, its goal should be 'die Welt ins Reine, Wahre,

Unveränderliche [zu] heben' (T 534). However, mimesis as Kafka conceives it, the production of a purified copy of the world, has its own problems, two of which can be deduced from an aphorism of 1920, in which Kafka professes to be recalling the desires he had entertained many years earlier:

Als wichtigster oder als reizvollster ergab sich der Wunsch, eine Ansicht des Lebens zu gewinnen (und—das war allerdings notwendig verbunden—schriftlich die anderen von ihr überzeugen zu können), in der das Leben zwar sein natürliches schweres Fallen und Steigen bewahre, aber gleichzeitig mit nicht minderer Deutlichkeit als ein Nichts, als ein Traum, als ein Schweben erkannt werde. Vielleicht ein schöner Wunsch, wenn ich ihn richtig gewünscht hätte. Etwa als Wunsch, einen Tisch mit peinlich ordentlicher Handwerksmäßigkeit zusammenzuhämmern und dabei gleichzeitig nichts zu tun, und zwar nicht so, daß man sagen könnte: 'Ihm ist das Hämmern ein Nichts', sondern 'Ihm ist das Hämmern ein wirkliches Hämmern und gleichzeitig auch ein Nichts.' (B 293–4.)

This passage expresses the mimetic ideal of producing a simulacrum of reality which corresponds to it in all essential respects while advertising its character as a work of art, 'ein Traum'. The first problem it raises is that the mimetic artist is even more prey to vanity than the expressive artist, for he wants to be praised on two counts. Since his activity is an ordinary one, like making a table or cracking nuts (the example used in *Josefine*, E 270–1), he wants to be praised by the standards that apply to everyone. But, since his activity is also art, he also wants to be praised by special artistic standards that apply only to him. Kafka considers the vanity of artists incorrigible, and makes sure that his fictional artists are punished for it. The starvation artist in *Ein Hungerkünstler* (1922) is punished by being allowed to accomplish superhuman feats of starvation only when the public has lost interest in him; while Josefine's punishment consists in the narrator's reflection that her so-called art is only an ordinary activity of which she reveals the 'eigentliches Wesen' (E 271) by doing it *less* well than other people—so that Josefine really deserves praise on neither of the above counts.

The second problem raised by the mimetic ideal of art is that it seems to make art unnecessary. Since we already have the world, what do we need a copy of it for? Kafka has sharpened this problem by making Josefine's squeaking indistinguishable from ordinary squeaking, except by its feebleness; and he has also suggested an answer. It is not Josefine's performance but the act of listening to it that matters. The mice who gather to hear it feel that they form a 'Volksversammlung' (E 277). Though Josefine would be mortally offended by the suggestion that her so-called art is no more than the pretext for a gathering of the people, its value evidently does consist in the 'Gefühl der Menge, die warm, Leib an Leib, scheu und atmend horcht' (E 274). Its importance, then, is not aesthetic in any accepted sense. Nor has it any transcendent meaning: it does not convey a message from the world of truth. Josefine's performance is valuable because, through its very ordinariness and feebleness, it expresses the spirit of her people: 'Dieses Pfeifen, das sich erhebt, wo allen anderen Schweigen auferlegt ist, kommt fast wie eine Botschaft des Volkes zu dem Einzelnen; das dünne Pfeifen Josefinens mitten in den schweren Entscheidungen ist fast wie die armselige Existenz unseres Volkes mitten im Tumult der feindlichen Welt' (E 278).

Josefine is, then, a profound and subtle meditation on the nature and value of art, analogous in its conclusions to the investigation of the basis of religion that Kafka carried out in the Zürau aphorisms. There he concluded that the real object of religion was the indestructible, vital core common to all human beings, and that belief in a personal god was simply a fiction masking 'das Unzerstörbare'. In *Josefine*, conventional ideas about the autonomy and value of art, even the ideas that a distinct aesthetic realm exists, turn out to be equally illusory. Josefine herself is under an illusion about her art, and the other mice preserve her illusion with great solicitude, but, despite her claims, her performances are simply the medium through which the individual communicates with the communal spirit of his people. No English word can convey the force of the word 'Volk' which recurs with such emphasis throughout Kafka's text.

We seem to have come full circle, for in Ch. 1 we saw that Kafka valued the Yiddish theatre because it created a sense of solidarity and national consciousness among its audience. The question therefore arises whether the mice represent the Jewish people. While the story certainly has universal significance, being, like *Beim Bau der chinesischen Mauer*, a meditation on the sources of national cohesion which would apply to any society, one need not hesitate to recognize in it a number of specific references to the Jews. Admittedly, some commentators have questioned this, pointing out, as Roy Pascal does, that the narrator states emphatically: 'im allgemeinen vernachlässigen wir Geschichtsforschung gänzlich' (E 277, cf. 291), and that the Jews, 'above all people, dwell in the ever-renewed memory of their past heroes, blessings and disasters'.[15] The mice, however, preserve the memory of their past heroes (E 291) in traditions and legends (E 269); what they lack is not consciousness of the past but history in the sense of historiography, and in this they do resemble the Jews. As Lionel Kochan has shown in detail, there was almost no Jewish historiography between the time of Josephus and the nineteenth century. The remote, semi-legendary past up to the destruction of the Temple was recorded, but subsequent Jewish history was no more than a catalogue of persecutions and was considered important solely as a prelude to the arrival of the Messiah, so that 'the phenomenon of total recall of the remote past co-existed with relative oblivion to the recent past'.[16] Leopold Zunz, who helped to inaugurate modern Jewish historiography by establishing the *Wissenschaft des Judentums*, wrote in the early nineteenth century: 'If the Jewish Middle Ages can show no historians or historical researches we should not be surprised. A nation *in partibus* performs no acts.'[17] In the previous century, Salomon Maimon, whose autobiography Kafka had read with enthusiasm, had planned to contribute to the Jewish Enlightenment by translating Basnage's *Histoire des Juifs* into German, but decided that the attempt would be futile, and wrote: 'Auch gäbe es, die Wahrheit zu sagen, keine eigentliche Geschichte der Nation; denn diese stand beinahe niemals in einem politischen Verhältnis mit andern zivilisierten Nationen; und außer dem alten Testament, dem *Josephus* und einigen Fragmenten von den Verfolgungen der Juden in den mittleren Zeiten finden wir davon nichts aufgezeichnet.'[18] From this source, and probably also from his visits to the Hochschule für Wissenschaft des Judentums, Kafka would have known about the absence of Jewish historiography. The reliance of the mice on legends, and their neglect of historical study, therefore constitute a pointed allusion to the Jews.

More generally, the wide area across which the mice are scattered, and the constant dangers to which they are exposed, make one think of Jewish life in the Diaspora: 'die Gebiete, auf denen wir aus wirtschaftlichen Rücksichten zerstreut leben müssen, sind zu groß, unserer Feinde sind zu viele, die uns überall bereiteten Gefahren zu unberechenbar' (E 279). They resemble familiar Jewish stereotypes in their economic concerns, mentioned here and elsewhere (E 276); in their practicality—'eine gewisse praktische Schlauheit, die wir freilich auch äußerst dringend brauchen' (E 268); in a critical spirit which makes them incapable of 'bedingungslose Ergebenheit' (E 275); in appearing timid (E 277); in their relative lack of interest in music (E 268); in being 'leidensgewohnt' (E 277); and perhaps in being gossipy (E 276), and humorous (E 275). The constant references to their national characteristics confirm that the 'Volk der Mäuse' is just as central to the story as Josefine.

If we are justified in regarding *Josefine* as Kafka's final statement about the position of the artist in society, and hence as full of personal implications, then the self-tormenting spirit of Kafka's earlier works has been succeeded by a mood of self-effacement. He does not deny the value of art, but he does conclude that its value is, and perhaps must be, something other than what the artist imagines. The 'Volk' understands art better than the artist does. In keeping with his aphorism, 'Im Kampf zwischen dir und der Welt sekundiere der Welt' (H 91), Kafka has taken the side of the people against the artist, and by doing so he has brought the relation between the two sides to a dialectical resolution, both inside and outside the story. Within the story we see that the artist, for all her vanity, is really very unimportant as an individual: her public, far from being subservient to her, tolerates her pretensions as good-naturedly as though she were a fractious child, and will not greatly miss her. In fact, the most recent news of her is that she has already vanished. Her disappearance means that the contradiction between her people's view of her, and her own view of herself, will be resolved, for after her death she will merge with the anonymous heroes of her people and exist not in history but 'in gesteigerter Erlösung' (E 291) as a portion of the spirit of her people, or, as Pascal puts it: 'she lives on in her people, not as a person or an individual memory, for this people of mice has no historical memory, but absorbed into the being, the nature and habits, of this people; personally forgotten but immortal in her contribution to the survival of her folk.'[19]

Outside the story, too, or rather through it, Kafka has achieved a resolution, for the story contains his most radical questioning of the nature and value of art and yet belongs among his unchallengeable artistic masterpieces. Not only is it full of subtle reflection and delicate humour, but in focusing sharply on the mice, and bringing their life vividly before us, he also manages to disclose historical vistas comprehending the whole of Jewish life in the Diaspora. Finally, the story is also an achievement on the most personal level. When he wrote it Kafka must have known that he had not much longer to live, so that in mentioning Josefine's disappearance he seems to be alluding to his own imminent death. If so, his absence of self-pity, and the gentle, beautifully controlled mockery he directs against Josefine's claims to be indispensable, testify not only to his artistic integrity but to his rare fineness as a human being.

Notes

Abbreviations of journals

Annali   *Annali dell'Istituto Universitario Orientale, Sezione Germanica*
CL   *Comparative Literature*
DVjs   *Deutsche Vierteljahrsschrift für Literatur und Geistesgeschichte*
FMLS   *Forum for Modern Language Studies*
GQ   *German Quarterly*
JDSG   *Jahrbuch der Deutschen Schiller-Gesellschaft*
LBY   *Leo Baeck Institute Year Book*
MAL   *Modern Austrian Literature*
MLN   *Modern Language Notes*
MLR   *Modern Language Review*
OGS   *Oxford German Studies*
ZfdP   *Zeitschrift für deutsche Philologie*

Chapter 1

1. Felix Weltsch, 'The Rise and Fall of the Jewish–German Symbiosis: The Case of Franz Kafka', *LBY* 1 (1956), 276.
2. Emil Utitz, 'Erinnerungen an Franz Kafka', in Klaus Wagenbach, *Franz Kafka: Eine Biographie seiner Jugend, 1883–1912* (Berne, 1958), 267.
3. Heinz Politzer, *Franz Kafka: Parable and Paradox*, 2nd edn. (Ithaca, NY, 1966), 9.
4. The following sketch is based on Wagenbach, *Biographie*; Christoph Stölzl, *Kafkas böses Böhmen: Zur Sozialgeschichte eines Prager Juden* (Munich, 1975); Gary B. Cohen, 'Jews in German Society: Prague, 1860–1914', *Central European History*, 10 (1977), 28–54; Hartmut Binder (ed.), *Kafka-Handbuch* (2 vols., Stuttgart, 1979); Cohen, *The Politics of Ethnic Survival: Germans in Prague, 1861–1914* (Princeton, 1981).
5. I have used this spelling throughout, but the documents reproduced in Klaus Wagenbach, *Franz Kafka: Bilder aus seinem Leben* (Berlin, 1983), show that Kafka's father spelt his first name in three different ways: 'Herrman' (p. 24), 'Hermann' (p. 33), and 'Herrmann' (p. 36).
6. On *Mauscheldeutsch*, see Heinrich Teweles, *Der Kampf um die Sprache* (Leipzig, 1884), 14–19; Fritz Mauthner, *Prager Jugendjahre* (Munich, 1918, repr. Frankfurt, 1969), 30–1; Wagenbach, *Biographie*, 86; and, for

much relevant information, Caroline Kohn, 'Der Wiener jüdische Jargon im Werke von Karl Kraus', *MAL* 8 (1975), i. 240–67.

7. Max Brod, *Jüdinnen* (Berlin, 1911, repr. Leipzig, 1915), 54. Cf. Pavel Eisner, *Franz Kafka and Prague* (New York, 1950), 27–8; Kurt Krolop, 'Zur Geschichte und Vorgeschichte der Prager deutschen Literatur des "expressionistischen Jahrzehnts"', in Eduard Goldstücker (ed.), *Weltfreunde: Konferenz über die Prager deutsche Literatur* (Prague, 1967), 51, 75.

8. Wagenbach, *Biographie*, 19.

9. See Carl E. Schorske, *Fin-de-siècle Vienna: Politics and Culture* (Cambridge, 1981), 146–75.

10. See Wagenbach, *Biographie*, 45; Binder (ed.), *Kafka-Handbuch*, i. 74–6, 280–6.

11. Hans Kohn, *Living in a World Revolution* (New York, 1964), 37. Cf. Weltsch, *Religion und Humor im Leben und Werk Franz Kafkas* (Berlin-Grunewald, 1957), 35; Brod, *Streitbares Leben* (Munich, 1960), 346–8.

12. S. H. Bergman [*sic*], 'Erinnerungen an Franz Kafka', *Universitas*, 27 (1972), 742. Cf. T 222.

13. See Wagenbach, *Bilder*, 33, where the invitation-card sent out by Kafka's parents, with the word 'Confirmation', is reproduced.

14. Hermann Kafka's point of view has now been presented by Nadine Gordimer in 'Letter from His Father', *Something Out There* (London, 1984), 39–56.

15. See Brod, *Über Franz Kafka* (Frankfurt, 1966), 46, 276; Paul Raabe, 'Franz Kafka und der Expressionismus', *ZfdP* 86 (1967), 161–75.

16. Brod, *Über Franz Kafka*, 108.

17. Cohen, 'Jews in German Society', 29.

18. The valuable book by Stölzl can easily give the opposite impression, and therefore needs to be read with some caution.

19. Lulu Gräfin Thürheim, *Mein Leben: Erinnerungen aus Österreichs großer Welt* (4 vols., Munich, 1913), ii. 48.

20. Heine's letters on the Damascus affair are in *Lutezia*, Erster Teil, in Heinrich Heine, *Sämtliche Werke*, ed. Ernst Elster (7 vols., Leipzig, 1893), vi. 129–300. See also Ludwig Rosenthal, *Heinrich Heine als Jude* (Frankfurt, 1973), 204–5.

21. Rohling owed his position to a pseudo-scholarly anti-Semitic work, *Der Talmudjude* (Münster, 1871), which had gained him the favour of the Catholic establishment. He was discredited in 1885 by the Viennese rabbi Josef Bloch, who challenged him to read and translate correctly any page in the Talmud. See P. G. J. Pulzer, *The Rise of Political Anti-Semitism in Germany and Austria* (New York, 1964), 163–4.

22. František Červinka, 'The Hilsner Affair', *LBY* 13 (1968), 147.

23. The Beilis affair was extensively reported in the Zionist paper *Selbstwehr*, which Kafka may have begun reading as early as 1911. See Binder,

'Franz Kafka und die Wochenschrift *Selbstwehr*', *DVjs* 41 (1967), 283–304; Arnold J. Band, 'Kafka and the Beiliss [*sic*] Affair', *CL* 32 (1980), 168–83.

24. Brod, *Über Franz Kafka*, 177.
25. Quoted in Gerhard Neumann, *Franz Kafka, 'Das Urteil': Text, Materialien, Kommentar* (Munich, 1981), 36.
26. Brod, *Über Franz Kafka*, 270; Weltsch, 38; Klara P. Carmely, *Das Identitätsproblem jüdischer Autoren im deutschen Sprachraum* (Königstein, 1981), 162–6.
27. See Brod, *Der Prager Kreis* (Stuttgart, 1966), 111–12; Bergman, 'Erinnerungen', 743.
28. See Brod, *Streitbares Leben*, 353.
29. Brod, *Über Franz Kafka*, 100.
30. See Helen Milfull, 'Franz Kafka—The Jewish Context', *LBY* 23 (1978), 227–38. This is a good introduction to the topic, and so, despite its mannered style, is Walter Jens, 'Ein Jude namens Kafka', in Thilo Koch (ed.), *Porträts deutsch-jüdischer Geistesgeschichte* (Cologne, 1961), 179–203. The best and most thorough study of Kafka and Judaism is Anne Oppenheimer, 'Franz Kafka's Relation to Judaism' (D.Phil. thesis, Oxford, 1977).
31. Martin Buber, *Briefwechsel aus sieben Jahrzehnten* (3 vols., Heidelberg, 1972–5), i. 473.
32. The passage in the second sentence of this letter, 'etwas Nutzloseres als ein solcher Kongreß läßt sich schwer ausdenken' (Br 120), is sometimes taken to refer to the Zionist Congress: e.g. Oppenheimer, 61. From the context, however, it seems clear that Kafka is referring to the conference on industrial safety, and only moves on to talk about the Zionist Congress in the next sentence.
33. T 88; Brod's MS diary is quoted by Wagenbach, *Biographie*, 233.
34. This can scarcely be more than a guess, for the difficulty of estimating the Jewish population is particularly acute during this period. Assimilation increased the difficulty of defining a Jew, and vast numbers were emigrating to America. According to the article 'Population' in the *Encyclopaedia Judaica* (16 vols., Jerusalem, 1971), 'in the course of merely 24 years, from 1890 to 1914, some 30% of all Eastern European Jews changed their residence to some overseas country, particularly the United States' (xiii. 893). The Russian census of 1897 gave the Jewish population of European Russia and Congress Poland as 5,190,000, while in 1900 that of Austria-Hungary was 2,069,000 and that of Romania 267,000. This makes a total of 7,526,000, of which we may assume that the majority was unassimilated.
35. See Samuel J. Citron, 'Yiddish and Hebrew Drama', in Barrett H. Clark and George Freedley (eds.), *A History of Modern Drama* (New York, 1947), 601–38.

36. Hutchins Hapgood, *The Spirit of the Ghetto*, ed. Moses Rischin (Cambridge, Mass., 1967), 137.

37. Alfred Döblin, *Reise in Polen* (Olten, 1968), 146.

38. See Shlomo Avineri, *The Making of Modern Zionism* (London, 1981), 23–35.

39. M. Pinès, *Histoire de la littérature judéo-allemande* (Paris, 1910). See 'Pines, Meyer Isser', *Encyclopaedia Judaica*, xiii. 533–4.

40. See *The Diaries of Franz Kafka*, tr. Joseph Kresh (2 vols., London, 1948–9), i. 224–7.

41. Letter to Ernst Ferdinand Klein, 29 Aug. 1782, in Moses Mendelssohn, *Gesammelte Schriften*, ed. I. Elbogen, J. Guttman, and E. Mittwoch, vii. *Schriften zum Judentum I*, ed. Simon Rawidowicz (Berlin, 1930), 279.

42. Theodor Herzl, *Gesammelte zionistische Werke* (5 vols., Berlin and Tel Aviv, 1934–5), ii. 195.

43. *Die Romantische Schule*, in Heine, v. 248.

44. Harold Bloom, *The Anxiety of Influence* (New York, 1971).

45. Roy Pascal, *Kafka's Narrators: A Study of his Stories and Sketches* (Cambridge, 1982), 48.

46. Gilles Deleuze and Félix Guattari, *Kafka: Pour une littérature mineure* (Paris, 1975), 46–8.

47. Brod, *Über Franz Kafka*, 102.

48. See 'A Friend of Kafka' in Isaac Bashevis Singer, *Collected Stories* (London, 1982), 277–86. Löwy is last heard of in the Warsaw ghetto, where he recited Hebrew poetry to keep up the spirits of his fellow prisoners; see Lucy Dawidowicz, *The War against the Jews* (London, 1975), 257.

49. For one of the most persuasive demonstrations of influence, that of Kleist's *Der Findling*, see F. G. Peters, 'Kafka and Kleist: A Literary Relationship', *OGS* 1 (1966), 117–24. Source-study dwindles into mere parallel-hunting, however, when Urs Ruf, *Franz Kafka: Das Dilemma der Söhne* (Berlin, 1974), 51, points out similarities between *Das Urteil* and Storm's *Hans und Heinz Kirch*, a story Kafka never mentions and may never have read.

50. Karlheinz Fingerhut, 'Ein Beispiel produktiver Lektüreverarbeitung (Max Brods *Arnold Beer* und *Das Urteil*)', in Binder (ed.), *Kafka-Handbuch*, ii. 278–82.

51. 'Nachwort' in Brod, *Arnold Beer: Das Schicksal eines Juden* (Berlin, 1912), 175.

52. Spinell's 'zart angedeutete jüdische Herkunft', as Jost Hermand calls it in *Der Schein des schönen Lebens: Studien zur Jahrhundertwende* (Frankfurt, 1972), 182, is indicated by his bearing the name of a jewel (cf. distinctively Jewish surnames like Goldstein, Demant, Sapir) and coming from Lemberg, a city where the majority of the population was Jewish.

53. Brod, *Beer*, 133.

54. Ibid. 170.

55. Ibid. 149.

56. Ibid. 143.
57. Franz Werfel, 'Die Riesin: Ein Augenblick der Seele', *Herder-Blätter*, 1. iv–v (October 1912), 41-3.
58. Binder (ed.), *Kafka-Handbuch*, ii. 282.
59. Ingo Seidler, '*Das Urteil*: "Freud natürlich"? Zum Problem der Multivalenz bei Kafka', in Wolfgang Paulsen (ed.), *Psychologie in der Literaturwissenschaft* (Heidelberg, 1971), 188. On Kafka's opinion of psychoanalysis see p. 204 above.
60. See Claudio Magris, *Weit von wo: Verlorene Welt des Ostjudentums*, tr. Jutta Prasse (Vienna, 1974), especially p. 71.
61. Neumann, '*Das Urteil*', 82-3.
62. For a good recent discussion of Georg's guilt, with a survey of earlier interpretations, see H. H. Hiebel, *Die Zeichen des Gesetzes: Recht und Macht bei Franz Kafka* (Munich, 1983), 117-20.
63. Gerhard Kurz, 'Einleitung: Der junge Kafka im Kontext', in id. (ed.), *Der junge Kafka* (Frankfurt, 1984), 22-3.
64. E. T. Beck, *Kafka and the Yiddish Theater* (Madison, Wis., 1971), ch. 5. For a summary of the action of *Got, mensh un tayvl* see ibid. 72-4; for summaries of *Di shkhite* and *Der vilde mensh* see Hapgood, 143-6.
65. Cf. J. J. White, 'Endings and Non-Endings in Kafka's Fiction', in Franz Kuna (ed.), *On Kafka: Semi-Centenary Essays* (London, 1976), 146-66.

Chapter 2

1. Walther Rathenau, 'Zur Kritik der Zeit', in *Gesammelte Schriften* (5 vols., Berlin, 1925), i. 11.
2. See C. A. Macartney, *The Habsburg Empire 1790-1918* (London, 1968), 616-19, 755-6.
3. See Norman Stone, *Europe Transformed, 1878-1919* (Glasgow, 1983), 79-81.
4. Rathenau, i. 13.
5. Georg Heym, 'Die Stadt', in *Gesammelte Gedichte*, ed. Carl Seelig (Zürich, 1947), 87. For comment, see Heinz Rölleke, *Die Stadt bei Stadler, Heym und Trakl* (Berlin, 1966), 127-31. Rölleke places Heym alongside Döblin on p. 194.
6. Alfred Döblin, *Aufsätze zur Literatur* (Olten, 1963), 66.
7. Rainer Maria Rilke, *Briefe*, ed. Karl Altheim (2 vols., Wiesbaden, 1950), ii. 483.
8. K. R. Mandelkow, *Orpheus und Maschine* (Heidelberg, 1976), 102.
9. See Rilke, *Sämtliche Werke*, ed. Ernst Zinn (6 vols., Frankfurt, 1955-66), i. 46-7.
10. They are reprinted in Wagenbach, *Biographie*, 281-337.

11. For a report of one such meeting, reprinted from a local newspaper, see Anthony D. Northey, 'Dr Kafka in Gablonz', *MLN* 93 (1978), 500–3.

12. See Wagenbach, *Biographie*, 148–9.

13. Brod, *Über Franz Kafka*, 76.

14. Ibid., 92. See Wolfgang Jahn, *Kafkas Roman 'Der Verschollene'* (Stuttgart, 1965), 63–6; Hanns Zischler, 'Maßlose Unterhaltung: Franz Kafka geht ins Kino', *Freibeuter*, 16 (1983), 33–47.

15. 'Die Aeroplane in Brescia', in Brod, *Über Franz Kafka*, 365.

16. Ibid., 366.

17. Edwin Muir, 'Introductory Note', *America*, tr. Edwin and Willa Muir (London, 1938), p. vii; reprinted in Dieter Jakob, *Das Kafka-Bild in England: Eine Studie zur Aufnahme des Werkes in der journalistischen Kritik (1928–1966)* (2 vols., Oxford and Erlangen, 1971), i. 109.

18. Klaus Hermsdorf, *Kafka: Weltbild und Roman* (Berlin, 1961), 62.

19. Wilhelm Emrich, *Franz Kafka* (Bonn, 1958), 227.

20. Politzer, 120.

21. Politzer was following a conjecture in T. W. Adorno, 'Aufzeichnungen zu Kafka', *Prismen* (Frankfurt, 1955), 333.

22. Kafka had also read *Little Dorrit* (F 746). See Mark Spilka, *Dickens and Kafka* (Bloomington, Ind., 1963).

23. So must the influence of Whitman, recently suggested by Alfred Wirkner, *Kafka und die Außenwelt: Quellenstudien zum 'Amerika'-Fragment* (Stuttgart, 1976), 30–40. Wirkner supposes that Kafka had read Whitman's prose works on American democracy, which were available only in English. Kafka did learn some English in 1906 in order to qualify himself better for employment, but since the only book he is known ever to have read in English is Macaulay's essay on Clive (Br 33), Wirkner's suggestion seems far-fetched.

24. The information that follows comes from Northey, 'The American Cousins and the *Prager Asbestwerke*', in Angel Flores (ed.), *The Kafka Debate* (New York, 1977), 133–46.

25. Johannes Urzidil, *Da geht Kafka* (Zürich, 1965), 15.

26. See Binder, *Kafka: Der Schaffensprozeß* (Frankfurt, 1983), 83.

27. Kafka refers to this poem as 'Die Grine' (H 424), but no poem by Rosenfeld with this title is known. Binder has identified it as the poem 'Di historishe peklakh' ('The Historic Parcels'), which he reprints in transliteration in *Kafka: Kommentar zu den Romanen, Rezensionen, Aphorismen und zum Brief an den Vater* (Munich, 1976), 400–1.

28. Arthur Holitscher, *Amerika heute und morgen* (Berlin, 1913). See the (incomplete) catalogue of Kafka's books in Wagenbach, *Biographie*, 257. On Kafka's use of Holitscher, see Jahn, 144–50, and Wirkner, 15–25. Another, minor source of information about America was a lecture by the Socialist politician František Soukup which Kafka heard on 1 June 1912 (T 279). Its contents can be gathered from the book on America

which Soukup published that year in Czech, and from which Wirkner has reprinted long extracts in translation: see Wirkner, 50–1, 91–104.

29. Brod, *Über Franz Kafka*, 75. Cf. his attack on the Taylor system in 'Zwei Welten', *Der Jude*, 2. i–ii (Apr.–May 1917), 47–51.
30. Hermsdorf, 69.
31. Ibid., 62.
32. On this motif, see Claude David, 'Kafka und die Geschichte', in id. (ed.), *Franz Kafka: Themen und Probleme* (Göttingen, 1980), 69–70.
33. See V 160, 210, 187, 224. These and other inconsistencies are mentioned by Gerhard Loose, *Franz Kafka und Amerika* (Frankfurt, 1968), 36, 81.
34. Emrich, 236.
35. H. C. Buch, *Ut Pictura Poesis: Die Beschreibungsliteratur und ihre Kritiker von Lessing bis Lukács* (Munich, 1972), 233.
36. W. H. Sokel, *Franz Kafka: Tragik und Ironie* (Munich, 1964), 59.
37. Kasimir Edschmid, *Frühe Manifeste* (Hamburg, 1957), 32.
38. Buch, 238. Cf. Jahn, 33–7.
39. See Jonathan Culler, *Structuralist Poetics* (London, 1975), 193.
40. Martin Walser, *Beschreibung einer Form* (Munich, 1961), 71.
41. Malcolm Pasley, 'From Diary to Story', lecture delivered in the Taylor Institution, Oxford, 25 Oct. 1983. See e.g. Kafka's description of Paris, headed 'Das gestrichelte Paris' (T 619-20), or that of the Jewish goldsmith from Cracow with whom he had a long conversation (T 621). Kafka's debt to Flaubert for the technique of rendering momentary impressions is also discussed by Binder, *Motiv und Gestaltung bei Franz Kafka* (Bonn, 1966), 253–62, and Kurz in id. (ed.), *Der junge Kafka*, 25–32.
42. Georg Lukács, 'Erzählen oder Beschreiben?', *Schicksalswende* (Berlin, 1948), 147.
43. Brod, 'Nachwort zur ersten Ausgabe', in Franz Kafka, *Amerika* (Frankfurt, 1953), 356–7.
44. Emrich, 247.
45. Quoted in Jahn, 148.
46. Kurz, *Traum-Schrecken: Kafkas literarische Existenzanalyse* (Stuttgart, 1980), 158.
47. Jahn, 98.
48. See Jahn, 147–8. More recently Binder, *Schaffensprozeß*, 90, has quoted from an article in *Bohemia* about the extravagant advertising stunts with which Barnum publicized his circus.
49. Holitscher, 367.
50. Wirkner, 81.
51. Binder, *Kommentar zu den Romanen*, 148.
52. For another realistic but much more optimistic interpretation, see Irmgard Hobson, 'Oklahoma, USA, and Kafka's Nature Theater', in Flores (ed.), *The Kafka Debate*, 273–8.
53. Bonaventura, *Nachtwachen*, ed. Wolfgang Paulsen (Stuttgart, 1964), 33.

54. Jahn, 14.

55. This sentence is significantly misquoted by Ernst Fischer, *Von Grillparzer zu Kafka* (Vienna, 1962), 317, as 'Alles in beiden Riesenstädten ist leer und nutzlos aufgestellt.' Fischer then maintains that this sentence conveys the essential truth of life in these cities. If he had quoted correctly, the subjectivity of Karl's judgement would have been too obvious to permit this conclusion.

56. Quoted in Binder, *Schaffensprozeß*, 92.

57. Jeffrey L. Sammons, 'Land of Limited Possibilities: America in the Nineteenth-Century German Novel', *Yale Review*, 68 (1978), 35–52.

58. Adorno, 333.

59. Gustav Janouch, *Gespräche mit Kafka* (Frankfurt, 1951), 78. For an entertaining exposure of the unreliability of these 'conversations', see Goldstücker, 'Kafkas Eckermann? Zu Gustav Janouchs *Gespräche mit Kafka*', in David (ed.), *Franz Kafka*, 238–55. Cf. Binder's assessment in id. (ed.), *Kafka-Handbuch*, ii. 554–62.

60. Kafka must have read this by November 1912, for its influence is evident in the opening of *Die Verwandlung*. See Mark Spilka, 'Kafka's Sources for *The Metamorphosis*', *CL* 11 (1959), 289–307.

61. Northrop Frye, *Anatomy of Criticism* (Princeton, 1957), 48.

62. Politzer, 124.

63. See e.g. Jürgen Jacobs, *Wilhelm Meister und seine Brüder* (Munich, 1972); Jerome Buckley, *Season of Youth: The Bildungsroman from Dickens to Golding* (Cambridge, Mass., 1974).

64. Quoted in Lothar Köhn, *Entwicklungs- und Bildungsroman* (Stuttgart, 1969), 1.

65. Alastair Fowler, *Kinds of Literature: An Introduction to the Theory of Genres and Modes* (Oxford, 1982), 37. Cf. E. D. Hirsch, *Validity in Interpretation* (New Haven, 1967), 68–126. For a defence of the taxonomic use of *Bildungsroman*, see Martin Swales, *The German Bildungsroman from Wieland to Hesse* (Princeton, 1978). The section entitled 'Gattungen des Erzählens' in Heinz Hillmann, *Franz Kafka: Dichtungstheorie und Dichtungsgestalt* (Bonn, 1964), 161–94, is a taxonomic classification unrelated to the concept of genre which is being used here.

66. See Jürgen Pütz, *Kafkas 'Verschollener'—ein Bildungsroman?* (Berne, 1983), 27, 30.

67. Ibid. 69.

68. Fowler, 55–6.

69. On Kafka's conception of justice as discipline, see Hiebel, 90-1.

70. Politzer, 125. Kurz, *Traum-Schrecken*, 153–6, represents Karl as a wily and ambitious character, but his argument depends on highly selective quotation.

71. Robert Walser, *Jakob von Gunten* (Zürich, 1950), 18. Walser's influence on Kafka has been discussed by Karl Pestalozzi, 'Nachprufüng einer

Vorliebe: Franz Kafkas Beziehung zum Werk Robert Walsers', *Akzente*, 13 (1966), 322–44, and Bernhard Böschenstein, 'Nah und fern zugleich: Franz Kafkas *Betrachtung* und Robert Walsers Berliner Skizzen', in Kurz (ed.), *Der junge Kafka*, 200–12, but neither mentions the reappearance of Benjamenta in Kafka's works.

72. See Leopold von Sacher-Masoch, *Venus im Pelz* (1869; repr. Frankfurt, 1968), 136–8. Cf. Peter B. Waldeck, 'Kafka's *Die Verwandlung* and *Ein Hungerkünstler* as influenced by Leopold von Sacher-Masoch', *Monatshefte*, 64 (1972), 147–52.

73. See Nike Wagner, *Geist und Geschlecht: Karl Kraus und die Erotik der Wiener Moderne* (Frankfurt, 1982), 138.

74. Letter of 8 July 1796, *Der Briefwechsel zwischen Schiller und Goethe*, ed. Emil Staiger (Frankfurt, 1966), 239.

75. First published in 1952 and now reprinted, with others, in Friedrich Beissner, *Der Erzähler Franz Kafka* (Frankfurt, 1983).

76. See John M. Ellis, 'Kafka: *Das Urteil*', *Narration in the German Novelle* (Cambridge, 1974), 188–211.

77. See Hans Robert Jauss, 'Interaktionsmuster der Identifikation mit dem Helden', *Ästhetische Erfahrung und literarische Hermeneutik I* (Munich, 1977), 212–58.

78. Fyodor Dostoyevsky, *Notes from Underground; The Double*, tr. Jessie Coulson (Harmondsworth, 1972), 127.

79. See Michail Bachtin, *Probleme der Poetik Dostoevskijs*, tr. Adelheid Schramm (Munich, 1971), 53–86.

80. Georg Simmel, 'Die Großstädte und das Geistesleben', *Brücke und Tür* (Stuttgart, 1957), 231.

81. W. H. Auden, *Collected Longer Poems* (London, 1968), 119.

82. See Thomas Anz, *Literatur der Existenz: Literarische Psychopathographie und ihre soziale Bedeutung im Frühexpressionismus* (Stuttgart, 1977), 85–9.

83. Though Marthe Robert probably goes too far when, in *Seul, comme Franz Kafka* (Paris, 1979), 28–9, she argues that Kafka responded to his father's remark about Löwy, 'Wer sich mit Hunden zu Bett legt, steht mit Wanzen auf' (T 139), by promptly writing a story whose protagonist got out of bed *as* an insect. This certainly oversimplifies the genesis of the story.

84. Elizabeth M. Rajec, *Namen und ihre Bedeutungen im Werke Franz Kafkas* (Berne, 1977), 58.

85. Emrich, 120.

86. Lukács, 'Dostoevsky', in René Wellek (ed.), *Dostoevsky: A Collection of Critical Essays* (Englewood Cliffs, NJ, 1962), 148.

87. Arthur Schnitzler, *Der Weg ins Freie*, in *Die erzählenden Schriften* (2 vols., Frankfurt, 1961), i. 957. Cf. Hugo von Hofmannsthal, 'Das Gespräch über Gedichte', *Prosa II* (Frankfurt, 1951), 97; 'Vorspiel für ein Puppentheater', *Dramen II* (Frankfurt, 1954), 496; Alfred Kubin, *Die andere Seite*

(Munich, 1909, repr. 1975), 148; also Anz, 106–12, and Gotthart Wunberg, *Der frühe Hofmannsthal: Schizophrenie als künstlerische Struktur* (Stuttgart, 1965).

88. See Peters, 124–33.
89. F. D. Luke, '*The Metamorphosis*', in Angel Flores and Homer Swander (eds.), *Franz Kafka Today* (Madison, Wis., 1958), 25–44.
90. See H 92; Allan Janik and Stephen Toulmin, *Wittgenstein's Vienna* (New York, 1973).
91. Fingerhut, *Die Funktion der Tierfiguren im Werke Franz Kafkas* (Bonn, 1969), 256–7.
92. Luke, 40.
93. Hermsdorf, 154.
94. Rathenau, i. 86–7.

Chapter 3

1. Theo Elm, '*Der Prozeß*', in Binder (ed.), *Kafka-Handbuch*, ii. 424–5. This approach goes back to Walser, *Beschreibung einer Form*, and has been most persuasively expounded by Horst Steinmetz, *Suspensive Interpretation am Beispiel Franz Kafkas* (Göttingen, 1977). For some welcome criticism of it, see Robert Welsh Jordan, 'Das Gesetz, die Anklage und K.s Prozeß: Franz Kafka und Franz Brentano', *JDSG* 24 (1980), 333–4.
2. Ingeborg Henel, 'Die Türhüterlegende und ihre Bedeutung für Kafkas Prozeß', *DVjs* 37 (1963), 50–70.
3. Brod, 'Nachwort zur zweiten Ausgabe', Franz Kafka, *Der Prozeß* (Frankfurt, 1950), 324–5; Eric Marson, *Kafka's Trial: The Case against Josef K.* (St Lucia, Queensland, 1975), 8. The most noteworthy variants are reproduced and discussed in this book, a valuable study which has received less attention than it deserves.
4. *The Trial*, tr. Willa and Edwin Muir (London, 1937); *The Trial*, tr. Douglas Scott and Chris Waller (London, 1977). The second of these is excellent, and can be warmly recommended to the reader without German.
5. For a bibliography of the controversy, see Peter U. Beicken, *Franz Kafka: Eine kritische Einführung in die Forschung* (Frankfurt, 1974), 371–3. Uyttersprot's arguments are discussed in detail by Binder, *Kommentar zu den Romanen*, 160–74.
6. See Marson, 93. There remains the problem that chs. 2 and 4 take place on successive Sundays, but this is not decisive, for K.'s word 'etwa' indicates that Kafka was concerned to supply approximate rather than precise chronological markers.
7. See Binder, *Kommentar zu den Romanen*, 162–3.
8. See Peter Cersowsky, *Phantastische Literatur im ersten Viertel des 20.*

Jahrhunderts (Munich, 1983), for an (at times overstated) account of the resemblances between the works of Kafka, Kubin, and Meyrink.

9. See Steinmetz, 67–71, where Kafka is associated with Beckett and Robbe-Grillet. For a similar view, see David H. Miles, '"Pleats, Pockets, Buckles and Buttons": Kafka's New Literalism and the Poetics of the Fragment', in Benjamin Bennett, Anton Kaes, and W. J. Lillyman (eds.), *Probleme der Moderne* (Tübingen, 1983), 331–42.

10. W. J. Dodd, 'Varieties of Influence: On Kafka's Indebtedness to Dostoevskii', *Journal of European Studies*, 14 (1984), 262–3. Cf. Wagenbach, *Biographie*, 254; Brod, *Über Franz Kafka*, 46. The most thorough study available of Kafka's debt to Dostoyevsky is Sissel Lægreid, *Ambivalenz als Gestaltungsprinzip: Eine Untersuchung der Querverbindungen zwischen Kafkas 'Prozeß' und Dostojewskis 'Schuld und Sühne'* (Bergen, 1980).

11. See Fowler, 41–3.

12. Konstantin Mochulsky, *Dostoevsky: His Life and Work*, tr. Michael A. Minihan (Princeton, 1967), 300, 290.

13. Feodor [*sic*] Dostoevsky, *Crime and Punishment*, tr. Jessie Coulson, ed. George Gibian (Norton Critical Edition, New York, 1964), 80.

14. Quoted by Donald Fanger, *Dostoevsky and Romantic Realism* (Chicago, 1965), 42.

15. Joseph Conrad, *The Secret Agent* (London, 1907), 87.

16. Fanger, 194–8. Cf. Mochulsky, 290-2.

17. Cf. Kurz, *Traum-Schrecken*, 191.

18. Peter Demetz, *René Rilkes Prager Jahre* (Dusseldorf, 1953), 107–8. Cf. Brod, *Über Franz Kafka*, 170.

19. Anz, 58–9. On the Gothic mode of the 'Prügler' chapter, see S. S. Prawer, *The 'Uncanny' in Literature* (London, 1965), 21–2.

20. See Kurz, *Traum-Schrecken*, 178; Hiebel, 180.

21. See Beissner, 42.

22. Henel, 'Die Deutbarkeit von Kafkas Werken', *ZfdP* 86 (1967), 250–66.

23. See Winfried Kudszus, 'Erzählperspektive und Erzählhaltung in Kafkas *Prozeß*', *DVjs* 44 (1970), 306–17.

24. Binder, *Kommentar zu den Romanen*, 187; cf. 192.

25. For a detailed and readable account of these events and their bearing on *Der Prozeß*, see Elias Canetti, *Der andere Prozeß* (Munich, 1969).

26. Sokel, 140.

27. Quoted by Werner Mittenzwei, 'Brecht und Kafka', in Eduard Goldstücker, František Kautman, and Paul Reimann (eds.), *Franz Kafka aus Prager Sicht* (Prague, 1965), 123.

28. Some striking parallels are listed by J. P. Stern, 'The Law of *The Trial*', in Kuna (ed.), *On Kafka*, 22–41.

29. Fischer, 294.

30. Georg Lukács, *The Meaning of Contemporary Realism*, tr. John and Necke Mander (London, 1963), 57.

31. Politzer, 166.
32. This character recalls the father-figures who appear in Kafka's earlier writings (see pp. 70–1 above). He is 'riesig' (P 284), walks arm in arm with K., and is occupied with 'Damenbekanntschaften' (P 285). For some weeks his ageing, unappetizing mistress lives with him, and he and K. talk in the room where she is reading in bed and waiting for Hasterer to join her; this recalls the hints of voyeurism associated with Mack and Delamarche in *Der Verschollene*. In a cancelled passage, K. caresses Titorelli's cheeks (P 294), as though Titorelli were yet another father-figure.
33. Politzer, 186, points out that these employees are respectively German, Czech, and Jewish, thus representing each of the three nationalities of Prague, and that 'Rabensteiner' includes both *Rabe* 'raven' and *Rabenstein* 'place of execution' (cf. e.g. Goethe, *Faust*, l. 4399), while *kulich* is the Czech for 'screech-owl', another bird portending death. Cf. Rajec, 136. One may add that the name 'Kaminer' is derived not from the German *Kamin* 'fireplace' but from the Czech *kámen* 'stone', so that, by a multilingual pun, Kullich and Kaminer together convey the same message as Rabensteiner.
34. A common foible of Kafka commentators, the treatment of ordinary images as though they were esoteric ciphers, is illustrated by Binder's gloss (*Kommentar zu den Romanen*, 205): 'Die Verbundenheit der Hände war für Kafka ein Ausdruck menschlicher Zusammengehörigkeit.' The handshake has the same range (and ambivalence) of meanings in Kafka's writing as it has in real life.
35. See Martin Jay, *The Dialectical Imagination: A History of the Frankfurt School and the Institute for Social Research 1923–50* (London, 1973).
36. It is misread thus by Keith Leopold, 'Breaks in Perspective in Franz Kafka's *Der Prozeß*', *GQ* 36 (1963), 36.
37. Binder, *Kommentar zu den Romanen*, 197.
38. On the contrast between the physical and the rational implied by the word 'Bauch', see Kurz, *Traum-Schrecken*, 178–9. This emphasis on the physical makes one query the distinction Sokel tries to draw between the 'social self' and the 'pure self' in Kafka, and makes it unlikely that the Court is trying to make K. adopt 'die Existenzform des reinen Ichs' (Sokel, 141).
39. Friedrich Nietzsche, *Unzeitgemäße Betrachtungen*, iii, § 1 (*Werke*, ed. Karl Schlechta (3 vols., Munich, 1956), i. 287).
40. Adolfo Sánchez Vázquez, *Art and Society: Essays in Marxist Aesthetics*, tr. Maro Riofrancos (London, 1973), 147.
41. Thomas Mann, *Gesammelte Werke* (12 vols., Frankfurt, 1960), viii. 515.
42. This point is made most clearly by Jordan; cf. Emrich, 259.
43. Failure to realize this has given rise to many divergent interpretations of *Der Prozeß*. Sokel, 154, thinks that K. is not guilty at the outset but

becomes so in the course of the story; Hiebel, 181–2, explains K.'s guilt away as an Oedipal sense of being in the wrong which the Court exploits to cast him in the role of culprit; while Politzer, 177, maintains that K.'s guilt is completely unmotivated and that the novel is therefore seriously flawed.

44. See Emrich, 181–2; Henel, 'Die Türhüterlegende'.

45. Contrast Sokel's view, 141–2, that K.'s submission represents the rigorous self-examination required of him by the Court.

46. Leo Tolstoy, *Iván Ilých and Hadji Murád*, tr. Louise and Aylmer Maude (London, 1935), 69. Kafka read this story, but perhaps not before Dec. 1921 (T 551).

47. Cf. Walser, *Beschreibung einer Form*, 52–3. Marson, 167, thinks they represent the positive value of humility.

48. Here Kafka has adapted a Dostoyevsky motif by detaching it from its realistic context. When Raskolnikov arrives at the police-office, the lieutenant reprimands him for being late: 'You were told nine o'clock and it is now twelve!' (*Crime and Punishment*, 82).

49. This has been most persuasively argued by Henel in the two articles already cited.

50. Franz Brentano, *Vom Ursprung sittlicher Erkenntnis*, 2nd edn., ed. Oskar Kraus (Leipzig, 1921), 8. Cf. Jordan, 340–2.

51. Salomon Maimon, *Lebensgeschichte*, ed. Jakob Fromer (Munich, 1911), 358–9. Attention was first drawn to this passage, and its possible relevance to *Der Prozeß*, by Malcolm Pasley, 'Two Literary Sources of Kafka's *Der Prozeß*', *FMLS* 3 (1967), 142–7.

52. Lanz is evidently a projection of K.'s repressed libido, like the red-bearded man who watches his arrest. Cf. Marson, 63.

53. They have been well described by Sokel, 167–8.

54. Sokel, 173, thinks that K.'s 'Verwandlung' would resemble Gregor Samsa's, and would be a punishment for his inquisitiveness. The mere recurrence of the same word, however, hardly licenses such a bold interpretation. Cf. 'Verwandlung', P 294.

55. Kafka's description of the atmosphere is indebted to *Crime and Punishment*, where Raskolnikov faints in the police-office (see Binder, *Kommentar zu den Romanen*, 216), and, more unexpectedly, to Casanova's account of his imprisonment in the lead chambers in Venice: see Brod, *Über Franz Kafka*, 92, and Michael Müller, 'Kafka und Casanova', *Freibeuter*, 16 (1983), 67–76.

56. The fullest explication is by Marson, 148–62.

57. Marson, 158.

58. Walter Benjamin and Gershom Scholem, *Briefwechsel 1933–40*, ed. Gershom Scholem (Frankfurt, 1980), 157–8.

59. The details of Block's humiliation recall the treatment of 'Gregor' in Sacher-Masoch's *Venus im Pelz*. In particular, Block's small, windowless

room recalls the hotel-room in Florence where 'Gregor' is lodged as Wanda's servant: 'ein schmales Zimmer ohne Kamin, ohne Fenster, mit einem kleinen Luftloch. Es würde mich—wenn es nicht so hundekalt wäre—an die venetianischen Bleikammern erinnern' (Sacher-Masoch, 77). The allusion to Casanova's prison may have helped this passage to stick in Kafka's mind.

60. André Németh, *Kafka ou le mystère juif*, tr. Victor Hintz (Paris, 1947), 112–13. Cf. Marson, 193.

61. Emrich, 280.

62. Marson, 254–5.

63. This story was probably suggested by a passage in *Furcht und Zittern* where Kierkegaard denounces those people whose spiritual cowardice makes them think that they will increase their chances of salvation by banding together to form a sect. It runs in part:

> Der Ritter des Glaubens ist als das Paradox der Einzelne, absolut nur der Einzelne, ohne alle Konnexionen und Weitläufigkeiten. Das ist das Entsetzliche, das der sektiererische Schwächling nicht ertragen kann. Anstatt nämlich daraus zu lernen, daß *er* das Große nicht ausführen *kann*, und dies dann frei zu gestehen (was ich natürlich nur billigen kann, da ich es gerade so mache), meint der Stümper, daß er es werde ausführen können wenn er sich mit einigen anderen Stümpern verbinde. Da stolzierte denn so ein Dutzend Sektierer Arm in Arm einher. [. . .] Doch in der Welt des Geistes gilt kein Mogeln.

Sören Kierkegaard, *Furcht und Zittern; Die Wiederholung*, tr. H. C. Ketels, H. Gottsched, and C. Schrempf, 3rd edn. (Jena, 1923), p. 76. Kafka had read this by Nov. 1917 at the latest (Br 190).

64. F. M. Dostojewski, *Die Brüder Karamasoff*, tr. E. K. Rahsin (Munich, 1914), 523. This was the translation Kafka read: see Wagenbach, *Biographie*, 254.

65. Dostojewski, *Karamasoff*, 517.

66. Robert, 160.

67. Wilhelm Jannasch, *Erdmuthe Dorothea Gräfin von Zinzendorf, geborene Gräfin Reuß zu Plauen: Ihr Leben als Beitrag zur Geschichte des Pietismus und der Brüdergemeine dargestellt* (Herrnhut, 1915). See F 677.

68. For interpretations of the 'Heidelandschaft' itself, see Emrich, 291; Hiebel, 219.

69. Quoted by Walter Benjamin, 'In der Sonne', *Schriften*, ed. T. W. and Gretel Adorno (2 vols., Frankfurt, 1955), ii. 97.

70. See Pasley, 'Two Literary Sources'.

71. Nietzsche, *Die fröhliche Wissenschaft*, iii, § 125 (Schlechta, ii. 127).

72. Ibid. (Schlechta, ii. 128).

73. See the review by Ernst Weiss, reprinted in Jürgen Born (ed.), *Franz*

Kafka: Kritik und Rezeption 1924–1938 (Frankfurt, 1983), 96; Benjamin and Scholem, *Briefwechsel*, 169.

74. Mochulsky, 621.
75. Dostojewski, *Karamasoff*, 522.
76. Bertolt Brecht, 'Vergnügungstheater oder Lehrtheater?', *Gesammelte Werke* (20 vols., Frankfurt, 1967), xv. 265.
77. See R. St Leon, 'Religious Motives in Kafka's *Der Prozeß*', *Journal of the Australasian Universities Modern Language Association*, 19 (May 1963), 21–38. Cf. *The Talmud: Selections*, tr. H. Polano (London, n.d.), 347. Brod, *Über Franz Kafka*, 233, tells us that Kafka owned a Talmud anthology, but we do not know when he acquired it, and his knowledge of Talmudic lore at the time when he wrote *Der Prozeß* must not be overestimated. The Talmud quotations in his diary (T 173, 177–8) come from Gordin's *Di shkhite*.
78. Giuliano Baioni, *Kafka: romanzo e parabola* (Milan, 1962), 164, confidently identifies this as an assembly of Hasidim.
79. *Vom Judentum: Ein Sammelbuch* (Leipzig, 1913), 281–4.
80. See Jakob Fromer, *Der Organismus des Judentums* (Charlottenburg, 1909), 64. Kafka read this book in January 1912 (T 242). The man from the country is identified as an 'am ha-'arets' by Politzer, 174–5; Urzidil, 33; Robert, 163.
81. Baioni, 180. The word 'tartarisch' seems out of place, but it may have been suggested by a passage in Maimon's summary of the teachings of Maimonides. Maimonides provides an allegory in which different levels of religious understanding are represented by different degrees of proximity to the royal palace. Those furthest from it, outside the royal capital altogether, include 'die herumstreifenden nordischen *Tataren*' (Maimon, 460), because they have neither a natural nor a revealed religion and therefore belong to the lowest grade of humanity, 'mit den unvernünftigen Tieren beinahe in gleichem Range' (ibid.). The doorkeeper, similarly, is on the lowest rung of a hierarchy, and unable even to enter the house of the Law.
82. Karl Emil Franzos, 'Der Ahnherr des Messias', *Vom Don zur Donau: Neue Kulturbilder aus Halb-Asien*, 2nd edn. (2 vols., Stuttgart, 1889), ii. 267. Cf. Simon Dubnow, *Geschichte des Chassidismus*, tr. A. Steinberg (2 vols., Berlin, 1931), ii. 288.
83. Martin Buber says intriguingly that Kafka, when visiting him in Berlin on 28 Feb. 1914, asked him for information about the oriental myth on which Ps. 82 is based. In this myth, God has entrusted the governance of the world to angels who have become corrupt and deliver false judgements; only the man whose mind is fixed directly on God can escape from the power of these ministers. Buber may be right in saying that Kafka adapted this myth in *Der Prozeß*, but, since the Court officials are not portrayed as supernatural beings, it seems to have played a part in the

genesis of the novel but not to appear in the text. See Buber, *Werke* (3 vols., Munich, 1962–4), i. 499–500.
84. Georg Büchner, *Werke und Briefe* (Munich, 1965), 62.
85. Dostojewski, *Karamasoff*, 456.
86. See e.g. Günther Anders, *Kafka: Pro und Contra* (Munich, 1951), 28; Stern, 35–6.

Chapter 4

1. Brod, *Streitbares Leben*, 135.
2. See Binder, 'Kafka und Napoleon', in Ulrich Gaier and Werner Volke (eds.), *Festschrift für Friedrich Beißner* (Bebenhausen, 1974), 38–66. The development of Kafka's image of the leader is surveyed in Oppenheimer, 64–77.
3. Kafka, *Diaries*, ii. 132–8.
4. For Goethe, see T 248 and Ch. 1 above; for Hebbel, F 274–5; for Dickens, T 60, 536; for Balzac, H 281.
5. See Binder (ed.), *Kafka-Handbuch*, i. 427–8, where Binder refers to an un-published medical study of Kafka made by Hugo Hecht, a school-friend, which argues that Kafka suffered from hypogonadism (underdevelop-ment of the sexual organs) and did not become sexually mature till about the age of 25. The gist of Hecht's study is given by Klaus-Peter Hinze, 'Neue Aspekte zum Kafka-Bild: Bericht über ein noch unveröffentlichtes Manuskript', *MAL* 5 (1972), iii–iv. 83–92.
6. 'Fletschern' is a technique of chewing one's food with extreme thorough-ness, recommended by the American doctor Horace Fletcher, which Kafka practised scrupulously (F 671).
7. See Kafka, *Beschreibung eines Kampfes: Die zwei Fassungen*, ed. Ludwig Dietz (Frankfurt, 1969); Sokel, 33–8; Jost Schillemeit, 'Kafkas *Beschreibung eines Kampfes*: Ein Beitrag zum Textverständnis und zur Geschichte von Kafkas Schreiben', in Kurz (ed.), *Der junge Kafka*, 102–33.
8. See Kafka's letter to Buber, in Buber, *Briefwechsel*, i. 491–2; Pasley, 'Kafka and the Theme of "Berufung"', *OGS* 9 (1978), 139–49.
9. The text of *Der Gruftwächter* in B is unreliable. An authentic text has been prepared by Pasley, but is at present available only in English translation in Kafka, *Shorter Works* i, ed. and tr. Pasley (London, 1973), 40–9.
10. Pasley's translation runs: 'this tomb represents the frontier of humanity', *Shorter Works*, 41.
11. As Oppenheimer, 197, has shown, these nomads were almost certainly suggested by the invaders who Jeremiah says will descend on Israel from the north (Jer. 6: 22), armed with bows and arrows (Jer. 6: 23) and speaking an unintelligible language (Jer. 5: 15).
12. The establishment of a district court at Trautenau (now Trutnov) in

Bohemia was a controversial project which the German parties in Austria unrealistically voted for in the summer of 1918, when the war had plainly been lost and the national councils in the former Imperial provinces had already been recognized by the Western powers.

13. David in id. (ed.), *Franz Kafka*, 66–80. On Kafka's imagery of decadence, see Peter Cersowsky, '*Mein ganzes Wesen ist auf Literatur gerichtet': Franz Kafka im Kontext der literarischen Dekadenz* (Würzburg, 1983), 67–70.

14. Hugo Hecht thought that Kafka's tuberculosis could have been cured if he had not undermined his health by a vegetarian diet: Hinze, 90–1.

15. See Pasley, 'Asceticism and Cannibalism: Notes on an Unpublished Kafka Text', *OGS* 1 (1966), 105–6.

16. See Euripides, *Bacchae* 735–47. There is a coincidental but noteworthy parallel in this account of a rite formerly practised annually in Tangier, quoted by E. R. Dodds, *The Greeks and the Irrational* (Berkeley, 1951), 276: 'A hill-tribe descends upon the town in a state of semi-starvation and drugged delirium. After the usual beating of tom-toms, screaming of the pipes and monotonous dancing, a sheep is thrown into the middle of the square, upon which all the devotees come to life and tear the animal limb from limb and eat it raw.'

17. See Binder, *Kafka: Kommentar zu sämtlichen Erzählungen* (Munich, 1975), 207.

18. Bergman, 'Erinnerungen', 742.

19. Wagenbach, *Biographie*, 62.

20. See Br 80; Brod, *Über Franz Kafka*, 79.

21. See Goldstücker, 'Über Franz Kafka aus der Prager Perspektive 1963', in Goldstücker, Kautman and Reimann (eds.), *Franz Kafka aus Prager Sicht*, 40–1. The banal remarks about capitalist oppression ascribed to Kafka by Janouch, *Gespräche mit Kafka*, 2nd edn. (Frankfurt, 1968), 205–6, are most unlikely to be authentic, though they have been quoted *ad nauseam* by Marxist commentators: e.g. Sánchez Vázquez, 152; Lee Baxandall, 'Kafka as Radical', in Flores (ed.), *The Kafka Debate*, 122; Evgeniya Knipovich, 'Franz Kafka', in Kenneth Hughes (ed. and tr.), *Franz Kafka: An Anthology of Marxist Criticism* (Hanover, NH, 1981), 189.

22. Michal Mareš, 'Wie ich Franz Kafka kennenlernte', in Wagenbach, *Biographie*, 270–6.

23. Brod, *Über Franz Kafka*, 79.

24. See Goldstücker, op. cit., 41–2. Brod, *Der Prager Kreis*, 105, describes Mareš as 'zur Phantastik neigend'. Cf. Binder (ed.), *Kafka-Handbuch*, i. 361–6.

25. Much is made of this in Wagenbach, *Franz Kafka in Selbstzeugnissen und Bilddokumenten* (Reinbek, 1964), 49; Gertrude Durusoy, *L'Incidence de la littérature et de la langue tchèques sur les nouvelles de Franz Kafka* (Berne, 1981). Scepticism is recommended by Sir Cecil Parrott, *The Bad Bohemian: A Life of Jaroslav Hašek* (London, 1978), 70–1, 109–15.

26. Michael Löwy, *Georg Lukács: From Romanticism to Bolshevism*, tr. Patrick Camiller (London, 1979), 23.

27. See his comments on the First Zionist Congress, 'Judenstaat und Judennot', in Achad Haam [*sic*], *Am Scheidewege: Gesammelte Aufsätze*, tr. Israel Friedländer and Harry Torczyner (4 vols., Berlin, 1923), ii. 45–67.

28. Quoted in Binder, 'Kafka und *Selbstwehr*', 283.

29. Max Nordau, *Zionistische Schriften* (Berlin, 1923), 48. Cf. Avineri, 101–11. On the meaning and associations of the terms 'ghetto' and 'ghetto Jew', see Steven E. Aschheim, *Brothers and Strangers: The East European Jew in German and German Jewish Consciousness, 1800–1923* (Madison, Wis., 1982), 5–7.

30. Quoted in Binder (ed.), *Kafka-Handbuch*, i. 392.

31. Adolf Böhm, 'Wandlungen im Zionismus', *Vom Judentum*, 143.

32. Martin Buber (ed.), *Ekstatische Konfessionen* (Leipzig, 1909), p. xv.

33. See Arthur Schopenhauer, *Die Welt als Wille und Vorstellung*, ed. Julius Frauenstädt (2 vols., Leipzig, 1923), ii. 218–19; Nietzsche, *Die Geburt der Tragödie*, § 1 (Schlechta, i. 23–5). Buber's debt to Nietzsche is pointed out by Dietmar Goltschnigg, *Mystische Tradition im Roman Robert Musils: Martin Bubers 'Ekstatische Konfessionen' im 'Mann ohne Eigenschaften'* (Heidelberg, 1974), 26–7, in a helpful study of Buber's mysticism.

34. Buber, 'Das Judentum und die Juden' in *Der Jude und sein Judentum: Gesammelte Aufsätze und Reden* (Cologne, 1963), 16.

35. Ibid. 17.

36. Buber, *Die jüdische Bewegung: Gesammelte Aufsätze und Ansprachen* (2 vols., Berlin, 1920), i. 68–9.

37. Richard Beer-Hofmann, *Gesammelte Werke* (Frankfurt, 1963), 654. On the popularity of this poem, see Hans Kohn, *Martin Buber: Sein Werk und seine Zeit*, 2nd edn. (Cologne, 1961), 96–7; Binder (ed.), *Kafka-Handbuch*, i. 374.

38. Buber, *Die Jüdische Bewegung*, i. 191.

39. Ibid. i. 68. Cf. Nietzsche, 'Zarathustras Vorrede', § 9 (Schlechta, ii. 289); *Zur Genealogie der Moral*, ii, § 17 (Schlechta, ii. 827). The image of the artist shaping human material was also used by Mussolini: see J. P. Stern, *Hitler: The Führer and the People* (Glasgow, 1975), 45.

40. Buber, *Werke*, iii. 961–73.

41. Buber, *Die jüdische Bewegung*, i. 59, 74, 157; *Der Jude und sein Judentum*, 18.

42. Buber, *Die jüdische Bewegung*, i. 199–200. Cf. *Briefwechsel*, i. 246.

43. Buber, *Werke*, iii. 967.

44. Richard Wagner, *Sämtliche Schriften und Dichtungen* (Volksausgabe, 12 vols., Leipzig, n.d.), v. 72.

45. Nietzsche, *Der Antichrist*, § 24 (Schlechta, ii. 1184); emphasis in original.

46. Quoted by George L. Mosse, *Germans and Jews* (New York, 1970), 43.

47. Jakob Wassermann, *Die Juden von Zirndorf* (Munich, 1897), 239. Kafka owned a copy of this book: Wagenbach, *Biographie*, 261.

48. See Sander L. Gilman, ' "Ebrew and Jew": Moses Mendelssohn and the

Sense of Jewish Identity', in Ehrhard Bahr, Edward P. Harris, and Laurence G. Lyon (eds.), *Humanität und Dialog: Lessing und Mendelssohn in neuer Sicht* (Detroit and Munich, 1982), 67–82.

49. Buber, *Die jüdische Bewegung*, i. 59.
50. Mosse, 91.
51. Ferdinand Tönnies, *Community and Society*, tr. Charles P. Loomis (East Lansing, Mich., 1957); first published in 1887 as *Gemeinschaft und Gesellschaft*.
52. Paul de Lagarde, *Deutsche Schriften* (2 vols., Göttingen, 1878), i, 79. Cf. Hans Kohn, *The Mind of Germany* (London, 1961); Fritz Stern, *The Politics of Cultural Despair: A Study in the Rise of the Germanic Ideology* (Berkeley, 1961).
53. Buber and Lagarde are compared by Mosse, 85. On Buber's *völkisch* ideas, cf. Kohn, *Living in a World Revolution*, 62–7.
54. Buber quotes his earlier remarks unrepentantly in 'Die Losung', *Der Jude*, 1. i (Apr. 1916), 2. For reactions, see the letter of 12 May 1916 from Gustav Landauer in Buber, *Briefwechsel*, i. 433–8; David Biale, *Gershom Scholem: Kabbalah and Counter-History* (Cambridge, Mass., 1979), 62–3.
55. T. J. Reed, *Thomas Mann: The Uses of Tradition* (Oxford, 1974), 182.
56. This account is based on Dubnow; Gershom Scholem, *Major Trends in Jewish Mysticism* (New York, 1946); S. Ettinger, 'The Hassidic Movement—Reality and Ideals', *Cahiers d'histoire mondiale*, 11 (1968), 251–66; Louis Jacobs, *Hasidic Prayer* (London, 1972); Bernard D. Weinryb, *The Jews of Poland* (Philadelphia, 1973).
57. Dubnow, i. 85. Cf. Geza Vermes, *Jesus the Jew: A Historian's Reading of the Gospels* (London, 1973).
58. Quoted by Scholem, *Major Trends*, 344. Cf. Scholem, '*Devekut*, or Communion with God', *The Messianic Idea in Judaism* (London, 1971), 203–27.
59. See the article 'Ruzhin, Israel', *Encyclopaedia Judaica*, xiv. 526–32. A less admiring account of the dynasty is given by Franzos, *Vom Don zur Donau*, ii. 251–70.
60. Buber, 'Mein Weg zum Chassidismus', *Werke*, iii. 964. *Rebbe* means a Hasidic rabbi, but not necessarily a *tsaddik*. This passage has been interpreted as expressing Buber's psychological need for a substitute for the father whom he seldom saw, since his parents were divorced when he was a baby and he lived mostly with his grandfather: see Gilman, 'The Rediscovery of the Eastern Jews: German Jews in the East, 1890–1918', in David Bronsen (ed.), *Jews and Germans from 1860 to 1933* (Heidelberg, 1979), p. 346.
61. See the letters of gratitude in Buber, *Briefwechsel*, i. 243 (Hofmannsthal), 321–2 (Zweig), 356 (Schocken); Pamela Vermes, 'The Buber–Lukács Correspondence (1911–1921)', *LBY* 27 (1982), 369–77; Aschheim, 121–38.

62. Scholem, 'Martin Buber's Interpretation of Hasidism', *Messianic Idea*, 228–50.

63. Buber, *Die Legende des Baalschem* (Frankfurt, 1908), p. ii. Cf. his reply to Scholem in *Werke*, iii. 991–8, and his preface to a German translation of the *Kalevala*, reprinted in Buber, *Die Rede, die Lehre und das Lied* (Leipzig, 1917), where he praises the dubious methods of Elias Lönnrot in assembling a 'national epic' by choosing and combining the most attractive versions of the songs he heard from Finnish minstrels.

64. Buber, 'Die Erneuerung des Judentums', in *Der Jude und sein Judentum*, 43.

65. Kohn, 'Der Geist des Orients', *Vom Judentum*, 9. See Werner Sombart, *Die Juden und das Wirtschaftsleben* (Leipzig, 1911).

66. Moses Calvary, 'Das neue Judentum und die schöpferische Phantasie', *Vom Judentum*, 107.

67. See Brod, 'Notiz über einen jungen Maler', *Herder-Blätter*, 1. iii (May 1912), 56.

68. Quoted from Jost Schillemeit (ed.), *Epochen der deutschen Lyrik 7: 1800–1830* (Munich, 1970), 358.

69. Extracts from the German translation of *Le Jardin des supplices*, which was banned on its publication in 1901 and is now very rare, are given in Kafka, *In der Strafkolonie. Eine Geschichte aus dem Jahr 1914*, ed. Wagenbach (Berlin, 1975); this quotation is from p. 83. Kafka's debt to Mirbeau was first noticed by Wayne Burns, '*In the Penal Colony*: Variations on a Theme by Octave Mirbeau', *Accent*, 17 (1957), 45–51, and is discussed further by Binder, *Kommentar zu sämtlichen Erzählungen*, 174–81, and Cersowsky, *Phantastische Literatur*, 204–8. Other sources have recently been pointed out by W. J. Dodd, 'Dostoyevskian Elements in Kafka's Penal Colony', *German Life and Letters*, n.s. 37 (1983), 11–23.

70. Mann, xii. 31. On the origin and development of the antithesis between *Kultur* and *Zivilisation*, see Fritz K. Ringer, *The Decline of the German Mandarins* (Cambridge, Mass., 1969), 83–90.

71. Nietzsche, *Zur Genealogie der Moral*, ii, § 7 (Schlechta, ii. 809); Pasley, 'Introduction', Kafka, *Der Heizer, In der Strafkolonie, Der Bau* (Cambridge, 1966), 17–21.

72. Pascal, 80, 82.

73. See Henel, 'Kafkas *In der Strafkolonie*: Form, Sinn und Stellung der Erzählung im Gesamtwerk', in V. J. Günther *et al.* (eds.), *Untersuchungen zur Literatur als Geschichte: Festschrift für Benno von Wiese* (Berlin, 1973), 480–504.

74. Pascal, 87–9.

75. See especially the chapter in *Der Zauberberg* entitled 'Operationes Spirituales', Mann, iii. 608–47.

76. This information is taken from 'Die Ostjuden in Prag', *Das jüdische Prag* (Prague, 1917; repr. Kronberg, 1978), 53–6; Moses Wiesenfeld,

'Begegnung mit Ostjuden', in Felix Weltsch (ed.), *Dichter, Denker, Helfer: Max Brod zum 50. Geburtstag* (Mährisch-Ostrau [Ostrava], 1934), 54–7. Wiesenfeld is no doubt the 'gewisser W.' mentioned by Kafka (T 465).

77. Brod, 'Erfahrungen im ostjüdischen Schulwerk', *Der Jude*, 1. i (Apr. 1916), 34.

78. Quoted in S. Adler-Rudel, *Ostjuden in Deutschland 1880–1940* (Tübingen, 1959), 50–1. Cf. Aschheim, 187–9.

79. Sammy Gronemann, *Hawdoloh und Zapfenstreich: Erinnerungen an die ostjüdische Etappe 1916–18* (Berlin, 1924), 50.

80. Buber, *Briefwechsel*, i. 388–9.

81. Hugo Bergmann, 'Der jüdische Nationalismus nach dem Krieg', *Der Jude*, 1. i (Apr. 1916), 9.

82. See Aschheim, 197–9.

83. Arnold Zweig, 'Das ostjüdische Antlitz', in id., *Herkunft und Zukunft* (Vienna, 1929), 142.

84. See the account of the Volksheim in Adler-Rudel, 51–6.

85. On Lehmann and his ideals, see Aschheim, 194–5.

86. Scholem, *Von Berlin nach Jerusalem* (Frankfurt, 1977), 102–4.

87. A. D. Gordon, 'Arbeit', *Der Jude*, 1. i (Apr. 1916), 39.

88. Alfred Lemm, 'Großstadtunkultur und Juden', *Der Jude*, 1. v (Aug. 1916), 322.

89. The best discussion of 'Jewish self-hatred' known to me is Peter Gay, *Freud, Jews and Other Germans* (New York, 1978).

90. See Roger Bauer, 'Kraus contra Werfel: Eine nicht nur literarische Fehde', in id., *Laßt sie koaxen, Die kritischen Frösch' in Preußen und Sachsen! Zwei Jahrhunderte Literatur in Österreich* (Vienna, 1977), 181–99.

91. Brod, *Über Franz Kafka*, 70. Cf. Binder, *Motiv*, 17–25.

92. Nordau, 51. Cf. S. Lehnert, 'Jüdische Volksarbeit', *Der Jude*, 1. ii (May 1916), 110: 'Wir wollen als Nationalisten nicht mehr wie bisher in diesem kalten luftleeren Raum leben, sondern wollen Boden unter unseren Füßen haben, wenn dieser Boden vorläufig auch nur ein Haus ist mit einer jüdischen Fahne darauf'; also Brod, *Beer*, 170; Robert Weltsch, 'Theodor Herzl und wir', *Vom Judentum*, 160; Kafka, Br 404, H 120, M 292.

93. Hans Blüher, *Secessio Judaica: Philosophische Grundlegung der historischen Situation des Judentums und der antisemitischen Bewegung* (Berlin, 1922), 20.

94. Ibid. 38.

95. Ibid. 56, 57.

96. This notorious forgery was first published in Russia as part of a book entitled *The Great in the Small: Antichrist Considered as an Imminent Political Possibility*, by a mystical writer, Sergey Nilus, and appeared in German in January 1920 under the title *Die Geheimnisse der Weisen von Zion*. See Norman Cohn, *Warrant for Genocide: The Myth of the Jewish World-*

Conspiracy and the Protocols of the Elders of Zion (London, 1967). Kafka read about the *Protocols* in a Catholic newspaper in Merano.

97. Quoted by Binder, 'Kafka und *Selbstwehr*', 301–2.

98. Jens Tismar, 'Kafkas *Schakale und Araber* im zionistischen Kontext betrachtet', *JDSG* 19 (1975), 306–23. Cf. Oppenheimer, 266–8.

99. Sokel, 345–51.

100. Friedrich Schiller, *Über die ästhetische Erziehung des Menschen*, § 6 (*Werke*, ed. H. G. Göpfert (3 vols., Munich, 1966), ii. 455).

101. Margot Norris, 'Darwin, Nietzsche, Kafka, and the Problem of Mimesis', *MLN* 95 (1980), 1233.

102. Herzl, ii. 12.

103. Nordau, 50. Cf. Rathenau, 'Höre, Israel!' (1897), in *Schriften*, ed. Arnold Harttung *et al.* (Berlin, 1965), 91; Döblin, *Jüdische Erneuerung* (Amsterdam, 1933), 10; Manès Sperber, *Churban oder Die unfaßbare Gewißheit* (Munich, 1983), 17.

104. Neumann, '*Ein Bericht für eine Akademie*: Erwägungen zum Mimesis-Charakter Kafkascher Texte', *DVjs* 49 (1975), 166–83.

105. Sokel, 341–2.

106. William C. Rubinstein, '*A Report to an Academy*', in Flores and Swander (eds.), *Franz Kafka Today*, 55–60.

107. Beck, 181–8.

108. Döblin, *Reise in Polen*, 74. On the compulsory adoption of surnames, see the fascinating essay by Franzos, 'Namenstudien', *Aus der großen Ebene: Neue Kulturbilder aus Halb-Asien* (2 vols., Stuttgart, 1888), i, 127–49; Benzion C. Kaganoff, *A Dictionary of Jewish Names and their History* (London, 1978), 20–30.

109. See Eisner, 41.

110. Brod, *Schloß Nornepygge* (Berlin, 1908), 139–41. Cf. the chapter 'Assimilation und Unsicherheit: Der *Graeculus* und der Clown' in Magris, 75–84.

111. Houston Stewart Chamberlain, *Die Grundlagen des neunzehnten Jahrhunderts* (2 vols., Munich, 1899), i. 241–4.

112. Wagner, *Sämtliche Schriften*, v. 73–4.

113. Heine, i. 433.

114. S. S. Prawer, *Heine's Jewish Comedy* (Oxford, 1983), 555. Cf. Gilman, 'Nietzsche, Heine, and the rhetoric of anti-semitism', in J. P. Stern (ed.), *London German Studies II* (London, 1983), 76–93.

115. There is an English translation, 'The Mare', in Joachim Neugroschel (ed. and tr.), *Great Works of Jewish Fantasy* (London, 1976). I am grateful to Dr Dovid Katz for giving me a copy of the Yiddish text. Whether *Di kliatshe* had any influence on Kafka's own work is doubtful: he probably knew it only through the summary in Pinès, 182–201, which is hardly enough to justify Patrick Bridgwater's assertion that Mendele's story

provided 'den Anstoß für Kafkas Erzählung': see 'Rotpeters Ahnherren', *DVjs* 56 (1982), 459.

116. These are the *Schreiben Milos, eines gebildeten Affen, an seine Freundin Pipi, in Nord-Amerika,* and the *Nachricht von den neuesten Schicksalen des Hundes Berganza,* both in E. T. A. Hoffmann, *Fantasie- und Nachtstücke,* ed. Walter Müller-Seidel (Munich, 1960). See Binder, *Motiv,* 151–66. Kafka was also fond of Hoffmann's *Lebens-Ansichten des Katers Murr:* see Dora Dymant's recollections, reported by J. P. Hodin, *Kafka und Goethe* (London and Hamburg, 1970), 28.

117. The title of the lecture is given in Scholem, *Von Berlin nach Jerusalem,* 102.

118. Micha Josef bin Gorion, *Die Sagen der Juden: Von der Urzeit* (Frankfurt, 1913), 24–5, 27–8. See Wagenbach, *Biographie,* 256.

119. Quoted in M. Friedländer, *Die religiösen Bewegungen innerhalb des Judentums im Zeitalter Jesu* (Berlin, 1905), 9. Kafka owned this book: see Wagenbach, *Biographie,* 255. He read about the same subject in Fromer, 37–8; cf. T 242.

120. Clement Greenberg, '*At the Building of the Great Wall of China*', in Flores and Swander (eds.), *Franz Kafka Today,* 77–81.

121. Nietzsche, ii. 675.

122. Otto Weininger, *Geschlecht und Charakter* (Vienna, 1903), 404. Kafka's one reference to Weininger (Br 320) expresses interest in a lecture which his friend Oskar Baum had recently given on Weininger, and implies that he had at least some second-hand knowledge of Weininger's ideas.

123. Zweig, 58.

124. The information that follows comes from Jiří Langer, *Nine Gates,* tr. Stephen Jolly (London, 1961), which includes Langer's own account of his experiences among the Hasidim and a memoir by František Langer, 'My Brother Jiří'; also Oppenheimer, 297–304.

125. Langer, *Nine Gates,* 4. Cf. Franzos's description of Belz as 'eine Art Mekka der Juden in Podolien und Volhynien', in *Vom Don zur Donau,* i. 162. On the Belz dynasty, see S. A. Horodezky, *Religiöse Strömungen im Judentum, mit besonderer Berücksichtigung des Chassidismus* (Berne, 1920), 180, and the article 'Belz' in *Encyclopaedia Judaica,* iv. 452–3.

126. Quoted by Oppenheimer, 303.

127. Brod, *Über Franz Kafka,* 137.

128. See Oppenheimer, 119–22.

129. See Binder, *Motiv,* 38–55; Oppenheimer, 121–2. On the origins and history of the Golem legend, see Sigrid Mayer, *Golem: Die literarische Rezeption eines Stoffes* (Berne, 1975).

130. The parallel is pointed out by Bianca Maria Bornmann, 'Tracce di una lettura flaubertiana in Kafka', *Annali,* 20 (1977), ii. 110.

131. S. A. Horodetzky [*sic*], 'Vom Gemeinschaftsleben der Chassidim. I', *Der Jude,* 1. ix (Dec. 1916), 592–3. Oppenheimer, 161, quotes this

passage in the context of an exhaustive study of *Ein Landarzt* in the light of Hasidism, 155–90.

132. Alexander Eliasberg (ed. and tr.), *Sagen polnischer Juden* (Munich, 1916), 109; quoted by Bluma Goldstein, 'Franz Kafka's *Ein Landarzt*: A Study in Failure', *DVjs* 42 (1968), 752, and Oppenheimer, 160.

133. Eliasberg, 40–4, 182–4.

134. Buber, *Baalschem*, 163–73.

135. See Dorrit Cohn, 'Kafka's Eternal Present: Narrative Tense in *Ein Landarzt* and Other First-Person Stories', *Publications of the Modern Language Association of America*, 83 (1968), 144–50.

Chapter 5

1. Pasley has noted that this title is based on a misreading of Kafka's text: Kafka wrote 'ein alltäglicher Heroismus'. See Kafka, *Shorter Works*, p. xii. I have put forward an interpretation of 'Die Wahrheit über Sancho Pansa' in 'Kafka und Don Quixote', *Neophilologus*, 69 (1985), 17–24.

2. Brod, *Über Franz Kafka*, 147.

3. See e.g. Achad Haam, ii. 48. Cf. Ch. 4, n. 91 above.

4. Ernst Troeltsch, 'Luther und der Protestantismus', *Die neue Rundschau*, 28 (1917), 1302.

5. Cf. the letter of 28 Nov. 1917 in which Bergmann thanks Buber for these two books: Buber, *Briefwechsel*, i. 514.

6. See T. J. Reed, 'Kafka und Schopenhauer: Philosophisches Denken und dichterisches Bild', *Euphorion*, 59 (1965), 160–72; Jost Schillemeit, 'Tolstoj-Bezüge beim späten Kafka', *Literatur und Kritik*, 140 (Nov. 1979), 606–19.

7. These words are in Kafka's notebook but have been omitted from the transcription in H, which contains many other major and minor inaccuracies. Some textual confusion seems to have resulted from Kafka's having subsequently copied out a number of these aphorisms, making a few changes in the process, as though he intended to have them published separately. The revisions in this selection (H 39–54) seem in Brod's edition to have found their way into what purports to be the transcription of the original notebooks. See Brod's note, H 437–8. Since my concern is with what Kafka wrote in 1917–18, I have corrected the major errors in Brod's transcription. I am very grateful to Sir Malcolm Pasley for allowing me to consult the manuscripts in the Bodleian Library.

8. O. P. Monrad, *Sören Kierkegaard: Sein Leben und seine Werke* (Jena, 1909), 59.

9. The image of the springboard may have been suggested by a passage where Kierkegaard represents the movement of faith as an acrobatic feat: 'Ich kann den großen Trampolinsprung machen, durch den ich in die Unendlichkeit übergehe', *Furcht und Zittern*, 32.

10. Sören Kierkegaard, *Buch des Richters: Seine Tagebücher 1833–1855*, tr. Hermann Gottsched (Jena, 1905), 170. Oppenheimer, 114–15, suggests that Kafka is here alluding to Joseph Karo, the compiler of the digest of Jewish law called the *Shulkhan Arukh*. For reasons given below, I doubt whether Kafka was so intimate with Jewish scholarship as this would imply. Besides, 'Karo' is as common a name for a dog in German as 'Diamond' is in English, so that the name does not necessarily require explanation.

11. See Brod, 'Nachwort zur ersten Ausgabe', Kafka, *Das Schloß* (Frankfurt, 1951), 488. Brod appears to have read into Kafka's text a theme with which he was himself preoccupied: cf. *Heidentum, Christentum, Judentum* (2 vols., Munich, 1921), i. 143.

12. S. S. Prawer, *Comparative Literary Studies* (London, 1973), 69.

13. Brod, 'Der Dichter Franz Kafka', reprinted in Jürgen Born (ed.), *Franz Kafka: Kritik und Rezeption zu seinen Lebzeiten 1912–1924* (Frankfurt, 1979), 158. Brod also published this essay, with slight changes, in Gustav Krojanker (ed.), *Juden in der deutschen Literatur* (Berlin, 1922). Oppenheimer, 114, misinterprets Brod's statement and as a result greatly exaggerates Kafka's knowledge of the Cabbala. Hulda Göhler, *Franz Kafka: 'Das Schloß'* (Bonn, 1982), 163, refers to 'seine kabbalistischen Studien', but fails to demonstrate that such studies ever took place; while Werner Hoffmann, *Kafkas Aphorismen* (Berne, 1975), 109, in speaking of the 'in seinem Wesen verankerte Beziehung zur jüdischen Mystik', seems to imply that he knew about the Cabbala without even needing to study it.

14. Scholem, *Major Trends*, 275.

15. Ibid. 284.

16. Quoted by Dubnow, i. 95.

17. Buber, *Baalschem*, 24.

18. The comparison is made by Henel, 'Kafka als Denker', in David (ed.), *Franz Kafka*, 54–5.

19. *The Metaphysical Poets*, ed. Helen Gardner (Oxford, 1961), 103–4.

20. Scholem, *Major Trends*, 275.

21. Quoted in Benjamin, *Schriften*, i. 495.

22. Brod, *Über Franz Kafka*, 89.

23. Wolfdietrich Rasch, *Zur deutschen Literatur seit der Jahrhundertwende* (Stuttgart, 1967), 17.

24. *Meister Eckeharts Schriften und Predigten*, tr. Herman Büttner (Leipzig, 1903), 34.

25. Schopenhauer, ii. 528–83. See Reed, 'Kafka und Schopenhauer', 165–6.

26. The introduction to Buber's anthology *Ekstatische Konfessionen*, 'Ekstase und Bekenntnis', was reprinted in Buber, *Die Rede, die Lehre und das Lied*, which Kafka probably read in Zürau.

27. Leo N. Tolstoj, *Tagebuch 1895–1899* (Munich, 1917; repr. Jena, 1923), 54. Cf. Schillemeit, 'Tolstoj-Bezüge', 611. By taking everyday phrases and metaphors literally, Binder, in id. (ed.), *Kafka-Handbuch*, i. 499–500, gives a very implausible account of Kafka's religious beliefs.

28. This information comes from a letter from Marianne Lask, Dora Dymant's daughter, to Mr and Mrs George Steiner, which Mrs Steiner was kind enough to send on to me. I have quoted from it in 'Edwin Muir as Critic of Kafka', *MLR* 79 (1984), 641.

29. The recent study by Helen Milfull, 'The Theological Position of Franz Kafka's Aphorisms', *Seminar*, 18 (1982), 168–83, though illuminating in detail, is based on questionable assumptions.

30. See Buber, *Werke*, i. 774–9.

31. This notion appears to have originated with the essay by Erich Heller, 'The World of Franz Kafka', *Cambridge Journal*, 2. i (Oct. 1948), 11–32, which has been reprinted without substantial changes in *The Disinherited Mind*, 4th edn. (London, 1975) and, as '*The Castle*', in *Franz Kafka* (London, 1974). It occurs also in Anders, 87, where a section is headed 'Kafka ist Marcionist. Er glaubt nicht an keinen Gott, sondern an einen schlechten.' This is not meant literally, however, for neither Heller nor Anders claims that Kafka actually knew the teachings of the second-century Gnostic Marcion. The statement that Kafka was directly influenced by Gnosticism occurs in Fischer, 309, and reappears in William M. Johnston, *The Austrian Mind: An Intellectual and Social History, 1848–1938* (Berkeley, 1972), as part of the contention that a 'gnosis which flourished at Prague between 1890 and 1930' and was 'reflected' in the works of Rilke, Meyrink, and Mahler and 'espoused . . . most fervently' by Kafka, Brod, Werfel, and the dramatists Paul Kornfeld and Paul Adler, 'resembled' the teaching of Marcion, so that 'Prague Marcionism' has become 'a commonplace of modernity' (pp. 270–1). Although it is not clear exactly what Johnston is asserting here, and he cites no evidence for his claims about Gnosticism, the gist of this is solemnly repeated by Franz Kuna, *Kafka: Literature as Corrective Punishment* (London, 1974), 45–6.

  Though I have not inquired further into the origins of this idea, it is true that Marcion was of some interest to Kafka's Jewish contemporaries, because he had rejected the Old Testament and its Law as the work of an evil god and had interpreted Paul's epistles in an anti-Semitic manner. His ideas were made known by the famous Protestant theologian Harnack in the book *Marcion: Das Evangelium vom fremden Gott* (Leipzig, 1921) and were certainly known to Brod and Weltsch, who would have reported any interest Kafka had shown in them. Instead, both repudiate Anders's and Heller's attempts to link *Das Schloß* with Gnosticism: see Weltsch, *Religion*, 62–3, and Brod, *Über Franz Kafka*, 305, 380–1. Brod (ibid. 71) even records a conversation in which Kafka rejected a parallel

Brod had tried to draw between Gnosticism and an idea expressed by Kafka.

32. Ludwig Feuerbach, *The Essence of Christianity*, tr. Marian Evans (London, 1854), 32. Kafka's conception of estrangement is equated rather too readily with Marxian alienation by Zbigniew Świat*ł*owski, 'Kafkas "Oktavhefte" und ihre Bedeutung im Werk des Dichters', *Germanistica Wratislaviensia*, 20 (1974), 97–116.

33. Especially by Neumann, 'Umkehrung und Ablenkung: Franz Kafkas "Gleitendes Paradox"', *DVjs* 42 (1968), 702–44. See the criticisms by Henel in David (ed.), *Franz Kafka*, 50.

34. Sabina Kienlechner, *Negativität der Erkenntnis im Werk Franz Kafkas* (Tübingen, 1981), 17.

35. Heinrich von Kleist, *Sämtliche Werke und Briefe*, ed. Helmut Sembdner (2 vols., Munich, 1961), ii. 122.

36. See Pasley, 'Introduction', Kafka, *Short Stories* (Oxford, 1963), 19; Binder, *Motiv*, 92–114; Lawrence Ryan, '"Zum letztenmal Psychologie!" Zur psychologischen Deutbarkeit der Werke Franz Kafkas', in Paulsen (ed.), *Psychologie*, 157–73.

37. The quotation comes from Kierkegaard, *Buch des Richters*, 112.

38. Franz Brentano, *Psychologie vom empirischen Standpunkt* (Leipzig, 1874), 35; also quoted by Binder, *Motiv*, 79. Extravagant and unconvincing claims for Brentano's influence on Kafka have been made by Wagenbach, *Biographie*, 107–16, and Peter Neesen, *Vom Louvrezirkel zum Prozeß: Franz Kafka und die Psychologie Franz Brentanos* (Göppingen, 1972). Cf. Binder (ed.), *Kafka-Handbuch*, i. 286–9.

39. See Fritz Mauthner, *Beiträge zu einer Kritik der Sprache* (3 vols., Stuttgart, 1901–2); Gershon Weiler, *Mauthner's Critique of Language* (Cambridge, 1970).

40. Kleist, ii. 342–5. Cf. Ralf R. Nicolai, 'Kafkas Stellung zu Kleist und der Romantik', *Studia Neophilologica*, 45 (1973), 80–103.

41. Schopenhauer, ii. 666, 693, and especially 698.

42. Kierkegaard, *Der Augenblick*, tr. C. Schrempf, 3rd edn. (Jena, 1923), 137–9.

43. Hans Joachim Schoeps, 'Theologische Motive in der Dichtung Franz Kafkas', *Die neue Rundschau*, 62 (1951), 37. On Schoeps's own theological position, see Mosse, 108.

44. Quoted by Jacobs, 59; also in Dubnow, i. 96–7.

45. Quoted from the MS. Kafka's original wording strengthens Reed's conjecture that he was alluding to the sub-title of Nietzsche's *Ecce Homo*, 'Wie man wird, was man ist': see Nietzsche, ii. 1063, and Reed, 'Nietzsche's Animals: Idea, Image and Influence', in Pasley (ed.), *Nietzsche: Imagery and Thought* (London, 1978), 216.

46. From Caroline Schulz's diary, in Büchner, 321.

47. Friedländer, 121.

48. Quoted by Brod, *Heidentum*, i. 142.
49. See the story 'Wahrheit' in Buber, *Der große Maggid und seine Nachfolge* (Frankfurt, 1922), 55–6.
50. *The Talmud*, tr. Polano, 277.
51. 'Vom Messias', in Buber, *Maggid*, 93.
52. Hiebel, 46.

Chapter 6

1. Schopenhauer, i. 316.
2. See 'The Metaphoric and Metonymic Poles' in Roman Jakobson and Morris Halle, *Fundamentals of Language* (The Hague, 1956), 76–82, and, for the further application of this typology to literature, David Lodge, *The Modes of Modern Writing* (London, 1977).
3. Sokel, 397.
4. SA 63. Cf. Binder, *Schaffensprozeß*, 306–21.
5. See Pasley, 'Kafka and "Berufung"', 146.
6. Brod, *Heidentum*, i. 142–5.
7. Nietzsche, *Zur Genealogie der Moral*, iii, § 26 (Schlechta, ii. 895).
8. See Brod, *Streitbares Leben*, 12–53. Brod's claim to have launched Werfel on his career has now been severely questioned by Karl S. Guthke, *Das Abenteuer der Literatur* (Berne, 1981), 295–309. On Kafka and Werfel, see Roger Bauer, 'K. und das Ungeheuer: Franz Kafka über Franz Werfel', in David (ed.), *Franz Kafka*, 189–209.
9. Scholem, *Von der mystischen Gestalt der Gottheit* (Zürich, 1962), 122.
10. See Brod, *Heidentum*, i. 318; Scholem, 'The Tradition of the Thirty-Six Hidden Just Men', *Messianic Idea*, 251–6.
11. See Friedrich Thieberger, 'Erinnerungen an Franz Kafka', *Eckart*, 23 (Oct. 1953), 52; Brod, *Der Prager Kreis*, 98; Binder, 'Kafkas Hebräischstudien: Ein biographisch-interpretatorischer Versuch', *JDSG* 11 (1967), 527–56; Oppenheimer, 302–3; Clive Sinclair, 'Kafka's Hebrew Teacher', *Encounter*, 64. iii (Mar. 1985), 46–9.
12. Brod, *Über Franz Kafka*, 172.
13. Weltsch, *Religion*, 38.
14. Now available in English as Yosef Haim Brenner, *Breakdown and Bereavement*, tr. Hillel Halkin (Ithaca, NY, 1971).
15. Brod, *Über Franz Kafka*, 122. Cf. Pasley, 'Two Kafka Enigmas: *Elf Söhne* and *Die Sorgen des Hausvaters*', *MLR* 59 (1964), 73–81; Breon Mitchell, 'Franz Kafka's *Elf Söhne*: A New Look at the Puzzle', *GQ* 47 (1974), 191–203; Peter Hutchinson, 'Red Herrings or Clues?' in Flores (ed.), *The Kafka Debate*, 206–15.
16. Brod, *Streitbares Leben*, 281, points out discrepancies in the chronology of

the novel and in the description of Amalia, who is first said to be blonde (S 52–3) and later dark (S 370, 387).

17. See Rajec, 152–72.
18. Brod, *Streitbares Leben*, 281.
19. Richard Sheppard, *On Kafka's Castle* (London, 1973), 76, 105.
20. e.g. Heller, *Franz Kafka*, 123.
21. Emrich, 300.
22. Göhler, 12, 52.
23. See Beck, 195. Cf. W. G. Sebald, 'The Law of Ignominy: Authority, Messianism and Exile in *The Castle*', in Kuna (ed.), *On Kafka*, 42–58.
24. For this and other examples, see G. B. Caird, *The Language and Imagery of the Bible* (London, 1980), 47–8.
25. Brod, *Heidentum*, ii. 126.
26. See Friedländer, p. xv.
27. See Scholem, *Sabbatai Ṣevi, the Mystical Messiah* (London, 1973).
28. See P. F. Veit, 'Moritz Spiegelberg', *JDSG* 17 (1973), 273–90. On Frank, see Scholem, 'Redemption through Sin', *Messianic Idea*, 78–141.
29. Wassermann, 3–86.
30. See Scholem, 'The Neutralization of the Messianic Element in Early Hasidism', *Messianic Idea*, 176–202.
31. Quoted from Horodezky, 66.
32. Moses Hess, *Rom und Jerusalem* (Leipzig, 1862), 4–5.
33. Quoted in Joseph Nedava, 'Herzl and Messianism', *Herzl Year Book*, 7 (1971), 12.
34. Herzl, v. 227–8.
35. Scholem, 'Towards an Understanding of the Messianic Idea in Judaism', *Messianic Idea*, 35.
36. See Sheppard, 127–88.
37. See Peters, 133–48.
38. Brod, 'Nachwort zur ersten Ausgabe', *Das Schloß*, 484.
39. Klaus-Peter Philippi, *Reflexion und Wirklichkeit: Untersuchungen zu Kafkas Roman 'Das Schloß'* (Tübingen, 1966), 215.
40. Maimon, 459; quoted and discussed by Pasley, 'Zur Entstehungsgeschichte von Franz Kafkas Schloßbild', in Goldstücker (ed.), *Weltfreunde*, 244, and Karin Keller, *Gesellschaft in mythischem Bann: Studien zum Roman 'Das Schloß' und anderen Werken Franz Kafkas* (Wiesbaden, 1977), 230.
41. Jan Amos Komenský, *The Labyrinth of the World and the Paradise of the Heart*, tr. Count Lutzow (London, 1905), 165–6. Kafka's debt to this book is discussed by Politzer, 233–4, and Pasley, op. cit. 243–4.
42. Schopenhauer, i. 118. Cf. Reed, 'Kafka und Schopenhauer', 168.
43. Kierkegaard, *Furcht und Zittern*, 61.
44. Kafka read this classic Czech novel in childhood: see M 22 and Wagenbach, *Biographie*, 44. Its influence is discussed and probably exaggerated

by Brod, *Über Franz Kafka*, 371–4; cf. Aloisio Rendi, 'Influssi letterari nel *Castello* di Kafka', *Annali*, 4 (1961), 80–1; Reed, 'Kafka und Schopenhauer', 171–2.

45. See Wagenbach, 'Wo liegt Kafkas Schloß?', *Kafka-Symposion* (Berlin, 1965), 161–80.
46. Philippi, 210.
47. Henel, 'Die Deutbarkeit', 259–60.
48. Pasley, op. cit. Cf. Nietzsche, ii. 845.
49. See Jonathan Webber, 'Some Notes on Biblical Ideas about Language: An Anthropological Perspective', *European Judaism*, 15. i (summer 1981), 21–5.
50. Maimon, 99.
51. Politzer, 235. Cf. Emrich, 310; Kurz, *Traum-Schrecken*, 161.
52. Robert, 91.
53. Nathan Söderblom, *Das Werden des Gottesglaubens*, ed. R. Stübe (Leipzig, 1916), 211.
54. Ibid. 64.
55. Ibid. 207.
56. Keller, 33.
57. Söderblom, 115–16.
58. See Reinhard H. Friederich, 'K.'s "bitteres Kraut" and *Exodus*', *GQ* 48 (1975), 355–7.
59. Keller, 60.
60. Nietzsche, *Zur Genealogie der Moral*, iii, § 15 (Schlechta, ii. 867).
61. Friedländer, 83–5.
62. Horodezky, 48.
63. Maimon, 321–2; quoted and discussed by Keller, 8.
64. Heller, *Franz Kafka*, 131.
65. Quoted by Jacobs, 9.
66. From the third octavo notebook. Brod omits it from the transcript in H but quotes it in *Über Franz Kafka*, 313.
67. Gustav Roskoff, *Geschichte des Teufels* (2 vols., Leipzig, 1869), i. 29.
68. Rajec, 159. Cf. Politzer, 383.
69. Eliasberg, 20.
70. Sheppard, 105.
71. There is an English translation, *Granny*, by Edith Pargeter (Prague, 1962).
72. Philippi, 73.
73. Weininger, 112. The affinity between Kafka and Weininger is discussed by Politzer, 197–200. Cf. Sacher-Masoch, 57.
74. August Strindberg, *Am offnen Meer*, tr. Emil Schering (Leipzig, 1912), 300. Cf. Rendi, 89–91.
75. Karl Kraus, *Beim Wort genommen* (Munich, 1955), 13. Cf. Wagner, *Geist und Geschlecht*; J. L. Hibberd, 'The Spirit of the Flesh: Wedekind's Lulu', *MLR* 79 (1984), 336–55.

76. Albert Camus, *Le Mythe de Sisyphe*, 2nd edn. (Paris, 1948), 183; Politzer, 272.
77. Brod, *Heidentum*, ii. 10.
78. M. D. Georg Langer, *Die Erotik der Kabbala* (Prague, 1923), 7.
79. Brod, *Heidentum*, ii. 11–12.
80. Langer, *Erotik*, 24.
81. Jacobs, 61.
82. Quoted ibid. 60; also in Dubnow, i. 96.
83. Brod, 'Nachwort zur ersten Ausgabe', *Das Schloß*, 488.
84. Cersowsky, *Phantastische Literatur*, 221.
85. Sheppard, 94–105.
86. Ibid. 96.
87. Brod, *Heidentum*, ii. 11.
88. Buber, 'Geleitwort', *Maggid*, pp. xxviii, xxvii. Kafka read this book with enjoyment in May 1922 (T 580).
89. Fromer, 10; Eliasberg, 10.
90. Sokel, 439.
91. Binder, *Kommentar zu den Romanen*, 293.
92. This was first noted by Németh, 46.
93. Dubnow, i. 98.
94. Scholem, *Von der mystischen Gestalt*, 123.
95. Cf. Rajec, 156.
96. Buber, *Maggid*, p. xxxiv.
97. Sheppard, 44.
98. Edwin Muir, 'Introductory Note', Kafka, *The Castle*, tr. Willa and Edwin Muir (London, 1930), p. ix; reprinted in Jakob, i. 87. I have tried to explain what Muir meant by 'allegory' in 'Muir as Critic', 644–6.
99. Emrich, 77–81. Cf. Brod, *Über Franz Kafka*, 169–70; Anders, 39.
100. Sokel, 122–3; Henel, 'Kafkas *In der Strafkolonie*'; Kurz, *Traum-Schrecken*, 132–5; Hiebel, 40–5. Cf. Fingerhut, 102.
101. e.g. Sokel, 122–3; Henel, 'Kafkas *In der Strafkolonie*'; Kurz, *Traum-Schrecken*, 132–5; Hiebel, 40–5. Cf. Fingerhut, 102.
102. Among recent studies of allegory, I have learnt most from Maureen Quilligan, *The Language of Allegory* (Ithaca, NY, 1979); Heinz Schlaffer, '*Faust Zweiter Teil': Die Allegorie des 19. Jahrhunderts* (Stuttgart, 1981); Gerhard Kurz, *Metapher, Allegorie, Symbol* (Göttingen, 1982).
103. Both definitions are quoted by Kurz, *Metapher*, 52, 70.
104. Schopenhauer, i. 283–4.
105. Quoted by Paul de Man, 'The Rhetoric of Temporality', *Blindness and Insight*, 2nd edn. (London, 1983), 190.
106. In drawing this distinction I follow Kurz, *Metapher*, 72.
107. This well-worn example is used by Schopenhauer, i. 282, and Brod, *Über Franz Kafka*, 169.

108. On the varieties of visual allegory, see Göran Hermerén, *Representation and Meaning in the Visual Arts* (Lund, 1969), 103–25.
109. See Kurz, *Metapher*, 35–6.
110. C. S. Lewis, *The Allegory of Love* (Oxford, 1936), 334.
111. Herman Melville, *Moby-Dick*, ed. Harrison Hayford and Hershel Parker (Norton Critical Edition, New York, 1967), 144, 264.
112. See Quilligan, 100.
113. Kurz, *Traum-Schrecken*, 132.

Chapter 7

1. Edwin Muir, 'Introductory Note', Kafka, *The Great Wall of China*, tr. Willa and Edwin Muir (London, 1933), p. xii; reprinted in Jakob, i. 94.
2. See the delightful anecdote in Brod, *Über Franz Kafka*, 338–9.
3. Brod, letter of 25 Jan. 1927, in Buber, *Briefwechsel*, ii. 278.
4. See Brod, *Über Franz Kafka*, 176.
5. Weltsch, *Religion*, 39.
6. Brod, *Über Franz Kafka*, 179–80.
7. See Emrich, 152–67; Fingerhut, 188; John Winkelman, 'Kafka's *Forschungen eines Hundes*', *Monatshefte*, 59 (1967), 204–16.
8. Steinmetz, 122.
9. See Brod, B 350. The consequences are worked out in detail by Winkelman.
10. Fingerhut, 184.
11. Cf. Steinmetz, 125.
12. Emrich, 166.
13. Binder, *Kommentar zu sämtlichen Erzählungen*, 278–80.
14. The usual German word for the squeaking of mice is 'piepsen'. Kafka˙ also uses it, along with the less common 'zischen', but seems to apply them specially to the sound made by young mice: 'die unübersehbaren Scharen unserer Kinder, fröhlich zischend oder piepsend, solange sie noch nicht pfeifen können' (E 280). In a letter he uses 'pfeifen' to denote the sound normally made by mice (Br 198: 'leise gepfiffen'), though since he also told Robert Klopstock that *Josefine* was an 'Untersuchung des tierischen Piepsens' (Br 521), the distinction cannot have been a sharp one. There seems no need to translate 'pfeifen' by 'cheep', as proposed by Pascal, 248.
15. Pascal, 230. Cf. Politzer, 315; Fingerhut, 203.
16. Lionel Kochan, *The Jew and his History* (London, 1977), 9.
17. Quoted ibid. 3.
18. Maimon, 300.
19. Pascal, 229.

Bibliography

Sections 2, 3 and 4 list only those works that are referred to more than once in the notes.

Section 1
Editions and translations of Kafka's works

Erzählungen, ed. Max Brod (Frankfurt, 1946) [= E]
The Diaries of Franz Kafka, tr. Joseph Kresh (2 vols., London, 1948–9)
Der Prozeß, ed. Max Brod (Frankfurt, 1950) [= P]
Tagebücher 1910–1923, ed. Max Brod (Frankfurt, 1951) [= T]
Hochzeitsvorbereitungen auf dem Lande und andere Prosa aus dem Nachlaß, ed. Max Brod (Frankfurt, 1953) [= H]
Beschreibung eines Kampfes: Novellen, Skizzen, Aphorismen aus dem Nachlaß, ed. Max Brod (Frankfurt, 1954) [= B]
Briefe 1902–1924, ed. Max Brod (Frankfurt, 1958) [= Br]
Short Stories, ed. Malcolm Pasley (Oxford, 1963)
Der Heizer, In der Strafkolonie, Der Bau, ed. Malcolm Pasley (Cambridge, 1966)
Briefe an Felice und andere Korrespondenz aus Verlobungszeit, ed. Erich Heller and Jürgen Born (Frankfurt, 1967) [= F]
Beschreibung eines Kampfes: Die zwei Fassungen, ed. Ludwig Dietz (Frankfurt, 1969)
Shorter Works, I, ed. and tr. Malcolm Pasley (London, 1973)
Briefe an Ottla und die Familie, ed. Hartmut Binder and Klaus Wagenbach (Frankfurt, 1974) [= O]
In der Strafkolonie. Eine Geschichte aus dem Jahr 1914, ed. Klaus Wagenbach (Berlin, 1975)
Das Schloß, ed. Malcolm Pasley (2 vols., Frankfurt, 1982) [Textband = S; Apparatband = SA]
Der Verschollene, ed. Jost Schillemeit (2 vols., Frankfurt, 1983) [Textband = V]
Briefe an Milena, 2nd ed., ed. Jürgen Born and Michael Müller (Frankfurt, 1983)

Section 2
Other primary texts, including books read by Kafka and memoirs by his contemporaries

Achad Haam, 'Judenstaat und Judennot', in *Am Scheidewege: Gesammelte Aufsätze*, tr. Israel Friedländer and Harry Torczyner (4 vols., Berlin, 1923), ii. 45–67

Benjamin, Walter, *Schriften*, ed. T. W. and Gretel Adorno (2 vols., Frankfurt, 1955)
—— and Gershom Scholem, *Briefwechsel 1933–1940*, ed. Gershom Scholem (Frankfurt, 1980)
Blüher, Hans, *Secessio Judaica: Philosophische Grundlegung der historischen Situation des Judentums und der antisemitischen Bewegung* (Berlin, 1922)
Brod, Max, *Arnold Beer: Das Schicksal eines Juden* (Berlin, 1912)
—— *Heidentum, Christentum, Judentum* (2 vols., Munich, 1921)
—— *Streitbares Leben* (Munich, 1960)
—— *Der Prager Kreis* (Stuttgart, 1966)
Buber, Martin, *Die Legende des Baalschem* (Frankfurt, 1908)
—— (ed.) *Ekstatische Konfessionen* (Jena, 1909)
—— *Die Rede, die Lehre und das Lied* (Leipzig, 1917)
—— *Die jüdische Bewegung: Gesammelte Aufsätze und Ansprachen* (2 vols., Berlin, 1920)
—— *Der große Maggid und seine Nachfolge* (Frankfurt, 1922)
—— *Werke* (3 vols., Munich, 1962–4)
—— *Der Jude und sein Judentum: Gesammelte Aufsätze und Reden* (Cologne, 1963)
—— *Briefwechsel aus sieben Jahrzehnten* (3 vols., Heidelberg, 1972–5)
Büchner, Georg, *Werke und Briefe* (Munich, 1965)
Döblin, Alfred, *Reise in Polen* (Olten, 1968)
Dostoevsky, Feodor, *Crime and Punishment*, tr. Jessie Coulson, ed. George Gibian (Norton Critical Edition, New York, 1964)
—— (Dostojewski, F. M.), *Die Brüder Karamasoff*, tr. E. K. Rahsin (Munich, 1914)
Eliasberg, Alexander (ed. and tr.), *Sagen polnischer Juden* (Munich, 1916)
Franzos, Karl Emil, *Vom Don zur Donau: Neue Kulturbilder aus Halb-Asien* (2 vols., Stuttgart, 1889)
Friedländer, M., *Die religiösen Bewegungen innerhalb des Judentums im Zeitalter Jesu* (Berlin, 1905)
Fromer, Jakob, *Der Organismus des Judentums* (Charlottenburg, 1909)
Heine, Heinrich, *Sämtliche Werke*, ed. Ernst Elster (7 vols., Leipzig, 1893)
Herzl, Theodor, *Gesammelte zionistische Werke* (5 vols., Berlin and Tel Aviv, 1934–5)
Holitscher, Arthur, *Amerika heute und morgen* (Berlin, 1913)
Kierkegaard, Sören, *Buch des Richters: Seine Tagebücher 1833–1855*, tr. Hermann Gottsched (Jena, 1905)
—— *Furcht und Zittern; Die Wiederholung*, tr. H. C. Ketels, H. Gottsched and C. Schrempf, 3rd edn. (Jena, 1923)
Kleist, Heinrich von, *Sämtliche Werke und Briefe*, ed. Helmut Sembdner (2 vols., Munich, 1961)
Kohn, Hans, *Living in a World Revolution* (New York, 1964)
Langer, M. D. Georg, *Die Erotik der Kabbala* (Prague, 1923)
—— (Langer, Jiří), *Nine Gates*, tr. Stephen Jolly (London, 1961)

Maimon, Salomon, *Lebensgeschichte*, ed. Jakob Fromer (Munich, 1911)
Mann, Thomas, *Gesammelte Werke* (12 vols., Frankfurt, 1960)
Nietzsche, Friedrich, *Werke*, ed. Karl Schlechta (3 vols., Munich, 1956)
Nordau, Max, *Zionistische Schriften* (Berlin, 1923)
Pinès, M., *Histoire de la littérature judéo-allemande* (Paris, 1910)
Rathenau, Walther, 'Zur Kritik der Zeit', in *Gesammelte Schriften* (5 vols., Berlin, 1925), I, 7–148
Sacher-Masoch, Leopold von, *Venus im Pelz* (Frankfurt, 1968)
Scholem, Gershom, *Von Berlin nach Jerusalem* (Frankfurt, 1977)
Schopenhauer, Arthur, *Die Welt als Wille und Vorstellung*, ed. Julius Frauenstädt (2 vols., Leipzig, 1923)
Söderblom, Nathan, *Das Werden des Gottesglaubens* (Leipzig, 1916)
The Talmud: Selections, tr. H. Polano (London, n.d.)
Vom Judentum: Ein Sammelbuch (Leipzig, 1913)
Wagner, Richard, 'Das Judentum in der Musik', in *Sämtliche Schriften und Dichtungen* (Volksausgabe, 12 vols., Leipzig, n.d.), v. 66–85
Wassermann, Jakob, *Die Juden von Zirndorf* (Munich, 1897)
Weininger, Otto, *Geschlecht und Charakter* (Vienna, 1903)
Zweig, Arnold, *Herkunft und Zukunft* (Vienna, 1929)

Section 3

Secondary literature wholly or partly on Kafka

Adorno, T. W., 'Aufzeichnungen zu Kafka', *Prismen* (Frankfurt, 1955), 302–42
Anders, Günther, *Kafka: Pro und Contra* (Munich, 1951)
Baioni, Giuliano, *Kafka: romanzo e parabola* (Milan, 1962)
Beck, Evelyn Torton, *Kafka and the Yiddish Theater* (Madison, Wis., 1971)
Beissner, Friedrich, *Der Erzähler Franz Kafka* (Frankfurt, 1983)
Bergman, S. H., 'Erinnerungen an Franz Kafka', *Universitas*, 27 (1972), 739–50
Binder, Hartmut, *Motiv und Gestaltung bei Franz Kafka* (Bonn, 1966)
—— 'Franz Kafka und die Wochenschrift *Selbstwehr*', *DVjs* 41 (1967), 283–304
—— *Kafka: Kommentar zu sämtlichen Erzählungen* (Munich, 1975)
—— *Kafka: Kommentar zu den Romanen, Rezensionen, Aphorismen und zum Brief an den Vater* (Munich, 1976)
—— (ed.), *Kafka-Handbuch* (2 vols., Stuttgart, 1979)
—— *Kafka: Der Schaffensprozeß* (Frankfurt, 1983)
Brod, Max, 'Nachwort zur ersten Ausgabe', Franz Kafka, *Das Schloß* (Frankfurt, 1951)
—— *Über Franz Kafka* (Frankfurt, 1966)
Buch, H. C., *Ut Pictura Poesis: Die Beschreibungsliteratur und ihre Kritiker von Lessing bis Lukács* (Munich, 1972)

Cersowsky, Peter, *Phantastische Literatur im ersten Viertel des 20. Jahrhunderts* (Munich, 1983)

David, Claude (ed.), *Franz Kafka: Themen und Probleme* (Göttingen, 1980)

Eisner, Pavel, *Franz Kafka and Prague* (New York, 1950)

Emrich, Wilhelm, *Franz Kafka* (Bonn, 1958)

Fingerhut, Karl-Heinz, *Die Funktion der Tierfiguren im Werke Franz Kafkas* (Bonn, 1969)

Fischer, Ernst, *Von Grillparzer zu Kafka* (Vienna, 1962)

Flores, Angel (ed.), *The Kafka Debate* (New York, 1977)

—— and Homer Swander (eds.), *Franz Kafka Today* (Madison, Wis., 1958)

Göhler, Hulda, *Franz Kafka: 'Das Schloß'* (Bonn, 1982)

Goldstücker, Eduard (ed.), *Weltfreunde: Konferenz über die Prager deutsche Literatur* (Prague, 1967)

——, František Kautman, and Paul Reimann (eds.), *Franz Kafka aus Prager Sicht* (Prague, 1965)

Heller, Erich, *Franz Kafka* (London, 1974)

Henel, Ingeborg, 'Die Türhüterlegende und ihre Bedeutung für Kafkas *Prozeß*', *DVjs* 37 (1963), 50–70

—— 'Die Deutbarkeit von Kafkas Werken', *ZfdP* 86 (1967), 250–66

—— 'Kafkas *In der Strafkolonie*: Form, Sinn und Stellung der Erzählung im Gesamtwerk', in V. J. Günther *et al.* (eds.), *Untersuchungen zur Literatur als Geschichte: Festschrift für Benno von Wiese* (Berlin, 1973), 480–504

Hermsdorf, Klaus, *Kafka: Weltbild und Roman* (Berlin, 1961)

Hiebel, H. H., *Die Zeichen des Gesetzes: Recht und Macht bei Franz Kafka* (Munich, 1983)

Hinze, Klaus-Peter, 'Neue Aspekte zum Kafka-Bild: Bericht über ein noch unveröffentlichtes Manuskript', *MAL* 5 (1972), iii–iv. 83–92

Jahn, Wolfgang, *Kafkas Roman 'Der Verschollene'* (Stuttgart, 1965)

Jakob, Dieter, *Das Kafka-Bild in England: Eine Studie zur Aufnahme des Werkes in der journalistischen Kritik (1928–1966)* (2 vols., Oxford and Erlangen, 1971)

Jordan, Robert Welsh, 'Das Gesetz, die Anklage und K.s Prozeß: Franz Kafka und Franz Brentano', *JDSG* 24 (1980), 332–56

Keller, Karin, *Gesellschaft in mythischem Bann: Studien zum Roman 'Das Schloß' und anderen Werken Franz Kafkas* (Wiesbaden, 1977)

Kuna, Franz (ed.), *On Kafka: Semi-Centenary Perspectives* (London, 1976)

Kurz, Gerhard, *Traum-Schrecken: Kafkas literarische Existenzanalyse* (Stuttgart, 1980)

—— (ed.), *Der junge Kafka* (Frankfurt, 1984)

Marson, Eric, *Kafka's Trial: The Case against Josef K.* (St Lucia, Queensland, 1975)

Németh, André, *Kafka ou le mystère juif*, tr. Victor Hintz (Paris, 1947)

Neumann, Gerhard, *Franz Kafka, 'Das Urteil': Text, Materialien, Kommentar* (Munich, 1981)

Oppenheimer, Anne, 'Franz Kafka's Relation to Judaism' (D. Phil. thesis, Oxford, 1977)

Pascal, Roy, *Kafka's Narrators: A Study of his Stories and Sketches* (Cambridge, 1982)

Pasley, Malcolm, 'Two Literary Sources of Kafka's *Der Prozeß*', *FMLS* 3 (1967), 142-7

—— 'Kafka and the Theme of "Berufung"', *OGS* 9 (1978), 139-49

Paulsen, Wolfgang (ed.), *Psychologie in der Literaturwissenschaft* (Heidelberg, 1971)

Peters, F. G., 'Kafka and Kleist: A Literary Relationship', *OGS* 1 (1966), 114-62

Philippi, Klaus-Peter, *Reflexion und Wirklichkeit: Untersuchungen zu Kafkas Roman 'Das Schloß'* (Tübingen, 1966)

Politzer, Heinz, *Franz Kafka: Parable and Paradox*, 2nd edn. (Ithaca, NY, 1966)

Pütz, Jürgen, *Kafkas 'Verschollener'—ein Bildungsroman?* (Berne, 1983)

Rajec, Elizabeth M., *Namen und ihre Bedeutungen im Werke Franz Kafkas* (Berne, 1977)

Reed, T. J., 'Kafka und Schopenhauer: Philosophisches Denken und dichterisches Bild', *Euphorion*, 59 (1965), 160-72

Rendi, Aloisio, 'Influssi letterari nel *Castello* di Kafka', *Annali*, 4 (1961), 75-93

Robert, Marthe, *Seul, comme Franz Kafka* (Paris, 1979)

Robertson, Ritchie, 'Edwin Muir as Critic of Kafka', *MLR* 79 (1984), 638-52

Sánchez Vázquez, Adolfo, *Art and Society: Essays in Marxist Aesthetics*, tr. Maro Riofrancos (London, 1973)

Schillemeit, Jost, 'Tolstoj-Bezüge beim späten Kafka', *Literatur und Kritik*, 140 (Nov. 1979), 606-19

Sheppard, Richard, *On Kafka's Castle* (London, 1973)

Sokel, W. H., *Franz Kafka: Tragik und Ironie* (Munich, 1964)

Steinmetz, Horst, *Suspensive Interpretation am Beispiel Franz Kafkas* (Göttingen, 1977)

Stölzl, Christoph, *Kafkas böses Böhmen: Zur Sozialgeschichte eines Prager Juden* (Munich, 1975)

Urzidil, Johannes, *Da geht Kafka* (Zürich, 1965)

Wagenbach, Klaus, *Franz Kafka: Eine Biographie seiner Jugend, 1883-1912* (Berne, 1958)

—— *Franz Kafka: Bilder aus seinem Leben* (Berlin, 1983)

Walser, Martin, *Beschreibung einer Form* (Munich, 1961)

Weltsch, Felix, *Religion und Humor im Leben und Werk Franz Kafkas* (Berlin-Grunewald, 1957)

Winkelman, John, 'Kafka's *Forschungen eines Hundes*', *Monatshefte*, 59 (1967), 204-16

Wirkner, Alfred, *Kafka und die Außenwelt: Quellenstudien zum 'Amerika'-Fragment* (Stuttgart, 1976)

Section 4
Miscellaneous

Adler-Rudel, S., *Ostjuden in Deutschland 1880–1940* (Tübingen, 1959)

Anz, Thomas, *Literatur der Existenz: Literarische Psychopathographie und ihre soziale Bedeutung im Frühexpressionismus* (Stuttgart, 1977)

Aschheim, Steven E., *Brothers and Strangers: The East European Jew in German and German Jewish Consciousness, 1800–1923* (Madison, Wis., 1982)

Avineri, Shlomo, *The Making of Modern Zionism* (London, 1981)

Cohen, Gary B., 'Jews in German Society: Prague, 1860–1914', *Central European History*, 10 (1977), 28–54

Dubnow, Simon, *Geschichte des Chassidismus*, tr. A. Steinberg, 2 vols. (Berlin, 1931)

Encyclopaedia Judaica (16 vols., Jerusalem, 1971)

Fanger, Donald, *Dostoevsky and Romantic Realism* (Chicago, 1965)

Fowler, Alastair, *Kinds of Literature: An Introduction to the Theory of Genres and Modes* (Oxford, 1982)

Hapgood, Hutchins, *The Spirit of the Ghetto*, ed. Moses Rischin (Cambridge, Mass., 1967)

Horodezky, S. A., *Religiöse Strömungen im Judentum, mit besonderer Berücksichtigung des Chassidismus* (Berne, 1920)

Jacobs, Louis, *Hasidic Prayer* (London, 1972)

Kochan, Lionel, *The Jew and his History* (London, 1977)

Kurz, Gerhard, *Metapher, Allegorie, Symbol* (Göttingen, 1982)

Magris, Claudio, *Weit von wo: Verlorene Welt des Ostjudentums*, tr. Jutta Prasse (Vienna, 1974)

Mochulsky, Konstantin, *Dostoevsky: His Life and Work*, tr. Michael A. Minihan (Princeton, 1967)

Mosse, George L., *Germans and Jews* (New York, 1970)

Quilligan, Maureen, *The Language of Allegory* (Ithaca, NY, 1979)

Scholem, Gershom, *Major Trends in Jewish Mysticism* (New York, 1946)

—— *Von der mystischen Gestalt der Gottheit* (Zürich, 1962)

—— *The Messianic Idea in Judaism* (London, 1971)

Wagner, Nike, *Geist und Geschlecht: Karl Kraus und die Erotik der Wiener Moderne* (Frankfurt, 1982)

Index

The index refers to the preface (excluding acknowledgements) and text, but not to the notes. Fictional characters are not included. Works of literature are listed alphabetically after their author; other books mentioned in the text are not specified in the index.